Immaculate Misconceptions

Immaculate Misconceptions

A Black Mariology

AMEY VICTORIA ADKINS-JONES

Great Clarendon Street, Oxford, OX2 6DP,
United Kingdom

Oxford University Press is a department of the University of Oxford.
It furthers the University's objective of excellence in research, scholarship,
and education by publishing worldwide. Oxford is a registered trade mark of
Oxford University Press in the UK and in certain other countries

© Amey Victoria Adkins-Jones 2025

The moral rights of the author have been asserted

All rights reserved. No part of this publication may be reproduced, stored in a retrieval system, transmitted, used for text and data mining, or used for training artificial intelligence, in any form or by any means, without the prior permission in writing of Oxford University Press, or as expressly permitted by law, by licence or under terms agreed with the appropriate reprographics rights organization. Enquiries concerning reproduction outside the scope of the above should be sent to the Rights Department, Oxford University Press, at the address above.

You must not circulate this work in any other form
and you must impose this same condition on any acquirer

Published in the United States of America by Oxford University Press
198 Madison Avenue, New York, NY 10016, United States of America

British Library Cataloguing in Publication Data
Data available

Library of Congress Control Number: 2024951027

ISBN 9780198950042

DOI: 10.1093/9780198950073.001.0001

Printed and bound by
CPI Group (UK) Ltd, Croydon, CR0 4YY

The manufacturer's authorised representative in the EU for product safety is
Oxford University Press España S.A. of El Parque Empresarial San Fernando de Henares, Avenida de Castilla, 2 – 28830 Madrid (www.oup.es/en or product.safety@oup.com).
OUP España S.A. also acts as importer into Spain of products made by the manufacturer.

Nigra sum sed formosa.

for Judah. you are my first poem.

THE BLACK WOMAN.S IMAGE

THE ONLY IMAGE —— of the preFEMININE
that EXISTS. The IMAGE —— THAT AN ENTIRE
UNIVERSE is reverse accelerating to reflect.
Reflection — does not exist.

THE ONLY IMAGE —
that A WHOLE earth is
SHATTERING itself
To BECOME.

THE ONLY IMAGE
that can CAUSE
—— the beginning and
the end of an Earth.

Waheed, Nayyirah. stream black
books (p. 450). Kindle Edition.

Lina Iris Viktor, Eleventh, 2018. Courtesy of the artist.

Contents

Theology Is Not a Luxury (An Introduction)   1
1. Black Virgin, Black Venus   20
2. In Search of Our Mother's Garden   39
3. Theotokos, Another Spelling of My Name   80
4. A Womb of One's Own   109
5. Women Are from Venus   139
6. Following the Condition of the (M)other—or, At the Rim of the World   168

Acknowledgments   199
Notes   203
Bibliography   229
Index   241

Theology Is Not a Luxury
(An Introduction)

I've always been taken by flowers that bloom in the dark. The unction of perfume a backdrop for a tree frog sonnet, soft petals unfolding to punctuate the sensuality of the stars. The permeating quiet of bloom unreliant upon a conspicuous quality of day—rather, a photosynthesis so deep, so precious, as to be kept hidden—a dance that can only be perceived among a palette of shadows. In the origin myths of Christian theology, God creates, and it is darkness that hovers over the deep. There, She, the Spirit—the breath, the wind, the life—of God, fluttered.[1] A reminder that we are all born in holy darkness, that the night shines with divinity, that in Blackness there are sacred blossoms.

Immaculate Misconceptions is a submersive work committed to bloom, to a Blackness that is fluid and capacious and generative as source, to a world that considers birth and creation as sacred and possible and true, and to the possibility of a Christian theological imagination that breathes life, even through wounds and scars. This book argues a fundamental premise for Christian theology writ large:

Mary is Black.

Take Me to the Water

Take me to the water
Take me to the water
To be baptized . . .

It is said that water has memory, and it seems that the Paraíba River that day recalled something far more ancestral and divine than her shores had previously spoken. It was an early October morning in 1717—Brazil still a colony of Portugal—when the three fishermen set out for their catch. It was an auspicious day, as their community prepared for the formal visit from the governor of São Paulo who was visiting the villages beset along the river. The fishermen were in need of great supply for the banquets to come, but the river would not cooperate, their skill failing them in a moment where it felt it deeply mattered.

Tired and disappointed, the family—João Alves, Felipe Pedroso, and Domingos Garcia—turned to prayer, and asked Our Lady of the Immaculate Conception to intercede on their behalf. One of the fishermen, Alves, decided to make one last cast. In a moment of miracle and relief, something had finally found its way into their nets, but it wasn't the bounty they'd expected. Instead, out of the river they raised the broken body of a small clay statue—a Madonna—turned Black in the water. Shocked by the discovery, the men let down their nets again, this time pulling to the surface the missing head. The fishermen cleaned and swaddled the statue with great care. The third time they cast down their nets, they lifted to find them overflowing with an abundance of fish—a miracle. Out from the depths she appeared, *Aparecida*, dark as the waters that held her, with provision and abundance in tow.

The men brought the Black Madonna home, where Silvana da Rocha Alves—Domingo's wife, Felipe's sister, and João's mother—melted wax to *re-member* Mary's body. She placed the image on a small altar in their home, in show of her respect and gratitude. There, a legacy of devotion was birthed, to the one first known simply as Mãe (Mother) Aparecida. She now stands ubiquitously and symbolically as the Patron Saint of Brazil; with millions of devoted followers and pilgrims, The Shrine of Our Lady of Aparecida is today the largest Marian shrine in the world (see Fig. I.1).

Like so much of the Americas, the Brazil we know today was carved out and colonized through the gross enslavement of millions of Black African and Indigenous peoples—Brazil's shores were the landing place of more enslaved

Figure I.1 Nossa Senhora Aparecida, *Our Lady of Aparecida*.

Africans than any other country in the world.[2] In this context, of the many miracles that Our Lady Aparecida has performed, one resonates with unique sonority. The story tells of an African-descended man, Zechariah, who was enslaved in Brazil and woefully recaptured after a failed attempt at escape. Zechariah was forced to return by foot to the plantation, the measures of retributive torture exacerbated by the heavy chains that shackled his body along this *via dolorosa* of return. Along the way, they passed the small sanctuary of Our Lady of Aparecida, where Zechariah requested an opportunity to pray to the Virgin. Still ensnared, he was allowed to offer his devotion from the chapel door. As he came to his knees, the miraculous happened—the shackles locked around Zechariah's neck and body were immediately broken, falling useless to the ground. At this sign, the man who had enslaved Zechariah made an offering to *Aparecida* at the ledger value of Zechariah as property; Zechariah left the chapel a free person. To this day, his chains remain on display in her Shrine.

The 'Queen of Brazil' is a Black Madonna, a breaker of chains, a dark body materialized from dark waters. Some mythologies surmise that her initial form was of a white statue of Our Lady of the Immaculate Conception, brought over from Portugal. But here, on the banks of Brazil, she took on the form she willed for herself, "Black and beautiful am I."[3] Here she rose, newly ascended, broken but impervious, and *become* Brazilian. Her apparition is particularly special—a Black Madonna in relationship to *Black people*, to the enslaved and those whose ancestors were enslaved—and her miracles yet testify as an emblem of justice. As Ivonne Gebara and Maria Clara Bingemer describe:

> The Virgin who had become "black" could not but be the same one who would break unjust chains, the chains that diminished human dignity, especially for millions of people who had been uprooted from African soil and enslaved to serve the economic interests of the privileged.[4]

For those who have found themselves among the oppressed, this is not something that can so easily be taken for granted. And for a church so deeply embedded in a Christian-colonial project of violence and expansion, often reifying structural sin and injustice, there is also much to be considered. There is something to be said in this typology of the Madonna, for Black becoming, or to say, for *becoming* Black. There is something to be said for *being baptized* in Blackness, in *becoming* Black as incarnational solidarity, in *being* Black as signal of divine witness and grace. There is also something to be said, for a call to conversion to Blackness, as a sign of miracle and abundance, and as a signal of solidarity with those who are poor, those who are oppressed, those who are in search of (and attempting to enact) liberation. What if the appropriate petition to Mãe Aparecida may best be, *Take me to the water*....

When the inimitable Audre Lorde wrote about the significance of poetry, she described it as "illumination, for it is through poetry that we give name to those ideas which are—until the poem—nameless and formless, about to be birthed, but already felt."[5] She writes that, for women, "poetry is not a luxury," precisely for the ways it beckons forth new life, new dreams, new possibilities, from those "places of possibility," shrouded spaces that instantiate strength and courage and the rising spirit of wisdom:

> dark because they are ancient and hidden; they have survived and grown strong through that darkness . . . an incredible reserve of creativity and power.[6]

Immaculate Misconceptions: A Black Mariology takes seriously the poetry of darkness, and considers that for Black women, *theology* is not a luxury. Not when Christian theology has been so deeply centered as the source for the violences of colonialism, capitalism, whiteness, maleness, and patriarchy. Not when Christian theological presence animates daily life for so many, particularly those imagined to be in this thing called 'the West', as the silent guise of ethics and law, the governance of human rights and dignity, the locus of bodily knowledges and created order interwoven with the invisible strings of Christian cosmologies. Not when colonial Christian enterprise docks upon soft moral palates, encircling the tongue with the subtlety and nuance that pirouette when crafting a world—viscous, aromatic, bloodthirsty. Theology is not a luxury, even if one does not explicitly profess Christ, for in the wake of modernity, it is likely a certain kind of Christ has already been professed for you.

Instead, *Immaculate Misconceptions* recasts vision and reclaims the significance of Mary through the constellations of the Black Madonna, as she who is often relegated to notions of whiteness and virginity within Christian-colonial enterprise and European-descended theological discourse, and often gravely overlooked beyond the confines of Catholic doctrine. The Black Madonna is, however, a critical site to think and theorize differently the algorithms of oppression that manifest from purity, otherness, racism, misogynoir, and sexual violence, from the theological anthropological locus on one who was *fully human*, but asked to mother the Divine. If Mary—the one asked to mother the One who will be crucified toward salvation—is Black, what accountability must we have for the racial and gendered violences within the Christian tradition? How do we account for the Divine within the theological imaginary around Black women's bodies and lives? And what dreams and visions emerge when we attest to the miraculous in her presence, and bear witness to her commitments to freedom? Staged as a Black feminist and womanist theological conversation between the Black Madonna in image and icon, this project is a rally against the loss of sacred Blackness.

Theology-in-Relation

> my
> mother
> was my first country.
> the first place I ever lived.
>
> nayyirah waheed

> Sometimes, by taking up the problems of
> the Other, it is possible to find oneself.
>
> Éduoard Glissant

Of the many names by which Éduoard Glissant is known, theologian is not typically one. Born in Martinique, Glissant is considered to be one of the most important and influential writers of the French Caribbean. His conceptualization of the world mingles theory and poetry, traverses race and diaspora, bifurcates geographies and space. It is terrifyingly beautiful to hear Éduoard Glissant speak, even as his voice echoes the hollow evils of the African slave reality. To open *Poetics of Relation* is to be thrust from the door of no return, finding oneself at once suspended in the choking blue of Atlantic abyss. His imagery of the slave ship evokes a historical nausea only heightened by the suffocating accuracy of its deadly description:

> Imagine two hundred human beings crammed into a space barely capable of containing a third of them. Imagine vomit, naked flesh, swarming lice, the dead slumped, the dying crouched....[7]

One cannot underestimate the formative institution that was the colonial slave ship, as it carries the deeply entrenched theological DNA that would mark the definition of bodies throughout modernity, the feelings of collapse, drowning, choking, and sinking, a definition of consciousness very much still at work in the making of worlds. What this gathered experience of abyss marks is the evidence of Relation, a shimmering quality of crossing with no investment in the aesthetic of such:

> People who have been to the abyss do not brag of being chosen. They do not believe they are giving birth to any modern force. They live Relation and clear the way for it. . . . For though this experience made you, original victim floating toward the sea's abysses, an exception, it became something shared and made us, the descendants, one people among others. Peoples do not live on exception.

Relation is not made up of things that are foreign but of shared knowledge. This experience of the abyss can now be said to be the best element of exchange. (Emphasis added)[8]

Glissant speaks specifically to the violence executed upon glistening brown bodies held in a formidable cruelty between African and American shores, the inauguration of a diaspora fed by Blackness and blood.

But the concept of Relation, as defying origin and definition, as an imaginary of what Ashon Crawley has brilliantly described as an "otherwise movement," what might be stated as an "otherwise theology," is one that shifts the optic for thinking the world.[9] Relation is not bound by a historical compass nor a linear temporality, but instead is energized at the intersect, the overlap, the assemblage, the collage of bodies, of spirits, compressed, collapsed, and united. Relation operates as Delta, the process of change.

Amid the horror and abjection marked by a purgacious horizon Glissant does not lose sight of the totality of human experience, the alternative modalities of existence, of Black life that inherently resists oppression. Glissant considers, that even being bound in and by the negation of abyss does not preclude the possibilities of a bonded sociality that births new epistemic regimes. Standing starboard on the last transatlantic oceanliner, the *Queen Mary II*, during a taped interview, Glissant gestures over the glassy surface that masks the bones of Black bodies beyond our view. As the mainland shores slip out of sight, Glissant tells us that we must begin with departure:

> It's the moment when one *consents not to be a single being* and attempts to be many beings at the same time. In other words, for me every diaspora is the passage from unity to multiplicity. (Emphasis added)[10]

The Christian tradition echoes the stories of strange people finding themselves in strange lands, in places unknown and unforeseen, encountering oppression, enacting resistance, engaging in a transformative poetics that catalyzes an intervention into the stories we think we tell. The narratives of such queer life, of spiritual strivings both historical and contemporary, have often (necessarily) operated through such alternative horizons of possibility. Christian theology claims that humanity exists always ever as creation-in-relation; both the creature and creation are inherently theological categories, never singular, unable to stand outside of relation to God such that, truly, what is theology itself if it is not *theology-in-Relation*? Relation defies origin, transgresses definition, is that which is both imagined and lived; it carries the past, dreams of a future, but acts—right now—as a different optic for considering the world, detached from a false sense of progress and time and instead patterns the spiraled assertions of place and space. Such a vortex birthed through the combustion of race and embodiment is a means for thinking the implications in general, the theological implications in particular, of theological exchange.

And such an idea of passage marked with ebb and flow from unity to multiplicity is a theological anthropological enfleshment of diaspora, one wherein it can be said that, as Fred Moten describes, "exhausted, exhaustive maternity is her pedagogical imperative."[11] I argue that such a pedagogical imperative is theologically envisaged in the pregnant body of Jesus's mother, Mary. Does not the nature of Mary's Relation to her own body represent not the singularity, but the multiplicity of existence as divinity wrecks itself upon the shores of the human? Is not her relation to her own pregnancy the agential consent of Glissant's Relation manifest in the squeezing together of bodies, a plunging into an unknown abyss, the refusal to be a single being when one's ethic of justice is rooted in the generation of Diaspora taking root within her, invoking Incarnational habitation from which the intimacies of Christian life come to be known? To consider this requires one launch through a door of no return, a memorial threshold, that takes seriously a claim to Christian theological thought from the aegis of the Black Madonna.

I begin with Glissant because the theology in this book is grounded in Black study and Black feminist thought, takes seriously the person and work of Mary for theological discourse in relationship to Black liberation and womanist theologies, and takes seriously the consideration of Mary—who is Jesus's primary human relation—as Mary-in-Relation. In the past decade, explorations of race and theology have charted much critical ground, exposing Christian colonial conquest in relation to the production of whiteness, and expanding the critical foundations of Black liberation theology, Latin American liberation theology, *mujerista* theology, queer theology, decolonial theologies, eco-theology, and womanist theology (to name but some of the constructive threads influencing this book). Such interventions have traced the roots of Christian election and supercessionism over and against Jewish identity, in relation to the emergence of race, not as collapsible, equivocal identities—as the fight for Palestinian life teaches us—but as displaying a circle of thought of prejudice and supremacy whose legacies persist today.[12] These analyses demonstrate that if the container of the postmodern are mirrored lungs, the horizon of Christian thought is the air respiring its life.

Immaculate Misconceptions uniquely, specifically, considers the theological impact of such colonial encounters for Black women, and how Black and Indigenous women were reduced to bodies and flesh by the theological gaze. Thus the book takes seriously the idea of the sacred image, the *icon*, as a source of theological reflection and praxis, that never seemed to positively extend to the materiality of actual people with dark skin, even if the image before them retained it as such. This project is a turn to the Black Madonna, formal and informal, and the economy of the icon, as a means to better narrate the realized effects buried beneath the justifications of Christian salvation and understand the theological unbecoming of dark skin from the definition of full humanity. Here, *Immaculate Misconceptions* thinks deeply the concept of purity—the *idea* and the *ideal*—as an imaginary tied to whiteness and reproductive control, that evolved as a means to account for racial difference as well as the female body and sexual desire, and to ground the logics of how certain *kinds* of bodies become available for consumption. And of course, the turn to Black Mariology is to honor the ways the Black Madonna continues to resist.

This requires a word about theology. *Immaculate Misconceptions* assumes that theological thought is not something that happened in cracked wooden pulpits, tucked between yellowed hymnal pages, dashed against the rocks of an organ's exhale. Theology, rather, was and is a way of seeing, of touching feeling, of mapping bodies against the starscape of an inexhaustible universe. It was as adaptive as human life itself, vast enough to account for the rising of the sun while still making meaning from every hair follicle rooted on one's head. It accounted for the riches of a nation as much as the spread of the plague. It sourced hope in the midst of despair, made meaning out of the infinitesimal of life. It was used to divide and conquer people and land, to calculate morality in direct proportion to the melanin content of one's skin. It defined truth, goodness and beauty against bodies who could ground such ideas through their incapacity. It occupied the already-not-yet, examined and filled the spaces between, phallic and otherwise. As Jesus was imaged with corresponding limbs open, his arms spanning the width of a cross, so too did Christian theological thought evoke a certain kind of embrace, her openness justifying justice, mercy, and love. But by the same grip came a choking exploitation, engulfing the Enlightened mind, disguising and revising local knowledges as her own, capturing the colonial imagination in a siren song of destruction. Despite her breadth, Christian theology has often remained unmarked, an invisible power potent but unnamed for those who find themselves positioned beyond an explicit Christian sphere. Or worse, weaponized politically and interpersonally, as the resurgence of Christian nationalisms and theologies of white supremacy have gained traction (as well as power, influence, and artillery) globally.

Which means it is long past time that our intersectional analyses, that our critical theoretical apparatuses and methodologies, take God, and those who consider themselves the people of God, quite seriously. Things do get tricky when speaking of faith and God as 'real', particularly when academic research and public interest have often born repeated witness to the split subjectivity of theology and 'the rest' of religious study, between theology and 'the rest' of critical theoretical discourse. In many ways, the theological academy is perceived as the hermitage sect of the more valid, more rigorous study of religion proper, and, anecdotal as it may be, there are those on both sides who prefer and vigorously defend the distinction. We presume safe distance, separate but equal, a necessary and natural split between the religious and secular. But this is a dangerous mythology.

What is Christian theology? If theology is defined, perhaps most simply, as 'the human logic of the divine Logos' (okay: maybe that definition isn't the most simple), then the operations of such logics in and of the world comprise that which is theological.[13] How people—to note the differentials of said belief when met with dimensions of power, or a desire for power, and access to resources—understand God and God's relation to the world, *matters for everyone*, regardless of whether or not you share in said beliefs. The specificity of my research and claims about the negotiations of race and gender and sexuality throughout this work rely on a broader sense of theological categorical expansion (some might call it 'constructive'). It encompasses the idea that theology, in both study and praxis, is far more pervasive than this thing called belief, that theologians are not the only ones in the world asking theological questions, and that there is a situated urgency of its claims only appreciated by an engagement of the theological and theoretical.

This project understands the theological as a category of composition, of the composite. The theological is an interdisciplinary art, an expression and an interrogation. It manifests across texts and liturgies, pages and sound waves, melodies and paints, the ascetic and the erotic. Which is why the method of this book, ecological in formation and rooted in Relation, is evidenced through the explorations of theology as a *genealogical genre*. Foucault described genealogy (as opposed to history, or origin), as, gray, meticulous, and patiently documentary. It operates in a field of entangled and confused parchments, on documents that have been scratched over and recopied many times; it must record the singularity of events outside of any monotonous finality; it must seek them in the most unpromising places, in what we tend to feel is without history—in sentiments, love, conscience, instincts; it must be sensitive to their recurrence, not in order to trace the gradual curve of their evolution, but to isolate the different scenes where they engaged in different roles. Finally, genealogy must define even those instances when they are absent, the moment when they remained unrealized.[14]

In terms of its patience, detail, and "vast accumulation of source material," this project is certainly marked by its genealogical approach, by "an analysis of descent," one that is "situated within the articulation of the body and history."[15] One might argue that the most theological understandings of Christ reflect an analysis of divine descent, one that certainly stands between the embodied breadth of creation and the space and time of its enactment. Manifesting stigmata is something of what we are trying to do; it is something theology *does*. But theology is least of all about locating the origins of wounds, of pointing to gaping flesh. It is instead about the hope that resides in nooks and crannies, glimpsing joy in the midst of sorrow, displaying resistance manifest in bruises and scars, embodying mercy, celebrating freedom, demanding justice, being love. It is the mess of life, the space in between. And the attention to the glances, the heartbeats, the instances available and absent is something to which genealogical method calls our consideration. Describing theology as a genre is "to think about it as something repeated, detailed, and stretched while retaining its intelligibility, its capacity to remain readable or audible across the field of all its variations."[16] Because there are modes and ideas that circulate, patterns, and forms. And yet, what has not been foreseen is the breadth of these namings. The fluidity of the unstable. (Because we all know that the anti-genre too quickly becomes a genre into itself.) But the problem with genre is to misunderstand its ever-changing conventions—that flux allows us to position ourselves in such a way as to not be so committed to an idea that we ignore the moments when it is employed in efforts that produces effects other than justice. Genre lends itself to a more expansive definition of the Christian theological imagination, one that resists strict evaluative modalities and rather makes space for a multiplicity of interrogations to be engaged as theoretical innovations. It does not exclude the claims to belief and faith, nor does it ever eschew them. But it lends itself beyond the definitions of confessional life, and takes account of the ways it must always be responsible in negotiating the production and tethering to that which is also *a*theological.[17] It takes seriously nuance between content and form, *logos* and *lexis*, while also resisting the artificial divide between the two, between the thing expressed and expression itself.

A natural extension of this analysis of descent, one that blossoms from the critical space of how embodiment *feels*, brings us to a methodology of Relation. Descent is an act of scouring new depths and boundaries; it is Relation that allows us to feel ourselves sinking, plunged, and submerged, of taking seriously Katie Cannon's sense of pursuing an "emancipatory historiography."[18] The Relation of descent asks us to challenge our depth perception, in as much as we challenge our perceptions of death. It is a reminder that power and life are at the bottom, that precisely out of chaos God brings forth new worlds. Arbiters of the divine and miraculous appear. *Aparecida*. I am asking that we descend beneath the waters of Blackness—through the icon—to imagine through Mary an "enfleshed freedom."[19] This is an effort to tell one chapter of one story in an infinite volume illuminating the Christian underpinnings of modernity, a chapter that continues to spread roots and give life to a moral hierarchy that subtends the machinations of everyday life. If anything then, this project takes up the confessional *content* of theological genre in order to express the *form* of theological genre in the world. In essence, genre allows theology to exist in the world, even when it is not of the world.

Not everything in this book is theology.
But everything in this book is theological.

And we begin with the Black Madonna, with Mary's pregnant body—and as I argue throughout this text, a Black, queer body signaled by friendship as a way of life—that takes on the abyss of eternity inside her womb, communicates the properties of human life through her flesh, binds, latches, and secures her blood to Divine presence. Such consent is an act of volition, to engage in the imaginative despite the encroaching shadows of passage. And it is Mary's fully affirmed humanity that stirs the waters of consent for those of us who might profess Christian faith. Moten reminds us of the precarity of such a notion: "Everybody I know," he says, "is driven to dissent from such a movement, where consent is inseparable from a monstrous imposition."[20]

And yet, Mary is a figure whose consent and participation has been colonized as part of an institutional structure of discipline and discipleship. (One might recall here, that Christopher Columbus's largest boat on the fateful 1492 expedition across the Atlantic was the *Holy Mary of the Immaculate Conception*.) So often Mary is imagined through the lens of being virgin territory, an unknown land of endless space, the very presumption of colonial capture following that because a land is unknown, that it must be available, that it can be consumed, that it may be adjudicated through the imagination of a greater good. It is the rendering of the womb as an empty surface, a tabula rasa upon which the Word of God can be inscribed, instead of through and with whom the Word of God might be spoken. Relation, a movement toward multiplicity between Mary and Jesus, resists the dismembering of Mary from her flesh and body, from her own womb, the false fragmentation of the subject that would alienate Mary from the image of Christ and her being in the world.

Something like a slave ship.
Which requires us return to the womb.

> Being white has never been enough.
> Not without being black.
> Denise Ferreira da Silva

To begin a theological discussion of the Black woman's body, to question how and where dark female flesh functions for (rather than fits in to) a theological canon of purity, is a task of thinking the taut relation between God, race, sex and desire. The survey of resonance between theology, sensuality, and the erotic is not in itself sufficient unless we consider thinking the relation of these, as the relation of *race* and *gender* themselves the powerful narratives whose "odd coupling," as Denise Ferreira da Silva describes, are themselves inherent to the evolving imaginary of the "others of Europe."[21] This pursuit does not simply ask how the category of race or gender becomes exclusive within a society, but instead, pushes us to see "how the racial combines with other social categories (gender, class, sexuality, culture, etc.) to produce modern subjects who can be excluded from (juridical) universality without unleashing an ethical crisis."[7] Questioning how racial subjection fails to incite an ethical response within modernity also suggests questioning how racial subjection failed to incite an ethical response in either the before or the after. It is my contention that theology not only is an important discourse to unlock the deeply embedded assumptions of morality and violence within contemporary United States society, but also that theology—as a discourse and at times, a system, that often moderates and drives ethical praxis—needs more accountability.

Contemporary Black feminist thought has readily located the ethical injury of Black women's sexuality imagined in terms of its lustful, insatiable appetite and excess, an exotic amalgamation of butt and breast, of explicit sexual secrets waiting to be unlocked and explored. The exploitation of such an imaginary has left Black women subject to harassment, degradation, consumption, and rape. But as Hortense Spillers describes, this exploitation was not inaugurated by the crucible effects of the institution of slavery itself, but rather by the unbridled exploitation of such an imaginary that the conditions of slavery provided:

> [Black American women's] enslavement relegated them to the marketplace of the flesh, an act of commodification so thoroughgoing that the daughters labor even now under the outcome. Slavery did not transform the black female into an embodiment of carnality at all, as the myth of the black woman would tend to convince us, nor, alone, the primary receptacle of a highly profitable generative act. *She became instead the principal point of passage between the human and the nonhuman world.* Her issue became the focus of a cunning difference—visually, psychologically, ontologically—as the route by which the dominant modes decided the distinction between humanity and "other."[22] (Emphasis added)

What takes the Black woman's body into the realm of the sexual as it crosses the threshold into the non-human? The "cunning difference" that Spillers describes here marks the *displacement* of the Black woman's body as "vestibular to culture."[23] As identities were untethered from land and geography, the relocation of the Black woman's body beyond the normative perimeters of femininity and whiteness exacerbated the violence of patriarchy, reifying this dislocation as a theological principle. Black women were the dictionary by which one could readily define the idea of "man" (patriarchal humanity) from the negative, *via negativa*; out of nothing, *ex nihilo*. This was a derived interpretation of an absence by its presence as it manifest in dark female flesh, as "the black person mirrored for the society around her what a human being was *not*."[24] This means that, while the mythology around the sexual pleasures and desires of the black woman's body had direct material consequences, the exploitation of Black women—sexual and otherwise—were nuances in a larger theological operation of ordering the world. More than a denial or degradation of the Black body, this operation was a denial of Black humanity.

But denials are not in themselves truths, even as they are building blocks in the making of worlds. And the witness of Black flesh itself does not bear the burden for testifying to this reality as a unilateral concept. It instead witnesses to this and to so much more, from outside, inside, beneath, below and within. As Fred Moten describes, Blackness is something "fugitive," as he puts it—an ongoing refusal of standards imposed from elsewhere. In *Stolen Life* he writes:

> Fugitivity, then, is a desire for and a spirit of escape and transgression of the proper and the proposed. It's a desire for the outside, for a playing or being outside, an outlaw edge proper to the now always already improper voice or instrument.[25]

The Incarnation is a moment carving an outlaw, sacred edge inside of the womb, and the theological concept of the *already-not-yet* (the sense of bearing witness to and participating in a divine reality that has not yet been full realized) is a fugitive imaginary, the transgressions of holiness by grace, driven by desire. This fugitivity is one that pushes through the remnants of survival to the possibilities of intimacy, healing, grace, joy, and a vision of thriving, untethered from consumption and rooted in collective. More than just liberation, we are in search of freedom, even if it is not discernible to those exterior to its existence.

Black Mariology

Black Mariology emerges when we consider the primary claim of this book: Mary is Black. Traditional Mariology is academically associated with the Roman Catholic Church and four dogmatic principles—Divine Motherhood, Perpetual Virginity, Immaculate Conception, and Assumption. These formulations have been, to say the least, "a matter that is ecumenically sensitive, morally problematic, and theologically challenging."[26] The thrust of this work is not necessarily to approach the history and proclamation of each these dogmas, but instead to take up the ways theological promulgation of Marian ideas do or do not take seriously her capacity for Blackness (which includes taking Mary seriously to begin with), and to consider how such dogma cannot simply exalt Mary in the ways she functions as exception, but must also "exalt precisely her poverty, her dispossession, and her simplicity," for "this is the only condition that will enable the church, which sees the symbol or figure of itself in Mary, to be . . . the church of the poor, those whom Mary declared liberated, fed, and exalted in the song of the Magnificat."[27] For when held in the arms of colonial expansion and conquest, the uses of the Virgin Mary that functioned to discipline and tame women's bodies, and later non-white bodies, throughout history found a particular swaddling in the imaginations of white male domination, a theological fissure rooted in exclusions. Though the iconic life of Mary was always varied and complex, the economy of her icon bloated through colonial expansion into the shape of an empire. This project thinks more distinctly about Mary as a figure of theological and theoretical reflection both within and beyond conciliar dogmatic claims, to more deeply consider the challenges presented when we take seriously the sacrality of the Black Madonna and what it means to bear God. I argue that the Black Madonna expresses being in-Relation—the womb, the birth, the touch point between humanity and divinity, between the election of the people of Israel and the salvation of the world. Within Mary are a multitude of possibilities for rethinking theology from the space of the theoretical, in ways that dialogue as much with 'the tradition' as they demand acknowledgment and often privilege the realities of embodiment beyond dogma. While much of Christian theology has at the least, obliquely, acknowledged the oeuvre of the Black Madonna tradition, we are left to grapple with the image of Black women and femmes as embodying sacrality.

To claim—or rather, *acknowledge*—that "Mary is Black," is to state both the personal and the political as they are entrenched in the theological. Such a plain truth, wrapped so deeply in refusal that her disguise is whiteness, domesticity, fragility of the most insidious kind. But, not only to claim, but to *know* that Mary is in fact Black, signals the questions of human dignity that mark the violences of our contemporary time, and an indebtedness to multiple theological inheritances, particularly those of Black liberation and womanist theological thought.

First, Black Mariology is premised in recognizing Black liberation theology's claims that Jesus is Black. Jesus's Blackness—"an ontological symbol and a visible reality that best describes what oppression means in America"[28]—was predicated upon understanding God as being on the side of the oppressed; in the Latin American liberation contexts, the parallel language emerged of the 'preferential option for the poor'. James Cone and others argued it was critical to imagine salvific presence and sacred essence inside of the communities that disproportionately face oppression, despisement, and violence, and in the United States in particular, Jesus had to be Black. Cone argued that "God has chosen to make the black condition *God's* condition!"[29] Black Mariology takes seriously that God has done so, through his mother.

Such a turn is a natural extension of several threads of analysis in womanist theology, which has perhaps missed a theological anthropological opportunity to engage more extensively with Mary as a theological figure, especially as an extension of a Black Christ—his flesh hewn so completely from hers, that which He himself created. This can be attributed to the ways Black liberation theology emerged first as a discourse arising from predominantly Protestant thinkers, and because the aura of her dogmatic imaginary (and as we will discuss, the inaccessibility of virginity as a primary marker of her identity) has often felt impenetrable. Noting the prominence of figures like Hagar for womanist theology and a dearth of (and possible reticence toward) extended reflection on Mary, Karen Baker-Fletcher noted that "There is something . . . important to learn from Mary. So many Korean women and black American women have lost children, sons, and husbands to violence like Mary. . . . Protestant womanist theology could deepen in wisdom by taking Mary more seriously."[30] This undoubtedly speaks to the need for a deeper communion among scholars and thinkers across Christian traditions, particularly for projects oriented around justice and freedom. Black Mariology is an explicit commitment to engaging in this task, which arguably is also but an extension of Delores Williams's contentions in her groundbreaking *Sisters in the Wilderness*. There she describes that:

> Womanist analysis ... suggests another kind of history to which black theology must give attention if it intends to be inclusive of black women's experience. This is *"women's re/production history."* It involves more than women birthing children, nurturing and attending to family affairs. Though the events and ideas associated with these realities do relate, "women's re/production history" has to do with whatever women think, create, use and pass on through their labor for the sake of women's and the family's well-being. Thus black women's resistance strategies belong to black women's re/production history—just as the oppressive opposition to these strategies from dominating culture belongs to this history. Through the lens of black women's re/production history we can see the entire saga of the race. (Emphasis added)[31]

The insistence on articulating a Black Mariology is to take seriously Black women's re/production history, at the site of the Black Madonna, as one through which we can see the entire saga *of the faith*, particularly as Christianity is bound up in global colonial and racial violence. Here we consider Mary, in her configurations in Scripture and beyond, as a figure whose lived experiences are analogous to those of Black women (though not *just*, or necessarily *all*, Black women; and to name explicitly that this book and its proximate contexts draw heavily from the experiences of Black women and theologians who live in the United States, though the implications attempt to inflect a global awareness and consciousness), and thus press to consider Mary as a site to rethink resistance, justice, survival, sustenance, and resurrection from despair.[32]

The notion of a Black Mariology is not one in which I am interested in simply adding race to the recipes of doctrine and dogma, but instead, as I will repeat again, to consider a theology arising *from* the condition of the Black Mother, a theology *following* the condition of the Black Madonna, a theology *for* the consideration of all those who pursue justice and life at the spiritual intersections of the world, questioning the 'legislative doctrine' around our perceptions of Mary, and perhaps extending conversations forward to consider the *what else* of life. This is not a claim of hierarchy or erasure, for Mary is not *just* or *only* Black.[33] But to claim Mary's Blackness is to ontologically stand against the logics of domination and supremacy of whiteness as it manifests as anti-Blackness. A Black Mariology must siphon through the past that is always present and never truly past, naming and thus attenuating the effects of the refusals and denials of Blackness beneath a sacred canopy.

For to think against sacred Blackness is an immaculate *misconception*. Here I am playing on the widespread misinterpretation of the Immaculate Conception, which invokes a significance in the lineage and genealogy of women—how Mary was conceived by her mother Anne, *not* how Jesus was conceived by Mary. But I here am also playing on the idea of conceptions as fixed theological ideas of God's relation to the world that go uninterrogated or revised. To be included in ways we have been *misconceived*, then, is to perceive Blackness as outside of the realm of divine goodness, and succumb to the collapsing of metaphors of light and dark as a spectrum of racial proximity to God. For some—for many—thinking about the Blessed Virgin Mary, the Theotokos, the Mother of God, Blackness is the least of what comes to mind. Blackness is not represented through her skin, through notions of purity and cleanliness, to visions of light and holiness—particularly in a world where Jesus continues to be imagined as white. And thus without paying attention, one can readily *mis/conceive*—do our theologies gestate and support conditions of life, fecundity, and freedom for all, including Black women?

Instead, *Immaculate Misconceptions* centers the theological body of the Black Madonna as a means to reconsider the female body, the Black body, the transbody, the cisbody, the reproductive body, in Relation to itself and to the world, a form of legibility of encounter and exchange across embodiments, with bonds neither finite nor transparent—accounting for the particularity and collectivity of this thing called sociality. And to attend to the theological capacity of the Song of Songs formulation, "Black and beautiful am I." It is an exercise in what Andrew Prevot has described as *doxological Blackness*, which:

> refers to an irrevocable fact of existence, which is not only rooted in the creative and redemptive actions of the triune God but which is also phenomenologically evident: namely that black is beautiful. This is simply—but also diversely and complexly—a given. To be black is ipso facto to reflect something of the glory and word of God.[34]

This is also an act of naming Blackness as icon, on calling this flesh, Beloved. As Prevot expounds, such an endeavor "can refer to those aspects of black culture, thought, or praxis that intentionally affirm this beloved relation to God in a doxologically rigorous manner."[35] If the Incarnation establishes the principle of Relation, the poetics of Relation, then perhaps we must return to the womb as hush harbor, birth as liturgy, and Black life as holy. To see what can be constructed from Black women's testaments of "intelligence and ingenuity in the midst of struggle, creating a culture of resistance."[36] To consider that the Black Madonna teaches us that "the 'Good News' is that the divine can occur within and between bodies."[37] A vision to hold the world itself as sacred, perhaps modeled by how a Black mother held the world within her. Cone, speaking on the content of theology, described the earnest theological task as one that must have "visions of the future because the present is unbearable."[38] Black Mariology, unsatisfied with the world as is, sings the songs of Zion.

The Chapters

The first chapter, "Black Virgin, Black Venus" offers a theological reading of the painting *The Rape of the Negress* (1632). Composed at the height of the Dutch Golden Age, I argue the reception history of this image (as well as it's canonical avoidance and elision) asserts the emergence of a white "master" gaze reflective of Dutch imperial ambitions across the globe. The image is a prototype of violence against a Black woman within the visual field, and marks this anonymous woman (and subsequently, Black female flesh) as licentious and available despite the cues of her physical resistance. Can an image capture the mechanisms of becoming a "master" in one's mentality? I argue that it can, and outline the Christian thought at play behind this profaning of the Black woman's body. I place this image in the context of the broader iconoclasm of the Dutch landscape, and the flight (fugitivity) and loss of the Black Madonna, to demonstrate the violence that occurs when we annihilate (holy) images that point us to the *imago Dei* (image of God) in Black flesh.

Chapter 2, "In Search of Our Mother's Garden," begins in *the* beginning, in a garden where Eve came to be (held) responsible for all that is wretched of the earth. Reading biblical narratives through Black study and the figure of the conjure woman, this chapter revisits the myths of the Garden of Eden as an origin story of God-ordained gender difference, anthropological truth, the subordination of women's bodies, and divine suffering. Here I demonstrate how Eve's reception prefigures other bodies that will be "marked" as disobedient, unruly, suspicious, and impure—one that upon colonial encounter will ostensibly be pathologized as Black. Eve reflexively formed the anchor for Mary's perfection—a polarity marked by obedience and disobedience, and movement from "darkness" to light—such that for Eve, "all of her sex" would bear the blame for the conditions of human sin and strife. I argue that part of the spinning of Eve's tale demonstrates the threat of her curiosity as proxy for sexual pleasure, agency, reproductive anxiety, desire—and eventually, miscegenation and purity of bloodlines. This chapter queers the negotiations of Eve in the Garden and describes how theological assessment of gender difference eventually inflects the color spectrum of race, evidenced by the theory of polygenesis in the work of Charles Carroll. The chapter turns to Harmonia Rosales's *Lilith and Eve* as a site of redemptive Black feminist reimagining, to consider that Mary and Eve are not actually opposites in the questions they ask, only in the answers they are imagined to hold.

Chapter 3, "Theotokos, Another Spelling of My Name," delves more deeply into the dogmatic formation of Marian identity, and the questions of virginity, purity, and reproduction that would signal Mary's exceptionalism. Mary was ground zero of how one could understand the person and work of Jesus Christ and the schema of redemption at the heart of the Christian faith. But the intense debates over the status of her body and sexuality (perpetual virgin), those over her title and name (*theotokos*), and those over her sinlessness (immaculately conceived) shifted her agency as well as her utility, and left a devastating wake wherein a divine sense of *misogynoir* could emerge. Picking up with the narratives of the New Testament, this chapter examines how paternal anxiety affronted claims to the nature of Christ, and the context of the Nestorian controversy, a tumult of fifth-century events leading up to the Council at Ephesus (451) that forced the question of the nature of Mary's body. This chapter presses the libidinal reticence and refusal of Mary's body through her dogmatic emergence as an apophatic gauge apart from other women and their wombs, a modeled perfection (and religious Jewish erasure) that signal the prehistory of how Mary became white, a model Christian European subject.

Chapter 4, "A Womb of Her Own," takes up the tangled web of purity logics in an extended meditation on the womb imaginary of Black life, and the configuration of Black birth and Black mothering in the American social landscape. The chapter introduces 'Three Mothers' with the consideration, after Bersani, "is the *womb* a grave?," to recognize the ways that both the concept of the womb, as well as the concept of the Mother/mothering, are infused with theological glosses around what one can or cannot do in service of reproduction. The questions of virginity discussed in the previous chapters lead us to think more specifically about the process of birth itself, and to think through how the question of pain and cleanliness around Mary's pregnancy and birth, as signifiers of purity and grace, must reckon with womanist theological interventions around suffering and surrogacy. The chapter turns to consider the figure of the *Mater Dolorosa*, and the visual witness of Black mothers in the United States who have lost their children (legacies stemming from Mamie Till-Mobley to the contemporary moment), in their shared pain, as those who perhaps only wanted to mother, not mother a movement.

Chapter 5, "Women Are from Venus," offers a theological rendering of the continued imaginary of Black female flesh through *the* Venus, the Venus Hottentot, Saartjie (Sara) Baartman. Marketed as a lucrative scientific curiosity, this chapter traces the connections between her race, gender, sexuality, and eroticized profitability as signaling a paradigm of the "sex-trafficked" subject in modernity. The chapter interrogates the *theological* constructions of Baartman's personhood and agency, as a group of white male Christian 'abolitionists' dismissed her for not being the right *kind* of confessing subject, in one of the oldest human trafficking cases on record. I connect the legacy of Black Venus with that of Black Eve, one positioned to be mouthpiece or minstrel, and argue Baartman's exploitation is elicited against the backdrop of the convergence of Christianity and whiteness, and of a sensibility of morality and duty that married sexual access and excess to Black female bodies. Reading Baartman as theological subject holds accountable the place of Christian missionaries in her life and elucidates the moral binary and purity narratives inscribed by the Eve-Mary citation, while theorizing Blackness, gender, and performance, theologically. To expand the story of Baartman's life is to challenge the question of her use in iconography as only a victim, and to consider the complexities of her icon through the lens of fugitivity and freedom, the ethics of a Black woman under constraint.

Moving from the analyses of Baartman as a theological figure, Chapter 6, "Following the Condition of the M(other), or At the Rim of the World" assembles the cumulative threads of Black feminist and womanist Marian analysis to begin to articulate a Black Mariology, one rooted in a moral imaginary of possibility, relation, complexity, hope, and joy, *otherwise*.[39] The chapter returns to the notion of 'consent not to be a single being' as an invitation to pilgrimage to and with the Black mother—*fugitive, friend, flesh, fire, free*. The analysis considers a number of capacious imaginaries of Scripture and constructive theology, to include the Annunciation and Trinity as moments of Black queer possibility, and (re)turns to the iconic tradition—specifically the Eastern orthodox icon, Mary of the Unburnt Bush, a vision of iconicity and birth from one filled with fire but *not consumed*. I conclude in litany and song, the Black Madonna as spiritual, as prayer, as invocation and invitation to new life, an approach to 'live Relation and clear the way for it', to follow the Black Madonna as a signpost to freedom.

There is a gift in theological thought that inflects certain modalities of Black study, Black feminism, liberation, and womanist thought—disciplines that demand and insist upon *life*, enact networks of support and care, and insist that horror and abjection are not ever the totality of a human experience, and most certainly that death is not the only horizon for Black life. What critical theories of social death and alienation and Afro pessimism (while important analyses) lose in their assessments are the alternative modalities of existence that inherently resist oppression, and the witness to ancestors who carried rice and seeds, buried beneath cartographies of plaited hair, who insisted we sow, even if we have been scattered; for even among the abyss, we birth. This is an exploration that theology not only makes possible, but attends as midwifery, as divine command. This is the hope of an empty tomb: commitment to bloom. And for Black women, for any who believe in freedom, this kind of theology is most certainly not a luxury. In a world where God is still too often seen as and only as the white Father—and increasingly the gatekeeper of political power that demands spiritual, social, economic, and intellectual impoverishment of the masses—may this work bring us down by dark riversides, a different 'door of no return.'

I invite you across the threshold of this work by quoting first none other than Jesus on the matter at hand.

Here is your [Black] Mother.

1
Black Virgin, Black Venus

Annunciations

To unveil the veil . . . is to veil the unveiling.

Elliot Wolfson

Every public exposure of an honorable virgin is (to her) a suffering of rape; and yet the suffering of carnal violence is the less (evil), because it comes of its natural office.

Tertullian

Our attentions are narrowed, swept across a luminous canvas to the animated struggle of a naked Black woman. She hangs askew, slightly right of center, alerting us that something is awry. Her right arm thrusts into the air, the sable outline of skin shadowed in soft strokes of grey, the imperceptible hum and blurred whirring of her mechanically urgent movements captured in warm hue. She is signaling, waving—no—struggling, fighting; her outstretched fingers splay in search of an assistance out of reach.

A white man sits naked at the edge of a mattress, holding the disrobed woman in his lap. He restrains her body, gripping her at the thigh and forearm. She twists awkwardly attempting to wrench herself away, but to no avail. Her feet hover just above the wooden planks of the floor, the weighted tension of her body torqued against her suppressor signals his leverage and her futility. Her contorted position intensifies the fear that has infused every detail of her face. Panicked and strained, her mouth gapes wide, frantic with shrieks we cannot hear—her eyes plead rage, petitions for a God we cannot see.

We are asked to look upon an unwilling sacrifice at the most ancient of altars, a bed unmade and undone, crude and cruel, a table prepared for what is to come. The man restraining her does not look at her, his disinterested gaze filled with flat apathy. Not *seeing* his prey, his eyes float toward his compatriot—a second white man, partially naked, pale thighs exposed beneath a crisply textured sheet he holds loosely around his waist. While one hand holds up the covering for his lower body, the other is raised, possibly "a nod to the religious tradition," as "the gestures made by the rapist's companions are a clear case of the devil quoting scripture to serve his own purpose."[1] Eyeing his audience with indeterminate expression, the casual glance over his shoulder breaks the fourth wall with mocking conceit, a sordid playback loop watching us watch his friend watching him. All of this looking, and still, even in her state of hypervisibility, no one *sees* the Black woman.[2] Both internal and external to the scene, he shepherds us from the border frame through the conglomerate obscenities of observance still refusing to acknowledge her subjectivity. Only a pointed index finger returns our eyes to the suspended moment of physical subjection. The body language, hand gesture, and facial expression offer no accusation, commentary, criticism, or disruption—they simply ground us in a violent present.

We do not know how we have gotten here, how he, the other men, or the woman have entered this moment in time, only that our gaze is collapsed in warped apprehension. There is a third and final man. Fully clothed in decorative costume, he stares through the shadow, angled behind the struggle centering the scene. He raises both hands before him, spreading his fingers in a declaration of innocence. His body language articulates surprise, surrender, and deflection from his own culpability in the matter, but as he maintains his voyeuristic posture, he consents to participate, his astonishment unmoored from an ethical impulse to intervene. The progressive states of undress between the three white men are revelatory in their unveiling, a detail of episodic discovery mimicked through the progressive gestures of their hands, a body language that heightens the inflections of their gaze. Collectively they offer a sustained fermata of the event, a teleological suspension that elides the past, penetrates the present, and anticipates a violent eschatology—an "already-not-yet" future end. Arrested by a suspended image that only mimics the suspension of time, a viewer cannot keep from crashing into the future it forebodes.

The men in this image are invariably white and invariably Dutch. They are not individual selves, but a gathered community with a shared ethos of collaborative violence reinforced by white supremacy. As historian Amanda Pipkin describes, even an "... optimistic analysis of [this] painting of three young white men raping a black woman is that it served to critique the debauchery of student life and the existing social and racial hierarchies where men could commit such crimes with impunity. . . ."[3] These are not sins relegated solely to the level of individual action, but of state sanctions. Their code of ethics and honor work themselves out behind the canvas. One as three, or three in one, they are a trinity of colonialist posture—chronicler/narrator, explorer/enforcer, and bystander/benefactor. Their depiction enacts colonial modalities of intrusion and consumption, in part because these men are not just white and Dutch—they are Christian. They pervert omniscience and omnipresence via a racial optic, a corruption of divine attribute.

Despite the fact that Dutch culture and life were suffused with a puritan sense of ethics, the art of the seventeenth century detailed a number of scenes that would confirm the Dutch "were not shy of erotic depictions."[4] Yet, even for a culture that regularly explored sex and violence in the visual field, art historians and commentators insistently note the conspicuous difference in content and tone of this image as an outlier; "This one goes beyond the usual bounds."[5] What are the 'usual bounds' of uninhibited artistic expression? Where exactly is the transgression defined? The attempted subtlety is but a stark reminder of the insistent refusal to name a deeply social and theological truth about violence at the intersections of race and gender, another way of not saying what must be said: that even in art, violence against Black women remains illegible before a normative white gaze. No one in the scene is looking at *her*. No one in the scene sees *her*. How then can we?

Avoidances

What's in a name? Of the disproportionately few historians and critics who have offered comment on this painting, *The Rape of a Negress* (see Fig 1.1) presents only a discomfiting enigma—it is unusual, but not egregious. On several fronts the painting is obscure, inciting clear prudence and clear reticence in its reception

Figure 1.1 Christiaen van Couwenbergh, *The Rape of the Negress*, 1632.
Oil on canvas, 105 × 127.5 cm. Museé des Beaux-Arts, Strasbourg.

as anomalous. Had the author included an inscription or title himself, perhaps we would know more about the visual he depicted. But for centuries this early portrayal of the Black body languished in the shadows of masterpieces much more celebrated, its creator left shrouded in anonymity among far more celebrated contemporaries like Rembrandt and Vermeer. Only in 1940 was the work identified as that of Christiaen van Couwenbergh, a well-respected history painter hailing from Delft.[6] Of the 88 paintings that have since been confirmed to comprise his oeuvre, there is nothing that compares to this, no scenes without direct and easy historical location, and no other paintings including, much less featuring, a Black figure.[7] The sheer expanse of the canvas nauseates, immediately intimating the wealth of its owner. Even in the free-market economy of Golden Age art, a painting of such measure would have been too great an expense to be undertaken without a sense of demand.[8] Discerning tastes required great discrimination and care, and the images adorning museum corridors, the emblems now memorializing times past, are those that "privileged male artists thought would appeal to potential buyers."[9] With excess of size and obscenity of composition, by every estimation this painting was meant for an audience.

The scene itself is crude and disheveled, reinforcing the emotions and interactions within the cloistered space. Little attention is given to detailing the background, daubed in muted tones of brackish light and heavy shadow. An unadorned pediment headboard reinforces notions of austerity. With sheets in disarray and straw springing from the worn mattress, the unmade bed suggests the disturbance of order and the disheveling of emotion; this is chaos, the sign of the reprobate. A sitting chair frame peeks from beneath the careless heap of clothes, hurriedly cast off, obscuring any sign of cushion or comfort.

An uncovered chamber pot rests on a tripod stool. A typical Dutch motif, the pot brings an element of documentary witness to the chamber interior. Usually stored beneath the bed, it too rests *in medias res*, oddly out of place.[10] Left uncovered and exposed, the pot speaks to a lack of decorum and discretion. A haptic, olfactory element evokes further disgust: the stench of sweat, bodies, wood, hay, urine, and feces encircle our nostrils, an epistemological miasma the reminder that to look here is to be caught in the process of *seeing* something foul, inappropriate for civilized public consumption. Like many contemporary still life portraits that depict rotting fruit with bugs or flies, so too this image foregrounds a kind of decay signified by the presence of filth. Sparseness heightens the unsettling gravity of the scene, the "*sentiment du déshabillé*" that implies this is something one would be mistaken to witness, not meant to be privy to as an audience nor subsequently, as participants.[11]

She has been stripped of her clothing, of any other markers that would distinguish her but for a small bonnet still tied to her hair, a possible sign of socioeconomic status. While head coverings frequently indicate servitude or lower-class stature for women in European paintings, Couwenbergh regularly prefers to style the women in his paintings with the braided, decorative hair styles of the time. However, in the one other depiction of a Black woman that Couwenbergh paints, she too wears a bonnet of similar style to the Black woman in this painting.[12] It seems that Couwenbergh intends to mark Black women, though the specific symbol remains opaque for a contemporary audience. The bonnet thus reminds us of the breach of modesty, the misrecognition of humanity at play, and of a definition of womanhood to which the Black woman does not have access.[13] To this point, Couwenbergh has dispensed with the diaphanous fabric that is typically depicted draped over the lap and genitals of a naked woman. The use of fabric would have been an opportunity to flaunt technique, its folds meant to flirt with the eye, the textured hint of erotic overture just beyond the veil of a translucent lens. Of course, the fabric that *suggests* nudity is not necessary to actually *depict* nudity—but its absence signals the gratuitous. The Black woman is not situated within the realm of the erotic save for her captivity. If the woman is experiencing the etymological breadth of *la rapt*—her rapture, her rape—then the viewer is implicated in the moment of her abduction.

Diane Wolfthal has contrasted this painting with Dutch Baroque depictions of white women within interior domestic spaces. Referencing the extensive scholarship on these painted environments, she notes that typical depictions feature "rooms [that] are sparklingly clean, 'beds spotless, unrumpled and without stain and suspicion,' [where] the domestic interior has been transformed into a sign of moral purity and domestic tranquility."[14] The medium infers theological themes of inner moral purity expressed not only through the body but through the environment. As the domestic was understood to be the domain of the female sex, the maintenance of cleanliness and order, of a well-kept household, was a sign of integrity. In these images, women depicted in organized interior spaces symbolize chastity, holiness, and honor associated with the recognition and capitulation to a proper created order, a moral standard where women are safe and protected when they are *in the right place*, the domestic domain. Women who were out of doors—too close to or caught looking out of windows, standing in open doorways, or actually, heavens forbid, on the street—were seen as problematically curious, inappropriately inviting, lacking integrity and morally deficient. Their artistic relationship to architecture and to the "outside" world were euphemisms for promiscuity and prostitution.[15] But the Couwenbergh painting depicts no door, window, or entryway; no indication of interruption or escape from the hostage of enclosure, of internment, of incarceration. This is not a domestic space, this is a domestic dungeon, and the Black woman is reduced to an accessory Other out of place. She does not belong here. Her disposal will not be disruptive. The precarity of Blackness is indexed by the inaccessibility of safe space, especially within the borders of domesticity.

The arrangement of bodies pendulum the eye as it ricochets off the surfaces of darkness and light, the balance between shadows—the woman's flesh, the man's costume—alternating with the light bouncing off the naked white flesh of the two others in the room. The narrator stands prominently to the left, his figure the brightest. The fabric sheet around his waist crisp and resplendent with white, its gleaming detail luminescent against the pale skin of its wearer in the textural study of realism, drape and fold. The influence of Caravaggio and the use of *chiaroscuro* are explicit in the subtext of shadows and contrast lurking throughout the scene, but where Caravaggio favored an unidentified source of light to illuminate a central figure, Couwenbergh overwhelms the foreground. White bodies efface the focality of light—the single source reflected in the surface of the chamber vase—juxtaposed with the absorbing use of black paint, the energy of the Black woman's flesh.

The pointing figure mimes a classic framing trope, instructing the viewer where to look. His pointing inversely draws attention to himself as *pointer*, an intentional sleight of hand that guides the trajectory of the gaze while staging the modalities of interpretation: *this is what you are to see*. His facial expression is smug, returning the "amused" look on the seated man's face: "grin[ning] in our direction, as if sharing a joke with us."[16] As it were, this figure is the artist in his own likeness.[17] The image is doubled over as Couwenbergh frames the stage first as the artist, then again as party to the scene itself—a strange simulacrum, even as the image only transfers the features of Couwenbergh's face into its likeness (not necessarily his body, nor his historical presence), disturbing our understanding of his "real" spatial relation to the scene. Historically, artists inserted themselves into their own paintings to align themselves with wealth, power, and prestige—what is the work of insertion in this context? Is this a copy or a simulation of an event? A myth or reality? A genre or a "sadistic erotic fantasy"?[18] It is impossible to know exactly what Couwenbergh means in projecting himself upon *this* canvas in *this* scene, but the mimesis questions how the artist perceives perspective, how (or why) he wishes to accommodate a certain optic. What is his relationship to the scene from the perspective of the painted man, from that of the artist, or from that of the viewer? Is he exploiting an opportunity or painting his complicity? We lose the story, the identity, the subjectivity of the Black woman in this painting, but we have not completely lost the artist as invisible hand. Rather, his insertion forces a return to his role, his attitude, his relation to this piece and those it seeks to represent. His presence returns us to the contexts of production, and the sustained refusal and discipline of the Black body.

As both artist and pedagogue, Couwenbergh thus implicates the viewer twice over; even the most prudent observer has been betrayed by him into an inhumane display. But this is not haphazard mistake; it is an invitation that instantiates the fields of colonial power. As Charmaine Nelson describes:

> The white body as viewer, to sustain its power, must constantly repel, redirect, erase or otherwise sublimate the other's gaze and sensory world as inauthentic,

uncivilized, unscientific and inadequate. This rupture between imagined and actual bodies—what the white subject perceives and wants to see and what is actually there—marks the inability of whites to see blacks outside of a racialized projection of their own bodily privilege. To this extent, within the context of colonial vision, white subjects suffer from a *strategic blindness*.[19] (Emphasis added)

Strategic blindness is the pondering, questioning, objectifying gaze that marks the illegibility and misrecognition of the Black subject. It is the very thing that reduces a Black *person* to a Black *body*, a Black *woman* to Black *flesh*.[20] *The Rape of the Negress* thus draws us into a particular optic, a process of seeing that is formative and pedagogical for the white audience for whom the painting was created. Because she could be from any place, practice any religion, or speak any language, there is an anonymity that transforms the materiality of her body into a floating signifier, and subtends the logics of enclosure that dispossesses the Black woman (and those who would view her in this moment) from identity and dignity, from place and time. As Nelson describes of Black female representation in Western art writ large, the painting captures a certain set of avoidances and erasures through representation:

> The critical point of intersection, that point of connection between the gaze and the image, is the process through which re-imagination becomes re-presentation; the process where what one "sees" is translated into an actual art or visual cultural object that represents another's body. But because it is the identity and subjectivity of the white artist that is the dominant structuring element of the black female subject, the archive of representations of the black female subject reveals the white body/subject as a constant haunting absence.[21]

At the level of nomenclature, Nelson's "haunting absence" is manifest through the insistence on rendering white male sexual violence against a Black woman invisible. These notions of refusal, of *unseeing* the image, function to uphold the cognitive colonial dissonance that makes the whiteness of the other subjects, and doubly of those who are collector-consumers of the Black woman's naked image, invisible and unquestioned. Such optometries of refusal are perhaps most nuanced in the shuffling of titles and interpretative analysis in the reception history of the painting, a limited archive that only until recently has failed to name both the subjectivity much less the pain of the woman imaged here. Rather than outrage, interrogation, or protest, avoidance has filled the gap for the historical questions of this painting that are so difficult to account for: Who is this woman? Who are these men? Was—*is*—this a scene of real life? There are no indications in the local archives that reflect a historical record of an event this painting may be capturing. There is no way to elucidate what Couwenbergh conjured in his own mind, whether from memory, fantasy, or an amalgamation of both and beyond. Because of this, more than one critic has suggested the scene is so graphic as to *only* be fictional, possibly inspired by a literary source—though plausible deniability seems to raise far less savory questions about Couwenbergh's personal imagination.

Several of the most prominent commentators, in their expertise, arguably come to harmfully ambiguous conclusions. Van Gelder did not assign a title at all. Instead, keeping it unnamed, he assigned it to the category of *genre*. Though the early part of the century witnessed a preference for historical paintings—those depicting scenes from mythology, Scripture, and literature—genre paintings catered to the "newly enriched bourgeoisie with an insatiable appetite for the pleasures and astonishments of 'real life.'"[22] Genre paintings served similar aims to contemporary advertising schemas, providing a means to "mirror back and promote certain ideals of domestic living to their viewers."[23] These reflections in these mirrors were not always exact, comprehensive or true, but they were carefully composed artifacts, the majority created for men, by men.[24] What does an image like this advertise? While there remains an adroit avoidance of naming this image, van Gelder's categorization at least retains the possibility the painting reflects *some* kind of contemporaneous life reality: if not an actual event, then an expression of white male fantasy of Black subjection.

Writing in 1972, Victor Beyer insisted the image simply could not have been the reportage of a contemporary event. Beyer thus suggested the chance possibility the image was a literary event drawn from two verses in Song X of *Os Lusíadas*, the Portuguese epic poem by Camões—this, however, only after first asking, "*Mais ce fait, quel est il?*" [But this fact, what is it?].[25] The poem tells of a Portuguese voyage of conquest and 'discovery', and depicts the story of Albuquerque, the conquistador who orders the execution of one of the ship captains as punishment for having sex with the enslaved Black woman on board. The narrator contends that the captain has not committed any crimes, as sex with a Black woman does not constitute rape or adultery—instead, given that she is a 'gift' to the queen of Portugal, the captain is only guilty of the violation of property.

Beyer soon admits that the reference to the song is in many ways unconvincing, requiring several suggestive leaps despite a number of inconsistencies between text and image, to say the least of the generalized randomness of the connection. What is significant is the tacit reticence to consider the most obvious interpretation—that this image is the rape of a Black woman. Even in this example, were the poem truly the source for the painting, there is still a latent archival commitment to *avoid* addressing sexual violence against a Black person on its own terms. As the poem describes, the sexual violence here does not play on par with the sins of 'abominable' incest, rape, nor adultery, but is reduced in a hierarchy of errors to a lapsing susceptibility without volition—a falling prey to the woman already marked reprobate and lascivious herself, thus indicting her as accessory to her own brutalizing (note that the poem itself reserves the capacity for rape as possible only in the context of whiteness—the "ruffian rape of virgin pure"—where the Black woman on board is described as "wanton slave-girl, vile, obscure.") Beyer's ultimate conclusion, fictive or not, resists the commitments and accountability of naming this as rape, and rests in an adroit and sanitizing ambiguity.

In his 1991 *catalogue raisonné* of Couwenbergh's work, Maier-Preusker argues the scene depicts a man preparing himself to bathe and also to 'whitewash' the Black woman.[26] The other white men laugh in jest at their friend's futility. Maier-Preusker suggests the joke references the biblical scene of Jeremiah 13:23, which asks whether or not a leopard can change his spots, or an Ethiopian his skin. Though there is no 'washing of the Moor' within the biblical canons, this colloquial reference is a modern conflation with Aesop's fable of the man who thought that the Ethiopian he enslaved had dark skin because it was dirty, and subsequently took to scrubbing him almost to death. Despite describing the painting itself as "crude," and the Black woman as "fearful" and "defensive," Maier-Preusker almost casually still concludes the intent is comedic, a ludicrous scene reflecting the shock and awe of a bathing test case, the innocuous jeers of explorations in exfoliating violence. This gesture towards an exegetical interpretation attempts to resolve the clear tension of the work, perhaps in part because, as several art historians describe, *biblical scenes of rape and violence were not viewed as particularly offensive.*[27] Moreover, there are other contemporary examples of biblical scenes redacted in paint, imaging newly sexualized female characters in scenes infused with gratuitous eroticism.[28] Does the violent attempt to wash the Blackness out of the woman's skin arouse sensual appeal for the viewer; does desperation evoke a sense of the erotic? The Jeremiah verse was often taken to infer doing something in vain, knowing it already to be an impossibility—is this fraternity simply seeing if the rumors of the Black body are true? While such violent exfoliation produces its own scenario of violence, the painting here includes no bathing accessories, no water. Quite the opposite; again, the single ceramic object present is the chamber pot, which would seem as much a baptismal mockery as the callousness of the white male characters—an ironic turn on who is in need of being cleansed. Associating the image with any biblical justification is a nuanced attempt to sanitize its contents, a subtle inflection that the image of a naked Black woman's body, in the presence of stripped white men, can be redeemed if linked to a vision of purification no matter how cruel or senseless.

Since Maier-Preusker, various references to the painting have found other ways to avoid associating the picture as its early adopters did with the term *rape*, instead preferring various iterations of a more innocuous description: *Three Young White Men and a Black Woman.*[29] The title is a clear attempt to avoid both a discussion and an admission of the subject of the painting, evading culpabilities that such an analysis might infer. While there were no clear laws against rape as sexual assault in the Netherlands at the time, the juridical notions of women as property were directly shifting to those marking women as violable subjects whose legibility was articulated through conceptions of honor and innocence.[30] And yet, the concept of rape was not absent from the Dutch imagination at all—as Pipkin describes, "rape was *fundamental* to the cultural construction of Dutch national identity during the first half of the seventeenth century..." (emphasis added).[31] If we note "an unflagging refusal" to address the topic of rape in this corner of the Dutch archive, it is not due to some sense of care for anachronistic preservation, but exists in direct relationship to race.[32] Blankert argues the problem of the subject matter is not that the depiction "is sexually explicit, nor [that] it shows a black woman being violated—which was not an offence, as we are told by the Portuguese Camões. But in seventeenth-century Holland a sexual liaison with a black woman was in itself a moral transgression, which, by today's standards, would of course be equally racist."[33] Which is to say, by any rendering, the painting is an affront that affords no dignity to the Black woman—in every scenario, she is the source of transgression. Her clear fighting and resistance are always left bereft of the indictment it presumes.

The Rape of the Negress paints a vision of its objects in relation, beyond mere recognition of who, or what, their bodies are. Whether horrified or (horrifically) aroused, innocence is drained from the viewer's standpoint, where perhaps it is true that "we feel as if we are either complacent bystanders or even accomplices."[34] Such is the power of painting a vision, of making it plain; We watch as *accomplice voyeurs*, irrespective of intention. If this is indeed the case, the unknown audience of this image provides more questions than answers: "Again, one wonders who ordered it."[35] A moral statement about the violence portrayed in the portrait is unnecessary to effectively communicate the portrayal of violence itself. Whereas claims that historicize the visual representation of Black women's bodies as productive of violence are indeed important to contemporary concerns about how Black women's bodies are treated in the world, what *this* image shows is an antecedent of that very narrative, the very disruption of the narrative itself. This image makes (some) historians and viewers uncomfortable, precisely because this Black woman demonstrates no willingness in this moment. There is no slack in her posture, no decorative attire, no relaxation of the muscles, no smirk or smile marking an ambiguous welcome to colonize her body. She is anything but desiring. This Black woman, however "eroticized" her resistance may be for the other characters in the painting, or even for the intended viewership, is not complicit in the act, nor in the viewer's consumption. The question of how such violence is named through the archive retroactively speaks to the continued inferences of power around how narratives of the *Black body* are shaped through a gaze structured by even the earliest anatomies of whiteness. I intentionally infer the *Black body* here to insist on the ways Black humanity is actively obscured through the image, disarticulated from a field of relations, and left as invisibilized as the power of the white gaze guiding the image itself. The men in this image do not see a *Black person*, certainly not someone with dignity or worth equal to their own, for this would require a robust and capacious doctrine of creation, and a vision of theological anthropology with God at the center, not themselves. This piece canonizes what is often presumed to be known, the *theo*-logics of race operating at the nexus of the imagined Black body's sexuality with the idea of the Black body as inhuman. The violence and brutalization of the Black (presumed female) body can be charged to no agent other than the inevitable, the (in)act(ion) of God, an ideological archive, a visual record of the unfettered access to bodies of the Other in colonialism and enslavement. And yet, the presumptions of divine distance that emerge within Couwenbergh's frame are not the only narrative of engagement for the image of Black flesh in Holland.

Alternatives (or Black Flight)

In 1630, six Carmelite nuns made a decision for the security of their lives and their faith. The winds of Reformation had not spared spinning the windmills of the Dutch provinces, a religious climate change that even the most robust of Catholic sisters could not stand to weather. In the thick of the first half of the seventeenth century, a young Dutch Republic was emerging into its own European identity among the power players on an increasingly discovered global stage. By this time an extended war had broken out between the Protestant and Catholic states of central Europe, with political motives and positioning parading itself as religious ideology. The Spanish, hoping to quell the spirit of dissent and revolt throughout their Dutch provinces, joined what would come to be known as the Thirty Years War (1618–48). This war across Europe was the feather in the cap of the Eighty Years War (1568–1648), or the Dutch War of Independence, that would formally manifest in the official founding of the Netherlands in 1648.

But the Dutch were on the imperial move even as they trudged the road to European independence. Founded in 1602, the Dutch East India Company (the *Vereenigde Oostindische Compagnie*, or VOC) would quickly secure a monopoly on trade between South Africa and South America. Eventually the VOC would control more than half of the entire world's ocean-based trade, becoming the largest commercial enterprise in the world. The port of Amsterdam grew with this expansion, blossoming into a global center for banking and trade. The VOC's sister, the West India Company (WIC), was founded in 1621 to advance Dutch presence in the New World. By 1624, the WIC laid claim to an ideal port island called Manhattan, an island "purchased" for only 60 guilders. By 1637, the Dutch would take over from the Portuguese the infamous Elmina slave castle-dungeons on the gold coast of Ghana, a key port of human cargo further solidifying the Dutch influence around the globe and the country's own claims to prowess and prominence.

And then there were the nuns. The beginning of the revolution that would result in the founding of the Netherlands in 1648 was precipitated by a wave of iconoclasm during the summer of 1566. The *beeldenstorm* ("statue storm"), which would spread like wildfire throughout Europe, was relatively brief but intense in its toll. Like many Protestants, the Dutch Calvinists were extremely skeptical of religious images and practices that were closely associated with the Spanish and the religious and cultural practices of Catholic devotion. The predominantly Calvinist response to Catholic rule, both theological and political, left innumerable images, statues, and paintings in Catholic churches destroyed.[36] By 1572, in the wake of the revolt against Spain, Catholic worship was outlawed in the emerging Dutch provinces, and all of the church's property was secularized. On September 14, 1629, the Spanish invaded and besieged s'Hertogenbosch (Den Bosch, or Bois le Duc, as it was also known), the city where the nuns lived.

From the fourteenth century, Den Bosch had long been known as a city of miracles, all attributed to the Madonna and child, and as such a well-known site for Marian pilgrimage. It was also one of the first cities to establish a Carmelite branch beyond the city of Antwerp. In 1624, just five years before the city would be invaded, Ann Doyne (Mother Ann of Jesus), Elizabeth Worsley (Sister Teresa of Jesus Maria), along with several Flemish novices were sent to Den Bosch to found the monastery there.[37] But the circumstances became exigent. Though there was a generalized agreement by the Prince of Orange and the Spanish invaders that the Church property would be left intact, vandalism quickly ensued throughout the city in 1630. Caught between more fights than they could follow, the brave Carmelite women participated in their own act of revolution, their own search for freedom. Leaving behind their mission, six of the Carmelite women together abandoned the city of in search of a refuge, crossing the border and pushing forward until they reached Köln (Cologne), Germany, a city where their Catholic faith would be well defended and safe.

But they didn't go alone. If the women were to flee, one of the miraculous statues of Mary was to flee with them.[38] And as it is told, the women carried with them a very particular statue of the Virgin Mary. The delicately carved wooden statue shows the regal form of Mary holding her son, the Christ child, in her left arm. Today she is a giver of mercy, a formal image of grace (*gnadenbild*) known to heal the sick and answer prayers. Housed at St. Maria in der Kupfergasse sanctuary in the center of Cologne, she is the Black Mother of God, one of the most famous Black Madonnas in the world (see Fig. 1.2).

Today there are over three hundred "formal" Black Madonnas, also called Black Virgins, in global existence, a majority of which pepper the European landscape. Their formality is described both by their broader recognition by the Roman Catholic Church, the miracles and Marian devotion attached to their presence, and their exotic presence amid landscapes of whiteness—these numbers do not acknowledge the countless Black Madonnas that have existed throughout Africa and Asia since the beginnings of Christianity, the traditions of the Ethiopian Orthodox Church, or the contemporary landscape and traditions that ascribe iconicity to figures of the Black Madonna (for example, the Ezilis of Haitian Vodou). Instead, the Black Madonna scholarship traditions, limited in breadth, primarily focus on the presence and apparitions of Black virgin figures that proliferated

32 IMMACULATE MISCONCEPTIONS

Figure 1.2 *Black Madonna,* seventeenth century. Linden wood statue. St. Maria in der Kupfergasse, Cologne. Photograph taken by author, 2017.

across the European continent during the medieval era, many between the twelfth and fifteenth centuries, where the dark flesh of these Marian icons were cited as the miraculous work of God. Their exegesis too came via the Song of Songs formulation—*Black and beautiful am I*—and stood as symbols of power, of protection, and of unintelligible yet material speech-act of God.

Though initially rendered theologically as sites of the miraculous, it was only in the wake of modernity that the appearances of Black Madonnas began to be scientifically "explained away" as either separately inculturated images, or simply the by-product of physical deterioration from exposure to smoke, a breakdown of minerals in paints, the consequences of wear and tear. With formal recognition, such sites of pilgrimage were often swallowed up inside of narratives aligned with church or state power and identity. For while Florensky described the power of the icon, the *holy image*, as "an energy,"[39] as a "work of witness,"[40] therein still lies a question of identity and discernment:

> An icon becomes truly an icon only after the Church recognizes that the image in it corresponds to its living spiritual Prototype; in other words, it is an icon only after She truly names it. And the act of true naming—i.e., of establishing the self-identity of the person in the icon—belongs *only to the Church*.[41]

But what if She who has power to name speaks the language of colonialism, rather than with the tongues of Pentecost? Though inconsistent at best, questions around whether or not images were copied with dark skin, or instances where images were lightened, still press the "validity" of the tradition—the Black Madonna's capacity for disruption both muted and quelled under the auspices of conversion.

Scholars have assumed that Mary was never *meant* to be depicted as an African, but this in and of itself is a tenuous claim. For one, we might question the notion of intent. To do so would lead one to then also question, what is the imaginary that presumes Mary to be white? Two, we might recall that authorial intent does not predicate interpretative experience. Which is to say, whether "Black skin" and "person from Africa" were completely and statically synonymous or not, how people viewed, interacted with, and prayed to Black virgins likely still intersects with the perception of Black skin and/or African peoples and their presence in Europe, or as Scheer describes, "how perception and aesthetic experience are determined by culture."[42] However, the debate around intent, and by extension plausibility, still "oscillat[es] between extremes of exoticization and denial,"[43] extremes that fail to take seriously a theological grammar of sacredness that encapsulates humanity without racial hierarchy.

The emergence of any image of the Black female body might be (at the least) juxtaposed with the shifts that index the incoherence of the Black Madonna traditions, and more particularly, the demeaning of her *Blackness* within the Christian theological canon. This is not to espouse the virginity of these Madonna images as a singular virtue, for the juxtaposition of Blackness and virginity means to expand the definitive lens of purity and holiness that may or may not be attributed to either quality, not to reify one with the other. Instead, such incoherence points us to note how the need to deny her Blackness and its materialization subtend a theological reification of *Black skin* as that marking a sexually available body. How can a Black woman's body be pure, be sacred, without disintegrating the boundaried discursive dogmas that constitute the very presumption of a thing that might be known as purity, or sacrality, unto itself? The phenomenon of the Black Madonna, then—whose apparitions, legends, and icons can be found at the center of numerous Marian cults that continue to attract millions of religious pilgrims each year—is arguably one of the most critically disruptive sites of the unorthodox within the presumed orthodox, of possibility within impossibility, that has shaped a significant portion of Christian history. Yet the Black Madonnas *of Europe* remain fugitive in their resistance, resisting a Christian theological imagination that aligned purity and election with white skin. This is to say, a Black Mariological intervention must insist upon a Christian theological precedent for Black flesh not as unrapable, but as inviolable—a canon that imaged Black *female* flesh as sacred, as a unique dimension worthy of veneration—that was denigrated and ignored amid the European Christian colonial project.

The story of the fugitive Black Madonna escaping the plunder and destruction on the burgeoning colonial stage is the religious background to the social imaginary that birthed *The Rape of the Negress*. What else might we dream, if we take seriously the image of the Black Madonna in her reverence and in her rescue, of the Black Mary in flight from the Dutch landscape in search of safety, as a metaphor for the shifting lens toward Black flesh, as a narrative of Black fugitivity that continues to resist the notion of holiness as only being reflected in mirrors of whiteness? As the contact with bodies of darker shades and hues increased throughout Europe, so too did the theological *un*becoming of dark skin from the definition of full humanity. On the Dutch stage, the backlash to the iconoclasm was a flurry of images, a flourishing of art in new ways and new forms as wealth amassed and contact with Black "others" increased. Here the invisible framed the visible, the representation of daily life, in ways that specifically mark the ideological baptism of the Black female body in the waters of the profane, in the aesthetic denials of sacred iconicity. The image of the unnamed woman in Couwenbergh's painting juxtaposed against the explanatory frustrations of the Black icon, index a fundamental incoherence of Black life, marked by the oscillations from the venerated status of virginity, to the denigrating conquest of Black flesh. We are returned to the scene of a Black woman held captive in the painting, to the decorated altar of a Black woman refugee, as scenes of Black feminist fugitivity. We are reminded that Black women have been running a very long time.

Assertions

Among the atrocities committed against the varieties of dark flesh on a global scale, there was certainly a register of sexual, gendered violence compounded through the lens of race, through what Moya Bailey has since termed *misogynoir*.[44] As many Black feminists assert, the genealogies of sexual violence against women of color are linked to the exotic mythologies of Black female sexual excess, but this notion of the body is deeply indebted to a white European Christian theological imagination. Physical violence and particularly sexual violence were justified by the idea of predestined predispositions, temptations, hypersexualized desires and behaviors. A "natural" sexual appetite attributed to peoples of darker skin, and theorized as a mark of their primitive, animalistic, and lower place in a hierarchy of God's creation. When it comes to those racialized Black and gendered woman, the social denials of agency, the assumption of rapable flesh, manifests through the denial not just of *what* we see, but *how* we see. In the process of their looking, the three men in *The Rape of the Negress* perform supremacy, structurally, on theological grounds. And yet, with particularity, they too perform the Christian-colonial work of naming. They determine and mark that which they see as property subject to their authority. As Nelson describes:

> As a colonial invention, Black Woman and her precursor Black Girl are a measure of white colonial fear/desire and the abject black female subject is revelatory of an imagined whiteness, equally fictive and reified through an incessant sociocultural and racist *collective narcissism* that builds this imagined racial purity through the perpetual exploitation and marginalization of black subjects.[45]

The problem is that Christianity itself must be called into question as an arbiter of this incessant "collective narcissism," as the institution that informed the way of (un)seeing, the incubator of an idolatrous *looking*. European colonialism breaks Black bodies. It is difficult to evade such captivity—whether captured, or captivated—by the coerced intimacy of the painting itself. The effects of consumption are inherent to the very act of looking. And yet, while there is meant to be no escape, there is still refusal.

After the iconoclast, Calvinism was a prevailing force throughout the Dutch provinces, with the question of moral purity and its representation taking their form in the new iconocism of the Golden Age. Calvinist belief reinforced a certainty about fate before God, a theology of predestination that manifest in the ideas of both race and class. As George Whitfield would one day write to John Wesley, predestination had a dark side, an intention equal but opposite in its determination of the body—reprobation.[46] As Willie Jennings describes of colonial encounters as they exploded across the globe, reprobation as theological calculus offers a more sinister reality than correlation and causation, reduced to "simply the state of existence opposite election; it is also a judgment upon the trajectory of a life, gauging its destiny from what can be known in the moment. Reprobation joins the Black body to the Moor body and both to the Jewish body. All are in the sphere of Christian rejection and therefore of divine rejection."[47] On the grounds of divine rejection, it is easy to condemn the body in life to the horrors certain to come in death, infusing the (im)moral imagination and the ethical horizons of the ordinary, of the everyday.

The Black woman here evokes the figure of Eve, splintered by surroundings barren and portending her death, her voice eclipsed by those who mock God, their mouths open, configured for consumption. *The Rape of the Negress* witnesses imperial power, a theology of reprobation that cemented "the logical conclusion of Black incapacity."[48] Here manifest anxieties and fantasies around the stabilization of that power with shocking clarity (as the refusal of the Black woman viewer simultaneously witnesses *against it*). In other words, the image becomes for the viewer a kind of "antidote for those who interpret colonialism as a process by which Europe brought 'civilization' to the Third World; it gives the lie to the myth that contact with white society brought . . . positive changes for Africans."[49] The white gaze is one that does not see, but rather chooses to look askance and away. We know how the Black body becomes object. Here we also see, *in medias res*, how the white body becomes subject, how white men (attempt to) become like God.

Theorizing the aesthetics of literary prose, Viktor Shklovsky suggested that "the purpose of the image is not to draw our understanding to that which this image stands for, but rather to allow us to perceive the object in a special way, in short, to lead us to a 'vision' of this object rather than mere 'recognition.'"[50] What Shklovsky observes in the modernist moment provides a helpful analogue for the reception history of *The Rape of the Negress* as a kind of text itself (noting the ironic search for its assumedly textual origins), as well as for its own reading. At first glance perhaps we know, or we think we know, only again to find that we know naught, know not, know *no* thing. We are faced with the whiteness of the men, the Blackness of the woman as qualities from which we are estranged, and yet drawn more intimately into by their being laid bare.[51] Shklovsky continues, noting that: "The purpose of imagery may be most clearly followed in erotic art. The erotic object is here commonly presented as something seen for the very first time."[52] The shock of effect is no less present than in Couwenbergh's portrait, as the rape (to note the violence of the 'erotic') carries the nuance of virgin sight, of a familiar yet inaugural moment of seeing and thinking a certain arrangement of bodies presented before one's eyes.

What can be done when there is so little we are given, when we know nothing about her, when the archive leaves us bereft of much more than epistemological violence? What can be done when we know nothing about her, when we know only her dispossession? And yet, "I want to say more than this. I want to do more than recount the violence that deposited these traces in the archive."[53] She is a fictive amalgamation of rapable flesh, and yet, this is not all she (re)presents. This is not an image centered on Black female flesh as hyper-erotic imaginary, but the perverse performance of white masculinity as it is expressed against Black female flesh. This is capture. And yet, the Black woman here resists. She has given no invitation, and her refusal is transparent through what might too quickly be assumed to be the opaque disposition of the white imperial gaze.

The idea of agency does not absolve the violence of the image, and yet how are we to hear the echoes of her screams? For, as Ashon Crawley notes in the context of the narrative of Harriet Jacobs, "To consider the sounds, those piteous groans, is to think about how sound can prompt movement toward escape."[54] If she is met with strategic blindness, what might be said through a rendering of strategic hearing? Can such "residual materiality" call us to listen *through* the captivity, to the sonic rendering of the terrible, to attend the Black woman's scream as "a desire, a provocation against such an institution?"[55]

It returns us to the opening narrative of the Carmelite nuns—what happens when Mary is made to flee? What are the sacred possibilities of fugitive Blackness? *The Rape of the Negress* provides a critical site not only for a kind of theological accountability, but to question the competing forces of how we see or unsee Black bodies as *iconic*, how to attend to a legacy of the sacrality of Black flesh, and how we might think alongside Black capacities for reproduction as signals of resistance and futurity even in the midst of abjection.

The Dutch Golden Age is marked by an intentional movement away from, if not the destruction of, religious iconography—a 'religious storm' against Black bodies presumed damned from their start. The secular presence of religious art remained only in connection to its existence as capital—the difference marked in the naming, the sanctity and the sacred depiction of human flesh. The upending of the world, the turmoil of the time emanated from the altars of the church, raising the issue of who, or what, is *iconic*. Which is to say, of who can bear the image of God. We imagine a cloaked Madonna, a Black Madonna, stolen in the night, absented from our minds, but where absence is also always presence. This figure of Mary, a person who theologically has navigated her own "kind of chiaroscuro."[56] Her loss signals more than an aesthetic, more than an ocular calculus. Rather, her loss is the composite of possibility, of multiplicity, of participation. Her loss is that of the *gnadenbild*, the loss of our grace.

What occupies the chasms between a Black Virgin and Black Venus? What triggers the expansion and contraction in the fissures of difference? Perhaps the distance between one and the other is not lacunose. Perhaps it lives buried beneath the expansive field of blue called the Atlantic, the signaling abyss, the peaks and troughs that pushed the spectrums of Black and white bodies toward new poles of (im)purity. It is felt in the murmurs, the plate tectonics of continents filing against one another, buttressing new worlds. Conquest and consumption begin with the voyeur, with the observation, with the look that does not see.

The Rape of the Negress, then, is a site where we can begin to name rape, name attendant complicities, and take seriously reparations for such violences. This image is perhaps a way to address the past that is never past, that sense of that 'haunting absence', that '*sentiment du déshabillé*', and to think again what would be required to depict and enflesh Black humanity. We return here with tension, torn between a horrific reality and the incessant problem of reinscribing Black pain for intellectual consumption, and yet resisting the gaze intended in effort to see the Black woman who is (still) there—to move beyond being bound to the expanding privileging of white male flesh, *iconocratically*, and an empire of the gaze. Out from the shadows, this painting captures the negligence, complicity, and culpability for the wake of violences across Europe and its empires. *The Rape of the Negress* is an object lesson in the relativity of proximity, in approximation, and in the fugitivity of Black resistance we glimpse when it seems no one else is looking—her resounding claims to her life, even when facing death. This is a canvas that depicts a cruel world, the witness of Black flesh as testified to—or rather, translated by—the white masculine optic. Through the imaginations of burgeoning imperial power, we bear witness to the Black woman's consumption as perverse *pieta*. Even in paint, she does not go quietly.

2
In Search of Our Mother's Garden

When beginning, He, God created...
While the Spirit of God, She was fluttering....

Genesis 1:1
Wil Gafney

What is found at the historical beginning of things is not the inviolable identity of their origin; it is the dissension of other things. It is disparity.

Michel Foucault

Subservience of any kind is death to the spirit.

Alice Walker

Never break them in two. Never put one over the other. Eve is Mary's mother. Mary is the daughter of Eve.

Toni Morrison

Deadname

It begins *in the beginning*, with the narrations of creation and fall found in the book of Genesis. You know this story well. Long before Mary and Jesus—*a priori* to any concerns of salvation and redemption—there stood in a garden Adam and Eve. The record of the world's first biopsy and excision, an exercise in non-reproductive reproduction, the evolution of a somewhat androgynous and ambiguous being of oneness becoming that of two:

"God created them."

For adherents of the Abrahamic religions, these stories of origin root humanity in a chronicle of creatureliness, intimately tied to a supreme being who is mindful enough to express love and desire as the Creator. As opposed to the oft-cited singular, more misogynistically rendered narrative that has acquired canonicity in Western Christian thought, the book of Genesis harbors not one but two unique accounts of creation.[1] Juxtaposed and in conversation they suggest the swirling,

Immaculate Misconceptions. Amey Victoria Adkins-Jones, Oxford University Press.
© Amey Victoria Adkins-Jones 2025. DOI: 10.1093/9780198950073.003.0003

discursive waters of origin and interpretation, understood in light of divine inspiration and intelligent design. The first chapter of Genesis offers not only an account of God-in-relation, but an account of male and female being created within the same temporal moment. In the beauty of quiet and glory of darkness, a God whose presence exceeds the boundaries of any gender or race, creates, manifests, produces, uniquely. God, the plural first-person pronoun "us," writes the icon of humanity in such a way as to inflect both a sense of equity and unity:

> [26] Then God said, "Let us make humankind in our image, according to our likeness; and let them have dominion over the fish of the sea, and over the birds of the air, and over the cattle, and over all the wild animals of the earth, and over every creeping thing that creeps upon the earth." [27] So God created humankind in his image, in the image of God he created them; male and female he created them. [28] God blessed them, and God said to them, "Be fruitful and multiply, and fill the earth and subdue it; and have dominion over the fish of the sea and over the birds of the air and over every living thing that moves upon the earth."[2]

Most scholars render this account a communal one. Of the four writing communities to which various parts of Genesis are attributed, this account was redacted sometime in the midst of Babylonian exile. The writers themselves were a school of priests, committed to remembering God in narrative amid a world filled with separation and loss. They wrote logically and copiously (as demonstrated through later textual genealogies and lists), and were clear and organized in format. Though it is marked with familiar traits of multiple ancient Near Eastern creation myths, the narrative carries the signs of experience, as if to hold fast to one truth: There once was a time when our exile was not; there will come a time when our exile shall be no more. In *this* creation story, *people*—regardless of genitalia and, in this way, without gender—emerge together in light and wonder from the land.

Still, our Christian imaginations have not been formed to hold the first chapter of Genesis at the forefront of our understanding of sex, particularly when the juiciest scandal is yet to come. It is the latter account of creation in Genesis 2 where God, noting that "it is not good for man (*ha'adam*) to be alone," places a lonely Adam within a divinely induced coma, excises his rib and fashions an unnamed 'suitable helper' (*ezer kenegdo*) to share in the experiences of human relationship, creaturely existence, and an eternal Arbor Day:

> [22] And the rib that the Lord God had taken from the man (*ha'adam*) he made into a woman (*ishshah*) and brought her to the man (*ha'adam*). [23] Then the man (*ha'adam*) said, "This at last is bone of my bones and flesh of my flesh; this one shall be called Woman (*ishshah*), for out of Man (*ish*) this one was *taken* [lit. built]." [24] Therefore a man (*ish*) leaves his father and his mother and clings to his

wife [lit. woman, *ishah*], and they become one flesh. ²⁵ And the man (*ha'adam*) and his *wife* [lit. woman, *ishah*] were both naked, and were not ashamed.³ (Emphasis added)

This is the elder of the creation stories, her prevalence matching her chronology. Attributed to the Jahwist, the account reflects the characteristics of singularity and solidarity of history, from the mountaintop of Jewish empire.[4] Amid the streamlined and definitive reflection on a certain God (YHWH) and a chosen people, the narrator exegetes via interjection in verse 24. As cited above, the parallelism of the text is easily lost between the translation of a man (i.e., not a husband) clinging to his wife (i.e., not a woman, person, or something other than an object of property). The text does not read wife at all, of course. It states that a man will leave and cleave to his woman. The possessive is still there—the idea of the woman being "his," but only with moments of narrative interruption that signal us to third-party interpretation. Adam does not have a father nor a mother to leave, so we as readers are pointed toward an already established idea of marriage (one of many present in the Hebrew Bible). But this is not to miss the crux of the insinuation not just of *who*, but *what* these two people together were:

One flesh.
Naked and unashamed.

Things fall apart when Woman-qua-Eve violates God's prohibition *not* to eat from the tree of knowledge of good and evil.[5] God gives the direct command to Adam (2:16) prior to the creation of Woman (2:22). But once she is alive, well, and alone, she is approached by the crafty serpent—the one of still mysterious ontological origin.[6] This agent provocateur mocks God, questions the logics of the fruit-taboo as well as the historical memory of what, exactly, God did or did not say about the theopolitics of eating:

> Now the serpent was more crafty than any other wild animal that the Lord God had made. He said to the woman, "Did God say, 'You shall not eat from any tree in the garden'?" ² The woman said to the serpent, "We may eat of the fruit of the trees in the garden; ³ but God said, 'You shall not eat of the fruit of the tree that is in the middle of the garden, nor shall you touch it, or you shall die.'" ⁴ But the serpent said to the woman, "You will not die; ⁵ for God knows that when you eat of it your eyes will be opened, and you will be like God, knowing good and evil."
> ⁶ So when the woman saw that the tree was good for food, and that it was a delight to the eyes, and that the tree was to be desired to make one wise, she took of its fruit and ate; and she also gave some to her husband, who was with her, and he ate.

Not that she couldn't move, work, or think autonomously, but Woman's unchaperoned dialogue with the serpent has been a particularly contentious aspect of the narrative. For one, as if watching a game of telephone unfold, Eve misquotes the original directions from God that she heard from Adam. Perhaps the more cautious one, she adds the prohibition of touch to the command, actually increasing the rigor of the command. Early interpreters wondered if this was her downfall, and thought this was the how and why of Woman's deception: having witnessed the serpent *touch* and not die, it may seem not only logical to probe Adam's words, but to respond in kind to the serpent's demonstration that the prohibition was false and, to eat. The sensuality of the moment is paramount to what will become prohibitions around touch, taste, and feel—the questions of permissible, acceptable, appropriate desire, even as the limits of what one "can" do still reflect the arbitrariness of the experience.

Perhaps most blatant, however, is how the prepositional phrase in verse six (translated as "with her") carries the baggage of a significant omission history. For centuries, this phrase, clearly present in multiple Hebrew manuscripts, was left completely untranslated as though it, like Adam, simply were never there.[7] The absence triggers a textual smoking gun pointed directly at the rogue insurgent: the Woman. In short order, Eve eats, offers to an unseen Adam who, cloaked in ambiguity, is either completely ignorant to the situation (all fruits look alike?), happily obliges his own desires and indulgences, or follows blind trust amid the carnality of hunger.[8] Either way, Adam is absolved for not executing first. The luscious experience of haptic arousal, and the associated eroticism that purportedly leads to death, transpires seamlessly.

But the knowledge of good and evil includes the affective quality of learning how to blush. With eyes wide shut Adam and Eve experience the spectacle of seeing their own loins, sartorially mending fig leaves as makeshift camouflage, a cheap concealer they hope will blend in among the unblemished. Realizing their own nakedness aligns them with both the awareness and the plummeting despairs of newfound shame, so much so that when they hear the nearness of God—seemingly taking evening rounds about the property—they are compelled to hide. It is a plight that gestures toward disgust, knotting the reality of their naked bodies as corrupted flesh.

Still, God does not mean for them to be alone, and makes known the voice of concern: "Where are you?" One would doubt that the omniscient and omnipresent God actually needs radar response to echo-locate the only two humans in all of existence, but God calls out specifically to Adam despite already knowing the foliage beneath which he lies. One can consider that in moments of embarrassment and indignity, it is good to be reminded that one's presence, regardless of the state of affairs, is missed. God thus "finds" Man and Woman and questions them. The interrogation transcript of Genesis 3:9–13 (format theatrically adapted) is as follows:

LORD GOD. *(to Adam)* Where are you?
ADAM. I heard the sound of you in the garden, and I was afraid, because I was naked; and I hid myself.
LORD GOD. Who told you that you were naked? Have you eaten from the tree of which I commanded you not to eat?
ADAM. The woman whom you gave to be with me, she gave me fruit from the tree, and I ate.
LORD GOD. *(to Woman)* What is this that you have done?
WOMAN. The serpent tricked me, and I ate.

To his credit, Adam can rightly be said to have confessed the truth: he obtained the fruit from she-who-will-soon-be-named-Eve. But the implications of his preface to that truth cast shades of bias not previously there. In referencing "the woman whom you gave to be with me," Adam implies the responsibility of God as haphazard Santa Claus in the makings of his predicament. Adam had already experienced a life alone and in charge, and already prefers solitary power over social connection. Though God saw that it was good to have human community, what more likely situation than this for Adam to regret God's goodwill?

Analyzing the genesis of women's oppression, Gayle Rubin's landmark essay "The Traffic in Women" describes how exactly a woman becomes an *oppressed* woman: "A woman is a woman. She only becomes a domestic, a wife, a chattel, a playboy bunny, a prostitute, or a human Dictaphone in certain relations. Torn from these relationships, she is no more the helpmate of man than gold in itself is money...."[9] Adam here is clear to establish himself as apart from Eve. In the moment of accountability, the relation of being one flesh collapses beneath the weight of their exposure. As Rubin remarks, a woman is a woman, full stop: for Adam, the 'ishah is an 'ishah, until she becomes something else; oppression takes root from relations bound within a hierarchy of power and shame. Though multiple readings of Adam's presence or absence have been offered over time, perhaps the most endearing of which suggest that the reason Adam ate the fruit from Eve (the subtext being his knowledge of its taboo) was because he was so deeply connected in intimacy to her.[10] This is a partner who would not let a loved one enter the unknown without being by her side. But Adam's defense before God is but a post-script of the prix fixe, as the eruption of flavor ruptures their friendship and introduces a new cultural affect to the text. In the moment of inquiry, motivated by shame and fear, Adam's shift in narrative marks a shift in relation. Adam's response is the first display in the trafficking in women. No longer "built" but now "given," Adam places Eve as a sign in exchange.[11]

What comes next is the eternal fate of the gendered body. God speaks first to the serpent, anointing the phobia of snakes and condemning the creature to slither for all time. Though marriage is never actually referenced within the account, the curse of death includes next as particular to the woman the "curse" of reproductive labor and toil in childbearing, as well as the desire for and subjection to the man who is her husband:

[14] The Lord God said to the serpent,

"Because you have done this, cursed are you among all animals and among all wild creatures;
upon your belly you shall go, and dust you shall eat
all the days of your life.

[15] I will put enmity between you and the woman,
and between your offspring and hers;
he will strike your head, and you will strike his heel."

[16] To the woman he said,

"I will greatly increase your pangs in childbearing;
in pain you shall bring forth children,
yet your desire shall be for your husband,
and he shall rule over you."

[17] And to the man he said,

"Because you have listened to the voice of your wife,
and have eaten of the tree
about which I commanded you,
'You shall not eat of it,'
cursed is the ground because of you; in toil you shall eat of it all the days of your life;

[18] thorns and thistles it shall bring forth for you;
and you shall eat the plants of the field.

[19] By the sweat of your face you shall eat bread until you return to the ground, for out of it you were taken; you are dust, and to dust you shall return."

(Gen 3:14–19)

Because of Man, having listened to (t)his Woman, the ground is cursed and he is cursed to care for it. No longer a source of provision, the land is both the marker and maker of danger and toil. Nature itself now occupies the place of surveillance and death as the logics of natural disaster are internalized. As if life in the Garden had been gluten free, now one must ask, must beg and work for the land to surely give, as the curse includes the manufacture of food, enforced carbohydrate consumption for survival, not pleasure. Alternatively, it is the land that always takes, receiving the sacrifice of death and bodily decomposition for nutrition, a circle of dependency. If one is ever colloquially 'blessed to be a blessing', the land is cursed to be *that which curses*. When European Christian colonists later encounter new-to-them lands, they will paint them in lines of naked, enticing female bodies as personifications of the need for feminized and colonial discipline, pillage, and civilization. Curses, again.

Now enmity between humanity and the land is reflected in the enmity between partners, as the relation between men and women becomes one of confrontation rather than communion. It is only here that this woman-whom-you-gave-to-be-with-me is actually named:

> [20] The man named his wife Eve, because she was the mother of all living. [21] And the Lord God made garments of skins for the man and for his wife, and clothed them. (Gen 3:20–21)

For the first time, we meet Eve, named by Adam in a way that mimes Adam's authority to classify and order the plants and animals of the earth. With one final comment upon the dire straits, God speaks to God's self, again as "us," to determine that all parties shall henceforth be bound to labor, toil, and eventually death as consummate of the human experience (3:22). The curtain falls as we realize the fate of our forebearers.

> *They are the first to be separated from God.*
> *They are the first to be separated from each other.*
> *They are the first to be separated from the land.*

In but a few sparse sentences we witness the symbolic divorce of the first family from God, but even more so the symbolic and linguistic divorce of Adam from Eve's presence. These textual displacements and narratives of loss will inherently "operate in the expansion of worlds."[12] From these moments of early diaspora forward, Eve, and eventually "all of her sex," are made to bear the blame for the sufferings that occur in human life. Breaking the flesh of a forbidden fruit is cemented as a perpetually unforgivable and unredeemable act, one that stands as the originary site of sex gender difference. The once bright stage of creation fades to black, ossifying the fallenness of the female subject as anthropological truth.

Exegeting the Vagina

> [P]alates can be trained.
> *Things Eve Learned from the Serpent*
> Sandy Supowit

Recounting the rise and fall of life on Earth has both overtly and subliminally injected the essence of sexual difference beneath the skins of our thinking. But cosmetological fillers are addictive to the ego, smudging the memories of our past and augmenting the realities of our present. Many readings have been offered in attempt to smooth the detailing of two disparate creations (we have yet to mention the non-canonical tale of the starter wife—Lilith), but such vanity only minimally obscures the textual crow's feet marking the complexity of our myths.[13]

When it comes to the instantiation of two separate and unequal sexes, a newly binary construction of gender, served with all the requisite trimmings, the germination of these ideas take root in a number of places beyond the plot of Genesis. The tales from paradise only complicate our conceptions of life and death, of sex and reproduction. The first-yet-latter account of creation, summed in "male and female, [God] created them," bears her own concerns. Innumerable arguments for male hierarchy draw on the order of creation (Adam first, Eve second) as a model for the social, cultural order of patriarchy. The Adam and Eve–less version of the story is rendered a much more positive account, the question of succession erased by temporal equity. There is seemingly no sense of social rank, no implication of hierarchy because there is only *male and female*, not male first, female afterthought. However, within this narrative still lurks an argument for complementarity of the sexes, which has pointed to the same concerns of identity stasis that many now question, protest, and resist.

Further, the command to "be fruitful and multiply" (though reconfigured in a contemporary world of scientific intervention that supports birth, however expensively, far beyond spontaneous conception) ultimately rests upon the premise of sexual intercourse between a biological male and female. Fulfilling the command requires an egg and a sperm walk into a bar and, apparently, only converse with each other. Though the command does not speak of sex or pleasure, does it preclude the possibilities of such? And are the male and female assumed to be exclusive partners?[14] When it comes to ethos around sex and relationship, the terms of engagement are far more nebulous a construction, and are certainly not reflective of a contemporary social construction of marriage and partnership, particularly when sex in the ancient world was not understood only in monogamous or heterosexual terms.[15]

The question turns on how we can think reproduction, and more specifically, *right* reproduction—the order of the desire, the social mores of intercourse, the progeny of the race, and how to appropriately engage in activity that is imagined in tandem with lesser virtue, impurity, and irrationality. Is the command one of sexual intimacy, or debased utility? Early on, interlocutors (who read the two creation accounts in concert, as opposed to offering separate treatment) considered whether or not Adam and Eve had (or would have had the opportunity to have had) sex in the garden. Augustine theorized that in Eden, Adam and Eve (who he argued did have a marriage) had reproductive organs that were something more akin to a pre-modern version of the appendix: present, seemingly purposeless, and only warranting notice when inflamed. The Garden provided an active firewall to the fleshly drives of lust and desire, and thus by Augustine's account, the first genitalia were completely subject to the rational mind and self-control.[16] By this reading, while God does perhaps distinguish genitalia, what God does not do is create gender. There are no gender roles assigned to fruitfulness and multiplication. No murmurings of sexuality. No discourses on mothering or maternal labor. Virility and lordship are not actors in the play of seven fantastic nights. So where do we place the penis and vagina in the landscape of Eden?

Genitalia also remain a complicated part of the equation in the second-yet-earliest account of creation, the tale of Adam and Eve. Here, we see the creation of an unspecified being, what Phyllis Trible aptly translates "the earth creature."[17] This androgynous doctrinal account of creation offers a critical point of contention when juxtaposed with an account emphasizing sexual difference, leveling a challenge to the presumed status quo of a presumed sex/gender binary. But androgyny does not immediately occupy the space of equity. Despite the attractive angle of the androgyne for many feminist and queer interpreters, many arguments maintain that because *ha 'adam*/Adam does not linguistically change after the creation of Woman—which is to say, that Adam as a term for man never changes after Woman is created—that the original earth creature was always in fact male. But what defines the male as such? Is it his naming power? Or, if Aristotle got it wrong, is the male the one who is defined by a lack (or a phallic excess)? Is it simply the presence of a penis? And if it is his genitalia, then can we speak to its purpose? In the moments between coma and creation, what *exactly* does it mean to have one's inner female unleashed?

What it does *not* mean is that Adam gave birth to Eve, insofar as Adam embodies seminal volition, or that hetero-sex is the exclusive means to understanding reproductive capacity. Again it is critical to note here that the creation of genitalia is not directly cited through sex or reproduction, but rather, as differentiation: Gender is not defined by genitalia. Sexual desire and sexual pleasure do not arise as punishment for Eve concerning reproduction. And, spoiler alert: God will take an asexual, or perhaps extra-sexual approach to reproduction again when Mary becomes pregnant.

Though an applicable and explicit metaphor at other moments throughout both the Hebrew Bible and the New Testament, God in this moment of natality is neither doula nor midwife. Rather, the God of this text is something more akin to a molecular biologist. The moments of silence in the garden are the inchoate intimacies of asexual reproduction. They manifest the makings of a divine parthenogenesis, of a cell division as it unfolds, the machinations of which challenge core assumptions about difference and identity. From one there are now two, but the emergence of Ish and Ishshah cannot be collapsed into the material embodiment of one's rib. While considering the logics behind how human beings understand

and articulate death, philosopher Jay Rosenberg offers an illustration that presses our own set of Edenic concerns:

> Let us take a well-fed, healthy amoeba alone in a drop of well-oxygenated pond water. I shall call it 'Alvin.' Alvin, let us suppose, lives happily through Tuesday and, precisely at the stroke of midnight, divides, producing two offspring whom I shall call 'Amos' and 'Ambrose.' On Wednesday, then, we find two amoebae—Amos and Ambrose—swimming happily about in our drop of pond water. But what has become of Alvin? One thing is quite clear: Alvin is not an inhabitant of our drop of pond water on Wednesday. Alvin is one amoeba; our drop of water contains two amoebae; and one amoeba cannot be identical to two amoebae.[18]

Adam need not be as to an amoeba to helpfully consider the before and after of divine dissection. Though the descriptors in Genesis do not point directly to single-cell organisms, there are broader implications. The amoeba experiences such depths of change that, in giving life to something new, its originary being is no longer. Rather, there are two new elements that come into being. The original amoeba does not die, and yet, it also ceases to exist. Stated differently, *birth* is not the only way to begin a life, nor is death the only way for life to end.

First, a death. Bataille's description of life and the discontinuity of being illumines how we might think the essence of such a relation. For Bataille, when there is a reproductive splitting of cells, "... the new entity is itself discontinuous, but it bears within itself the transition to continuity, the fusion, fatal to both, of two separate beings."[19] The story of Adam and Eve is a story of two people who have been severed not *in* their existence, but *as* their existence. This is the tear that the grammatical continuity of *ha 'adam* cannot alone suture. But it doesn't need to. In the garden, a certain kind of death—in the sense of death as the ceasing of a known form of life—overtakes Adam. While under anesthesia, who he knows or thinks himself to be becomes but a requiem for a dream. He who awakens will never be the same.

If fatality and natality are qualities inextricably bound, the resuscitation of Adam *births* new knowledges and ways of being. It is the end of the nascent world as he knows it. In some way, shape or form, from Adam, *'ishash* is created. Perhaps the cells split. Perhaps Eve arises from a unique cloning experiment. Either way, when *'ishash* comes into being, Adam is not the same flesh Adam was before. Adam can no longer be who he was because the moment that births Eve is also the moment that births Adam's relation to Eve. In and through this relation, Adam is known anew to himself, a person also changed in constitution. In other words, it is the creation of Woman that constitutes the creation of Man. It is a relation of revelation, of new life together.[20]

In the encounter with the serpent we witness another end of life, this time finalized in the painful loss of continuity with the Creator. We come to understand its gravity when the nakedness in the garden is no longer a sign of nature but of nurture. The moment of realization that something has changed, marked by the shock of realizing one's body in a new way, culminates the climactic eating of forbidden fruit. As Bataille describes, "most creatures in a state of nakedness, for nakedness is symbolic of this dispossession and heralds it, will hide."[21] And they did. Nakedness amplifies the resounding confusion, embarrassment and fear that come with being flung into the cruel terrors of the everyday. Bare bodies crystallize the umbilical break between humanity and God, electrocuting Adam and Eve's consciousness into a denuded awareness of themselves. Adam and Eve are extracted into a world, one wherein they have *become* naked, their genitals exposed. The garden is the killing field of innocence, the death of perfect union between God and human.

In "The Garden of Eden and the Heterosexual Contract," Ken Stone questions the breakup between God and, specifically, Adam: "To the extent that the human creature is initially created in relationship, then, the relationship in question is much closer to a homoerotic than a heterosexual one. That is to say, an ambiguously male human character and a(n ambiguously) male divine character are the only beings in existence."[22] Stone speculates that, while the Yahwist writer may not have explicitly intended to counter accusations of divine-human sex allegations, that there was a latent "discomfort" with the ambiguities of intimacy and relationship absent of Eve. *Ha'adam* sounds increasingly like "he" might more aptly identify across a sexual spectrum than within the narrow confines of a heterosexual contract. While there are clear counters to the problems of the presumed maleness of the Lord God (none of which are lost on Stone), Stone acknowledges the unsettling, antagonistic nature of Eve's creation and fall as presented within the text. Without reading physical sex into the argument, it would certainly seem that for Adam, Eve's presence disrupts a certain intimacy, a certain continuity that he uniquely experienced *alone* with God. We have already elaborated that in the first creation account, the reproductive assignment is not coupled with gendered instructions. This only exacerbates Adam's change in reference to Eve, from describing her as his own object, to the person he was stuck with, that reads patriarchal performance through the sex of the Woman.

In *Gender Trouble*, Judith Butler delineates the critical nuance between gender and sex, explaining that:

> Gender ought not to be conceived merely as the cultural inscription of meaning on a pregiven sex [...] gender must also designate the very apparatus of production whereby the sexes themselves are established. As a result, gender is not to culture as sex is to nature; gender is also the discursive/cultural means by which "sexed nature" or "a natural sex" is produced and established as "prediscursive," prior to culture, a politically neutral surface *on which* culture acts.[23]

Butler's critique of the fabled distinction between sex as biological, and gender as cultural, surmises that *both* sex and gender are constructed entities. She later describes that "*woman* itself is a term in process, a becoming, a constructing that cannot rightfully be said to originate or end."[24] Though she is not particularly interested in the biblical creation myths, her description maps almost directly onto the text itself: we do not actually know from whence Woman comes (please don't respond "Adam's rib"), and what we are witnessing is less a clarity around her creation, and instead the much stickier process of her becoming. As the text recounts the death of Adam but never the death of Eve, we also find we know nothing of her end. What we see in these early discursive moments are the apparatuses of production, the emergence of a sex and gender paradigm that has its roots in patterns of exchange rather than divine command.

The dominant narrative of creation has soldered gender performativity into our minds precisely because Eve was attempting to enact a certain kind of *pre*-gender trouble. Within the Abrahamic traditions, it seems that the search for a gender origin is triangulated through the acts of the sexed body of 'ishah. Seduction, sexual danger, destruction, unwieldiness—these are the threats that become tied to the essence of the female body. When God pronounces the curse, the rectifying gender performance of accountability is enacted as an illusory means of stabilizing gender as a binary category. The curtain of the curse belies performative acts, the expressions of gender that only pretend as facts.

God's curse does not serve to create gender hierarchy, but is read as codifying the traits and problems already seen as being inherent to the Woman sex. Gayle Rubin describes that "gender is not only an identification with one sex; it also entails that sexual desire be directed toward the other sex."[25] And so while God does not create gender, God becomes the purveyor of gendered performances: a Woman's desire shall be for her Man. Of course, this again does not speak to whom, exactly, Man's desire shall be for. Nor of the multiplicities of either's desire. But such culturally wrought gender performance is given primacy because it is assumed to bear the divine economy, despite the inconsistencies therein.

Placing blame is an arduous task to shoulder. Though the weight often falls to Eve, when the realization of the transgression occurs, it seems that God places responsibility with Adam:

> [22] Then the Lord God said, "See, the man has become like one of us, knowing good and evil; and now, he might reach out his hand and take also from the tree of life, and eat, and live forever"— [23] therefore the Lord God sent him forth from the garden of Eden, to till the ground from which he was taken. [24] He drove out the man; and at the east of the garden of Eden he placed the cherubim, and a sword flaming and turning to guard the way to the tree of life.
>
> (Gen 3:22–24)

Yet the reception history points to mixed messages of blame, or at least a marked shift toward naming the woman.[26] The once enslaved Jewish historian Josephus, whose writings offer critical insights into early Christianity and late Temple Judaism, wrote that:

> Adam then began to make excuse for his sin and besought God not to be wroth with him, laying the blame for the deed upon the woman and saying that it was her deception that had caused him to sin; while she, in her turn, accused the serpent.[27]

At first it seems that Adam is held particularly accountable for his shifting of blame, but the onus shifts in Adam's favor as Eve is rhetorically emphasized as the source of fault:

> Thereupon God imposed punishment on Adam for yielding to a woman's counsel.... Eve He punished by child-birth and its attendant pains, because she had deluded Adam, even as the serpent had beguiled her, and so brought calamity upon him.[28]

Never, never listen to the woman, Adam. Otherwise, you deserve what's coming. Already we can detect the theological impulse that has to both account for Eve as a source of deception, while yet resisting according the equal status between men and women that such a power might intimate. The coals of condemnation seem to increasingly heap upon the head of Eve, with early Christian exegetes latching on to interpretations that consistently cited Eve as if the source of sin itself: "From a woman was sin's beginning, and because of her, we all die."[29] Of far lesser significance was the perspective that because of Eve, we have all been born and thus live. Rather, by the advent of Christianity, the assertions of the afterlife of the fall were the wayward doings of Eve. As Philo asserted (despite acknowledging Adam's culpability in the matter elsewhere), "[W]oman becomes for him the beginning of a blameworthy life."[30] He not only elaborates the blame of the Woman in general, but tied her presence and Adam's downfall to the problem of pleasure, as the Woman inspires in Adam erotic desire (*pothos*):

> and this desire likewise engendered bodily pleasure, that pleasure which is the beginning of wrongs and violation of law, the pleasure for the sake of which men bring on themselves the life of mortality and wretchedness in lieu of that of immortality and bliss.[31]

If Jewish exegetes of the first century were faced with theologically interpreting the loss of the Temple, early Christian thinkers were continuing to grasp the ethereal meaning behind the loss of their Messiah, and the meaning of his first enfleshed coming as well as his highly anticipated return. The latter scholars thus turned to narratives that understood the events in the Garden in relationship to the salvific work of Jesus Christ as the climax of a theodrama written from the beginning of time. For some, Eve was readily effaced from genealogical mention:[32]

> For as by a man came death, by a man has come also the resurrection of the dead. For as in Adam all die, so also in Christ shall all be made alive. (1 Cor 15:21–22)

The questions of sin and the nature thereof were keys to understanding Christ's death and Resurrection. If Christ died for the forgiveness of sins, surely the origins and conditions of sin were under examination, not only for the first man, but for all men. Addressing the story of Adam and Eve provided continuity to the chiasmus of humanity's fall and Christ's rise, for we all have to die for the transgressions of divine estate, and death is what makes atonement necessary. As Paul writes in his Letter to the Romans:

> [5] For if we have been united with him in a death like his, we will certainly be united with him in a resurrection like his. [6] We know that our old self was crucified with him so that the body of sin might be destroyed, and we might no longer be enslaved to sin. (Rom 6:5–6)

The Incarnation of Christ marked for Paul, and for the early Christian church, a disruption of both space and time. The divinity and humanity embodied in the flesh of Jesus Christ represented a new world order, one that challenged every status quo, and freed humanity from the shackles of sin and the terrors of death brought upon ourselves by our own doing. But the Apostle Paul continued to reference Adam and Eve as models of disobedience, not redemption, a side eye reminder of the old versus the new, who embody distraction from the pursuit of a new life in Christ.[33] Eve is only mentioned twice in the New Testament, neither time in high regard:

> But I am afraid that as the serpent deceived Eve by its cunning, your thoughts will be led astray from a sincere and pure devotion to Christ.
>
> (2 Cor 11:3)

> Let a woman learn in silence with full submission. I permit no woman to teach or to have authority over a man; she is to keep silent. For Adam was formed first, then Eve; and Adam was not deceived, but the woman was deceived and became a transgressor.
>
> (1 Tim 2:13–14)

Beyond naming Eve, Paul's writings about women, sex, and marriage seem to highlight a broader ethos of suspicion around the female body. Though Paul espouses a newfound freedom in Christ—one that might suggest resisting the hierarchies imposed by the first curse—he is unable to think fully beyond the cultural categories in which his own thinking has been formed. With a Pauline foundation in place, early Christian interpreters came to understand Eve as "gullible, dumb, beholden to the desires of her senses, and desirous of taking Adam with her when she falls."[34] But perhaps more concretely, Eve's identity as a consumer, marks a transgression and deception of the body writ large, an alloy of appetites that adulterates one's devotion to the Divine. At some point the consumption of fruit becomes synonymous with sexual promiscuity, a lurid narrative of the loss of virtue. Somehow the questions of agency, exploration, and curse that follow from eating the wrong thing, function to moralize desire and demonize agency, ideas that will come to bear the brunt of racialized anxiety.

Black Girl Magic

> There are the eaters, and then there are the eaten;
> Similarly, there are eaters, and then there are the hungry.
> Kyla Wazana Tompkins

Opening your mouth can get you killed. For as some say, the power of life and death is in the tongue (Proverbs 18:21). The axiom is often used colloquially to describe the power of the things we choose to say (almost at the level of incantation), but in the case of Eve, being demonized, discarded, overdetermined, hypersexualized, and at so many interstices written off throughout history, has as much to do with opening one's mouth to *speak* as it does with opening one's mouth to *partake*. As we are told and retold of the curse stemming from the food crossing the palate of Eve's open mouth, we are pushed all the more deeply into the foregrounding of sexual intercourse as carnal lust, and the simultaneous transgression of an open vagina now drowned in the waters of theological prohibition. Open mouths and open legs become gratuitously aligned with temptation, and will be stretched even further at the site of those whose bodies are read to approach that of a woman, and whose skin is complected as inferiorly dark.

Which requires pointing to the grave irony that the instances in the Garden make no explicit mention of sexual intercourse or of sin. Sexual intercourse is not mentioned until Adam and Eve are beyond the garden walls, where the verb connoting sexual intimacy (*yada*, "to know") is first used between the two (Gen 4:1). The first sin is not qualified as such by name until Adam and Eve's son, Cain, murders his brother Abel a few verses later (*chat'ah*, "to fail, to miss the mark," Gen 4:6–7). For many early Jewish interpreters, humanity's fault was not found in an 'apple' bite (the specific fruit is unspecified), but with the description of human wickedness in Genesis 6, which includes God's grief and regret over having created humankind to begin with. Though much scholarship has heavily cited the discrepancies of associating Genesis 3 with a kind of sexual deviation more broadly, such notions have not made significant headway in the cultural production and animation of Eve as seductive and sexually fallen woman, a warning of the dangers of promiscuous behavior. But for whom, and to what end?

We must remember that eating fruit is not in itself an act of sin. Neither, then, is sex. As others have described, the eating of the fruit cannot be an immoral act, because Eve does not have access to the knowledge of moralities prior to her eating.[35] So what does Eve actually do? Is misinterpretation directly disobedience? And is disobedience inherently unethical or immoral? What is the warning of death in a fruit tree to someone who does not yet have knowledge of evil, nor the ethical or experiential discernment to evaluate the two? And did not God also create any sensations of pleasure and desire? When thought more closely, it becomes clear that the acts in Eden are rendered as acts of transgression primarily because they connote that which is in excess of prohibition, in excess of boundary and limitation. But excess is not morally neutral, and conceptually must be considered for the ways it is theologically invoked to mark certain kinds of people. The scenes of consumption are the scene of a crime, and thus intimate a certain kind of criminality inherent to human nature. To follow this to its logical end, the inequity of the world beyond the walls of Eden reflect a curse deserved—the world itself as the first carceral state, with sex the shackles of the first degree.

Though this line of thinking has antecedents throughout Judeo-Christian history, Augustine is perhaps the most critical and influential theologian for moralizing consumption and instantiating connections between varying carnal appetites as contra one's most intense devotion to God. Most famously narrated in his *Confessions*, the prolific Bishop of Hippo lived several lives before fully committing vocationally to the call of God, which he reflected deeply through his experiences and conclusions drawn from his own sense of desire and sex.[36] His fourth-century thinking laid the foundation of one of the most extensive and ubiquitous doctrines in the Christian church and, subsequently, the expansion of Western thought: the idea of *original sin*.[37] Though hinted at by previous Christian thinkers and traced through the writings of the Apostle Paul, the doctrine of original sin understands the inherently good nature of Adam and Eve in the Garden to have been irrevocably corrupted in their acts of disobedience. But these acts were not theirs alone. For Augustine, humanity experienced a kind of *curvatus*, a scoliosis of the soul with wrongly directed desire and longing. As such, as Adam and Eve produced offspring—by sexual intercourse—they too transmitted to all subsequent generations the degenerative disease of selfish longing and desire known as *concupiscence*. Original sin, then, is "an infection which propagates itself from father to son through the act of generation which, being an act of organic trouble caused by the sin, is a sin itself and determines the transmission *ipso facto* of the sin to the new creature."[38] Despite the gendered language invoked here, more specifically, it would seem the disease of sin is transmitted from mother to child through the womb, a kind of stain now tainting the entire human race (the question of the purity of the womb will become critical for later Christological thinking).

Original sin then is *the* primary characteristic of a species. When Adam and Eve pridefully disobey, the "beginning of all sin" already taken root in their hearts, they subsequently fall away from God through the perversity of their desires, for the want of the wrong things. From then on, human beings are "born fundamentally disoriented, so that only grace can challenge sinful desires."[39] According to Augustine, this dire fate seals the nature and condition of humanity for all time; "man could not be born of man in any other state."[40] As such, the lust and desire associated with sexual arousal and pleasure (detailed in Augustine's writings down to the lack of rational control that males experienced over their erections) were reflections of the concupiscence associated with original sin. Sexual intercourse become synonymous with sin, when invoked for any purposes other than procreation. This teaching and understanding continues to drive certain theological injunctions around sex outside of marriage, erotic pleasure and enjoyment, as well as the use of birth control or other forms of family planning.[41] It also instantiates a notion of marriage limited by the confines of heterosexism and patriarchy.

But it is Augustine's allusion to that fateful day with Eve in the garden that so famously undergirds the explicit and implicit theological sinews uniting eating and sex. In the semi-autobiographical-tell-all that is *Confessions*, he recalls a neighborhood pear tree. He allegorically spins a tale of adolescent mischief through the lens of Edenic immaturity:

> Close to our vineyard there was a pear tree laden with fruit. This fruit was not enticing, either in appearance or in flavor. We nasty lads went there to shake down the fruit and carry it off at dead of night, after prolonging our games out of doors until that late hour according to our abominable custom. We took enormous quantities, not to feast on ourselves but perhaps to throw to the pigs; we did eat a few, but that was not our motive: we derived pleasure from the deed simply because it was forbidden.[42]

Elsewhere, I have rendered this account, particularly in its misdirection and disappointments, in terms of Annamarie Jagose's analysis of the fake orgasm. The fake orgasm, or the counterfeit pleasure of the text, considers the pleasure that comes from the labor(s) of pleasure, the pleasures of performance that is itself the manifestation of desire, as opposed to the assumed telos of a different destination and endpoint of a particularly (imagined) climax.[43] Which is to say, regarding the text of Augustine's *Confessions*:

> Where one eagerly awaits pornographic detail, one inevitably receives nothing more than a pear tree—an ugly one, at that, with fruit that doesn't even taste good. Not to mention, Augustine isn't even hungry. There are no descriptions of even

the sensual pleasure of holding, grasping, swallowing the fruit he has so deviously acquired and savors—he merely takes a few bites and throws the rest to the pigs. He goes to so much trouble to steal a pear that he doesn't even want to eat.[44]

Eating is undoubtedly a corporeal pleasure, but how does forbidden fruit become consonant with forbidden sex (which already assumes a heightened sense of pleasure in transgressing a boundary)? What Augustine's self-characterized lust for forbidden fruit helps us understand are the sleights of hand by which eating fruit becomes euphemism for a broader economy of libidinal impulse. While the act of desire for Augustine is enough to playfully flaunt his lack of chastity, for Eve, it is not the consideration of the fruit, but the taking pleasure in the fruit that most sternly indicts her character. It is the horizon of her desire that corrupts her heart. Eve's eating of an unspecified object is likened to her succumbing to the temptations of lurid sexual desire, precisely because she invites by mouth the seeds that Augustine understands take root as sexual desire. Her tempting is one that destabilizes the heteronormative resonance of the text, as her desires are directed away from God, God's word, and the assumed purveyor of that word, Adam.

Tina Beattie makes note of this trajectory of interpretation by illuminating the Temptation of Eve in Michelangelo's *Sistine Chapel* (see Fig. 2.1). Citing the continued pondering throughout the Renaissance (as in all times) of sex in the garden, she sees in Michelangelo's illustrative schema of interpretation the moment of *coitus interruptus*—

> There is a bold sexuality hinted at in the image of Eve's temptation. Adam stands over her as she reclines on the ground. She turns her head to take the fruit from the serpent, and yet were she to turn back towards Adam, she might take his penis in her mouth instead. There is a hint that sexual foreplay is frustrated and deferred by the Fall.[45]

But such sexual foreplay lays claim to other pornotropic imaginaries. Augustinian rhythm method aside, this *coitus interruptus*, as it were, is one of queer disruption. Michelangelo's framing of the moment of truth considers a different moment of choice: *fellatio* or *fruit*?

Different but not *unlike* the pleasures Augustine experiences between himself and a pear tree, Eve presents herself as somehow queer within her excessive desire. While Augustine doesn't seem to have an appetite himself, Eve's insatiability is one of sloth. Is *she* even hungry? This is a Woman who inhabits a continuum of pleasures—she wants multiple joys, and she is willing to share. Despite the fact that the linguistic "gender" of the serpent in the Genesis text is decidedly male, Michelangelo has rendered the voyeuristic basilisk as a woman, as well, further intimating the spectrum of Eve's attentions. Eve pleasures herself—and then has the nerve to pleasure Adam—with the prohibition. She does so in front of a

Figure 2.1 Michelangelo Buonarroti, *Expulsion from the Garden of Eden*, 1509–10. Fresco, 280 × 570 cm. Sistine Chapel, Vatican.

(gender queer?) serpent who liked to watch. And when Eve eats, she likes it. She finds nourishment and delight. She lavishes. She is generous. She is both selective and greedy, invoking what Kyla Wazana Tompkins so helpfully describes as "queer alimentarity," the resonance between eating and the erotic that "signal[s] the alignment between the oral pleasure and other forms of non-normative desire."[46] In the midst of the realm of the Edenic alimentarity there is a disciplining of desire that secures a heteronormative posture: Eve is problematically queer because her indulgence, her lack of control, her provocative excess of desire is both aberrant and blatant. Her presence signals a shift in libidinal economy—the exploratory act of eating raises the question not just about the controlling of desire as a thing itself, but of policing the agency and expression of desire within a framework of normative conditions.

Tompkins's broader investigation centers the ways that eating itself is inherently tied to racial identity, and more specifically, the critical significance of the moments when "acts of eating cultivate political subjects by fusing the social with the biological."[47] Though speaking specifically to the long nineteenth century and the United States context, Tompkins's analysis offers a logic by which we can better understand the ways the queering of Eve's eating arguably takes the same shape of that which, in a racialized and capitalist world, fashions Black, fat, erotic, sexual, sexualized, differently-abled bodies to be seen as excessive, non-normative, out of control, and in need of disciplinary apparatus. The notion of Eve's excess and control returns us to Tompkins's analysis of the open mouth, particularly of Black people, as signaling a set of dangerous flirtations—speaking with, thinking with, considering, inviting, and eventually entertaining deception—as the corollary to swallowing, ingestion, and consumption. Perhaps this is why the woman in the Couwenbergh painting has an open mouth that is not unheard, but silenced? The difference between speaking and being heard, a different take on the scriptural reminder, that the power of life and death is in the tongue.

Our Eve of the text entertains the considerations of the serpent, the generic word (*nachash*) for which is the same as that meaning divination or enchantment—Eve is speaking not just with a snake, but with a being that has access to (implied nefarious) spiritual power.[48] However, it is Eve's volition in speaking with the serpent, presumably from a position of power *over* the serpent, that marks her complicity—her claims to trickery are insufficient to absolve her of eating. The turn to the Enchanter, to a form of wisdom beyond the cosmology of her Creation, suggests (as varying literary and artistic tropes will come to explore) Eve as consorting with the 'darkness' of the demonic. In her turn away from God, Eve becomes culpable for what comes, for Eve is caught messing with magic.

Yvonne Chireau's description of the problem of "magic" within the contemporary (and I would argue, heavily Christian theologically imprinted) imaginary almost directly recalls the scene in the Garden:

> Magic is a particular approach or attitude by which humans interact with unseen powers or spiritual forces. In contrast with religion, it is efficacious, with its spells, curses, incantations, and formulae. Magic is used for specific, personal ends. It operates mechanically—as opposed to prayer, which is communal, devotional, and noncoercive. "Magic," notes a famous treatise by the nineteenth-century Scottish classicist James George Frazer, "often deals with spirits," but "it constrains or coerces instead of conciliating or propitiating them as religion would do." Religion is, accordingly, a public and social activity; magic is private, manifested in solitary, focused events, and has no church or sustained collective.[49]

The contemporary imaginary fails to consider the ways that magic, "generally characterized as the antithesis of religion . . . seems just as often to reflect the latter, to be its mirror image," which is helpful to see "the arbitrary nature of the categories."[50] Chireau goes on to quote Suzanne Preston Blier's summation: "Stated simply, magic is . . . the religion of the other."[51] Eve embodies the religion of the other, her exploration aligned conceptually as witchcraft, especially as a woman.[52]

The problem with "magic" has never been reducible to a purity of concerns around the ethics of ontology or deontology, but rather, alloyed dynamics of who deserves to possess power and subsequently wield it. What does it mean that Eve is despised for her *aptitude* for transgression as much as the transgression itself? For asking questions, for "dealing with contested notions of belief?"[53] Eve, and the problem of the open mouth, represents more than the arbitrary ethics of speaking with snakes (or even the reliance on "divination" or "experience" as translated elsewhere in the biblical texts), but a certain question around power itself.

In other words, Eve embodies the proto-imaginary of the conjure woman. Kameelah Martin helpfully describes the term *conjurer* as:

> an umbrella term that encompasses the individual vocations of root worker, fortune-teller, midwife, herbalist, two-head doctor, spiritual medium, persons born with second sight, and others who are gifted with verbal and/or visual communication with the invisible world. As such, the term comprises the various forms of healing and spiritual praxis with expressly African derivations rather than a catchall phrase for the occult.[54]

The emphasis here would highlight Eve as having access to communication with a source—however alternate, or witnessing alterity—in her conversation and communion with the snake. But as Martin intimates here, the image of the conjurer—specifically the African descended healers and workers who found themselves literally captive to settler-colonialists across the "dark" heart of Africa, or those who found themselves physically captive across plantations throughout the Americas—were often wrongly demonized, discarded, overdetermined, and read as purveyors of "black" magic and "dark" arts. Instead of being imagined as having the power to access the divine, of bearing epistemologies of healing and wellness, as being vessels of the sacred, they were often written off as witches, devil-worshippers, and minions—a narrative necessary to diminish the claim to powers higher than those who would enslave them, and to resist encouraging any defiance inherent to ritual practice.

What then to imagine Eve's exploration through the lens of queer, racial anxiety? What then to imagine Eve as first embodiment of the evocative Black girl magic?

This line of inquiry situates the heightened interest in the pursuit of biblical evidence of polygenesis (that is, a theory of *multiple* creations) that emerged by the mid-nineteenth century in the United States, as a means to theologically justify enslavement, theorizing the existence of Black people as a species entirely distinct from *white* humans. Indeed, a wide swath of American theologians, biblical theorists, and scientists invested in and promulgated this colonial, Eurocentric, white Christian nationalist doctrine, and readily "returned to the Biblical scene of the Garden of Eden as the setting for their racist imaginings."[55] It would seem that Eve's consorting with an "other" would provide much theological fodder for the anti-Blackness already at play in the minds of a number of white American men, with both the notions of Eve's sex and gender (as then conflated) and her racial(ized) identity playing key roles in the story and its meaning.

Whereas the earlier reference to Michelangelo's Renaissance interpretation of the encounter between Adam, Eve, and the serpent makes the temptress a decidedly *female* deceiver (which some interpret to be Lilith), Mason Stokes points to how American writers "arrived at a reading of the temptation in which the 'serpent' was either an ape or a human, often black, and usually male."[56] Introducing Blackness at the *site* of transgression interpolated Blackness as the *source* of transgression, an inference to understanding Blackness as inferiority, juxtaposed with the mythologies of Black excess—regarding sexual desire, reproductive capacity, size of genitalia, and virility—as sources of temptation and the impurity of miscegenation. This trope, which should read now as unoriginal and unsurprising in its triteness, centered fear around Black phallic capacity (usually without any acknowledgment much less interrogation of white desire), and relied on the idea of interracial intimacy as not only sin, but race betrayal: "Their concerns with the question of so-called racial purity made this black man's proximity to Eve the cause for alarm."[57]

Stokes's research further describes how this Black pathology of Eden not only divided Black and white people as separate species (confirmed by the theory of polygenesis), but read Eve's tempting in a way that served "to buttress the hysteria over the issue of miscegenation ... if Eve's tempter was a black man (or black woman), then original sin was not located in her eating of the apple, but in her far more grievous crime of heeding the seductive words of a black tempter."[58] This reading reiterated the imagined danger and threat of anything other than white nationalist purity and theologically justified segregation, with the biblical backing of proslavery arguments, protracting "... the mysterious relationship between Eve, 'our' great white mother, and that darker force, capable of bending her desires to his own."[59]

But while racial anxiety is expected in imagining a white Eve overtaken by the deception of a Black man in the garden, Stokes points out the theology visualized in Charles Carroll's work *The Tempter of Eve—or—The Criminality of Man's Social, Political, and Religious Equality with the Negro, and the Amalgamation to which these Crimes Inevitably Lead* (see Fig. 2.2). In Carroll's depiction, the serpent in the garden is decidedly *not* the Devil or some puppet of a great force of evil. Instead, Carroll's design of the garden imagines the serpent as a Black woman, "a *negress*, who served Eve in the capacity of maid servant."[60] Eve is rendered through the lens of white naïveté, "the unsuspecting woman in the simplicity of her nature," who's greatest crime was the subtlety of her fragility: Eve allows herself to receive *counsel* from the Negress (the purported iniquity that Eve should aspire to gender equality

IN SEARCH OF OUR MOTHER'S GARDEN 61

FIG. 9. EVE AND HER TEMPTER.

Figure 2.2 Charles Carroll, *Eve and Her Tempter*, 1902.

with her husband, and subsequently, be equal to God) rather than asserting the proper *control* over her.[61] Carroll essentially presents a framework that posits the problem of trusting 'the help', becoming sympathetic or friendly to someone of an inferior station in life, and the evil that transpires when a white woman fails to put a Black one in her place. There is a theological violation, for the white woman to

62   IMMACULATE MISCONCEPTIONS

not exert her rightful dominion *over* the Black woman, as per any of the other animals. She thus debases herself in the process—it is this seduction and lowering of one's station and one's guard that opens the gate to the real social evil—the false sense of equality that would lead to amalgamation.[62] The appeal to a divine order of raced being is not simply about separation, but discipline. Where thinkers like Augustine named Eve and Adam as sources of disobedience to God, Carroll's white hegemonic imagination centers disobedience as a failing to maintain and enforce ordained apartheid.

And yet, Carroll, despite portraying Eve as the demure and weaker sex, struggles to completely disrobe Eve of agency and fully maintain an uncorrupted picture of her innocence. This (white) Eve is still the beginning of the violation of God's law for (white) humanity. Marking the serpent figure as a Black woman subverts speculation that this picture of Eve, a white woman, would have any desire directed toward a Black male tempter (the queer potentiality of the Garden otherwise does not figure here for Carroll). Stokes offers a close reading of Carroll's visual rendering of the moments of temptation featuring the Black woman temptress, worth quoting at length:

> [The image's] primary emphases are on the stark white / black contrast and the participants' nudity, a nudity always assumed in the accounts of the temptation but seldom rendered graphically. Eve's femininity is obvious, though hidden from the viewer by a rather surprising shock of hair that flows down her front. This hair, meant to hide breasts and genitalia from the viewer, does nothing, however, to cloak Eve's body from the tempter, as the partial appearance of Eve's left breast makes clear. The hair preserves the reader's modesty—not the tempter's, and not Eve's. In contrast to Eve, the tempter's gender is less obvious, and thus less in need of cover (a need rendered doubly unnecessary by "the Negro's" supposed lack of modesty). There is nothing very "feminine" about the tempter's appearance. The lines are straighter, in contrast to Eve's obvious curves, and there is the appearance of facial hair. The artist has attempted to bestow breasts on the tempter, but the effect is closer to that of well-developed pectorals.[63]

Stokes's analysis elucidates Carroll's failed attempt at "the erasure of black male sexuality," precisely as the Black tempter's arm functions both as partially erect penis extending forth from the groin, as well as (if one notes the angular figuring and pointing of the tempter's hand) mimicking a serpent itself in striking position.[64] Stokes helpfully contrasts the strange performance of gender in this illustration, and the disappeared yet reappearing of the Black masculine to a number of significant ends (all not yet to be explored here). But for our purposes here, Stokes names that the fluidity of the "female" in this photo hearkens to the comparative image of Sarah Baartman as the "Hottentot Venus." As we will come to discuss more extensively of Baartman in Chapter 5, the absence of the exaggerated features of the Black woman's buttocks, breasts, and genitalia that stereotypically signal the pathology of bodily excess we have discussed in the context of Eve's desire, are an important juxtaposition. Stokes will conclude that:

> The fact that Carroll's tempter is far removed from this conventional iconography of black female lasciviousness further demonstrates that his interest in this black woman is to some extent a dodge—a cover for his greater interest in the sexual temptation of black masculinity. Giving us this "mannish" female tempter rather than the exaggerated, pathological, and more easily recognizable femininity of the Hottentot, Carroll keeps black masculinity relatively intact and retrievable.[65]

Despite both Eve and the Tempter being named as *kinds* of females, they are not indebted to the same registers of gendered legibility—a visual register again marking the ungendering of Black female flesh from Hortense Spillers's notion of patriarchal femininity.[66] Here, the white mistress is named Eve but is the performative extension of the person of Adam. Eve's stance is one that, though deceived, somehow remains undefiled. She maintains the position of purity and superiority, she honors the banners of virtue and whiteness, she is the one whose tears tell a tale of deception when perhaps there was none. *This* Eve, the white American woman braced against the Black female snake, maintains distance through color contrast, through a less feminine, less attractive, less kempt, Black *non*woman. A Black *non*femme. Dialectically opposed. By Stokes's reading this drawing reveals several realities around the threat of Black masculinity and virility, but only in conjunction with a subtending concern around white women's sexual desire. Within a theological cartography of the United States, Eve's proximity to Blackness—and more so, to a Black woman—represents "an alliance that threatens both patriarchy and white supremacy."[67] *This* is the threat of a Black woman's magic—a capacity for politics, for pleasure, and an interrogative gaze toward the parameters of paradise. The disciplinary invocations of the garden, then, are not simply theological truisms, rather, evolve as gendered technologies to discipline Eve (now synecdoche for "all of her sex"). And as socially constructed ideas of gender and sex evolve in relationship to race, the theologies of Eden become technologies for reproducing whiteness. Opening your mouth can get you killed, and in either case, there is an insistence that one must not dare hear the Black woman speak.

Breaking the Hymen

> Awake, arise or be for ever fall'n.
> *Paradise Lost*

> It is better to be alone than unwelcome.
> Eve
> *Diary of Adam and Eve*

Writing about her journey of return to the continent of Africa as a descendent of enslaved Africans in America, Saidiya Hartman describes the taut knot of liminality that far too often gags those formed racially between two worlds. Treading across the surface tension of the Atlantic, retracing the voyages, the memories, the flung, the chained, the drowned in the sea, Hartman returns. She finds the permanence of instability, the truth that there are some things lost in exile that are gone forever. As she returns upon shores that she may have, once upon a time, in another life, called home, she notes the reality of the stranger, the estranged:

> Being a stranger concerns not only matters of familiarity, belonging, and exclusion but as well involves a particular relation to the past. If the past is another country, then I am its citizen. I am the relic of an experience most preferred not to remember, as if the sheer will to forget could settle or decide the matter of history.[68]

In order to think well about Mary, the person who birthed and mothered Jesus Christ, we must also take more care in thinking about Eve—both figuring so prominently within the Christian theological landscape, yet also so isolated from themselves, relics we prefer to forget or perhaps to save away until they again become useful in some reference or ritual. Can we imagine the *strangeness* of these women's situations? Can we imagine the *estrangement*? Hartman describes that:

> The most universal definition of the slave is a stranger. Torn from kin and community, exiled from one's country, dishonored and violated, the slave defines the position of the outsider. She is the perpetual outcast, the coerced migrant, the foreigner, the shamefaced child in the lineage.[69]

On a bridge between starshine and clay, Eve had no models. She, too is thrust from a door of no return, "a place emptied of beginnings,"[70] torn from her home and severed from her kin. Ridiculed in her partnership. Pathologized in her parenting. The dust of the curse settled against her. She, too, will lose a son to the senseless violence of greed and scarcity. East of Eden, one wonders if her heart is ever able to find that which is both kin and kind, a new home, clarity or peace amid a forced diasporic consciousness. Hartman states:

> "Stranger" is the X that stands in for a proper name. It is the placeholder for the missing, the mark of the passage, the scar between native and citizen. It is both an end and a beginning. It announces the disappearance of the known world and the antipathy of the new one. And the longing and the loss redolent in the label were as much my inheritance as they were that of the enslaved.[71]

Eve X.
Mary X.

In essence, paradise lost. The subtlety of this line of thought—the scar of Eve's transgression—is one organized around the questions of a created order, what we might now reflect on as an explicit exercise in hetero-patriarchal logic as the trajectory of Eve's transgression is made possible only in reference to the prehistory of the knowledge of good and evil. What is such prehistory or prelapsarian goodness, other than that of Eve's virginity? Virginity, canonically understood as being "lost" by the insertion of a penis into a vagina, is and only is something that can be violated—and thus resisted—within the confines of heterosexual sex. Thus the loss of innocence for Eve is related to her enactment of queer desire, a desire imagined through the framework of pride and perversion. Virginity now functions to discipline signs of queerness in the garden. Where Adam linguistically infers women as signs in exchange, virginity will become the physical sign of exchange in the trafficking of women. And while Eve is perhaps not yet white, the imaginary of purity and virtue will ground the racialization of transgression, the eliding of wrongful appetite and desire with miscegenation and amalgamation, the fall of the white race of Adam. As Patricia Hill Collins writes:

> African or Black sexuality becomes constructed as an abnormal or pathologized heterosexuality. Long-standing ideas concerning the *excessive sexual appetite* of people of African descent conjured up in White imaginations generate gender-specific controlling images of the Black male rapist and the Black female jezebel, and they also on myths of Black hypersexuality. Within assumptions of normalized heterosexuality, regardless of individual behavior, being White marks the normal category of heterosexuality. In contrast, being Black signals the wild, out-of-control hyperheterosexuality of excessive sexual appetite.[72] (Emphasis added)

While Hill Collins writes of pathologized heterosexuality, I would consider the signaling of wildness, uncontrollability, and excessive desire a pathologizing of queerness, for in the same ways that Hortense Spillers theorizes Black women's exclusion from the categories of patriarchalized gender, we must also consider that there is a racialized sexuality of enslavement that shifts categories of heteronormative function, desire, and consent. Which is to say that Tompkins's argument of eating and ingestion as racially performative acts help us foreground the ways that Eve's presumed pathology itself is racialized. The notion of autonomy is one that almost directly produces racial, sexual anxiety. Far east of Eden, the work of inoculating humanity from Eve's viral pandemic will find a theological anthropological locus in the body of the Virgin Mary. And in the light of a pure, redemptive, obedient, and eventually "white" Virgin Mother, Eve will almost inevitably figure as Black.

When we see Eve *othered*, in both gender and in race, we see that Eve's actions—her body, her life; her strangeness, her *estrangement*—have been rendered in terms of a disobedience inherent to Blackness. Eve's body—and more specifically her mouth and tongue as sites of entry and sensual experience, are battlegrounds of spiritual turmoil, situating both appetite and consumption as possessing the capacity for cosmic upheaval. She marks a genealogy of humanity, and more specifically Christian thought and life, wherein a woman in particular in unable to indulge appetite of any kind without a fear of (further) falling from grace. Eve represents a kind of proto-conjure, if not *the* conjure woman, particularly as her narrative names the significance of her autonomy.

But what if we imagine such freedom as sacred, and return to Eve her ability to act for herself, and to have it be a neutral exploration, if not even a good thing, to be able to differently discern knowledge and evil, rather than to heap the coals of all humanity upon her head? What to imagine, even that her autonomy is a grace from God, particularly if we can consider that "the source of [the conjure woman's] divinity falls outside the jurisdiction of Satan, extending it then to the far reaches of the universe and dating it to a time before creation?"[73] How is Eve's 'Black girl magic' different from the kind of sacred intervention that would impregnate a virgin? Is it the source or the site that separates magic from religion?

How do we remember the stories of creation and creativity when they are stitched together by lineages of pain? To recall, the culturally infused understanding of women's bodies through the mythology of Eve are a narrative warped with attempts to make sense of the circles of life and death. And while the recitations of Genesis events have a history of multiple interpretations, the dominant narrative of Eve and women, particularly with the rise and spread of Christian thought, was easily secured in her desire and excess as qualitatively transgressive. It is this understanding of the female body, then, as inherently sinful almost from the point of conception (not unlike the later idea of Blackness as a mark of inherent failure and pathology) that presents itself as a conundrum from within the theological debates of the early church and Patristic era.

From the earliest moments of the Christian faith, the person of Jesus Christ was something of a conceptual roadblock—how can a person who claims to be the Son of God be crucified, but come back to life? How is one to make sense of a God-Man claiming to be the source of salvation? How can the perfection of God take on the material imperfection of humanity? And as such, how to consider the materiality of the female body, given a tradition that would find it "unthinkable that God would enter the world through a vagina?"[74] Some of our earliest and well-circulated Christian theologians were compelled to account for this obvious hole in logical thought. Without any means to access the divine aspect of Jesus's nature, the taxis of this early church debate logically turned to Mary as the source of Jesus's flesh, blood, and bone. Very quickly, they too realized that there is no way to make sense of the theological-anthropological investments in the female body of Mary, *theotokos* ("God-bearer"), the virgin mother of Christ, apart from underscoring Eve, the mother of all living, as her negative complement.

We don't know much about Mary, much less the material realities of her body. Though Mary does find reference in brief glimpses throughout the unfolding of Jesus's life, there is surprisingly little information about the mother of Christ within canonical Scripture. The letters of Paul, which predate the Gospel accounts of Jesus's life, make no mention of her barred a lone oblique reference in Galatians, noting that Christ was "born of a woman."[75] Though Mary is present in all four Gospel accounts, they each differ in their emphasis, particularly with regard to the matter of virginity. Only the books of Matthew and Luke, which are the only two books that contain infancy narratives of Christ, reference Mary not having previously "known" a man. Within the New Testament canon itself, she is never given the title of Virgin, and certain scholars question if the virginity narrative was even known to the other gospel writers.[76] Such ambiguity has not stopped Mary's sexual status from becoming paramount to her identity.

The more elaborate account that we have of Mary, specifically detailing the events of her Annunciation and the Magnificat, comes from the book of Luke. The Gospel of Matthew, while focusing more on Joseph's reaction to the news that "they" are expecting, is the one that causes some confusion. The author recounts in his first chapter the story of Joseph finding out about Mary's pregnancy:

> [20b] [A]n angel of the Lord appeared to him in a dream and said, "Joseph, son of David, do not be afraid to take Mary as your wife, for the child conceived in her is from the Holy Spirit. [21] She will bear a son, and you are to name him Jesus, for he will save his people from their sins." [22] All this took place to fulfill what had been spoken by the Lord through the prophet:
>
> [23] "Look, the virgin shall conceive and bear a son, and they shall name him Emmanuel," which means, "God is with us." (Luke 1:20b–23)

Verse 23 directly quotes a prophecy from the book of Isaiah (7:14), which is where the translation issues are muddled. The author of Luke chose to quote the Isaiah verse from the Septuagint, the popular Greek translation of the original Hebrew text. Through the translation of a translation, we are left in English and in Greek with the word *parthenos*, a term specifically referencing a young virgin. However, the original Hebrew word *almah* refers more generically to an unmarried woman or to a young adolescent girl (either states can imply virginity or inexperience). Though elaborate debates have taken place over the etymology at play, the importance of one or two words reflects the kind of gravity that only comes with having so few details to draw upon.

The majority of more popular stories about Mary's childhood and life prior to giving birth to Christ are actually traditions based on the narratives in *The Protoevangelium of James*, a later, extra-canonical source written around 150 CE. Here we find the narrations of Mary's life that are perhaps most well known and (now) dogmatically proclaimed—her own immaculate conception, her dedication as a virgin to the Temple (though virginity and asceticism of this type were unusual for Jewish worship at the time), and eventually her consecration to the care of a much older (and assumedly impotent) widower, Joseph. Still, Mary's virgin conception, however rumored and partially recorded, is something that many felt had to be established as a means of verifying the claims to the divinity of her son.

Necessarily so, for by the second century, all bodies were being called into question. These years saw the rise and spread of Gnosticism, a religious sect that understood all physical matter to be fallen and representative of darkness. Adherents to the sect interpreted the words of Christ as intimating a secret knowledge needed to escape from the bonds of the flesh, the dark, evil materiality that stood in opposition to the light of the spirit. However, this notion threatened the theological grounds of understanding Christ as the son of God, for the evil ascribed to all materiality undermined the very possibility of an Incarnation. For Gnostics, the pure and holy God would not be soiled by the filth of the world, an idea that was unacceptable for the keeper of the faith. The focus naturally turned to the Incarnation, and the logical emphasis on Christ being a real human being. The theological implications and subsequent attention given to the meaning of Mary's virgin womb expanded in correspondence to this defense, as the claims to Jesus as the Son of God utilized virginity to concretize theological claims about sexuality and the female body more broadly.

Known for his unrelenting witness to his faith despite his arrest and death sentence for the cause, Ignatius of Antioch was an early apologist refuting the Gnostics claims to the inherent evil of the body. His account notes the importance and reality of Mary's body as uniquely life giving, bearing the true and holy flesh of Christ:

> Mary then did truly conceive a body which had God inhabiting it. And *God the Word was truly born of the Virgin*, having clothed Himself with a body of like passions with our own. He who forms all men in the womb, was Himself really in the womb, and made for Himself a body of the seed of the Virgin, but without any intercourse of man. He was carried in the womb, even as we are, for the usual period of time; and was really born, as we also are; and was in reality nourished with milk, and partook of common meat and drink, even as we do.[77]

Ignatius espoused that Christ's birth, Christ's death, and Mary's virginity were the three secrets God kept from the Devil, a unique trinity of holy mystery.[78] And yet, in the letters he wrote while being marched to his martyrdom, meant to encourage various churches and believers in keeping their faith, his thoughts on what threatened the church hearkened back to Eve: "Let no one be anointed with the bad odor of the doctrine of [the prince of] this world; let not the holy Church of God be led captive by his subtlety, as was the first woman."[79]

As the third century dawned, so too did the influence of a young bishop from Lyon named Irenaeus. Thrust into the institutional role, Irenaeus returned from a mission to Rome to piece together the remnants of his home after a severe persecution, and to take the place of the bishop who lost his life during the resistance. His claims to authority, however, were substantial—he had learned from the teachings of Polycarp, who had learned from the teachings of Saint John. As such, he stood in direct apostolic succession, and played an incredible role in the forming of Christian thought. Accessing Mary's body to further his treatise against the Gnostic heresy, it is Irenaeus who first links Eve and Mary in a bound dichotomy.

In his effort to explain Christ as the "second Adam" (a theme we noted in the writings of Paul), Irenaeus aligned Eve and Mary through the critical typology he cited as *recapitulation*. For him, Eve and Mary share in common their unspecified complementarity to key male figures, precisely as their bodies have been instrumentalized as female. Irenaeus does not explore the implications of the different roles of their relations, one as "wife" and one as mother, an oversight that might have yielded some interesting questions for his analysis. Despite his noticing this, however, he does see in the Eve-Mary typology two methodological problems that only Mary—or his rendering thereof—can solve. First, he must address a logical inconsistency in his newly organized framework—how can Adam and Christ be aligned if Eve was created from Adam, but Jesus was created from Mary? There must be a way to find continuity in the inversion, lest Mary be to Adam as Eve is to Christ. Irenaeus turns to Mary's virginity as the key to this puzzle, for as "the first Adam was taken from the [virgin] earth and fashioned by the Word of God, [so also] it was necessary that the Word himself, working in himself the recapitulation of Adam, possessed a like origin."[80] In this moment, by linking the *virginity* of the earth from which Adam was taken to the *virginity* of Mary's flesh, Irenaeus establishes virginity as the prerequisite condition for God to create. In the case of both the earth and the womb, God indubitably fashions, but only from blank, pure, previously unused materials. God does not *do* sloppy seconds. Mary's virginity is the necessary ingredient for chosenness, the reason that she is favored, exalted, and greeted as "blessed are you among women" (Lk 1:42).

Relating Eve and Mary through their status as both female and virgin, Irenaeus exegetes not simply the idea of their gendered embodiment, but the very potentiality of their bodies. He continues: "So too the knot of Eve's disobedience was loosed by Mary's obedience, for what the virgin Eve had bound by her unfaith, the virgin Mary loosed by her faith."[81] Eve's lack of virtuous obedience is the suffocating, lynching noose that has severed humanity from the fullness of grace. Her negative body becomes the anchor and contrast to Mary's purity and obedience. Note here that Eve's *theo-ontological Blackness*, if you will, does not depend on biological fact, but instead emerges through the lens of patriarchy and order, as contrast between the notions of purity and chastity associated with white people, and the degenerate, sexually demoralized bodies that come to be associated with Black people.

Irenaeus thus moves from the "hetero-citational" link between Adam-Eve and Mary-Christ the hierarchal suturing together of subjects that functions, as Clare Hemmings describes, without equity as a relationship "of inheritance and debt [that] is consistently represented as such," to a "homo-citational" link between Eve and Mary.[82] This new link is no less hierarchical and no less indebted in its female valence. By the second century, Mary's virginity, purity, and holiness already stand in stark relief to Eve's sinful embodiment. They are the metaphorical realities for the sacred and profane. Irenaeus only improves upon the point when he aligns Mary and Eve through the narration of Mary's *obedience* versus Eve's *disobedience*. If Eve and Adam "partnered" in the fall (Adam's being "given" the fruit from the tree, thus instrumentalizing his body in effecting disobedience), then Christ and Mary "partner" in redemption (Mary being "given" the fruit of her womb, thus instrumentalizing her body in effecting obedience).

There is something to be said for the power of a rhetoric venerating Mary at all. To be sure, promoting virginity in society carried its own form of equity and empowerment, freeing women from laws forcing them to marry and begin families in Roman society. To venerate Mary as a woman of any kind was not a small feat, and Irenaeus claimed that Christ receives everything from Mary, a real woman who gave birth to Christ's real, human flesh. Arguing the redemption of humanity through Christ's flesh subsequently redeemed Mary's significance and presence from any detractors.

But while this may have been a rather feminist statement in the early fourth century, even here we see remnants of a theology inadequate to account for the female body. Irenaeus achieves the prominent reverence of Mary only by citing her through Eve, and in accordance to their respective virginities. The juxtaposition of virginities is one that prioritizes virginity as the measure of virtue particular to the female body (as a site of obedience), and as the locus of evaluation within the ecclesial community.[83] While Irenaeus attempts to liberate Mary (and women in general) from the cursed disobedience of Eve, he turns the female body against itself. Mary becomes the pure rendering of the female body who loosens the knot of sinfulness permanently marking Eve's body. Though this reversal is supposedly one of redemption, it actually is one only of narrative recapitulation, restating the facts of the female body within the story of redemption as still tethered to production and labor, the sacrifice of one's womb as mere instrument of Christ's coming.

While Irenaeus's typology seemingly depicts Mary's faithfulness as an overturning of Eve's shortcomings, Mary's redemptive qualities do not theologically find any application for women's lives. Rather, Mary becomes an indictment against women, period. Irenaeus's contemporary Tertullian, the Father of Christianity in the West, elucidates this ideology. Tertullian converted to Christianity after seeing the gruesome, moving persecutions of Christians in Carthage. He was committed to the defense of the minoritized group of believers called Christians, but his compassion did not extend to Eve in the least. His fervor did. Writing early in the third century, he states:

> And do you not know that you are (each) an Eve? The sentence of God on this sex of yours lives in this age: the guilt must of necessity live too. You are the devil's gateway: you are the unsealer of that (forbidden) tree: you are the first deserter of the divine law: you are she who persuaded him whom the devil was not valiant enough to attack. You destroyed so easily God's image, man. On account of your desert—that is, death—even the Son of God had to die.[84]

For Tertullian, it is not Judas, Pontius Pilate, or even the Roman government that is to blame for Christ's crucifixion. No, the blame belongs to Eve, to all women. The womb-body is the gateway of the devil, the wormhole to Hell. As the "unsealer," Eve contaminates not only herself, but *all* of *man*kind. Her virginal innocence is penetrated by her quest for knowledge, spoiling her, ruining her. Tertullian famously narrates the dictum of the Eve-Mary dichotomy: Eve is not only a comparative virgin—a ruined virgin; she now also embodies the motherhood emblem as well—a mother of a bastard:

> For it was while Eve was yet a virgin, that the ensnaring word had crept into her ear which was to build the edifice of death. Into a virgin's soul, in like manner, must be introduced that Word of God which was to raise the fabric of life; so that what had been reduced to ruin by this sex, might by the selfsame sex be recovered to salvation. As Eve had believed the serpent, so Mary believed the angel. The delinquency which the one occasioned by believing, the other by believing effaced. But (it will be said) Eve did not at the devil's word conceive in her womb. Well, she at all events conceived; for the devil's word afterwards became as seed to her that she should conceive as an outcast, and bring forth in sorrow. Indeed she gave birth to a fratricidal devil; whilst Mary, on the contrary, bore one who was one day to secure salvation to Israel, His own brother after the flesh, and the murderer of Himself.[85]

Conception, which is to say paternal anxiety and reproductive capacity, resonates strongly with Tertullian, from whom the threat of phallic snakes creeping into docile women's ears is still very real. Tertullian's digression against women, then—as all women are "an Eve"—angrily drowns the already culturally low view of women into the baptismal waters of Christian imagination, minting Mary and Eve as two sides of one patriarchal coin. The currency, though, is in virginity, that key link that "signif[ies] the *recycling* that Mary effected for Eve" from the trash of sin, desire and the shame of nakedness that comes from being known and exposed in the garden of Eden.[86] The Eve-Mary bond is one meant to celebrate Eve's redemption, but this is the story left untold. The early Church Fathers effectively stage Mary and Eve in direct opposition to one another, but Mary does more than recycle. She does not simply repurpose Eve's essence and assumed mistakes into something new. Rather, the emphasis of Mary's virginity in contrast with Eve's performs a complete erasure of everything that is "woman" about her. She is completely recast as a blank slate, except this time she is made available to man's creative powers, not God's.

Which is perhaps why the great orator, scholar, and world traveler Jerome summed his thoughts on the matter with enviable brevity: "Death through Eve, Life through Mary."[87] It is the perfect slogan (catchy enough to be repeated in one of the key Catholic documents from the Second Vatican Council, *Lumen Gentium*, in 1964) hailing the goodness of the Virgin and the harrows of her predecessor. Establishing this relation between life and death, between Mary and Eve, does the work of producing the female body as the ontology of sin. The scale of purity, then, is one that places the value of a woman not in reference to one's proximity to Mary, but rather, to the distance one might maintain from Eve.

The immense anxiety around the bodies of Eve and Mary reflects the Madonna-whore complex at the heart of Christian theology.[88] This trope, noted throughout Sigmund Freud's writings on sexuality, requires the organization of the female body as a psychoanalytic function of the Oedipal complex:

> The whole sphere of love in such people remains divided in the two directions personified in art as sacred and profane (or animal) love. Where they love they do not desire and where they desire they cannot love. They seek objects which they do not need to love, in order to keep their sensuality away from the objects they love.[89]

Theologically, Eve-Mary represents the way women are subtly divided in "two directions." The Christian man cannot love an imperfect, lustful, deceiving Eve. Eve does not necessarily function as the desired taboo, rather, she is the taboo that embodies desire. The Christian man also cannot desire the virginal and holy Mary, their Mother—and so she becomes most venerated of all women.[90] Freud analyzes the confusing sexual development of male children while they are still in the period of nursing. Noting the erotogenic zones of both the mouth as correspondent to the genitals, a mother would inherently deny any sexual possibilities for biological necessities—breastfeeding, cuddling, etc.—narrating them as "asexual, 'pure' love."[91] But the arousing intimacy inevitable with a suckling child leads the male adult to dichotomize women in their lives, the extreme poles of this dichotomy manifesting in the categories of mothers and whores.[92] As if Christianity were set up with the Madonna-whore complex in mind (one thinks here even of the complementary Mary Magdalene), attention to the theological rendering of women's bodies exposes the superfluous nature of such a choice. The idea of the virgin versus the whore caters to patriarchy in the sense that it is a sexual assessment of worth between men; but this is all the more insidious a process as it invites women to actively participate in the objectification and exclusion of other women. The "hom(m)o-citation" disguises the reality, that regardless of the category, the woman in every situation is objectified. The complex categorization is didactic, teaching women how to be held in the gaze of a same-other, teaching women that they are meant to be *looked* upon.

Again we see the emphatic nature of this dichotomy expressed theologically: "And Eve [had necessarily to be restored] in Mary, that a virgin, by becoming the advocate of a virgin, should undo and destroy virginal disobedience by virginal obedience."[93] This need for destruction marks a looming conundrum. Surely Eve's fall away from her virginal, pure state cannot be elided with the postpartum, post-virginal state of Mary. If Mary's virginity is disrupted, her womb then signifies the same corruption by sin that dooms Eve.[94] It quickly becomes imperative that Eve and Mary remain permanently disarticulated, especially at the juncture of their virginities. The tension of the Madonna-whore conflict ensures that an attempt must be made to "seal the womb, so to speak, by emphasizing virginity and condemning sexuality as a whole."[95] The spectrum here again must be seen in its historical moment, as well as expanded to the kinds of comparison and demarcations the sexual logic will encompass when tied to racial logic and questions of blood purity.

The best way for the Fathers to seal the womb was to enshrine it, and the theologies of the Patristic era around the perpetual virginity of Mary is one of the longest defined dogmas of the Catholic Church, officially declared at the Fifth Ecumenical Council at Constantinople (553), clarified at the Lateran Council (649), and reaffirmed during Vatican II (1964). For the Church, Mary maintains her Virgin status ante-, peri-, and post-partum for all eternity—she is *aieparthenos*, ever-virgin. Theologically, one virgin is exchanged for another; one body sealed as to correct the unsealing of all. It is the final stitch in the suturing of Eve and Mary:

> As one whose virginity is never lost, Mary remains forever outside the symbolic order that represents the language and meaning of our fallen condition, signified by the phallus and constructed around the binary knowledge of good and evil. As one who loses her virginity, Eve is penetrated by the knowledge that the phallus represents, so that even retrospectively, she has been understood as a patriarchal symbol....[96]

Paradise lost is actually something more akin to virginity lost, sexuality lost, freedom lost. Eve and Mary are equally silenced by the abstract functions of something called virginity, something solely applicable to the passive female body. It is this kind of body that "signifies a condition of physical liminality," incomplete and unachieved in relationship to the male body.[97] Mary's perpetual virginity is the chasm that separates her from Eve, from women who are liminally confined by their self-imposed imperfection, subject to "physical determinants making them second-class citizens."[98] If Eve is queer in her excess, Mary is meant to occupy the further oppositional point; heterosexual performance is not enough, so she is rendered completely asexual to be sure to thoroughly counter the effects of the first Woman. The image of Mary is held before women as the ideal feminine, whose emulation is necessary to atone for being created a sinful female.[99]

The problem is not that Mary is a mother, nor that Mary is a virgin. Rather, the detrimental blow to all women is that the ideal form can only be obtained by manifesting both qualities *simultaneously*. The sealing of Mary's womb allows for an inscrutable hatred of all women's bodies as constant reminders of primitivity. Even as the paragon of female embodiment, the Virgin herself remains as "Aristotle's incomplete male . . . a danger to herself and to society. [Her virginity] functions as both a means and a sign of purity" that are nothing less than entrapment, even as the very conditions of her status are not equitably available (even if undesirable) within society and culture.[100] Mary is split wide and emptied of her own body, to include her Son, for while "Mary's bodily essence is constructed on the hymen and the womb . . . both serve to distance her from it."[101] The exegesis of the vagina ends in poor translation, a story foreclosed from a happy end. Freshly replete with phallocentric conceptions in service to patriarchy, Mary is completely severed from her own body.

Lose Your Mother

What if Mary's bringing forth of Christ relates to God's bringing forth of Adam not in terms of virginity, but in the capaciousness of the womb? It is from the womb mind of God that the waters of the earth are divinely inspired and parted to bring forth, literally, *'adam*—the dust from which Adam is formed and for which Adam is named. This is the Genesis account of creation. In parallel, in the womb of Mary waters are divinely parted to bring forth, literally, a new kind of *'adam*. Thinking through typology in these terms moves emphasis away from the anthropologically derived terms of purity and virginity, and instead prioritizes the volition and love of the creative relation. Such a logic resists opposing Eve's virginal disobedience and Mary's virginal obedience as lateral claims. As such, the creation of humanity and the coming forth of Christ to redeem the world would not be bound to the sexual rendering of the female body, or the instantiation of fallenness as embodied in Eve's body and actions. Rather, it recalls the notion of interdependence, that the center of covenants were relations—or, perhaps, again, Glissant's "consent not to be a single being."

Of the many things that are absent from the church's configured relation between Eve and Mary, then, one of the most important continues to be found by considering the significance of space. Which is to say, perhaps Irenaeus makes an apology where there need be none. Recapitulation is a theory, not a praxis. Irenaeus works so myopically to map recapitulation upon the body that he does not realize his lens toward the *body* of Christ insists on a logic of the individual. When Irenaeus types Adam and Eve with Mary and Christ in terms of their virgin becoming, he delimits the potentiality of both the body *and* the land. But this is a story not of virgin soils, but the fluidity, and thus the expanse, of intimacy. Of the boundlessness of relations. Are there gardens of these theological mothers we take for granted?

Mari Kim argues that the events in Eden actually embody an abiding and unfolding faithfulness emanating from and under the aegis of Eve. Kim's work argues that the events of the garden can be read as demonstrative of three key theological frames—"benevolent creation, erotic faithfulness, and a praxis of beauty."[102] Insisting the Genesis text is rooted in an understanding of all of God's creation named as good (*tov*), Kim helps us imagine beyond the fictive scarcities of curse, dominion, toil, and sweat, to consider what else is possible if we start from the premise of *tov*—how does the narrative change if the serpent is good, if the tree is good, if Eve's journey is one that does not seek perfection, but yet manifests a kind of relational seeing, a discernment rooted in the delight, the goodness, the beauty, and the truth of the other. For Kim, Eden is experienced through the lens of goodness and hospitality—a hospitality that extends beyond death or expulsion, drawing us more deeply toward one another, to all living kind, and to the heart of God. As Kim describes:

> The certainty of mortality fails to mar the striking revelation that in her praxis of beauty, the woman enables humanity to imitate the benevolence of loving relationality ascribed to God throughout Genesis 1—the seeing and delighting in the tov of Creation. Thus Genesis 3 presents the woman as inaugurating humanity's vocation as "God-bearers," as she realizes humanity's capacity to manifest the likeness to the divine. And for her faithfulness, the woman is fully deserving of the name Eve. She is rightfully honored as "mother of all living" for faithfully embracing the praxis of beauty that inaugurates humanity's likeness of God.[103]

If we return to the questions posed earlier—What then to imagine Eve's exploration through the lens of queer, racial anxiety? What then to imagine Eve as first embodiment of the evocative Black girl magic?—Kim's analysis responds by returning us to a Garden where love, truth, goodness, and beauty, where virtue itself, can be cultivated and yet bloom, even as humans are asked to take those skills out into the world. In order for such beauty and benevolence to emerge, Kim's framework attends deeply to the erotic, the "contemplative *eros*" as necessary for inscribing a sacral imagination.[104] These premises of sacred imagination are profoundly

76 IMMACULATE MISCONCEPTIONS

illumined in the eloquent and sagacious rendering of Eve *against* expulsion in Harmonia Rosales's *Eve and Lilith* (see Fig. 2.3).

Part of a series of works that challenge the narrative of overrepresented Eurocentrism in art by both artist and subject, *Eve and Lilith* counters Michelangelo's vision of expulsion by centering Eve and the serpent/Lilith as Black women interlocutors. From the outset of the title, Rosales claims the pastiche of Michelangelo's suspected amalgamation of Lilith as the serpent, but expands the symbolic imagery to impress consciousness of Africana religious traditions and the implications of a Black Eve upon the viewer.[105] Though not mentioned in the biblical texts, Lilith is the fabled and failed first partner to Adam, who refused obedience and subservience to him, primarily on the grounds that they were created equally, of the same clay. Lilith chooses to leave the Garden rather than live life as second-class citizen, and flies away only to be chased by angels who threaten to drown her in the sea.[106] Lilith's prominence expands in the Middle Ages, as her archetype becomes increasingly synonymous with that of a demon, and specifically as a ruthless tormenter of mothers and their infant children. (One can already see how a Lilith-Eve dichotomy parallels an Eve-Mary bifurcation, particularly as part of Lilith's iconography becomes associated with a murderously violent anti-mothering aesthetic.) Like many powerful figures of female divinity, Lilith is confident, resilient, independent, and fierce. Subsequently, this means that her image is weaponized—she is depicted as inherently dangerous, possessing a seductive beauty, the source of cunning deceit—familiar gendered invectives that make vice out of what, when male embodied, would otherwise represent bold wisdom and charismatic virtue.

Rosales's image centers Eve and Lilith together, by name, with a conspicuously absent Adam. In this rendering, Lilith is vibrant and mighty, her largess irrefutable in both stature and in spirit. Resplendent scales of cobalt and indigo bricolage the lower half of her body, their thick gloss echoing light across the frame, glistening in memory of what may be water nearby—the source of creation, and perhaps the new home from which Lilith would have come. The realism of Lilith's figuration here summons several diasporic allusions, hearkening to a pantheon of female-identified spirits in Africana religious traditions—for example, Mami Wata—who in various iterations are able to communicate with snakes, and take on bodily forms with scales and tails (often represented as mermaids, or various forms of fish or snakes). Lilith's eyes gaze across the sheen of her own lamina, as if surveying her body and life in real time. Her left hand rests gently on Eve's right shoulder, the other arm cradling the Tree of Knowledge. Echoing the cradle of civilization, Rosales's depiction seems to reference the African baobab tree, whose branches look like roots, and whose mythology often describes the inversion of its growth, an intentional nuance of her own recapitulation of the scene. The unexpected entanglement of the branches are further animated by the concentric coiling of Lilith's tail, whose end slides softly against the back of Eve's foot. Where the biblical

Figure 2.3 Harmonia Rosales (b. 1984), *Eve and Lilith*, 2020. Oil, 24k gold, and iron oxide on wood panel, 36 × 24 in. The image appears courtesy of the artist.

curse pronounces enmity between the serpent and Eve, and promises that she will (presumed, violently) strike the serpent's heel, Rosales paints a vision of intimacy and caress between creation.

Eve does not stand apart from Lilith nor does she rest in passive recline. Rather, her posture is bold and assured, standing upright as she stretches forth and elongates her body to grasp the nearby fruit. There are no demure gestures to the nakedness of her form, for accurately, this Eve is unabashed and without shame. She gazes warmly at Lilith, her mouth parted, perhaps both mid-conversation and in preparation to eat. A red nimbus, used in orthodox iconography to mark the *alpha*, or beginning, of writing an icon, encircles Eve's head. It is gilded, but the absence of the white *omega* line that would mark this work complete, indicates an ongoing revelation—a work *in media res*, a reminder of the open-ended possibilities yet to extend forth from this encounter. There is no further distinction other than the vermillion outline between the gold expanse that floods the entirety of the scene's background, a blurring of the nuances of a paradise paved with gold, and Eve's definitive halo. Here, Eve's holiness is of the same substance and texture as all of Eden.

The catalogue description of *Eve and Lilith* describes Rosales's "representation of Lilith as a force of good, instead of terror, that works to overturn Christianity's misogynistic presentation of women as originators of sin and seduction."[107] Rosales captures the capaciousness of an ethic of care and mutuality in the Garden, the same insistence on goodness described in Mari Kim's argument for benevolent creation. Rosales paints *against* terror, and thus against subjugation or domination, with a scene that images embrace and connection. In an Instagram post detailing the process of the image, Rosales writes of the two women, "we are one and the same."[108] Instead of the twin intimations between Lilith and Adam, there is a sacred duality in creation between Lilith and Eve, these *ere ibeji*, these *marassa*.

Eve and Lilith move us closer to a theological anthropology that takes seriously Blackness, womanness, Wisdom, community, and desire as serious tenets of sacred being. Rosales's image resists the overdetermination of the demonic, and asks a question that *should* go without saying, but speaks to the inability of some to grasp her work: what if *this* is a truer image of the Garden? What if, in the beginning, there were Black women? What if the narrative we have is not the *only*? For certainly this is what holy iconography is meant to do, to shift the optics beyond the limitations of creaturely vantage, and consider differently both God and the world... no?

Rosales's reconfiguring of Eve and Lilith reiterate the problem of what I have described here as Eve's *theo-ontological Blackness*, but more significantly, subtend the possibilities for a Black gaze of the Garden, and for what else might be birthed, theologically, if we begin with the premise of goodness, with Black women as sources of the divine. What fruit—instead of famine—might such contemplation of desire bear? In her work, Kim will further claim that Eve's pursuits are evocative of her—and our—highest vocation, "to be 'God-Bearers' engaged in the work of co-creating with the Divine."[109] Seeing Eve wholistically, and expansively—laying claim to her title, as Mother of All Living—reconsidering her Blackness as marking her as sacred—and considering that she sings in concert as God-Bearer, with Mary, Theotokos—reframes the dignity not just of Black women, but of all of humanity as well as the non-human that we together inhabit. Such is a different theological vision of tethering and embrace, a citation rooted in vocation and kindred, not separation and distance.

Yet history continues to echo the hallways of theological thought, aligning Mary and Eve as archetypes of female embodiment and existence along a spectrum of negation. Eve is still Bad. Mary is still Good. The discourse around Mary's body maintains dissonance between her body and all other women's bodies, and in *their* tethering, Eve and Mary are left constantly producing each other. These are narrations of a gendered, sexed *ordo salutis*, one that will diagram nations, races, classes, and sexualities in the centuries to come. The theological codification of the female body through the figures of Mary and Eve will frame the paradigm within which Christians map private, domestic, and colonial space—and, of course, racial hierarchy.[110] Virginity lay concretizing claim to the salvation of the world when theological chastity was under assault, Eve's maternity pathologized against the beacon of Mary's impossible and inaccessible state, a light shining not from Heaven, but through the burning ash of valorization that left scorched earth in both wakes. And despite the theological rhetorical commitment to leave the hymen intact, in truth, its elusive rupture had only just begun. What does it mean to free Eve, to free Mary from the impositions of sin, as sin itself? What then to reclaim them both, Black Eve, Black Madonna (and perhaps even Black Lilith, too), in the lands of their own tending and flourishing? What if we trusted their bodies, their Gardens, as their own?

3
Theotokos, Another Spelling of My Name

> It is the images of women, kind and cruel, that lead me home.
> Audre Lorde

What makes a *real* woman? Is it a box marked at birth? A gender presentation? A vulva, a dress, a role one takes in one's home? Is it one's proximity to manufactured objects—makeup, hair, nails, lashes, and breasts? Is there a percentage threshold by which to measure a majority stakeholder? Or does one simply need to achieve plurality by which to say that they are more "real" than their competitor? The publicly staged "realness" of a woman is a measured constitution of an imagined reality, a performance that conscripts external and internal standards of being bound to a binary set of expectations. These performances trope implicit and explicit assumptions about gendered norms as well as the inhabitation of virtue, the unknown known of "womanly" essence that makes a claim to its own auspices of authenticity. These assumptions frequently ground biological genitalia as evidences of truth, rehearse cis-gendered privilege and desire, and veil a standpoint of internalized patriarchy, whose rewards only manifest as a lopsided location along a polarizing ideological spectrum.

What makes a woman *real*? The passion and emotion of such claims raise the question of impetus. How do we trace genealogies of yearning, the undertones of desire that lust for acknowledgment, recognition, and validation within a cultural formation that itself produces the concept of the real? If the contemporary moment inflects the defensive mechanisms of a pervasive and violent beauty culture, of filter-induced insecurities and augmented realities that threaten to undermine the institution of authenticity itself, what then happens when we come to the realization that being "real" may be inadequate to the economy of the real, may be inadequate to achieve recognition, must less to incite desire. Who, or what, then, does authenticity approximate, and who—by virtue of capital or color—has access to her realm?

The early Church Fathers could not have anticipated the movies and makeup, fillers and filters that are now so common to daily life, the debates and refusals around sex and gender, the feminizations or masculinizations, the racialized notions and economic injunctions around, the perverse transphobia behind claims to something *natural* as considered to be *real*—a nod to virtues of purity, and what is good, beautiful, and true. But they had no shortage of their own commentary to offer around authenticating and ritualizing the performance of their bodies and lives. Yet the content of their theological suppositions and explorations so many centuries ago is something we find both familiar and strange, perhaps because the debates and dramas of the early church would have made perfect reality TV. Shackles, bondage, martyrs fed to lions, a hostile Constantinian takeover, and endless cycles of verbal disparaging, scandals, exiles, anathemas, and intellectual brutality constitute the context, if not the content, from which the Christian faith emerged.

And not unlike the contemporary motifs, a dispute about "real" "womanness" was one of the most trenchant discussions of the fifth century. For those working to theologically secure the future of the Christian church, it was of the utmost necessity that there be a *real* woman around to give *real* birth to the Son of God. With a wholly divine Father, it followed that this Son must have, at minimum, an incredibly anointed Mother, one who could guarantee the claims to Christ's human flesh, yet who could stand out from the crowd of all women, so real as to also be the exception to the real.

That exceptionality came in the form of Mary's virginity. The supernatural birth of a child from a pure virgin specimen was a centripetal theme woven into the early Fathers' theological systems. Mary's virgin birth was a means to guarantee the pure, sinless, and divine nature of Christ in his incorruptible flesh. As a generous kickback, the virgin birth would simultaneously be the sign of transformative, redemptive motherhood previously sullied by the woman Eve. If Eve had come to represent sexual deviance and corruption, Mary represented sexual chastity and integrity. Where Eve was damned to give birth in pain and anguish, Mary was exalted to give birth in triumphant defeat of an ancient curse. Mary wasn't just any woman. She was the true exemplar of all that women could (and should) aspire to be in this life.

In Chapter 2, I described the textual and dialogical frameworks of a Mary-Eve dichotomy as a two-way mirror, a lens that captured the narration of the female body as well as her signifying parts. Traversing the reception histories discerning what exactly happened when Eve ate the ignominious appetizer to the downfall of the world, I highlighted the struggle emerging discourses of Christianity encountered in configuring the role of a woman in the salvation of that same world, and the continued racialization of the characters and "appetites" at play. In the effort, the homocitational practice binding Eve and Mary established purity as an accumulating measure of distance between the two women, a gender binary that would eventually inflect the color spectrum of race. This redaction effectively collapsed an entire genealogy of women's narratives and experience into a flat modality, and encouraged a moral category that reduces and indexes the female body within the solitary confines of its walls. But even as Mary was tethered to a disparaged and vilified Eve, her growing prominence and importance for the Church made sure to cut ties away from this other Mother, She of All Living, entirely.

"Theotokos, Another Spelling of My Name" explores this advent of Mary's renown. We pick up with the genesis of a New Testament, with the gospels and letters that contextualize Mary's life as the questions of paternal anxiety comingle with those of the nature of Christ. The ripple effect of these stories, particularly reading the pregnancies of Mary and Elisabeth against patriarchy, help to foreground the Nestorian controversy, a tumult of fifth-century events that forced the question of who Mary was and what her body did. Here, in the moments leading up to the Council at Ephesus (451), the heightened attention paid to the sexual status, virginity, and purity of Mary bore miraculous witness to the life of Christ, but not without making a calculated set of political claims toward the body. This chapter examines the contours of those claims by theorizing the ideological structure of the womb as a battleground for narrating gender, race, and sex, and linking the *making exceptional*—which is to say the M(othering)—of Mary as "alone of all her sex." As Mary stands as an apophatic gauge apart—the real(est) Virgin, the real(est) Mother, and the real(est) Woman—then we must consider the material repercussions that take root in this (theo)logical fallacy of modeled perfection, a divine motherhood linked to misogyny, ethnic erasure, and what Gay Byron describes as "symbolic Blackness," and the theological prehistory of how Mary became white.[1]

In Vitro Fertilization

Do you know a real woman when you see one?

For those living in the inchoate moments of the New Testament narrations, both cultural and religious practices made discernment of real womanhood quite the easy task. For at least a significant part of a definition, the expectations of a "real" woman included giving birth to children, preferably sons to be suitable heirs for their husbands. A woman's identity was (and for some, still is) tied to her womb, and divine favor was associated with reproducing maleness for progeny and legacy. When these conditions of possibility were not met in the biblical texts, there was then no biological data to demonstrate that men are often the infertile half of a heterosexual pair. Instead, women predominantly bore the weight of both inaugurating and executing a pregnancy. Wombs were vast spaces, uncharted territories either lush with fecundity or scorched by sterility. It was far easier task to blame the land for rejecting the gift of the seed, to hold the land responsible for its own circumstances of barren oppression, and to locate the volition of a procreative divine will at ground zero—the female body.

The Hebrew Bible features numerous stories that acknowledge barrenness as an inevitable condition of (fallen) humanity, but what are most memorable are the examples that describe barrenness as an affliction that can be corrected through the intervention of God. Early in the Torah texts, God promises that, if obeyed, "no one shall miscarry or be barren in your land."[2] This promise is so great as to extend to both human and non-human creaturely life. A womb considered closed was a sign of punishment and displeasure, the uninhabitable conditions and collected cobwebs of a deserted shelter signaled a cursed land. This space was double jeopardy, a curse of *the* curse—a womb whose failure to suffer the pains of childbirth in order to be fruitful and multiply mocked for the desire and need to not suffer appropriately. All this, precisely because God was understood to "open" and "shut" the womb at will.[3] The miraculous event of finally becoming pregnant after extended infertility is so frequent a motif in Scripture that it almost becomes mundane, were it not for the impassioned responses of new mothers insistently expressing their relief from the spiritual and social critiques of their childless state. Compared to the hostile early church juxtapositions of Eve and Mary we discussed previously, the Gospel of Luke introduces an alternative juxtaposition of female bodies and kinship between Mary and Elisabeth. We do not first come to know Mary at the moment of Annunciation (or even her own Immaculate Conception), rather, the way we come to know Mary is in relation, and with a birth story that begins with one of barrenness.

Picture a kind and gentle couple, aging with wisdom and grace among the Jerusalem hills. They are the sort of couple who might appear on a greeting card, exuding warmth and light, their eyes beaming with the same radiance as their smiles. They are outstanding citizens known for their integrity, role models of righteous living, community leaders who live a life above reproach. Everyone knows their names, especially at the Temple, and they never forget a face. He is a priest of utmost rapport; she is generous and kind; together they are devout and reverent, their lives a delicate balance of humility and approbation. And yet, despite their respected status, their disciplined adherence to all of the laws of God, they exist in a world unforgiving of their one conspicuous shortcoming. They, rather, *she* is barren.

They are Elisabeth and Zechariah. In Hebrew, their names respectively tell of a God who remembers promises and fulfills oaths. After only a few words of self-introduction, the author of the Gospel of Luke brings our attention to the deferred dream they share. On a day like any other, Zechariah is preparing for his responsibilities as a member of the priest corps on duty at the Temple. Serving the innermost parts of this most holy place was serious work, and by the cast of lots, Zechariah was on call to burn incense at the interior. He alone would perform the holy rituals inside while those outside assembled in worship. The work was both sacred and solitary, precise and exacting, careful and complex, rote and remarkable. Zechariah moved quietly among the dim shadows cast from flickering candles and the fading end of day. The familiar hum of a faintly murmuring crowd just beyond the Temple walls would have harmonized the careful liturgical movements marked by the sound of his own breathing whiffs of ash and perfume.

Suddenly Zechariah is not alone. According to Luke, an angel of the Lord, a messenger of this God who remembers, appears before Zechariah with greetings of his newly answered prayers. Which prayers, exactly, does this angel herald? Those most fervent; those asking for a child. Behold, Elisabeth is going to have a son. As readers of these texts, we are never privy to witness Zechariah, Elisabeth, or so many others before them in the moment of their trials and tears, their agony of anticipating a pregnancy that has no advent. No narrative devices are present to remind us of the last time either of them had even bothered to ask God about it, or to show us the stage of this wound and scar. What we do know about Zechariah and Elisabeth is that they have aged out of hope, their bodies far beyond the limits of what basic biology would indicate to still be possible, reasonable, or desirable. And here, an angel appears.

One question escapes Zechariah's lips, asking what we as readers now do not have to: "How will I know that this is so?" It seems innocent enough, but this messenger called Gabriel is apparently concerned with the shades of skepticism detected in Zechariah's voice. Gabriel chastises Zechariah for his unbelief: "Because you did not believe my words, which will be fulfilled in their time, you will become mute, unable to speak, until the day these things occur."[4]

A womb opened and a mouth closed. Ancient narrations of the womb often typologized what was imagined as a symmetrical, anatomical correspondence between the upper mouth orifice and the lower genitalia. The related pairing often signaled an attunement to divination, as virgins were imagined to be especially powerful vessels who could relay prophetic messages, their mouths open and filled by divine presence given the sanctity of their bodies. Inversely, Zechariah's closed mouth uniquely aligns him in partnership with Elisabeth. The forcing of Zechariah's silence can be read as punishment and the foreclosure of questioning, but this seems to suggest a contested relation, one that does not account for the legacy of devout witness that characterizes Zechariah's life. Zechariah literally has no mention in any other gospel account, so his presence at all seems to point to a nuance other than his playing literary foil to a bossy Creator. For this reason it is interesting to also consider the vibrational possibilities resonant within silence itself.

Throughout Scripture, silence operates as a recurring theological condition that animates God's creative impulse. *Are not all of God's greatest works wrought in silence?* Such silence takes on a haptic materiality of shining brilliance that deafens, a making deaf affected by the sonority of holy presence. The residual of the pause, this break, is demonstrative of the way silence operates as the insistent denial of that which has already been thought to have been heard, "a cutting and abundant refusal of that closure."[5] Such closure and refusal of closure are at once necessitated by the operation of God's timing and will, which speak themselves through a quiet that gives way to encounter, to God's presence and primacy that speaks itself through silence.

Silence is sound, sound that transforms desire by what it can and cannot articulate. It is the condition for amplifying, for opening new worlds of possibility that cannot simply be spoken for, but must be heard. Perhaps then the silence of Zechariah is a displacement of the will to sound, inferring the sonic space required for more attentive practices of listening. Gabriel's rebuke would condition early hearers of this text (there were few readers), positioned with and beside Zechariah, to attune more clearly to the *re*sounding of the Lord, as heard in the Temple, as heard in the elsewhere echoes of a heart beating as its valves and chambers formed inside of Elisabeth's body. The angel pauses the patriarchal claims to this baby's body by closing not just Zechariah's voice, but the symbolic representation of his voice as that which speaks on behalf of the religious institution that would limit the operation of God's will.

Elisabeth does indeed become pregnant and hides herself in seclusion for five months. Theologians have speculated numerous reasons for this, from Elisabeth's angling for a more emphatic "reveal," to a guided psychological weariness of having a history of miscarriages that caused her to shield herself from exposure to ridicule. Perhaps it was a way for her and Zechariah to simply experience the quiet of the miracle alone. Again, it is never made completely clear why she turns inward in a moment where one might be expected to immediately boast the miraculous work of God, but what is clear is that this matters to her, and it matters deeply. She expresses the importance of this moment in her own words, particularly as her now mute mate cannot: "This is what the Lord has done for me when he looked favorably on me and took away the disgrace I have endured among my people."[6]

Elisabeth has lived with the incredible irony of her desire, a desire for the curse of Eve. What would Elisabeth not give to have her body rocked with contractions, shivering with the pain and pressure of child labor. When weighed against the options, it makes sense. The duress of labor is finite, limited to a fraction of time, a few hours collapsed into moments by the hindsight of memory. But the torment of sterility in the early centuries would have been endured through a lifetime of humiliation. Perhaps the struggle across trimesters makes one damned if you do, but there is no reward of new life, of kinship, of social acceptability when you are damned if you don't.

Elisabeth's travail over her disgrace is now dissipated for eternity, the sense of her shame displaced by an opportunity that is complex in its form. She will have the child she wants; she will also have a different sense of normalcy, now conformed to the normative social expectations bestowed upon a woman. It is a brief moment whose gravity can be missed, because for now, the birthing person (rather than just the one who will be birthed) actually occupies our attention. She is still part of, and not just party to, the miracle. We are given insight into Elisabeth's own feelings about what this will do for *her* heart, the gratitude she feels for *her* life. It is not a surprise then that she worships God for the opportunity to break the curse of barrenness, even as it embraces what is technically the curse of her female body. Perhaps the strictures of desire and the limits of opportunity are really where curses lie.

The dialogue at the beginning of Luke circles back, folding in on itself to spring a new offshoot stretching parallel to the narrative thus far. This time, we encounter a diametrically opposed protagonist found in Mary. It has not been six months since that fateful day in the Temple. One might think of Elisabeth, who is clearly "showing," as noticeably more rosy and round. She has been out of hiding for one month now with the imminent birth of her son. Ready to transform yet another ordinary day in the life, Gabriel dances across the stage of Scripture as the preeminent messenger of God, announcing another child to be born. But this time, the angel makes a visit to the virgin (*parthenos*) Mary.

"Virginity" is the only constitutive descriptor of Mary we have at this point. It is not in itself much of an introduction to the beloved young girl, not that she really needs one. By this time, our attentions have already been directed toward the miraculous by the chiastic literary elements of déjà vu too blatant to ignore. We anticipate the divine realm on collision course for conception when the foreshadowed ethereal being greets Mary with a double entendre that now resonates in the hearts and minds of people of faith around the world—"The Lord is with you."[7]

Artists have interpreted the emotions of this moment with everything from holy fear and trembling, to the contours of Mary's likeness displaying inimitable calm and poise. Similarly to Zechariah's response, Mary is "much perplexed" and "ponders" what is happening to her. The angel moves to clarify with prophetic certainty:

> [30b] Do not be afraid, Mary, for you have found favor with God. [31] And now, you will conceive in your womb and bear a son, and you will name him Jesus.

But bearing God can be no ordinary task, and even Mary finds this an occasion for questioning. She asks the logical question of the angel, "How can this be, since I am a virgin?"[8] Here, the repetition of the word *parthenos* emphasizes this aspect of Mary's life, a building resonance in the Book of Luke despite, as discussed elsewhere, the lack of clarity around Mary's virgin designation.[9] Given the announcement of Mary's pregnancy mirrors the announcement of Elisabeth's, Luke's attention to Mary's virginity makes logical sense in qualifying Mary's question of "How?," affirming the centrality of divine intervention in the narrative. As Mary was already mature enough to bear children by natural means, something extraordinary amid the ordinary must point to the supererogatory nature of Christ's coming. A pregnant virgin certainly accomplishes this goal. But while Luke explicitly recounts Mary's virginity, there are no theological claims or inferences to "the transmission of original sin as it was related to the sexual nature of human propagation," nor the "incarnation of a pre-existent being," the latter of which will soon become a vital doctrinal concern.[10]

Likewise, Luke does not reveal Mary's own inclinations about her virginity, which will be a foil for the angelic statement of Christology.[11] As Jerome, one of the most distinguished Fathers of the Church, described it, Mary's reaction of being "terror-stricken and unable to reply" at the Annunciation was the modest and apposite reaction for the pious woman who had "never been saluted by a man before."[12] Apparently for him, Mary had experienced her own share of being sequestered, even from her fiancé Joseph, never mind that seeing a phantom prestige may have just actually been a terrifying experience. Jerome's interpretation reflected the emerging cultural mores of virtual conduct for women in a post-Constantinian church, "a Mary characterized by a quiet voice and demure behavior."[13] Comparatively, Jerome doesn't seem to consider that Zechariah, who would not have at all been unfamiliar with greeting other men, was equally startled and gripped by fear when an angel of the Lord appeared to him.

But there are cues on the matter present in the text of Luke itself. Whereas Gabriel is insulted by Zechariah's inquiry into the machinery behind the prophesied miracle—and subsequently punished for his lack of faith—the angel does not read any further into Mary's befuddlement at what seems a preposterous claim. Jerome likewise lauds Mary's nature by the irony of reaction, the young woman terrified by the presence of whom she thought was a mere man (Jerome leaves no room to consider Mary might have thought Gabriel a woman or wholly alien altogether) has no trepidation speaking to a divine messenger. The messenger Gabriel would seem to concur, as Mary's objection receives a much more patient and hospitable reply:

> 35b The Holy Spirit will come upon you, and the power of the Most High will overshadow you; therefore the child to be born will be holy; he will be called Son of God.

Gabriel substantiates the claim with a sign, revealing to Mary that God has elsewhere been working in a similar fashion, even within Mary's own lineage. It would seem that God's favor runs in the family:

> 36 And now, your relative Elisabeth in her old age has also conceived a son; and this is the sixth month for her who was said to be barren. 37 For nothing will be impossible with God." 38 Then Mary said, "Here am I, the servant of the Lord; let it be with me according to your word." Then the angel departed from her.

Mary immediately goes to visit Elisabeth, who has just turned the corner on her third trimester. Upon being greeted by Mary, Elisabeth feels her son "leap" in utero. Luke interjects the meaning of this, as Elisabeth is "filled with the Holy

Spirit," which leads her to vibrantly exalt her young relative and her wondrousness as it unfolds:

> [42-45] Blessed are you among women, and blessed is the fruit of your womb. . . . And blessed is she who believed that there would be a fulfillment of what was spoken to her by the Lord.

It certainly takes one to know one. Two women find themselves in quite the unusual predicament, and Elisabeth's voice dances analogously to the baby in her womb, both feeling the nearness of their similitudes as Mary's body nurtures the Christ to come. Praise is contagious and Mary, apparently moved by the exclamations of her own blessedness, breaks in turn to her own song blessing the Lord, the sacred and renown Magnificat:[14]

> [46] And Mary said, "My soul magnifies the Lord, [47] and my spirit rejoices in God my Savior, [48] for he has looked with favor on the lowliness of his servant. Surely, from now on all generations will call me blessed; [49] for the Mighty One has done great things for me, and holy is his name. [50] His mercy is for those who fear him from generation to generation. [51] He has shown strength with his arm; he has scattered the proud in the thoughts of their hearts. [52] He has brought down the powerful from their thrones, and lifted up the lowly; [53] He has filled the hungry with good things, and sent the rich away empty. [54] He has helped his servant Israel, in remembrance of his mercy, [55] according to the promise he made to our ancestors, to Abraham and to his descendants forever."

This is Mary's fiat, her renown "yes" to the will and work of God. Her words are repeatedly cited as those of a revolution; Mary is the first disciple of her own firstborn. She stays with Elisabeth for three months, right until the time when Elisabeth will give birth, before returning home.

The community, friendship, love, and vocality of Mary and Elisabeth, their kinship, and the joy they experience in the presence of the Holy Spirit, that is, in intimate communion with God—remind us again of the absence of paternal perspective. In their togetherness they center the joy of their pregnancies on their own terms, against patriarchal interference, and beyond the limitations of heteronormative claim. Strangely in absentia here, only the Book of Matthew expounds upon Joseph's reaction—a move couched by Matthew's genealogy of Jesus traced through the lineage of Abraham down to that of Joseph, where the appearance of an angel to Mary goes without mention. Instead, this retelling indicates that Mary and Joseph were engaged, but certainly not yet living together (and by implication, not having sex), when she became pregnant. Matthew specifically mentions that

Mary was found to be with child by the Holy Spirit, placing up front the corrective, clarifying knowledge only an omniscient narrator can possess. At the time, Joseph was not privy to such clarity about the supernatural nature of Mary's pregnancy, but "being a righteous man and unwilling to expose her to public disgrace," he planned to dismiss her quietly.[15]

It would only seem logical, much less equitable, to inform both Mary and Joseph of their partnership in the miraculous, particularly given the social constructions of the time. So while sleeping, an angel appears to Joseph, saying:

> [20b] . . . do not be afraid to take Mary as your wife, for the child conceived in her is from the Holy Spirit. [21] She will bear a son, and you are to name him Jesus, for he will save his people from their sins.

With noted brevity Matthew recites the curt comments before he closes the scene, carefully giving interpretive measure to what exactly we are witnessing—

> [22] All this took place to fulfill what had been spoken by the Lord through the prophet: [23] "Look, the virgin shall conceive and bear a son, and they shall name him Emmanuel," which means, "God is with us."

Matthew characteristically marks this moment as the fulfillment of a long-awaited prophecy of the coming Messiah. Joseph wakes from the dream, marries Mary, but "had no marital relations with her until she had borne a son,"[16] whom he obediently names Jesus. It is important to note the looming ambiguity of the text, and the ongoing question over whether or not Joseph *ever* came to be sexually intimate with Mary, but for now, the case is clear. In stark contrast to Luke, Matthew focuses his energies on a masculine narrative, underscoring the paternal anxieties that are evinced in narratives of Jesus's birth and Mary's virginity.

To this point, Howard Eilberg-Schwartz argues that divine intervention and causation are insistent reminders of a God who asserts masculine power over and against that of human men. He describes:

> If it is the divine father who is responsible for opening a woman's womb, it is not clear at all what role the human father plays. The deity is sometimes regarded as competition for human males, since the human male's ability to reproduce is dependent upon the will or participation of the deity. To be sure, the human husband contributes the seed. But this alone does not guarantee pregnancy.

Citing the numerous examples of this in the Hebrew Bible, Eilberg-Schwartz takes an Oedipal view of the relationship between a gatekeeping God and the human male. Men, in a sense, need permission to impregnate. This jeopardizes the identity of the male subject, that is the human husband as anticipated father, whose virility is displaced by the divine masculine. The formulation raises several moments of contention, including the ways that such a relation as described would necessitate the volition of God in the traffic of women, and would severely curtail any positive consideration of Mary's voice or agency in the matter. But even if we eschew the suggestion of a (hu)man versus God competition, Eilberg-Schwartz highlights a critical contention that sex, no matter how procreative in intention, does not itself guarantee pregnancy and progeny. Virility may be at risk, but no more so than a woman's fertility.

A reminder then, of the miracle. When fetuses grow in the womb, the uterus muscles expand alongside the child, making space for a child who is at once making space for themselves. The fireworks of exploding synapses, the grip strength in the sinews of toes, the malleability of placental walls whose porous sieve provide nourishment, transfer and contact, a blessed choreography between mother and child. How the more so for a child who created the world and then chose to inhabit it? We will return to this line of thought, but here it reminds us that Mary's miraculous impregnation, her semen-less insemination, functions from the start to make a specific genealogical claim. God absents any human father of her unborn child, and as such marks the fulfillment of a long-awaited prophecy of the coming Messiah. But what is this thing? This womb of Mary? How can one explain its capacity and possibility, its materiality and ethereality?

Flesh of My Flesh

For a moment, we have a brief hiatus, a distilled silence that is filled with the voices of women. This moment is not blithely absent of fathers themselves, but is rather absent of the patriarchal formulation of the virile male as father, one who was not born but rather made, one who is equally produced within the oppressive structures of subjectivity. But the father we do have is not done yet. The close of the Annunciation comes with the fulfillment of a promise. Elisabeth gives birth to her son. While there may have been tears in his eyes, Zechariah is kept silent, though words so often fail us in our most tender of moments anyhow. As was customary, eight days after the birth, Elisabeth and Zechariah's family gathered to name their child. Logically they suggested naming him after his father, but Elisabeth heard this and protested, "No; he is to be called John."[17] Zechariah had not let Gabriel's instructions to him be overlooked.

But these were different times (or perhaps not—listening to new mothers seems to be a transhistorical concern), and their families surely thought that Elisabeth was being disrespectful if not suspicious. They reminded her that none of her relatives had this name and, refusing to heed her desires for her own child, went to get Zechariah to settle the matter. Someone brought him a writing tablet, on which he promptly wrote: "His name is John."[18] In that exact moment, the lock on Zechariah's tongue was broken, striking fear and wonder into the heart of all of his neighbors. Zechariah had learned to not become captive to his questions, and more so, be bound by an unnecessary cycle of patriarchy, and immediately focused his new found voice on praising God. Thus we hear our second song of praise from the old man, the new father inspired by the Holy Spirit:

> [68] Blessed be the Lord God of Israel, for he has looked favorably on his people and redeemed them. [69] He has raised up a mighty savior for us in the house of his servant David, [70] as he spoke through the mouth of his holy prophets from of old, [71] that we would be saved from our enemies and from the hand of all who hate us. [72] Thus he has shown the mercy promised to our ancestors, and has remembered his holy covenant, [73] the oath that he swore to our ancestor Abraham, to grant us [74] that we, being rescued from the hands of our enemies, might serve him without fear, [75] in holiness and righteousness before him all our days. [76] And you, child, will be called the prophet of the Most High; for you will go before the Lord to prepare his ways, [77] to give knowledge of salvation to his people by the forgiveness of their sins. [78] By the tender mercy of our God, the dawn from on high will break upon us, [79] to give light to those who sit in darkness and in the shadow of death, to guide our feet into the way of peace.

Zechariah's song reminds us that if something can be divinely closed, it can be divinely opened. It can be divinely stretched, reimagined, and repurposed for something new. It can be empty yet filled, silent yet resounding. The juxtapositions of structure, song, and capacity in the opening chapter of Luke question not only who speaks, but who listens; not to mention, the when, where, and why of it all. What takes place in Mary's body is not a single, individual action, but a communal enterprise, an embodiment of social conditions and relations that foreground the revolutionary as it manifests in and through her. She and her community—her Palestinian Jewish community—are impacted, touched, challenged, and changed first, with the entire world to follow suit. This family makes space for a multiplicity of bodies and relations within what will come to be known as the church, and recalibrates thinking around what it is to be chosen by God to do God's work. Through Mary, and not just Mary's womb, we are brought together toward the body of Christ, the irruption of Divinity into the flesh of humanity, who will dismantle every normative claim to the body itself.

We turn to the question of Mary's life as a Palestinian Jew because it is a critical matrix through which Mary's purity—and subsequently, the purity of the Christian "race"—will be considered. In the expansion of the institutional guild of the Christian faith, the questions of who and how one speaks, of the tensions between agency and the foreclosing of language, of the marking of flesh, of the surveillance and narration of the body, can only be considered against the backdrop of Jewish election. For it is the erasure of Jewish flesh that explains the roots of the instrumentalization of Mary's body religiously and culturally, and the erasure of her Palestinian identity that asks contemporary questions of race, settler-colonialism, and genocide. Both are deeply rooted in constructions of identity, divine notions of inheritance and superiority, commitments to violence, and at root, the political axis of propaganda and shifting narratives. For this we turn to one of the most critical and cut-throat debates that would arise in the early Church around the Virgin Mary—the Nestorian Controversy.

Delayed Insemination

> If Mary is not, strictly speaking, Theotokos, then the one who is born from her is not, strictly speaking, God.
> Cyril of Alexandria

> Let me thus say, Theotokos.
> Nestorius of Antioch

There are times where it is better to agree than disagree. Times where it is more beneficial to concede a nuanced point and closely discern which battles you are most prepared to fight. Times where unity prevails over disunity, where reconciliation and peace can be worked out in the name of Christian community. When the Emperor Constantine reversed the illegality of Christianity and inaugurated the Holy Roman Empire after the 312 Battle of Milvian Bridge, he baptized an entire world beneath the placard of such a universal reconciliation. But opening the threshold of Christianity did not suddenly set all Christian feet upon the same rock. There had always been pluralities of thinking and multiple brands of worship and art amalgamated beneath this sign of the cross, but the sudden event that made Constantine's beliefs law had conquest, not community, as core value. Legalizing orthodoxy may have changed the game, but it did not necessarily shift the investments of the players.

The fifth century would see a number of theological veterans and rookies wax and wane in the political game of Christendom, players who very quickly found themselves with very different allegiances. There were key rivaling dissensions between the schools of Alexandria (Egypt) and Antioch (Syria), with a rift fissuring around the nature of Christ. Where Alexandrian theologians emphasized the unity of Christ's nature, Antiochenes stressed the important differences between the divinity and humanity of Christ. These were not limited nuances, they were ideas that staked claims to an entire way of seeing the world, with the requisite theological battles fought as if life and salvation itself depended on it. And Christian leaders were particularly brutal. As one scholar would put it, "to cast the ancient hierarchs in the mold of twentieth century western European gentlemanly churchmanship is a peculiarly misinformed canon of judgment."[19] In but one of the ways time has not brought about change for Christianity as an institution, injury, anathema, and exile were part and parcel of theological truth claims.

In 428, Nestorius was thrust from his monastic moorings into the peculiar stadium lights of sorted church leadership. With the sudden death of Sisinius, Emperor Theodosius II chose Nestorius to be installed as the new Bishop of Constantinople. Born in a Roman province of Syria near what is now Maras, Turkey, the erudite had been rigorously formed by the local theological sands of Antiochene faith before himself becoming a monk and eventually priest at the monastery of Euprepius, just beyond the city walls. This "stranger from Antioch"[20] was an unlikely candidate for the position, but the ambitious Nestorius would quickly inherit the traditions of the apostolic Fathers, as well as the longstanding dissension among their ranks. There was no way he could have known the weight of the battles brewing on an imperial stage, not when he had his own local forays to fight, and not if his intentions were to wield the full power of his office while he could. Within days of being seated in his bishopric, Nestorius was already staging the conditions under which he would soon find himself under orthodox siege.

The first thing to do when you move into a new house is clean it, and Nestorius wasted no time getting down and dirty in his new digs. Though poised as an ardent defender of the faith, he had much to learn about decorum, about the ways and means of being a little too eager, and the political problem of moving too quickly to create change "before he had tasted the water of the city."[21] Immediately after his ordination, the newly minted bishop ascended to the throne to promptly declare the famous first of the lasts of his vocational promises: "Give me, my prince, the earth purged of heretics and I will give heaven as a recompense. Assist me in destroying heretics, and I will assist you in vanquishing the Persians."[22]

Promising the emperor that winning the spiritual fight for orthodoxy would mirror results in the political fight of continued conquering, Nestorius staked his claim with a sweeping approach to reform, but not without offending many with his impetuous attitude. The "hammer of heretics" boldly launched his campaign by threatening to destroy the one remaining Arian chapel in the city.[23] Ordering a "demolition squad" to destroy the Arian chapel was considered by most to be "an unnecessarily dramatic and tactless way of proceeding."[24] Rather than be humiliated by Nestorius, the Arians felt they had no choice but to set fire to the chapel themselves, burning down several nearby structures in the process—the blame for which fell to Nestorius. From those ashes would rise Nestorius' new sobriquet "*purkaia*," an epithet akin to "Torchie" or "Firebrand" that offered a hat tip to his incendiary nature and his erroneous actions alike.[25] The name would prove a prophetically accurate description of the way Nestorius' reputation would soon go up in flames. But at the time, for the inchoate leader, it would take more than the destruction of one chapel to squelch the embers of a heresy he sensed throughout the region. Focused so intently on fanning his own flames, one of Nestorius' greatest mistakes was miscalculating the fury of a woman scorned. Specifically, that of the sister of Theodosius II, Augusta Aelia Pulcheria.

Pulcheria was immensely popular and well respected in the political and ecclesial circles of the time, and was known for her deep devotion and emulation of the Virgin Mary, but this meant little to Nestorius and his mission to clean up Constantinople. From his first celebration of the liturgy at the Great Church in Constantinople, Nestorius continued to make clumsy moves in the game of thrones. Traditionally, the emperor and emperor *alone* was allowed to take Eucharist in the sanctuary—no other lay person would be extended such a privilege, and certainly not a woman. But Pulcheria had taken these privileges upon herself and enjoyed them freely while Sisinnius held the office. Both royalty and devoted virgin, she partook of the holy sacrament by her brother's side without interruption, despite the fact that she was not the emperor, and despite the fact that women were relegated to the separate *gynaikeia*, segregated galleries from which the women would worship separately from any men.[26] As a result of the "conclusions Pulcheria herself drew from her emulation of Mary and from the Eve/New Eve synthesis," Pulcheria defended her new practice by "evoking the mystical birth of Christ in her own flesh and her consequent Marian dignity."[27] When Nestorius heard that Pulcheria intended to enter the sanctuary, he ran to the door and denied her entry. Though it was her longstanding custom, when an irritated Pulcheria asked to enter the sanctuary, Nestorius informed her that only priests (men, of course) could walk through the sanctuary. When Pulcheria asked "Is it because I did not give birth to God?" Nestorius yelled at her "You? You have given birth to Satan!" and drove her out of the church.[28]

For Nestorius, the claim to Marian dignity or authority was a moot point, and nothing would trump or redeem the sacrilege of Pulcheria—a lay person and a woman—daring to enter the Holy of Holies. Pulcheria obviously took umbrage to the sudden imposition, but the liturgical assault continued. Refusing to serve her in the sanctuary was one thing, but Nestorius allegedly defaced the portrait of her that hung above one of the church altars.[29] In a show of public dishonor and disrespect, he removed Pulcheria's robe, one that she actually wore and gifted to the church, from the altar table. The insinuations were clear that even her clothing and offerings were tainted, lacking sacrality and hinting that she was perhaps not as consecrated as she claimed to be. His actions laid claim to Pulcheria's ordinariness, of her no-placeness within the space of the sacred, of her need to know her proper place and act accordingly so. Indeed, skeptical of her social calendar, of a woman being in places when and where she should not be (even beyond the walls of the church), Nestorius struck out against Pulcheria and the female ascetics and aristocrats who kept her company. Aiming to "keep [the] prominent women of Constantinople under control," Nestorius forbade women from participating any longer in any vespers or evening ceremonies or services, claiming that these were opportunities for women to be promiscuous.[30] This was but another means by which Nestorius insultingly questioned Pulcheria's merits as a virgin, at various points insinuating that she had enjoyed multiple illicit encounters with men and demonstrating his beliefs with his holy acts. Indeed, "for a public refusal by the bishop of her claim to consecrated virginity needed only a little elaboration in the bazaars of the city to become no less than a public slur against her chastity."[31] By the time of his embittered hindsight written in the Book of Heraclides, Nestorius will have accused the "belligerent" Pulcheria of adultery and innumerable wiles, painting her as the Jezebel behind his downfall.[32] But one wonders the extent of the interpersonal undertones peeking through the skimpy disguise of Nestorius' disdain, of what happened between he and the young woman he claimed was once his friend.[33] Whatever the more intimate details of their fallout, Nestorius' public distaste for the alpha women in his city manifest through the multiple efforts to put these women in their rightful, humbled place. Almost naturally, his quest required he more resolutely clarify and place their role model, the Virgin Mary, as well.

So when two dissenting groups of Antiochene Christians (one of which was very likely patroned by Pulcheria) brought before Nestorius an expanding lexical debate, he intervened, but not without having more than one pair of hungry eyes trained in his direction. If the dual nature of Christ had been settled in the century before, the question had turned to what one should call Mary, and by what theological descriptor she would be known. Was she the Mother of God (*Theotokos*), or was she the Mother of Man (*Anthropotokos*)? The latter 'anthropos' camp referred to the former as 'Manicheans,' insinuating that the title focused too squarely on Mary giving birth to divinity, and as such aligned with the historical, heretical beliefs of a God who only *appeared* in human flesh without daring to *assume* it— the divine in disguise. The former 'theos' camp reduced the latter to 'Photinians,' accusing them of treading the path of another heresiarch who denied the incarnate being of Christ—a mere mortal as Messiah. Given Nestorius' outlined program against heresy, each wanted to witness the condemnation of the other's terminology. And like most responsible bishops fulfilling their office might seek to do for their congregants, Nestorius moved to ameliorate the situation at once with clarity and resolve.

Like many Antiochenes, Nestorius understood the humanity and divinity of Christ to be two subjects of independent existence, the divine Logos and the human Jesus conjoined as one *prosopon* (lit. person). For Nestorius, the distinctiveness of the two natures of Christ was essential to ensuring human salvation. He noted that both terms had enough orthodox potential so as to not out rightly dismiss either as completely heretical, but he thought a better solution was to be had. If *Anthropotokos* didn't do enough to emphasize that the baby Mary birthed was more than just a man, and if *Theotokos* didn't do enough to nuance that Mary could not give birth to an eternal God, the solution would be found in a neologism that guarded against the misinterpretation of either term. Nestorius offered up the term Mother of Christ—*Christotokos*—as a descriptor that would remedy the heretical tendencies that both of the presented options seemed to accommodate.[34]

The incendiary had an irenic spirit, but he had created too much smoke around himself for anyone to ever see his diplomatic side. No one was impressed with his third way, and both parties left convinced that their suspicions of the bishop had been warranted. His most vocal opponents interpreted his solution as outrightly denying the full affirmation of the Virgin Mary and undermining the Christological confession of the very person and work of Jesus Christ. But what cannot be miscounted is whether Nestorius' reticence toward the *Theotokos* title signaled less about his Christology, and more about the boundaries of place that he felt a woman could be afforded.

At this point, the Alexandrian school, with the cunning Cyril at her head, was aware of the floundering Nestorius, and continued to keep watch as the drama unfolded. There were plenty in Nestorius' own city that would find his proposals an intolerable affront to Mary's own dignity, to include Pulcheria's friend and confidant, the acclaimed orator and bishop Proclus. Proclus himself had been an early contender for the ecclesiastic throne when Sisinnius first came into power. He was well connected in the Imperial City, which is perhaps the reason why Theodosius II didn't choose Proclus for the throne once Sisinnius died. Surely embittered by the political tide of the time, Proclus readily and critically instigated the *Theotokos* question by adding propane to Nestorius' fire.

Though the exact dates are unknown, what is certain is that between the end of 428 and the early spring 429, Nestorius initiated a series of public sermons that included exhortations against the use of *Theotokos* as a title for Mary. It was a measured response to the uproar in the city, beginning with the exclamations of Anastasius, who asserted, "Let no man call Mary Mother of God for she was but a woman, and it is impossible for God to be born of a woman."[35] The attempt to systematically explain that Mary was not a goddess, and that God did not experience change in undergoing birth, was lost on the audience. Proclus, however, knew what to do. While in a liturgy held in the presence of Nestorius, Proclus executed a masterful bait and switch. In what would become one of the most famous homilies on Mary and the Incarnation, Proclus rose to begin a seemingly innocuous ode in honor of the holy Virgin, only to then praise her directly as *Theotokos* in front of the patriarch:

> The reason we have gathered here today is the holy Theotokos Virgin Mary, immaculate treasure of virginity, spiritual paradise of the second Adam, workshop of the union of [Christ's two] natures, marketplace of the saving exchange, bridal chamber in which the Word was wedded to the flesh, living bush that was not burned by the fire of the divine birth, the true light cloud that bore the One who, in his body, stands above the cherubim, fleece moistened by celestial dew, with which the Shepherd clothes his sheep.[36]

Proclus was not shy, and ended the sermon with gusto and vigor, dropping the proverbial microphone of antiquity. "Behold," he effused, "Holy Mary is openly declared *Theotokos*." Though the details of the panegyric itself are worthy of extended consideration, the entire speech was a starting bell declaring open season on that which was an invocation, a commendation, and most of all a provocation, all at once. Nestorius found himself sitting front row and center to it all, and did not fail to respond to the incitement to discourse. Rising from his seat he approached the pulpit and began to dismantle the points of Proclus' outline, but it is doubted he was even heard after the thunderous applause the congregation gave to Proclus.[37]

In an instant, any levees of respectability holding back the theological waters between the two cities were broken; there would be no turning back. Nestorius continued his attempts to educate the masses against the use of *Theotokos*, but by that spring, public demonstrations were being carried out in the Constantinople squares alleging Nestorius' status as a heretic. Pulcheria had opened her own church for the protesters to worship in and receive sacraments away from Nestorius. And as it still seems to do today among congregants, word quickly spread, falling on less than sympathetic ears. One pair belonged to the savvy and brilliant Cyril. In the annual paschal encyclical letter announcing the 429 date of Easter for the Egyptian church, Cyril subtly referred to Mary as *Meter Theou* ("mother of God"), a clear synonym for *Theotokos*.[38] Having understood the conversations among the monks in Egypt as canonical precedent for intervening in the situation (the controversy was now officially affecting his province), Cyril shortly thereafter wrote the "Letter to the Monks" to be circulated in Egypt as well as Constantinople. There, after two opening sections praising the pursuit of orthodoxy he witnessed among the monks, his tone turns cold:

> I was greatly disturbed to hear that some dangerous murmurings had reached you and that certain people were circulating them, destroying your simple faith by vomiting out a pile of stupid little words and querying in their speech whether the holy virgin Mary ought to be called the Mother of God or not.[39]

The monks were concerned that the title of *Theotokos* was neither present in Scripture, nor in the formal statements of the Nicene Creed (as it had been revised and finalized at the first Council of Constantinople in 381). As such, Cyril refutes the question of whether or not the term appeared in Scripture, instructing that the divine nature of Christ necessitates the inspired term, which had been used (however vaguely) by a number of Church Fathers before. He explained this paradoxical notion with a simple analogy. Although earthly mothers produce the physical bodies of their children, and the "ineffable workings of God" provides the spirit of who a child is, mothers are nevertheless not described as giving birth to only a part of a child. Rather, they give birth to an entire being consisting of body and soul, not the same but not unlike the manner of the natures of Christ. Rather, "If anyone should want to insist that the mother of such and such a person is the 'flesh-mother' but not the 'soul-mother,' what a tedious babbler he would be."[40] This first apologetic was the inaugural discourse of a full-blown crisis.

From there things deteriorated quickly. In February of 430, Nestorius drew more lines in the sand by putting his words in the mouth of his friend Bishop Dorotheus of Marcianopolis, "If anyone says mother of god, anathema."[41] After the sermon Nestorius celebrated communion and ended the liturgy, pronouncing a blessing on the position. Almost concurrently, Cyril was writing his second letter to Nestorius, and by the summer had pre-empted Nestorius in sending letters to Pope Celestine, including dossiers of the two rivaling bishops' correspondence. Cyril's agents had carefully reported on everything Nestorius was preaching, which gave him the opportunity to exegete his statements and carefully craft a thoughtful argument against Nestorius' position. By the end of the summer, Cyril released *Against Nestorius*, a forceful five-volume counter to his rival.

Birth Pangs

Nestorius tried to explain his concerns with *Theotokos* in his letter to Pope Celestine—"this word is not appropriate for her who gave birth, since a true mother should be of the same essence as what is born of her."[42] Yet he indicated he was open to discussion of the nomenclature, as long as the meaning of the term was specifically outlined and clarified; "But the term could be accepted in consideration of this, that the word is used of the Virgin only because of the inseparable temple of God the Word which was of her, not because she is the mother of God the Word—for none gives birth to one older than herself."[43] For Nestorius, the use of *Theotokos* itself as a term was an issue of the identity of being a mother, what it means to bear a child, and what it means to give birth. The contours of the biological find their way into the theological, which register a "taut intimacy between thingness and personality."[44] For Nestorius, there is a conceptual roadblock in thinking the person and work of the Holy Spirit, having come upon and imbued the person and work of Mary, that cannot be abstracted from the thingness of the woman's body (virgin or otherwise).

For both Cyril *and* Nestorius, the flurry of letters and politics move so quickly that it is easy to miss the critical notion of birth and birthing that center their logic. Much like Nicodemus in the Gospel of John, who marveled at the possibility that one could be born again, the mystery of birth is something so readily assumed that it is difficult to disarticulate from the social conditions of time and space. Interestingly, when Cyril countered Nestorius in his third and final letter in late November of 430, he too returned to the idea of birth, "lest Christ should be thought of as a God-bearing man."[45] This unique comparison situates Mary and Christ together through the idea of pregnancy. Cyril is asserting the nature of Christ to be one, a hypostatic union (not a prosoponic one) between God and man that reflected the natural union of the body and soul. Christ is not simply a surrogate of the divine, a "God-bearing man." Just as body and soul were only separated in death, so were the Divine Word and material body of Christ united together from the moment of conception in Mary's womb. Christ, then, "taking flesh of the holy Virgin, and making it his own from the womb,"[46] now beautifully incarnate will "recapitulate human birth in himself."[47] Cyril was concerned with a salvation history that always involved the work of God, One who is innumerable and immeasurable, but who even inside of Mary's womb "filled all creation as God."[48]

To be submitted to the experience of birth is a much more interesting point not just to discuss the nature of Christ, but to discuss the nature of birth. The recapitulation of human birth returns us to the question of place, to the creation of being and the space of creation, and thus to the vessel, to the thing itself. In naming Mary in this particular way, what Cyril points to here is the disruption of the curse, that is, the transgression of the supposed boundaries of the biogenic. It is an opportunity to extend the thought of Irenaeus, to think through the recapitulation of the reconstruction of the idea of *birth* itself. For Cyril, *Theotokos* grounded a hypostatic union that left intact God's full experience of humanity, a necessity for the plan of redemption. The full experience of humanity, then, included the incarnate God-Man submitting himself to the experience of birth, "therefore we say that she is *Theotokos*, not as though the nature of the Word had the beginning of its existence from flesh . . . (nor that the Word needed human birth, but that by accepting it he blessed the beginning of our existence, and removed the curse from it)."[49] What Cyril points to is a recapitulation that is not a reinstantiation, but instead gestures toward restitution and restoration. The unique possibility of this need not elide Mary's "identity" as a woman, a virgin, a mother. Rather, it signals the critical nature of embodiment beyond identification. However, though Cyril would win the day, we will also come to see that his own brand of politics was not without problem, particularly when it came to one identity in particular—the Jewish other.

Though Nestorius, Theodosius, and Celestine could not necessarily see it at the time, history would not be kind to Cyril—not just for the ways and means of the Nestorian years, where he was heralded for defending the faith—but for the *longue durée* of his far more unsavory dealings. Long before Cyril ever set his sights on deposing Nestorius, he established himself at length for his brash, acerbic, and often irrational pursuit of orthodoxy and power. In fact, as Susan Wessel describes, in the first few years of his rule, "Cyril paid little attention to the problem of Christian heretics, directing much of his invective instead towards Jews."[50] Cyril's early Festal letters, which were circulated widely among the Christian community and viewed as instructive documents, repeatedly invoked anti-Jewish polemic and cautionary tales as an anchor to the aspirations of Christian identity and practice.[51]

From 414 to 418, Cyril bolstered a negative Christian lens of the Jewish faith and practice, as a means to wield and reinforce the unity and identity of the Christian community in Alexandria. Tellingly, in 415, a series of convoluted events led to Cyril's expulsion of the Jews from the city, furthering the rifts between the Jewish and Christian communities in the area. According to Socrates, under the duress of increased tensions between Jews and Christians in Alexandria, and in response to the discriminatory limitation of Jewish rights in the city, a group of Jewish residents near the main church of Alexandria rebelled, running through the streets asserting that the church was on fire. The false alarm was a pre-meditated ploy to attack the Christian residents, who unknowingly ran to the rescue only to find themselves taken off guard and ambushed.[52] The incident led to the expulsion, and set the stage for the event that "has imprinted an indelible stain on the character and religion of Cyril of Alexandria," the gruesome and infamous murder of the virgin philosopher, Hypatia.[53]

Hypatia was a prominent aristocrat and renown neo-Platonist philosopher, who taught everything from mathematics and astronomy to literature and rhetoric. She was a preeminent scholar with an unprecedented following (including two future bishops), particularly as a woman. History remembers her as having been as incredibly beautiful as she was wise, and an embodied model of high standards of *sophrosyne* (temperance), of cleanliness, virtue, and moral purity she held for herself as an example to her students—"in complete sexual continence, in her famous virtue of chastity, which, to be sure, strengthened her reputation for holiness spread by her disciples."[54] According to historian Edward Gibbon, it was Hypatia's sensibility as a modest and erudite maiden "in the bloom of beauty, and in the maturity of wisdom," that drew the jealous ire of the less intelligent Cyril.[55] According to some, several of Cyril's more zealous followers took umbrage with Hypatia, and figured that she was the source of a compounded set of problems between Cyril and Orestes, the imperial prefect who represented the Jewish faction who rioted against Cyril in the months before the expulsion.[56] Somehow, Hypatia became the scapegoat of the populace, who figured that her pagan teachings were the real thread of discord in the city connecting the dots between Orestes and Cyril. The events of her death are recorded in several places, but the brutality can be summed as such:

> On a fatal day, in the holy season of Lent, Hypatia was torn from her chariot, stripped naked, dragged to the church, and inhumanely butchered by the hands of Peter the Reader, and a troop of savage and merciless fanatics: her flesh was scraped from her bones with sharp oyster shells, and her quivering limbs were delivered to the flames.[57]

It was a heinous and shocking event that shook the city, a perversion of the Paschal right in the midst of Lenten remembrance. Did Cyril order the hit on Hypatia?

Did he know in advance what his associates planned for that day? The macabre occasion was never tied directly to Cyril, but even today Cyril's legacy is marred by the accusations of the heinous act, and left an indelible mark on his character as a bishop, a moment of deep disgrace for the entire Christian community.[58] A remarkable collateral for Cyril's disdain for non-Christians, and an important lesson on the capacities for violence among any zealously faithful.

Years before Nestorius would despise the power of Pulcheria, Cyril despised the power of Hypatia. In every way except a Christian confession, Hypatia seemed to embody her own *imitatio Mariae*, a powerful and brilliant teacher who was a paragon of purity and wisdom. Yet somehow, she found her end in the Way of the Cross. One cannot help but notice the liturgical significance of her death, in the midst of a community fasting and praying with the approach of Christ's Passion. To think, a group of devout religious men who were meant to be liturgically remembering the sacrifices of Christ, found time to accost one who they deemed a false teacher on the road. Never once did they consider the irony of their efforts as they surrounded her, tried her in their own eyes, led in slaughter and denial by a man named Peter. Hypatia was dragged through the streets, stripped naked, humiliated, and savagely crucified in the sanctuary of the city. Cyril's championing of the woman *Theotokos* cannot be thought apart from his washing his hands of Hypatia's murder.

In all truth, Cyril's own anti-heresy agenda, unyielding resume and reckless tactics might have found he and Nestorius, in another time and another place, linked allies rather than foes. But against the backdrop of the violently sectarian city of Alexandria evinces a sordid undercurrent in Cyril's turn against Nestorius, exacted by Cyril's tagging Nestorius as 'an unbelieving Jew', an epithet first invoked in his Festal briefs.[59] In doing so, Cyril drew on several centuries worth of Patristic supercessionist thought, as well as an entire imaginary of anti-Jewish sentiment he himself had cultivated throughout the empire. More than trading insults, the rhetorical method invoked the most apposite and lurid theological accusation available to most thoroughly slander his opponent.

Cyril chose his words carefully in a way that would accomplish the "*reductio ad haeresim*,"[60] aligning Nestorius as a heretic. Preaching the fifth homily against Nestorius during the summer of 431, Cyril exhorted against his rival: "These are the accusations of the ancient Jews against our Savior, and those who emulate their impiety and desperate folly bring an accusation [once] again, saying, 'Why do you, though a human being, make yourself God?' O witless and loathsome one, you have not grasped the mystery!"[61] What greater blasphemy than to be aligned with the terrorist profile of antiquity—the murderers of Christ, and those whose ultimate failure was the damnation of unbelief.

Like much in Cyril's campaign, the propaganda of his rhetorical prowess yielded tangible results. By the time news that Nestorius was deposed spread to the imperial city of Constantinople, the rousing populace (no doubt fans of Pulcheria) began celebrating the news with chants of "Nestorius the Jew, Nestorius the Jew!"[62] Another crowd was later recorded yelling joyous shouts of confirmation that "Nestorius and the thirty men are Jews."[63] The willingness of a gathered crowd to heartily celebrate the fall of an unfortunate Nestorius cannot only be credited to the rhetorical techniques and skill of Cyril. Rather, their ease of joining the chorus of outing a "Jew" is demonstrative of a well-established retort, a strategy well floated along rivers of a robust social context.

But did the slander of the time carry further implications? Did the purity of one's faith proclamations determine the purity of one's body? It is important to note that the use of "Jew" as label was libel, presuming the horizon of one's moral commitments, and perhaps more readily, one's moral deficiencies. By this point in Christendom, Jews had been referred to as ignorant, wicked, carnal, harlots, lustful, rapacious, and as "lascivious wolves in pursuit of innocent Christian sheep."[64] Such caricatures seeded justifications of abuse, torture, and murder for centuries to come. Applying anti-Jewish invective against an identified opponent of Christian orthodoxy was never limited to the habits of one's worship, but also offered an extended commentary on the true innermost nature of who a person really was.

As Susanna Drake's study in *Slandering the Jew* demonstrates, the theme of heretical sexual identity found in the Pauline correctives of Christian sexual practice became aligned in the early centuries of the church with the flesh, and more specifically, with Jewish flesh.[65] Sexual practices were invoked as markers of difference and virtue for Christian theologians like Justin, Origen, and Chrysostom. While the idea of sexual virtue had long served as a pious identifier of civilized, elegant culture in contrast to barbaric practices of hedonism, the Christian brand of sexual slander incited a trope that would only increase in strength and vitriol. What emerges is "the creation of an orthodox Christian attitude toward the body thus coincided with the construction of an abject 'heretical' sexuality."[66] In other words, hurling Jewishness as an epithet carried a subtext that included the deviant sexuality of the Jewish body. Under any circumstances, "sexual heresy—however defined at a particular cultural moment—serves as a way to rationalize the domination, disenfranchisement, torture, or obliteration of the heretic."[67]

These were the discourses intertwined with the emphatic consideration of the sexual and generative status of the Blessed Virgin Mary, lest the subliminal messaging around her body perform another unique sleight of hand. If Cyril's aims, invectives, and actions were all "necessary" to protect Mary from those who would threaten her status and reduce Jesus to a mere mortal man, perhaps he thought he did what he had to do. But without a doubt, his arguments were predicated on forgetting one very important thing: Before she was anything else, Mary, too, was a Jew.

As the details of who Mary gave birth to were debated, the church was also birthing who Mary herself would be. Arguably, it is *Theotokos* that draws our attention to the processes of gestation and birth that honor—not prioritize—the embodiment thereof. It is this title that instantiates the unique "consent to be more than a single being."[68] Raniero Cantalamessa narrates the work that *Theotokos* accomplishes as such:

> ... the title *Theotokos* places greater emphasis on the second stage, on the giving birth (*tikto* in Greek means "I am giving birth") ... [the moment of] the giving birth, belongs exclusively to the mother.[69]

While one reading of Cantalamessa would interpret his reconstruction as creating a new hierarchy, his point is to transition our thinking of Mary and the maternal body as a theological crux. The idea that the title of *Theotokos* and the shift of weight toward a kind of maternal exclusive in general (that is, the presence and process of the birth canal), does not yet account for the maternal exclusive state of Mary's conception. The value of this realization is less about the heightening of maternal virtues, but rather, a claim that in Christ, the presumed commonalities of both sex and conception are completely disrupted. In Mary's body there is a reconditioning of procreative sex; in her pregnancy with Jesus, Mary inhabited a new set of possibilities inside the heteronormative expectation of reproduction, that transgresses the heteronormative capture of sexuality. As such, might this inhabitation be the condition of possibility for birthing life, relationships, energy, imagination, and vision, far beyond the tangible notions of race and kinship, beyond the alliances of blood and peoplehood? Is this not what the blood of Christ, which is at once and always Mary's blood, signifies?

This is where we must take pause in the flurry between Cyril and Nestorius to return to the context of the Annunciation, the critical notions of barrenness and fruitfulness, of consent and willfulness. The burden of infertility was doubled over as a curse within a curse for women, a worse cultural situation to bear than the average daughter of Eve. Which raises an interesting consideration: Does one inhabit the fullness of the curse only in certain states of socially constructed relationship? If women who are single (as in, not married), queer-identified (as in, not having heterosexual and poorly defined "reproductive" sex), or unable to conceive (as in, biblically "barren"), are excluded from this categorical curse of "woman"? What if one is a consecrated virgin? If we consider the nature of virginity at this time, particularly in the privileged situation of wealth and power that Hypatia once laid claim to, or that which Pulcheria enjoyed, we see that "virginity" was a claim that enabled political power while also extending one's social and cultural freedom. As an explicitly Christian expression, Pulcheria's *imitatio Mariae* demonstrates how the public practice of virginity functioned as a kind of social loophole to the original curse upon all women, insofar as it was a mechanism that subverted the social obligations of patriarchy. To be a virgin meant that a woman would not be subject to the rule of a husband, nor governed by the presumption of heteronormative desire. To be a virgin meant that a woman had the capacity to inherit and maintain one's own wealth, could wield public influence and carry out civic duties, and could lead her own household legally. Being a virgin also meant that a woman—if socially *understood* as a woman, for again these categories do not extend to those who are sexed female and also enslaved, etc.—would not be subject to the labor of birth and the commitments of mothering.

However, while it is certain that one could actually abstain from sexual intercourse as a dedicated virgin, it is clear that the "virgin" identity did not actually, only mean that one did not engage in or experience sexual arousal or pleasure, either by one's own devices or with various partners. In either case of a choice of actual chastity or the use of one's claim to chastity, it is clear that the idea of moral or ethical actions attached to a virgin identity have multiple subversive uses. Being a virgin need not be "real," in the sense of denying oneself sexual pleasure either by one's own devices or with various partners, to experience its social benefits (though it must also be noted that, regardless of one's sexual engagements, "women's pleasure" was not of great concern at the time).

This is critical because Proclus' famous sermon heralding Mary comes on the occasion of the "Virgin's festival," a celebration not only of Mary but of all of the women in the city (virgin and otherwise). As Proclus opened, "What we celebrate is the pride of women and the glory of the female, thanks to the one who was at once both mother and virgin. Lovely is the gathering!"[70] When we look more closely at Nestorius' reaction, one wonders about the nature of his insult. When Nestorius slandered Pulcheria's virginity, he not only attempted to dishonor her public image by marring the reputation of her virtue, but expressed a fundamental frustration with a woman who had, perhaps, found a way to have her cake and eat it too. Pulcheria's virginity was not that of a quiet, subdued woman who was cloistered away from society. She was incredibly smart, vocal, strategic, and knew with confidence her opinions as well as her wealth and power. Her commitment to Marian worship, particularly her record of service, and the work she did to introduce Marian shrines, relics and piety while establishing Marian churches in the region, all point to a devout sense of self and a high standard of obligation to the Virgin Mary. And yet she still drew incredible ire from Nestorius, whose most vicious attacks involved sexual slurs, and the accusation of her body bearing Satan.

The point here is not only to capture the complexity and intrigue of this ancient political and theological battle, but to take seriously the way that the arbiters of the Nestorian controversy considered *women*—an enigmatic but foregrounded Hypatia for Cyril, an emblematic Pulcheria for Nestorius, and of course, for both, an ethereal Mary. Things did not come to a neat or fair close. Despite the literary onslaught from Cyril, Nestorius held steady in his fight and made a solid attempt to wield his own political savvy where he could. Cyril did offer at least one feather for Nestorius' cap. When Cyril sent his dossiers in the form of *De Recta Fide* to Theodosius, he sent separate letters to Pulcheria and the royal household. Even from afar Cyril recognized that Pulcheria held several purse strings within the empire. But Theodosius was offended by the move and Cyril's appearance of scheming to undermine him. Sending letters to Pulcheria and the other empresses not only implied that the emperor's house was or could be divided, but held emasculating implications, as if his sister's thought and power were independent from or even stronger than his. Nestorius knew the feelings of his friend Theodosius, and confident in Cyril's missteps, organized for there to be a meeting between the bishops. But Cyril outplayed Nestorius, for Pulcheria had the synod moved to Ephesus, a city under the patronage of the Virgin Mary, and held the gathering in the church there, the great Marian shrine. The *place* of Mary would have a clear effect on the outcomes of the gathering.

By the time everyone got to Ephesus, more had been set in motion than could ever have been anticipated. The council was meant to be a neutral gathering to resolve the Christological differences dividing the empire, but in the chapel of Saint Mary, the outcome was prescient. Along with Memnon of Ephesus, Cyril readily led the council of bishops in their proceedings. The only problem was that he refused to wait for the bishops from the East as they traversed the 600 miles of unforgiving desert terrain to join their brothers. Instead, Cyril moved to depose and excommunicate Nestorius, which he successfully did, deeming his doctrine heresy. John of Antioch and the Antiochenes convened a counter-synod on the spot that immediately deposed and excommunicated both Cyril and Memnon. When the dust cleared, the now two-party system had drawn deep lines in the sand. Two councils had come to two contradictory positions, and Theodosius II—be it cowardly or just confusingly—affirmed the findings of both. Eventually, under the sway of his city, a great number of whom were thoroughly committed to Pulcheria, he succumbed to the pressures and removed Nestorius from the bishopric. Nestorius returned to Antioch in exile embittered, having been caught in a political hailstorm that escalated too quickly for him to find cover. "The Jew" was exposed as a heretic and made to pay for the sins of his unbelief.

Woman As We Are

What's in a name? *Everything.*

Mary would be called *Theotokos*. The debate around the conditions of the conception of Christ anchored an unprecedented amount of theological attention given to both a woman and her womb. The gravitas accorded her apposite description highlights the narrative constructions that imagined what a sacred and holy female body would look like, particularly as the reigning representation of woman had been a singular vision of Eve. But the words by which Mary would be properly referred are not to be confused with the consideration of her flesh, and of that made flesh within her. As Margaret Miles describes of the Christological debates, despite their rigor, "The question was not whether, and how, Mary was to receive recognition for her role in the incarnation; it was over how Christ's divinity and humanity were to be conceptualized."[71] Instead, Mary's material body foregrounded how we would think of Christ and the nature of Christ's being far beyond her.[72] When we consider Marian dogma, we must consider how Mary is theologically instrumentalized.

It is interesting to think how Mary, as Jaroslov Pelikan so aptly notes, "has provided the content of the definition of the feminine in a way that [Jesus] has not done for the masculine."[73] Despite the instrumentality that the *Theotokos* debates may have rehearsed (a critique we do not miss), even if Mary's title was the means to a very specific end, there is something to be said that Mary is the *only* means to that end. Mary's most orthodox title tilt-shifts our lens of the Incarnation. As a metanarrative, the Incarnation was a claim to God dwelling in, with and among all of humanity. But the notion that Christ saves what Christ assumes raised the profile of male flesh in a unique way relating back to the accusations of Eve. Pulcheria poses several critical questions. As she claimed her lineage, association, and sameness with the Virgin Mary, she inaugurated a female definition within the faith. She never sought to be a priest, nor to stand in direct competition with her brother. Yet, when she attempted to align herself with Mary's body, a non-divine entity, Nestorius turned to the apophatic anthropology of the woman, to the negative derivation of distance. For Nestorius, Pulcheria's claims of proximity to Mary were demonstrative of her perversion of Mary.

And yet, as Miles notes, the proclamation that was offered at the Council of Ephesus "contains the only generic use of 'woman' in the history of Christianity. The all-male Council declared: The blessed Virgin was woman as we are."[74] But what does this mean? It is a paradox within a paradox that, given Cyril's vision for the *oikonomia*, the acknowledgment of Mary as *Theotokos* affirms the sinfulness of humanity. For Cyril's vision of the divine economy much relied on the Fall, the necessary counter fact to Redemption. The thinkers at Ephesus were not yet invested in the sinlessness of Mary as removing the stains of human sin, but that was a doctrinal thought on its own way. Perhaps the idea of "woman as we are" held out, however briefly, a promise to reconsider what it means to be body and flesh. But the continued purification of Mary's body, and the pursuit of her exceptionality, would lead otherwise.

The fallout from the Council at Ephesus and the Formula of Reunion left lasting rifts in the church community. As such, the Council of Chalcedon (the Fourth

Ecumenical Council of the Church) formally reaffirmed the two natures of Christ. But the statements of the council also made a claim in their references to the nature of Mary's virginity. The letter that Pope Leo I had written to Flavian in 449, known widely as 'the Tome,' was brought forth at the Council for its doctrine of Incarnation, in which he stated: "Doubtless then, He was conceived of the Holy Spirit within the womb of His Virgin Mother, who brought Him forth *without the loss of her virginity, even as she conceived Him without its loss*" (emphasis added).[75] Briefly thereafter, he refers to Mary as *aeiparthenos*, or "ever virgin." This was an term referring to Mary's virginity at the time of her conception, during the course of her pregnancy, *in partu* or while giving birth, and postpartum. Though it was not the point of the document, the claim about the nature of Mary's virginity was included as part of the broadly accepted statement on the Incarnation at the Council of Chalcedon in 451. The terminology appeared increasingly in official documents of the church, and 200 years later, during the First Lateran Council (649), Pope Martin I officially declared that:

> If anyone does not in accord with the Holy Fathers acknowledge that the holy and ever-virgin and immaculate Mary was really and truly the Mother of God, inasmuch as she, in the fullness of time, and without seed, conceived by the Holy Spirit God the Word Himself, who before all time was born of God the Father, and without loss of integrity brought him forth, and after his Birth preserved her virginity inviolate, let him be condemned.[76]

Arguably the development of Mary's iconography and representation becomes increasingly an approximation of both humanity and divinity in the nearness, which is to say the distance, of her own emanation from God. Eventually Mary would be the exemption to the Fall—"like Eve before the fall," she who is "immune from all stain of original sin."[77] As Luce Irigaray would note, "A commodity—a woman—is divided into two irreconcilable 'bodies': her 'natural' body and her socially valued, exchangeable body, which is a particularly mimetic expression of masculine values."[78] The irreconcilable bodies of Mary and Eve are forced in polar directions, and Chris Weedon elucidates how the continuum of hyper-spiritualization of Mary's body functions inside of this aesthetic: "Patriarchal reason denies feminine otherness, reconstituting it as male-defined. This results in the denial of subjectivity to non-male-defined woman."[79] Eve steps beyond the boundaries of "male" definition, she is permanently denied agency and full subjectivity. Despite the insistent narration of her body inside of patriarchal categories—Mother, Virgin, Woman—Mary yet embodies a certain autonomy, a freedom *from* patriarchal patterns of exchange and kinship. But because Mary's pregnancy operates outside of the traditional boundaries of kinship structure in the traffic of women—that is, if "Mary is a woman who has access to the sacred outside the patriarchal family and its control"[80]—then patriarchal logics would continue to resist Mary's subjectivity, as it must still be denied in some form. The conflation of her identity as woman into that of the Virgin Mother achieves the desired effect. So, "in order to give paternal uncertainty its symbolic coup de grace, the church fathers needed a super virgin—one whose virginity can be certified as permanent."[81] Not due God's paternal uncertainty, but their own.

There is power in a name, and *Theotokos* brought Mary to the brink of both that which is human and divine. But what the Christological debates and their outcomes have shown us is that the restructured taxonomy of Mary's body is subtended by the question of the anthropological purity of Christ, and the reducibility of that purity to reproductive organs. Does the "purity" of Christ function independently of the contextualized environment of his gestation? If we return again to the Proclus homily, we come to see that Mary—the immaculate treasure of virginity, the marketplace of saving exchange—is already being bound up in a set of logics that instantiate virginity as a transactional event. And purity is a productive set of relations, both as *idea* and as *ideal*, one that cannot be defined, only imagined across the landscape of a theological anthropology met with market calculation.

Moving forward, then, purity travels due north, apparently from the imaginary hymen into the uterus itself, the categorical distinctions of virginity and inviolability blooming past the confines of the biological into the supernatural. But what happens when election follows exclusion, and exceptionalism becomes party to separation? Here we turn to examine the space of the womb, and the proverbial elephant in the room—the place of Mary's Palestinian Jewish identity in consideration of Mary's experience of birth. In the same ways that understanding the gendered production of Eve and Mary are critical to understanding the Blackness of Mary, so too the refusals of Mary's Blackness cannot be understood apart from the refusals of Mary's Palestinian Jewish identity—in other words, the ways Mary is *made Christian* corresponds to the way Mary *becomes white*. Mary's body will not just be subjected to new names, but to new narratives around pain, suffering, cleanliness, and purity that reflect a Christian eschatological vision of superiority and supremacy. If Mary literally carries Diaspora within her—granting Jesus not only his human flesh, but his Jewish identity—we turn to consider the narration of Mary as not just reproductive, but generative. The question remains, what kind of theology will she really be made to travail?

4
A Womb of One's Own

Is the Womb a Grave? (or, Three Mothers)

> *The slave ship is a womb/abyss.* The plantation is the belly of the world. *Partus sequitur ventrem*—the child follows the belly. The master dreams of future increase. The modern world follows the belly.
>
> Saidiya Hartman

In February 2011, an austere billboard shouldered its way among the crowded Manhattan skyline. With a background that faded into the crisp skies of a New York winter, a pair of dolefully enlarged brown eyes held a steady gaze into office windows and city traffic (see Fig. 4.1). The shoulder ruffles on her raspberry pink dress were accented by the off-center bow alighting her natural coils. If someone encouraged her to "say cheese" for the photo, she had clearly hesitated or resisted, her fixed mouth puckered in both quirk and inquisition. She was 4, maybe 5—or was she 6, perhaps 7, her smooth tawny skin betraying the presence of wisdom in the absence of furrows. Even a Photoshop novice could create the banal glow that haloed the outline of her image, an easy manipulation to convey innocence, or to blur whatever original background had once been there. The girl wore a crown of crisp, luminescent font, radiating the sanctity of a singular message, one "almost poetic in its brutal honesty." *Almost.*

THE MOST
DANGEROUS PLACE
FOR AN AFRICAN AMERICAN
IS IN THE WOMB.

The now infamous billboard was sponsored by Life Always, an anti-abortion organization who cited statistical data on the disproportionate amount of Black female pregnancy terminations in New York City as critical incitement for the affronting awareness campaign. When alarms of racism and sexism were signaled, the organization turned to their African-American members to speak out in defense of the ad. These leaders refuted opponents of the message, and instead advocated for an interpretation of the abortion statistics as signaling the enduring historical lineage of targeted eugenic practices neatly hushed and prepackaged for the contemporary

Figure 4.1 Life Always Billboard, 2011. New York.

moment. Proponents argued that this was an effort to thwart "a genocidal plot."[1] Ardent opponents to the message argued that the incendiary interpretation of questionable percentages was a racist, sensationalist ploy that targeted both the physical bodies and moral character of Black women writ large. The messaging implied that Black female reproduction was an exercise in self-harm, and that Black women could not be left to their own devices regarding pregnancy and the choices surrounding it. The discussion was bolstered by clerical representatives, Black and white, who argued both for and against the removal of the message. The cacophony of mixed theological, ideological, and political interests created immediate chaos and reaction, going viral and signaling that the campaign had indeed been successful.

The broiling controversy made the image an icon that was readily cemented in the mind of the downtown public. The billboard, intentionally timed to coincide with Black History Month, was quickly taken down from its SoHo neighborhood perch, but the memory left in its place could not be so easily resolved. Ironically, given the image presumed a conversation about mothering, rights, protections, and consent, it turned out that the young model's mother had never been asked permission for the use of her daughter's image. The appropriate politics of reproduction, particularly around wombs like *hers*, had not warranted inclusion in the conversation. Despite this anomaly and against the protests and civil actions of the mother, Trisha Frazier, around the image of her 4-year-old daughter, Anissa, the billboard continued to suspiciously appear in other locations around the country less urban, witnessing to the defiance and insistence of the mysterious organization who imagined the advertisement in the first place.

Long before the 2022 Supreme Court ruling to overturn *Roe v. Wade* (1973), the legislation that protected the constitutional right to abortion care, the topic of abortion rights circulated regularly through the media and political cycles of the contemporary United States, particularly as the philosophical and theological questions of conception, the "beginning" of "life," and the practices of sanctity, were theologically touted through interpretive lenses of faith, religion, and the absolutes of moral clarity (though often without historical context, medical precision, or nuance), particularly for the Christian right. The imaginary of conception, of what does or does not count as "life," and of what does or does not count as "death," together mark a sordid history of moral ethics bound by politics of space, place, and identity. The Life Always billboard traded in familiar fear tactics nourished by the social delusions of safety, all in the uniquely supposed interest of Black life. And yet, it paraded the image of a little Black girl to do that work on their behalf. This was not, by any means, a statement of how Black life matters.

The messaging of this "pro-life" campaign, far outside of the politics of abortion care itself, makes an interesting set of claims about the womb as a particular kind of place, one of precarity imagined through the lens of racial optic. Note that the ad did not cite traditional institutions, abortion clinics, or healthcare providers as the arbiters of danger. Unplanned pregnancy and reproductive choice were not distilled as questions determinable by a theological-moral compass (however conservative). Rather, a certain kind of place, in a certain kind of body, was located as the space of death, a fertile ground turned toxic wasteland, poisoned by a failed sense of rationale and virtue. It was a distinctly Black space, a space of destruction and the denial of life. A threat that needed alerting to, naming the individualized and personal protections of certain bodies at the expense of those imagined to be who we need to be protected from. Could the most volatile, violent and life-threatening place for human life really be GPS calibrated to, so fragile and corruptible a thing that must be protected, even—if not especially—from the Black woman who embodies it?

In 2020, the Centers for Disease Control and Prevention (CDC) published their findings that the maternal mortality rate in the United States had continued to worsen, with disproportionate effects on Black women. Specifically, in 2020, the maternal mortality rate for Black women increased 26 percent, from 44 deaths per 100,000 live births to over 55. By comparison, that was roughly three times the rate for white women. The data only confirmed what many already witnessed and knew. In a series titled "Lost Mothers," *ProRepublica* had reported several years earlier on the testimonies and public health data that indicated the gross inequity in places like New York City:

> Even when accounting for risk factors like low educational attainment, obesity and neighborhood poverty level, the city's black mothers still face significantly higher rates of harm. . . . Of note, Black mothers who are college-educated fare worse than women of all other races who never finished high school. Obese women of all other races do better than Black women who are normal weight. And Black women in the wealthiest neighborhoods do worse than white, Hispanic and Asian mothers in the poorest ones.[2]

Black birthing people in the United States live the multiplicity of endangered lives, both of themselves and the infants they carry. In contrast to the anti-abortion campaign, which signaled the dangers of Black women's ineptitude as autonomous subjects (beneath the fear tactics of eugenicist trigger), it turns out that, perhaps, the most dangerous place for an African American, is . . . *America*. For Black women and Black babies in utero, the most dangerous place may in fact be a hospital birthing ward. What does one make of the supposed "sanctity" of life in a world committed to Black death, curtailed at the site of Black birthing people?

While the statistics and realities of such precarity are enraging, there also remains a question around the performative political responses to said crisis. In *Birthing Black Mothers*, Jennifer C. Nash asks a necessary question as to "how and why resilience and trauma seem to be the necessary frames for making visible Black mothers' political agency and visibility."[3] Her book outlines the functioning of *Black maternal politics*, and names how the symbol of the suffering Black mother comes to function as "political commodity":

> While crisis has made the precarity of Black mothering newly visible—if not remedial efforts—it has also tethered Black maternal flesh to disorder, even if it is not the disorder of earlier eras, namely pathology and poverty. It is precisely because Black motherhood is now cast as suffering rather than pathological, as tragic rather than self-destructive, as traumatized rather than deviant, that the crisis frame can be both deeply seductive and rhetorically effective. Yet the rhetoric of crisis is part of an enduring and troubling tradition of rendering Black women generally, and Black mothers specifically, into symbols, even if now Black mothers are symbols of tragic heroism rather than deviance.[4]

Black birthing people—with particular precarity around how the notions of the "woman" complicate the frame of birth for those who do or do not identify as such—and their Black babies are subject to danger and thus made *crises* due to multiple exacting mechanisms of systemic racism and prejudice against their bodies. These tropes include epistemological suspicion of Black women's knowledges of their own and their baby's bodies; mythologies around Black women's capacity for strength, endurance, and feelings of pain; caricatures of Black women as "dramatic" that may lead them or their partners, family members, or doula support to be labeled as "difficult" or "noncompliant"; transphobia against Black birthing people who are not women; implicit bias and preferential options for non-Black caregiving; medical ignorance, general negligence, misogynoir, and the like. Thus, while the idea of being a "tragic hero" would seem more humanizing than being labeled "deviant," the pathos of the Black maternal health "crisis" seems to do little to create change *in situ*, nor to center framings of joy, possibility, imagination, justice, or intervention for those pregnant, parenting, or being parented. As Dorothy Roberts wrote presciently in *Killing the Black Body*, "Race has historically determined the value society places on a woman's right to choose motherhood. The devaluation of Black motherhood gives the right to decide to bear a child unique significance."[5] One must inquire, what becomes of these "mothers" made martyrs via malpractice?

In the pioneering book *In the Wake: On Blackness and Being*, Christina Sharpe includes the narrative of Aeriele Jackson. Sharpe draws our attention to the ways Jackson appears strangely and curiously in a 2010 documentary on shipping containers, a precursor to current conversations around supply chains, global capital, and wreckage. The film, *The Forgotten Space—A Film Essay Seeking to Understand the Contemporary Maritime World in Relation to the Symbolic Legacy of the Sea*, turns to discuss the ports of Long Beach, California, but somehow

Figure 4.2 Stills of Aereile Jackson from *The Forgotten Space*, 2010. Courtesy of Doc. Eye Film Amsterdam.

turns its lens toward the residents of a tent city nearby. When asked about this, the filmmakers suggest the interviews offer "insights of those people who have been ejected from the system."[6] There are three interviews in total. The first two feature white, middle aged men—one who will be identified as a *former building contractor*, the other identified as a *former mechanic*. The final interview is of a Black woman, who speaks with great pain and sorrow. Sharpe transcribes Jackson's oration:

> This is like a slap in my face to me and my family. I'm not on drugs ... I have, these are my dolls I picked up so don't think I'm mentally ill or anything like that.

I picked these up. I have a tent full of stuffed animals and dolls. This is the only thing that I have to hold on to for me to remember my children. I lost a lot and I'm homeless and I haven't seen my children since I was unable to attend court because I had no transportation. The court was way in San Bernardino and I'm way in Ontario and I lost out on my children and I haven't seen my children since and this is since 2003 and here it is 2009 so I've lost a lot. I'm trying... I'm hurt. I'm trying to figure out am I ever going to get the chance to be a mother again with my children I already have. I don't have my children. I'm over here in the dirt, getting darker and darker and darker. And my wig is because my hair comes out, you know, mysteriously my hair comes out, and it wasn't like that at first but I get over here and I take my hair out to wash it and stuff and it's coming out, you know. In patches. Like someone is shaving my hair off. That and I've gotten overweight to where I'm just starting to handle my weight in the hot sun and I can barely walk to the corner without getting hot and without getting hot flashes. So I'm trying to deal with my weight and my situation at the same time.[7]

A former building contractor, a former mechanic, and as the documentary identifies here, Aeriele Jackson, *former mother* (see Fig. 4.2). What to make of the vocational identity of a previous life? As Sharpe contends, a consideration of the humanity of Aeriele Jackson, juxtaposed by her configuration as former mother, evidences the myriad ways a Black mother's suffering remains incomprehensible inside the systems of power and abjection that constitute the multitudes of her loss—a signifier of the ways that Black life, writ large, continues to be unthought. The sense of her, as mother, as *former*—abdicated, or removed—fail to consider how the violence(s) enacted are those that trudge beneath the surface legacies of the Atlantic slave trade, how even in print (and even more so when heard on screen) her voice is both haunted and haunting.

Aeriele Jackson is marked by the temporal adjectival narration that does no justice, but instead elides the capacity for reproduction, for maternal care and desire, for societal failure, for capacities for attending fully to Black life even as it is plagued by death, within the (il)legibility of her suffering: former mother. Such an honorific, determined by loss, expresses the liminal space of Nash's notion of crisis that still stands at the threshold of pathology and deviance, the incomprehensibility wrought from the darkest hollows of a womb imaginary of Black life and already interred, with "seemingly no sense of the longue durée of that term à la partus sequitur ventrem and its afterlives."[8]

A tale of three mothers.

One, potential, but incapable.
A danger.
pre-partum.

Two, pregnant, but incapacitated.
Endangered.
peri-partum.

Three, posthumous, and imperiled.
Pathologized.
post-partum.

The womb, the belly, the bottom; Bloodshed from hollows signifying death, or life; Beating waves of baptismal font; space to swim or drown; Battleground of bloodline futurity. The womb historically presents a problem for the racial imaginary, a site of disastrous miscegenation, a palace of purity tied uniquely to the maintenance of racial blood lines, a technology of reproduction embedded in and concomitant with property, wealth, social capital, social control, and the inheritances thereof.

This extended meditation on the womb imaginary of Black life, and the configuration of Black birth and Black mothering in the American social landscape, is a means by which to recognize the ways that both the concept of the womb, as well as the concept of the Mother/mothering, are infused with theological glosses around what one can or cannot do in service of reproduction. Black life, particularly the imaginary of its essence as stewarded by those configured through the matrix of the Black maternal body, is stalked by death—named as pathology, as threat—and endangered from the moment of conception. Black pregnant bodies, and by extension Black birthing people, are seen as violent harbingers—the womb is not safe, and specifically not safe from the one who holds it. And yet, it is not (inherently) safe to give birth as a Black person in the United States under the visage of the state. And it is not (inherently) safe to raise a Black person, surviving birth being only the first of an intolerable struggle to maintain one's right to simply exist in the world while being, also, Black. One is pressed to inquire as to those held between the crisis of Black maternal mortality and those whose children have been murdered by the state (under any name), the fraught remnants not only of Nash's Black maternal politics, but of *Black maternal pathologies*, which I would argue extend to the expectation of loss without recourse for the systemic violences that are the conditions of possibility, or rather, the conditions of necessity for incessant mourning, of what Sharpe describes in the broader social sphere of Black death and dying, an interminable grief.[9] It is a reckoning with what it means for so many Black mothers that "inherited a world that was haunted by survival tactics shared in faded whispers of mothers in coffles, on the auction block, stolen away in the night, and those separated from their capacities to mother by the imposition of force."[10] We live in a moment where it has become popular parlance to, via hashtag or sweatshirt pronouncement, "Protect Black Women." But to whom does this invocation appeal, is this cry made? Who is vested with such a task? And how might such a slogan be reframed in such a way that *we warrant inclusion in the conversation*? What then, to riff on Leo Bersani's formulation, that "It may, finally, be in the [woman's womb] that [s]he demolishes her own perhaps otherwise uncontrollable identification with a murderous judgment against her." Which is to say, one must consider, for the Black woman, if the womb is, in fact, a grave.[11]

We begin here with three Black mothers, to frame the evolving conversations of Mary's body and reproductive organs with the material realities of what it means for us to image the M(other), and to consider the theology of mothering that takes seriously our narrations of birth as much as the birthing person—for what is a womb, and the *womb*-man who harbors it? To begin with the womb is to also then return to the ways that Mary—mother of Jesus, *Theotokos*, Blessed Virgin—and more specifically Mary's *body* continued to be in the spotlight of Christian theology from the early centuries of the church, and the way the Fathers (as we have less so the witness of the Mothers of the time) of the early church were particularly interested in *protecting* her womb. Protection, of course, manifest in securing and policing the dominant narratives of what went in and what came out of that womb, of carefully determining which technologies this womb was exposed to. Where exactly could the Christian God call a gestational home? In what place could God be kept *safe?* There were no midtown billboards in the early church, but the message was just as clear: Placing the Christian God in the wrong kind of womb could shatter the order of salvation.

This chapter describes how theologically, the womb as a racial imaginary emerges first through the refusals and separations of Mary's Palestinian Jewish identity, as Jesus's Jewish life is slowly elided in his configuration as Risen Christ. The questions of virginity discussed in the previous chapters now lead us to think more specifically about the process of birth itself, and the theological legacy of purity as an ideal. Drawing on visions from Hildegard of Bingen and Bridget of Sweden, the chapter demonstrates how questions of pain and cleanliness during the birth of Christ must be considered alongside womanist theological critiques of both suffering and surrogacy. The chapter turns to consider the figure of the *Mater dolorosa*, and the pierced heart of the Black mother in the United States, who share the grief of children killed by state violence, and who, in their shared pain, must be considered as those who perhaps only wanted to mother, not mother a movement.

An Intolerance for Pain

While there is no singular, cohesive tradition around the circumstances of Mary's birth (and very little scriptural detail to the process of that birth at all), there emerge on the medieval horizon two provocative narratives worth considering. These narratives are interesting not only for their content of their description, but because they are characterizations uniquely made by prophetic women writing and recording their holy visions of the birth of Christ.

One of the most popular accounts of Mary's birth was recorded as a vision from Hildegard of Bingen. Hildegard (1098–1179) was a twelfth-century mystic, poet, and prophet of great renown. From her skillful musical compositions to her scholarship in the natural sciences, she is considered by many to be a polymath of her time, whose contributions to the church have earned her immeasurable esteem. Of the 35 saints honored with the title of Doctor of the Universal Church, she is one of only four women to be included in this holy canon.

Hildegard began experiencing holy visions while in her early forties, which she felt divinely compelled to record. In what is perhaps her most popular work, *Scivias* ("Know the Way") records several of her visions, including an interlude detailing the complete process of Christ's conception and birth. Her reflection starts with the intensity of the Annunciation and the further purification of Mary's body by the Holy Spirit.[12] As her vision reveals, the Holy Spirit "caused a small clot to coagulate" [from the] "utterly pure and chaste blood ... and this coagulum became flesh in the form of an infant."[13] While scientific discoveries of the sperm and the egg are attributed to the seventeenth century, the manifestation that Hildegard describes is a fascinating insight into the smallness that is the start of life, likely inflected by her own biological study and research observations.[14] And yet, the description of blood she offers as "pure" and "chaste" bodily fluids, assign key descriptors that signal understandings of Mary's biology as transcendent, a subtle theological inference that ties sanctification to the absence of sex.[15] In the same way that Mary's body must be virginal, there is a virginal essence that Hildegard also transfuses into Mary's own blood.

Elsewhere Hildegard writes in ways that demonstrate appreciation for the female body—she thinks deeply about the physiological nature of women's bodies, about blood and menstruation, as well as the experiences of women's pleasure. Her writings and musical compositions even afford Mary sensual experiences of her body and fertility (though, from experiences outside of sexual penetration), and at times, it seems that "Hildegard is actually celebrating the female body and female fertility."[16] But Hildegard's vision in *Scivias*, and it's more explicit claims to Mary's conception, raise an important question of the notion of pure blood, for Hildegard's articulation sets Mary's blood, as part of her body, *apart* from that of the rest of humanity, aligning blood purity as parcel to a paragon of female embodiment. But the exception of the general requires the exception of the particular, as well. The blood of Christ is understood to be that which washes sins away, a material theology of purity, chastity, and fulfillment of another Isaiah prophecy: "though your sins are like scarlet, they shall be like snow."[17] In Hildegard's explicit vision of Mary's conception, does the purity and chastity imply a cleansing of Jewish lineage?

To be clear, Hildegard does not here comment explicitly on Mary's Jewishness, nor does she make a direct claim about the proto-miscegenation of ethnic chastity. But she does elsewhere lament the fallen state of humanity, born into mixed or comingled blood (*in ortu mixti sanguinis*).[18] And like many Christian thinkers in the Middle Ages, Hildegard maintains ambiguous and even derogatory depictions of Jews in her writing—*Scivias* was not only one of the earliest sources to identify the beast in the book of Revelation as the anti-Christ, but invoked tropes that aligned the demonic power of the figure with the Jewish faith.[19] The revival of the German mystic's works in the twentieth century was associated with the rising anti-Semitic ressentiment spreading throughout her home country and Europe, a note not intended to implicate Hildegard in contemporary events, but to point out what is demonstrative for thinking about the misuses of reproduction and purity.[20]

The Marian exceptions are significant. In the section "concerning birth" (*de partu*) of Hildegard's *Causae et curae*, her observations of childbirth are traumatic, if not realistic—"an event that causes the entire woman to 'tremble in terror' (*in terrore hoc tremet*), emit 'tears and shrieks' (*lacrimis et eiulatu*), and suddenly fear that the end of the world (*in fine temporum terra*) is nigh."[21] Hildegard's description of the travail of labor and delivery invoke a "metaphor that depicts the humoral disposition of the sexual and generative female body as a result of women's essential 'openness.'"[22] This differs significantly from Hildegard's description of Mary, who she lyrically describes in her closure:

> O how precious is the virginity of this virgin who has a closed gate, and whose womb holy divinity suffused with its warmth, so that a flower grew in her. And the Son of God came forth like the dawn through her secret.[23]

There is a theological mystery of Mary's body around the flow of traffic and her womb as enclosure. Thus, when we return to the vision from *Scivias*, the recurring motif of purity (and subsequently, the experience of pain) extend to a physiological register—both Mary's genitalia and reproductive organs are completely circumvented for Christ to emerge from her body:

> When the blessed Virgin was a little weakened, as if drowsy with sleep, the infant came forth from her side—not from the opening of the womb—without her knowledge and without pain, corruption, or filth, just as Eve emerged from the side of Adam.[24]

Mary's theological sedation and side-birth rehearse the typologies of Adam and Eve, reinventing the tropes of creation where Eve is brought into the world from a sleeping Adam. While many theologians assumed or agreed that Jesus experienced a vaginal birth, an experience which would logically require a claim about Mary's virginity *in partu*—a virginity that must be left intact is a virginity that was, through the birthing process, somehow at risk. Hildegard's vision however, expands upon the set of traditions that suggested Christ was born from the side, or from Mary's right breast, circumventing contact with the vagina altogether. As Hildegard elaborates:

> [Christ] did not enter through the vagina, for if he had come out that way there would have been corruption, but since the mother was intact in that place, the infant did not emerge there.... And no placenta covered the infant in the Virgin Mother's womb, in the manner of other infants, because he was not conceived from virile seed.[25]

This stands in stark contrast to the birth of the anti-Christ later described in *Scivias*, black, monstrous, covered in excrement and inaugurated with pain and filth—Mary's birth of Christ imitates the very opposite.[26] But this is also quite the reversal from the emphasis on the fecundity of Mary's body and the full circumstance of her birth that were so necessary to expressing Christ's nature in earlier centuries.

In the third century *On the Flesh of Christ*, for instance, Tertullian asks a pertinent question: "Pray, tell me, why the Spirit of God descended into a woman's womb at all, if He did not do so for the purpose of partaking of flesh from the womb. ... He had no reason for enclosing Himself within one, if He was to bear forth nothing from it."[27] Where Tertullian readily discusses bodily fluids, refers consistently to blood and milk, and describes a baby Jesus covered in the "ornaments" of his afterbirth, Hildegard's vision is of a Marian twilight. The lack of any blood or vaginal contact in her vision, for one so scientifically interested, deserts the body of its fecundity. The lack of a placenta denies a need even for the nourishment of Christ's body, or of marking the physiological connections between mother and fetus.[28] A novice with most basic knowledge might question if Jesus's body had a belly button, lest the umbilical cord be a source of sin. In Hildegard's vision of nativity, there is no comingling, no mixture, no touching of even Mary's own pure and chaste blood upon the young Christ. The demands of a *real* birth, of grave concern in the earlier centuries, no longer takes theological precedence.

We juxtapose Hildegard with one of the few other visions we have by a woman, Bridget (Birgitta) of Sweden (1303–73). Before becoming a nun as a widow, Bridget lived an interesting life as a wife and mother. She gave birth to eight children, six of whom survived (a miraculous number for the time) beyond their stages of infancy. Having experienced herself the travail of physical labor and the realities of infant mortality, her revelation of Christ's birth is all the more remarkable. As she describes, Mary does not moan and writhe through oncoming contractions, but instead enters labor while in worship:

> And while [Mary] was thus in prayer, I saw the One lying in her womb then move; and then and there, in a moment and the twinkling of an eye, she gave birth to a Son, from whom there went out such great and ineffable light and splendor that the sun could not be compared to it.... And so sudden and momentary was that manner of giving birth that I was unable to notice or discern how or in what member she was giving birth. But yet, at once, I saw that glorious infant lying on the earth, naked and glowing in the greatest of neatness. His flesh was most clean

of all filth and uncleanness. I saw also the afterbirth, lying wrapped very neatly beside him.[29]

Bridget's ephemeral account is filled with light, but only in the noticeable avoidance of any contact (eye, infant, blood, or otherwise) with the Christ child. Similar to Hildegard, there is a certain avoidance of the physicality of birth, and certainly no emergence from the vagina. Though Hildegard is able to give us some account, Bridget sees nothing of an actual delivery, as if time and body fast forward in a prophetic twinkling of an eye. But what is interesting in Bridget's account, is what she *does* see and recount—the surrounding formalities, even pleasantries of the event. She notes the ease of Mary's experience, the tidiness of the timing, even the cleanliness of the baby's flesh. There is no vernix or meconium—there isn't even *sound*. The overt neatness even extends down to the afterbirth, neatly folded and organized, likely *clean*, as if prefiguring the burial cloth the Risen Christ will leave folded in John's account of the Resurrection.[30] There is not chaos, only order in this moment. And for Bridget, the purity of Jesus at birth will manifest retroactively in Mary's recovery, the spiritual equivalent of a contemporary "snapback":

> And the Virgin's womb, which before the birth had been very swollen, at once retracted; and her body then looked wonderfully beautiful and delicate. . . . Then, sitting on the earth, she put her Son in her lap and deftly caught his umbilical cord with her fingers. At once it was cut off, and from it no liquid or blood went out.[31]

The immaculateness of Mary's giving birth is preserved by her body, absent of blood and fluid, retracted and preserved by God without the "corruption" of a swollen uterus, stretch marks, sore breasts, or certainly vaginal tearing.

Which is then to perhaps ask, in all of this cleanliness, in the absence of the stuff that makes the body, in the absence of water and mucus and blood, what has Mary given to her Son? While theoretically Mary's flesh and blood are constitutive of Christ's body incarnate, Maria Mar Perez-Gil makes a timely observation about the physical characterization of the *Theotokos*: "Mary's blood appears to be removed from some of the main evidences that accompany maternity."[32] Taking Hildegard, Bridget and others as examples, Perez-Gil describes the removal of Mary's blood from her maternal embodiment as the making of Mary's "white" blood. She draws upon Luce Irigaray's use of the term *sang rouge* (red blood) to describe a maternal genealogy, a blood kinship originating in the womb that connects a daughter and mother, but that is supplanted in a patriarchal society that demands a daughter leave to take on the role of wife and mother herself.

For Irigaray, the *sang rouge* is constantly under threat, and readily dismantled because there is a symbolic loss of the mother's body within patriarchy. Theorist Margaret Whitford highlights both the literal and literary significance of Irigaray's deployment of the term: "the *sang rouge* is opposed to the semblant, or the 'other of the same', which is a homophone for *sang blanc* (white blood)."[33] White blood represents, then, a male genealogy that replaces the symbol of the womb with that of the Father, suppressing the maternal, female body from symbolic representation. Perez-Gil plays off of Irigaray's psychoanalytic understanding of the cultural and symbolic loss of the maternal body, to analyze and critique the theological loss of Mary's maternal, sexual body. As she describes it, the narrative shift from a bloody, chaotic, and recognizably material birth, to a clean, neat, and light-filled anomaly, mirrors the preference for patriarchy over matriarchy, of white blood over against red blood. Perez-Gil does not do this as a means to simply switch the maternal for the paternal, but instead, for her, these claims are the groundwork for a theology of the body that takes seriously female sexuality and reproduction.

What Perez-Gil's illumines is how Irigaray's thought applies to Marian consideration. For Irigaray, the maternal universe of flesh and blood is replaced "by a universe of language and symbols that has no roots in the flesh and drills a hole through the female womb and through the place of female identity."[34] Where Perez-Gil creates space to consider the disappearance of a maternal genealogy, I would take this point to think along the lines of a genealogy of the womb that is not suppressed, but rather that is *cleansed*. What must be considered as well, then, is that such sanitizing of the womb not only sterilizes against the notion of Jewish genealogy, but will come to sterilize the very notions of sin and sinfulness attributed to a Black Eve—the threats of Jewishness will be maligned as the same *kinds* of threats to the womb, the threat of women (or womxn's) experience of sexual pleasure or desire (not in service to lineage and reproduction), the threat of Black reproduction to white lineage, the structuring of Christian notions of morality in service to white lineage, and the evilness assigned to Black women's bodies at the intersections of such labors.

What might be further considered here are the ways the Doctrine of Immaculate Conception—which again, refers to Mary's conception in the womb of her mother, St. Anne—not only reified Mary's purity as one whose privilege it was to be kept from the stain of original sin, a Christological claim—but also perhaps emerged from a long-standing tradition of, to use Irigaray's term, figuring a way around the problem of Mary's *sang rouge*.[35] That concern of womb-purity extended not only from Jesus's gestation in Mary's womb, but for understanding how Mary's purity as a vessel would come about. Instead of relying on the traditions of sanctification at the moment of Annunciation, the encyclical *Ineffabilis Deus* (1854) affirmed that Mary never participated in and was conceived without original sin. Instead, she received sanctifying grace from the moment of her inception that would last the entirety of her life, a "singular grace and privilege granted by Almighty God."[36]

There is a sense, then, by which the Immaculate Conception bilaterally disrupted the placental connection of Mary *to both her mother and her son*. Perhaps not by idea of the doctrine itself, but the social conditions of its expression and interpretation that necessitate the doctrine are those that set off an alarm—a cleansing genealogy of women's wombs. How far back must one be able to trace

Holy Motherhood, beyond Anne? Where are "the roots in the flesh?" Where is the "place of female identity?" If Mary is made to undergo exception after exception to human experience, particularly given that the humanity she gives to her Son is critical to his identity, then such removals of her material body indeed abstract her into a symbolic realm. One might consider the entendre of ways Mary's womb has been, symbolically, whitewashed. Mary's blood, too, is bleached, white as snow. Symbolic of sinless, stainless aspiration, the maternal genealogy that would build solidarity and connection between Mary and Eve—the supposed source of sin—and Mary and her Jewishness—a connection to a people—is, quite literally, exsanguinated. The possibility for Mary's body beyond whiteness is bled to death.

Purity Myth

In her classic reflections on purity, anthropologist Mary Douglas was one of the first to approach the expression or purity as a means of surveillance and maintenance of social norms. In *Purity and Danger*, engaging the question of religious concerns with hygiene and defilement, Douglas centered purity by analyzing its coordinate operations of dirt, cleanliness and the organization thereof. The genius of this analysis is the surprising intangibility of dirt itself. From the start she asserts: "There is no such thing as absolute dirt: it exists in the eye of the beholder."[37] What is powerful about this statement is that it frames an analysis of purity, which has no absolute reality, and manifests in the terms, conditions, and perceived reality of its enactment. So how to think of dirt? As Douglas describes, "Reflection on dirt involves reflection on the relation of order to disorder, being to non-being, form to formlessness, life to death."[38] If the idea of dirt inflects a way of making sense of the world, and understanding the interplay of that world, the interplay of life, then the idea of purity inflects the same nuance with a different lens. For our purposes here, it is important to know that purity is not a form. Rather, purity is a relation.

A relation of purity is most cohesively expressed via social reference to presupposed normative qualities, expectations, behaviors, and accounts. As we have already discussed, normativity is a proliferation of ideas that scaffold performance of ritual and identity. It is a construction wherein the concepts of wholeness, and the ideal of perfection, translate into the meticulous surveillance over the *acts* of the body, and the disciplinary operations of that body. Douglas's descriptions illuminated the ways that systems of purity perform themselves through scales of calculation. Because she understands dirt as an offensive idea that undermines the potential for order, she claims that "ideas about separating, purifying, demarcating and punishing transgressions have as their main function to impose system on an inherently untidy experience."[39] Recall to mind Bridget's vision of the afterbirth of Christ, neatly folded and clean beside him.

The purity idea, or more precisely, the purity *ideal*, exists to organize and mediate the concerns of the social body. Collective concerns of the political, religious or cultural are all easily graphed on the canvas of the individual. Such meditation upon the body would find itself manifest in both the making and taming of what Foucault described as "docile bodies."[40] Foucault first describes docility as resulting from the subjection and transformation of bodies punished in relation to the state, and thus imagined as bodies that "may be subjected, used, transformed and improved."[41] In our examples, we must recall that Foucault's emphasis on these elements of a punitive society have refrains for the Christian conception of the female body, for whom the pains of childbirth are punishment for transgression against a Sovereign will. From this, there are ways that Christian theology presumed female, reproductive bodies as docile bodies according to a natural order of salvation. Such a permeable idea was well suited for the proliferation of a relation of purity, which can be a mechanism, a technology even, for maintaining a status quo.

As a reminder of the discussions in earlier chapters, the fifth century bore witness to a trenchant, prideful, and prolonged dispute about the "real" nature of Mary as one who could guarantee the claims to Christ's human flesh, yet whose own body had to be exegeted as suitable to carry Christ within her. Mary needed to be real and truly human to fight the Gnostic claims that demonized Christ's flesh, but she also needed to be an exception to the rules of the flesh that governed the rituals of purity and propriety of the time. That exceptionality came in the form of Mary's virginity. The supernatural birth of a child from a pure virgin specimen was a centripetal theme woven into the earliest of theological systems (and not unique to Christian thought). Mary's virgin birth was a means to guarantee the pure, sinless, and divine nature of Christ in his incorruptible flesh. As a generous kickback, the virgin birth would simultaneously be the sign of transformative, redemptive motherhood previously sullied by the woman Eve. If Eve had come to represent sexual deviance and corruption, Mary represented sexual chastity and integrity. Where Eve was damned to give birth in pain and anguish, Mary was exalted to give birth in triumphant defeat of an ancient curse. Mary wasn't just any woman. She was the true exemplar of all that women could (and should) aspire to be in this life, even if the goalpost was perched on an impossible cliff to scale.

Douglas' analysis continues to elucidate the relational aspect of purity—and by our extension, the need for Mary's virginity—when she theorizes practices of ritual purity, taking as classic examples the purity and holiness codes present in the Book of Leviticus. For Douglas, the stringent mandates around food, animals, cleansing, and purification are anything but arbitrary. Rather the codes are highly organizational, and instituted to establish clear boundaries and classifications of the world as the community knew and understood it. Perhaps this details why virginity alone was never enough to combat the wages of sin, why the sanctity of Mary's womb would also need to be secured, lest the genealogy of the uterus pose a threat to the incarnate Christ. If the curse of Eve and geneaology of original sin made *birthing* the first autoimmune disease, this would require dogmatic clarification and continued organization. Yet even once located rightly, such womb-honor was still in need of defense. *This* womb was subject not only to the heretical slander of those who would denigrate the divinity of Christ, but also to the encroaching threat of "illegal" thoughts sneaking across the borders of Incarnational dogmatics. What Mary's womb really needed was a wall around it, to be clearly separated from anything that would penetrate its purity. Her womb literally needed *fixing*—to be set, permanently, as a kind of *fixture*, apart from any person, place, or thing that lent itself to the very imaginary of difference and election. It was then and now remains a tenuous theological challenge to maintain the claims of Mary's *real* body and real birth on the one hand, while still asserting the exceptionality of her chosenness that marked her as pure enough—or at least *purified*—on the other.

Douglas' work asks us to consider then how the question of normativity is entangled with the concerns of boundaries and classification at the site of Mary's body and the purity concerns that emerge when something cannot be understood within the logics of a strict category. In Douglas' assessment, when purity is involved, the imaginary of things that exist as hybrids, that exist at the boundary or border of a classifying logic, is incredibly limited. Instead, examples that could not be organized were often barred with a prohibition. These examples were considered unclean, a strange instance of a borderland that might be open to transgression and, as such, contamination. As Gloria Anzaldúa has elsewhere described:

> Borders are set up to define the places that are safe and unsafe, to distinguish us from them. A border is a dividing line, a narrow strip along a steep edge. A borderland is a vague and undetermined place created by the emotional residue of an unnatural boundary. It is in a constant state of transition. The prohibited and forbidden are its inhabitants.[42]

The borders around Mary's body, her womb, her vagina, and her blood in theological discourse operate as rhetorical markers of her purity, but they fail to more deeply account for the ways that Mary is innately required to exist as the point of contact between the human and the divine *against* purity. Her Jewish womb is the borderland, her body hybridized in mothering God. She is a confounding body, both Virgin and Mother, one who stands at the precipice between fallenness and the prelapsarian condition. This was the very question at the center of the Christological controversies, how to make sense of the pure and holy daring to make intimate contact with the flesh and blood of the human world. As Brian Bantum describes, Jesus is the contamination of the "purity" of God with the "impurity" of flesh:

He is the presence of what cannot be contained within the limitation of a body. ... In these moments, the conventional language of boundaries and identities and assertions could no longer be adequately applied to this man. Jesus' very presence in the world transformed the boundaries of identity and thus the possibilities of how identities might be configured in the world, but especially within his own body.[43]

For Bantum, the Chalcedon definition is one that marks a certain kind of "hybridity" in the Incarnation because Christ's body refuses the stability of a fixed identity, of a containable personhood. Christ is already a source of transgression and hybridity—humanity and divinity, flesh and spirit, Jewish Messiah and Christian Savior.

Like Mother, like Son. In as much as Jesus Christ is considered to be fully human and fully divine, *Theotokos* implies that Mary, too, in her state of pregnancy, epitomizes a valuable hybridity within her very body, the liminal space of interstitial reality, an internalization of the borderland. While she is fully human, even to the extent of granting Jesus his human flesh and Jewish identity, she carries contact with the Divine, she carries within her the fullness of Divinity, the *Imago Dei* itself. And yet, she is not allowed to bear blood, hypothetical or literal. Mary is not allowed to be a *bleeding* body, despite the power of the blood that flows from her child.

Here we return to the proclamations of Mary's virginity in perpetuity. As discussed, the conversations on the Incarnation that emerged in Chalcedon (451) were deeply invested in questions of Mary's status as a virgin, *without loss*, that came to be clarified at the First Lateran Council (649). For She who is Holy, Ever-Virgin, and Immaculate, emphases on integrity, incorruptibility, preservation, and inviolation come as logical, even necessary descriptors. But even the best of apophatic normativities evoke their cataphatic, antinormative anchors, each affirmation offering a formula of negation. In moving to stress the "ever-Virginity" of Mary, what the statements of the First Lateran Council (649) imply are a certain idea of what is divine and miraculous in opposition to the female body: "the Holy, Ever-Virgin and Immaculate Mary ... with integrity brought Him forth (incorruptibly bore Him), and after His Birth preserved her virginity inviolate."[44] The physical conditions of virginity and purity were reflections of the spiritual condition of a person's soul, the holiness of a bodily vessel. As such, the spiritual quality of purity was deeply rooted in a static understanding of bodily integrities and proprieties. The enduring nature of Mary's virginity without corruption and without change demonstrate the need for a miraculous sign of divine intervention, but they simultaneously taint and undermine a world teeming with life, the very precedent of creation and regeneration itself. As Sarah Jane Boss describes:

Within the multiplicity of creation, acts of generation and fruitfulness always involve the breaching of boundaries. Seeds break out of the walls of fruit, chicks break open their eggs, and cows struggle to push calves from inside their bellies to the outside world. All these processes are acts of change which leave ruptures and scars on the organs that bear that change.[45]

It is an interesting paradox that within the tradition of Mary's inviolability, her body will not bear the marks of this creativity, of the birth and generation of Jesus Christ, for the sake of a body immutable. There are perennial questions here, as to the presentation of Mary's youthfulness (as tied to an idea of her beauty and purity), and the perfection of her body, without blemish or wrinkle, given her Son's body is one that will bear wounds and scars. Where are the signs of Mary's life, that at least to say, of her pregnancy and labor? Why is it that we do not wish Mary to have stretch marks, chaffing, body hair, secretions—and certainly, not ever, to imagine a Madonna who has been made to bear the scars of the whipping tree? This is not to claim suffering or pain as theologically productive, and certainly not necessary or inherent to a claim to redemption or grace, but to say that *experience* is constitutive of human life, of growth and change. Boss speaks to this with a theological understanding of an infinite God, a divinity that exceeds the containment of walls and boundaries:

> In God, however, there is generation and procession that does not entail any rupture or the crossing of a boundary ... for God is one, with no division and no boundary or limit of any kind. There is no 'end' to God, so there is no 'outside of God', and consequently no 'inside' either.... And there are no 'parts of God': God is not made up, or composed of lesser units, such as atoms, or bodily organs.[46]

In a sense, Boss is describing a vision of God *against* anti-normativity. "In collating the world," *God* gathers up everything, including the spatiality that would reference a periphery or a center at all.[47] The immutable and eternal nature of God perdures even through what humanity would imagine as change, precisely because God constitutes both the inside and the outside of space, and transcends any bounds to the continuum of time. Boss extends this logic to describe how the body of Mary came to be thought, and the critical theological symbolism at work in the doctrine of perpetual virginity. When imagined as *Theotokos*, thinkers extended the logic of generation and procession to explain (without explanation) that bearing the Christ child was an event that left Mary's body unchanged in the process.

But what are the consequences to such an understanding of the Incarnation? While there are innumerable helpful interpretations of Mary's virginity (and Boss in several places offers important contributions to such a project), it is also important to critically engage how resistance to transgression manifests as a problematic logic of the body. The very theological argument of Christ's body, the Word made flesh who "dwelt among us" presupposes a radical contact between the human and the divine.[48] In the Incarnation, God violates time and space across multiple schemas, transgresses the boundary of purity in order to demonstrate that created flesh, flesh bearing the image of God, is inarguably redeemable.

Again, when Christ is resurrected, the Gospel accounts do not characterize redemption of the body in terms of aesthetics or integrity, but instead speak of the stigmata Christ continues to bear. The Apostle Thomas is often evaluated for his doubt of Christ's return because he asks to place his fingers inside of Christ wounds, touching to feel that the man before him is real.[49] Hymns and sermons in the Christian tradition continuously refer to a Christ that still bears these marks, as well as to a Christ who retains the scars from his crucifixion. Yet Mary is evacuated from the experience of *this* impossibility, as the spotlessness of her body is still thought prerequisite to qualify the suffering of her own Son.

The question of aesthetics extends to experience, as well. The insistence on a static virginity includes the traditions that Mary did not experience pain during her childbirth. Pain is a uniquely creaturely experience, and it is the specific physical sensation (and not the emotional trauma) that Mary is kept from. As noted throughout this text, the doctrine of original sin is a socio-temporally located origin, that names the locus of the pain of childbirth within a genealogy of sin. The book of Genesis pronounces that the pain and suffering of the female body while giving birth are the result of female transgression committed, bestowed and transmitted through Eve once she and her partner Adam were expelled from the garden. If sin is thus tied to desire, pleasure and shame in as much as it is tied to parturition, pain, breach and boundary, the miraculous birth of Christ would necessarily circumvent the experience of pain. The one who came to rid the world of corruption could not enter the world through corruption. Mary, as she would be considered to be free of sin, would logically be spared and thus extended a certain grace from the materiality of birth.

As Boss suggests elsewhere, perhaps Mary's freedom from birth pangs serves as the scapegoat from Oedipal guilt: "... the teaching that Mary gave birth without pain, and even without loss of her virginity, provides devotees with a mother whom they have never wounded, and who therefore does not seem to have cause to reproach them simply for being alive in the world."[50] But circumventing such reproach again fails to be commensurate with the figuration of Christ as the sacrificial lamb in a tradition where suffering becomes part of an ascetic ideal. Instead, the view towards Mary's body is already imagined on its own terms, with what seems to be a gendered bias toward fragility and embodiment. Mary will even come to defy the bodily corruption of death with her dormition and assumption—a complete bodily preservation even unto death.[51]

The insistence on Mary's virgin sexual identity and the gloss of her Jewish ethnic identity converge here, in the phallic imaginary of circumcision. At the hands of the Church Fathers, Mary's body has been subjected to a *kind* a female "circumcision."[52] The figurative cutting off of her sexuality or any symbol thereof is a sacrifice that bleeds out onto eternity.[53] The suturing of access to her womb, desires, and pleasures perform the machinations of kinship alliance expressed through the body. The investments in Mary's purity and spiritual essence as a disciple of Christ require her Jewishness, quite literally, be *cut out*.[54] The notion of Mary's presence as the first disciple—the first to believe and follow her own firstborn—elides the complexities of and realities of a kind of multiple religious belonging, an erasure that inevitably contributes the machinations by which Mary becomes white. As the historical nature of circumcision functioned as entrance into the holy elect, the theological "circumcision" of Mary functions in a similar way by instantiating the claim to her chosenness. The removal of her Jewish covering, the spiritual foreskin of flesh and blood, symbolize her commitment to God's commandments to raise up a Savior. In her absolute obedience to God, she shifts from Mary-Israel to the consummation of the people of Israel. As Eugene Rogers describes, "For Israel, consummation is the main plot. . . . In Mary the consummation and redemption plots coincide."[55] Much like the circumstances of her relation to Eve, her relation to Israel is a surpassing that signals a severing. Mary will now come to symbolize the figure of the Church. In this way, how could her psychic circumcision not also be required? Her virgin womb, hermetically sealed; her access to sexual pleasure, involuntarily sterilized. Both now function as the primary marker of her identity—it is a supreme irony. The spiritual circumcision of Mary, instead of constituting Mary's Jewish identity, makes a utilitarian paragon of Mary's feigned Christianity.

We turn to the question of Mary's Jewishness (and in relation to birth and pain) because it is a critical matrix through which Mary's purity will be considered. In the expansion of the institutional guild of the Christian faith, the questions of who and how one speaks, of the tensions between agency and the foreclosing of language, of the marking of the flesh, of the surveillance and narration of the body can only be considered against the backdrop of Jewish election. For it is the erasure of her Jewish flesh that grounds the instrumentalization of Mary's body, and foregrounds the longstanding battle for the claims to Mary's purity—a purity, religious, that will inevitably become racial in its enactment.

Our M(other)

For years, I've cried for other women's children.
Valerie Castile
Mother of Philando Castile

Beloved Mother, so stricken with grief, help us to
bear our own suffering with courage and love so that
we may relieve your Sorrowful Heart and that of Jesus.
prayer from the 7 Sorrows Rosary

The infinitude of Mary's virginity belies a question not just about her womb (and by extension, her mother's womb) but about what community she does or does not belong to, and the inability to consider Mary as a critical nexus of multiple religious belonging. Similarly, the refusal to name her subjectivity through the lens of hybridity, which is to say, a kind of multiplicity, is to force a narrative of her body as holy and ordained *crisis*—quite literally, carrying the crisis of the Cross within her—so as to not be a site of *deviance* that would undermine any Christological claim. As her womb is purified and exceptionalized in the early church, the logics of purity and cleanliness function to circumvent the Jewish religious (*cum* ethnic—for we have since seen the resistance and refusals to be accountable to Mary as Palestinian) identity and election that are genealogically carried through her body—a matrilineal line—as the only human contributor to Christ's DNA. There is a collective calculus by which the Jewishness of both Mary and her singular, deity offspring are disappeared. Mary is displaced from the Jewish community and severed of its flesh, in service to an ideal of unadulterated Christian discipleship.

Here we can learn in retrospect, for Hortense Spillers offers a critical analysis that demonstrates the crux of such a Jewish-Christian distinction, and the ways that Mary, according to the Christian spirit, took precedence over Mary according to the Jewish flesh. Though taking the Black woman of mid-Atlantic slavery as her specific temporal context, Spillers' theorization of the flesh is theologically infused, as she delineates with critical distinction how flesh operates away from the body:

> I would make a distinction in this case between "body" and "flesh" and impose that distinction as the central one between captive and liberated subject-positions. In that sense, before the "body" there is "flesh," that zero degree of social conceptualization that does not escape concealment under the brush of discourse, or the reflexes of iconography.[56]

For Spillers, captivity functions as both a logic of desire and of identity that imbibes the social, and arguably the theological, narration of human meaning. The distinction between body and flesh that Spillers describes is not unlike the Pauline distinction between the flesh and the spirit, between Paul's modulation of Jewish adherence to the Law against the new spirit of the Christian life, as a central distinction between a captive position subject to the flesh, and a liberated position renewed in and through the body of Christ. However, Spillers' conceptual organization is the inverse of Paul's. Though she is outlining the modern racial, Spiller's frame elucidates the Christian theological distinction between being enslaved and being free, that aligns flesh as a preceding liberated position. We must seriously consider the ways purity and virginity as valences of Mary's *Christian body*, function as the ground of her identity, in order to supplant her *Jewish flesh*, which lies in accordance with the argument around the *Blackness* of Eve, the narratives of purity ultimately crafting an image of Mary that supercedes her originary counterpart through the logics of purity masquerading as whiteness. Spillers work here is not only critical to understand the Black woman's gender, body, and life—but also illumines the significant shift that happens when we consider the treatment of Mary's *Jewish body*, in relationship to her creation and gestation of Christ, as the Word *made flesh*.

As Spillers suggests, the evidences of this marking manifest uniquely in the linguistic realm. Spillers begins the essay with a litany of names—Peaches, Brown Sugar, Sapphire, Earth Mother, Aunty, Granny, Holy Fool, Miss Ebony First, Black Woman at the Podium—but only after the invocation of acknowledgment: "I am a marked woman."[57] The list of names, this "locus of confounded identities, a meeting ground of investments and privations in the national treasury of rhetorical wealth," signal the haste with which one's identity—particularly when identified as a woman—can be determined by the needs of the social setting to which one is subjected. Again, this is critical to our understanding of what is taking shape when it comes to understanding the confounded identity of the Mother of God. Mary, too, is a marked woman. In this transition, the spiritual significance of Mary's linguistic marking foils the fleshly marking of Jewish identity. The linguistic representation of her identity—Virgin, Mother, Theotokos, Holy, Ever-Immaculate—manifests both a captive and captivating understanding of her body in relationship to Christ.

Virginity itself, then, retains a certain capacity for surrogacy. It provides the footing by which intimacy and relationality can be disarticulated from material witness, and instead promulgate theology bound by "discourses of displacement."[58] And it situates a theological consideration of the Black birthing body through the theological lens of surrogacy as a structure of domination unto itself.

As Delores Williams describes in *Sisters in the Wilderness*, the story of Hagar in the book of Genesis helps enlighten the histories of oppression for Black women in the United States and elsewhere, who through histories of colonial laws and enslavement have not been entitled to their own bodies, much less any sense of reproductive justice, access to parenting or mothering without imposition, and the delimitation of choice that reduced reproduction and birth to the frame of surrogacy.[59] For as Hortense Spillers described, the "New World, diasporic plight marked a *theft of the body*—a willful and violent (and unimaginable from this distance) severing of the captive body from its motive will, its active desire. Under these conditions, we lose at least *gender* difference *in the outcome*. . . ."[60] Williams turns to the theological resonances of Black wombs and the loss of such gender difference in this way, detailing Black women's roles as surrogates through both biological and social forms, and describing the antebellum period as marked by *coerced* surrogacy (and the generative notion of the Mammy). The Mammy, servant of all, was indeed "empowered (but not autonomous)" in whatever privilege she was granted, though still within the confines of enslavement. The position of the Mammy differed from the coerced surrogacy of those Black women forced to displace access to a domestic realm or performance of gendered roles in order to labor in the field—as Spillers describes, those "masculinized" or "ungendered" for raw production. It differed as well for those Black women who were raped, those who were subject to the unimpeded desires of their white enslavers (both men and women), and those continually made to become pregnant and give birth in a system of enslavement that relied on Black women's reproduction to sustain itself in absence of unfettered Atlantic passage. In every regard, no form of coerced surrogacy existed outside of exploitative violence as means to maintain the logics of slavocracy.

While these aspects shifted in the postbellum era, Williams notes the scriptural relevance of Black women now navigating new systems that still delimited freedom and choice.[61] Theologically this becomes a critical question not only for Black women's imaginary of the sacred (while Williams speaks specifically to Black women in the United States, the *theo*-logic she infers is not organized by the geographic boundaries of this country alone) and particularly the ways histories of surrogacy have taught Black women to "image redemption."[62] As Williams names, once we get to the notions of the Cross:

> Jesus represents the ultimate surrogate figure; he stands in the place of someone else: sinful humankind. Surrogacy, attached to this divine personage, thus takes on an aura of the sacred.... If Black women accept this idea of redemption, can they not also passively accept the exploitation that surrogacy brings?[63]

Which is perhaps a reason we must consider the Black Madonna, and the ways that both theologically *coerced* surrogacy, however empowering but not autonomous, and theologically *voluntary* surrogacy, however conceded but not apart from impositions of duress, are questions of theological anthropology that consider the proximate contexts of freedom that point to *Black life*. As such, Williams questions a theology of atonement that *requires* the Cross—suffering—as the locus of Resurrection, but instead sees in the Cross the multiple *resistances* that inhibited access to life, and that also, ultimately, failed.

What world would be possible, then, if we could seriously consider Mary's womb as reference to the flourishing of Black life, as a site of theological resistance? To fully consider the question not of her body as gestational carrier of the Divine, nor as surrogate mother to Divine Incarnate, but as truly *Theotokos*, Mother of God? Any theologian who considers seriously the proclamation of a Black Christ might thus also extend this sacred category to consider the proclamation of Mary a Black mother, particularly given the proliferation of Black mothers whose children have been unjustly murdered at the hands of the state. Here we note that the legacies of Mary's *painless* birth are reminiscent of the ways pain is misread or ignored for Black women–imagined as something fictive and other–that often leaves Black women bereft of their own affect and embodiment, an ungendering reflex of captivity. And yet, there must be something beyond the capacity for suffering that honors a mother.

Here we consider the Marian tradition of the *Mater dolorosa*, Our Lady of Sorrows, whose motherhood mirrors the torments of the *via dolorosa* of Christ's Passion (see Fig. 4.3). This iconic and representational tradition emerges most

Figure 4.3 Felipe del Corral, *Virgen de los Dolores* (Virgin of Sorrows), 1718. Sculpture. Capilla de la Vera Cruz, Salamanca. Photograph by Zarateman, 2014.

heavily during the medieval periods. The figure, depicted frequently with tears, seven swords piercing her body (reflective of the prophecy she received of the inevitable suffering of her child), or with a bursting (and implied, *breaking*) heart is almost completely absent from the already dearth filled depictions of Mary within the Protestant canon. Maximus the Confessor, whose seventh-century *Life of the Virgin* is considered the first Marian biography, predates the widespread devotion to the *Mater dolorosa* in the fourteenth century significantly, but graphically marks Mary as an active participant in the sufferings of Christ, particularly in the events of the crucifixion. This pain, however, is not befitting of her experience of birth, which as he describes, is as if to have had no experience at all, no experience of any "maternal conditions and pains."[64] Rather, tying together the conclusions of Mary's pregnancy as being without seed as requiring it also be without corruption, and thus also without pain, he describes Mary's "painless birth":

> ... not only that she avoided the pains of motherhood and appeared as a mother and was preserved as a virgin, but also that she did not feel the birth. Behold the economy of divine activities and the transformation of natures, for the wondrous son did not make known to the immaculate mother the knowledge of his birth, and in an instant he was inexplicably found outside her womb and settled in her lap, so that just as her conception took place without seed and without awareness, so also the birth took place without corruption and without awareness.[65]

Maximus continues, describing that Christ:

> entered into the Virgin's holy womb silently and painlessly, so he did not make known his ineffable coming forth to the immaculate mother, but he put on human flesh from her, and so he went forth easily and supernaturally, the one who did not make his birth known, not only to others but even to his own mother.[66]

The silence, hiddenness, and denial of enfleshment emphasizes the implied immutability of Mary's physical body as demonstrative of its sinless and uncorrupted state. Maximus however, shifts considerations of sin, corruption, and suffering *away* from Mary's womb, by diverting the pain of labor to Mary's agony at the foot of the Cross. Here—in death, instead of birth—are the moments where Mary "shared his pain."[67] It is on account of Mary's humanity (and the limitations thereof), that Maximus even further describes Mary as the one who "suffered more than him and endured sorrows of the heart."[68] While this suffering is explicitly not redemptive in Maximus writings, Mary's "fountains of tears" are undeniable, "her sons nails wound[ing] her heart as spears."[69] Mary has unfeelingly carried the Christ in her womb, but now she will feel every violation on the Cross in her heart. She displays overwhelming grief (though for Maximus, this is yet with a kind of decorum and appropriate sense of restraint—she does not display the rage one might also expect), as she witnesses the torture and death of her flesh and blood.

The shift in the absence of pain in birth to the presence of pain in death does little for Mary's body itself, much less her emotional experience of suffering. Maximus will still relegate the entire "maternal condition," to name his indications from conception through pregnancy and birth, as aspects of the sinful condition of humanity. There is no joy, celebration, or indulgence offered to Mary's experience—as if to experience bodily affect here might too closely be a source of defilement, too reminiscent of experiencing bodily desires and pleasures writ large. Her womb is not a grave, only insofar as she is kept, for Maximus, from even having one, or being alerted to and aware of its operations. The question for Mary turns on the suitability of pain, as a kind of apposite response to the pronouncement of her grace. Mary's painless birth is imagined as a kind of freedom and overcoming not only of the boundaries of the human body, but the spiritual ascension above the curse handed down to Eve. Pain is not something Mary *deserves*, and as such, she supercedes the conditions of labor.

But escaping the dangers of the womb will not escape the dangers of the world. And it is here that Mary's grief and lament have their true demonstration, the capacity for love matched and proven more deeply by the capacity for suffering. As we have intimated at different points throughout this text, the mythology of strength is not one that offers dignity for the Black woman, and the latent resistance to hear Black women, and to systemically deny them the capacity for pain, is rooted in a racist mythology that denigrates their humanity and relegates their position as reprobate. Perhaps it is a deeper accompaniment with the Black Madonna, and Black women's experiences as *Mater dolorosa*, that posit for us a broader capacity for experience of the fullness of maternal experience and human dignity.

Here it is pertinent to recall Mamie Till-Mobley's resounding demand that the devastated body of her son, Emmett Till, be returned to her, and that his casket be left open during his funeral to bear witness to what whiteness did (see Fig. 4.4).[70] Till-Mobley's unadulterated grief pierces the photograph, the viewer haunted by the youthful face of the son she sent to Mississippi, and sickened by the grotesque mutilations (the photographs would be widely circulated) so as to be seared in memory, wounds screaming for justice from the casket. We are faced with a different sonic of horror, the silky white sheets of funerary custom, the fluted fabric inside of the casket, a Black women held by hands not meant to restrain as much as support the incalculable reactions of the body through grief. Pain winces across her face; "*in the sound of the photograph: childless mother.*"[71] As Courtney Baker describes, "We can intuitively understand this response as the desire of a mother to bestow upon her deceased son the caring look of humane insight."[72] Her notion of humane insight is one that moves beyond a look or a gaze, to instead demand an ethical praxis, an observance that "turns a benevolent eye, recognizes violations of human dignity, and bestows or articulates the desire for actual protection."[73] She

Figure 4.4 Mamie Bradley grieving over the casket of her son, Emmett Till. September 3, 1955.
© Chicago Sun-Times Media, ST-17600658, Chicago Sun-Times Collection, Chicago History Museum.

describes Mamie Till-Mobley's capacity for such insight as something not simply innate to motherhood, but "significantly informed by her ability to perceive via the spectacle of her son's injured body her own body's potential response to torture."[74] Where a common theme of atonement considers Christ's experience of torture as taking the place of sinful humanity, Baker highlights the ways Mamie Till-Mobley, despite not having been there to witness the violence against her son, "can see herself in the body of the tortured and imagine herself in her son's place. Her alignment of her body with his reaches its peak when she is able to identify with his sense of fear as she discovers, suddenly, that she might be able to see with his eyes."[75] Here in real time, what is denied in birth and in life, is unrelentingly shared in death. The *Mater dolorosa* reiterates the misconceptions that deny material solidarity between Black mothers and the Black Madonna. As Stephanie Buckhanon Crowder argues, we must take seriously the ways Black women are distanced from an isolated and limited vision of mothering, particularly when repeated experiences of targeted violence and denial find Black mothers in concert with someone more like the figure of Rizpah, whose children King David kills for political strategy, and who is forced to alone "protect and secure her children, her dead children."[76] Crowder's exegesis of Rizpah points to the ways Black women are left alone to orchestrate their grief, for Rizpah is a figure who "shows the reader how mothers learn to literally dwell in death."[77] What does it mean to be made to dwell in death, at both life's beginning and it's end?

This requires we reconsider the Cross. Though the economy of Mary as Mother of Sorrows subsumes the entirety of her life as a mother—from the prophecy from Simeon to Mary proclaiming the sword piercing her heart, to her witness of the sword piercing her son's side—at the foot of the cross Mary, too, embodies the pain and suffering of Jesus. Here at the cross, Mary feels the pain of the sins of the world. Mary, the *pre-peri-post-partum* Virgin, prefigures our opening consideration of Three Mothers, calls to mind the "humane insight" in the shared experiences of Mamie Till in her son's torture. Mary, sole progenitor of the *Word made Flesh*, somehow too stands only *"in the flesh*, both mother and mother-dispossessed."[78] Somehow, while she is espoused as the paragon of the traditional symbolic of female gender at its epitome and apex, she is actually "a different social subject," even in her grief. And in this moment, I wonder about the different social subject, to return to what Sharpe and Nash have noted, of the Black mother bound to crisis, the ones labeled "former mother," or perhaps, even more unrelentingly, "mother of the movement." What does it mean if the legibility of the Black mother, still unholy, and still marked and excluded by pathology, is made ever slightly more legible, *only when she stands at the foot of the cross*? I am interested in what Alexis Pauline Gumbs has described as "the texture of her loss," which is another way to describe, the sacrilege of her surrogacy.[79]

At the foot of the cross, Mary is transformed from an *a*political subject to a political one through her suffering and her grief. But must actual Black women—and more specifically, Black mothers in the United States and across the diaspora, only bear witness there? Is the testament of grief—and the legacy and fulfilled prophecies of trauma—forever the site of legibility and theological attention? Whose pain matters, and how? As Black mothers like Samaria Rice have articulated, must she be conscribed to political leverage, abstracted phenomena, and gross capitalistic gain in the name of advocacy, amplification, and something feigned as justice?[80]

This chapter began in the womb, and the illegibility of it walls as porous with possibility, whose very amorphousness and sovereignty were a conundrum for a theological and political system. But the ways we do (or do not) account for Mary's capacity for pleasure and pain leave theological legacies for how bodies-with-wombs are theologically, and thus socially, perceived. Virginity cleared Mary from causing any sanitary hazard to the Incarnation, but in her relation to other women, Mary mirrored a dilemma similar to that of her Son. How could the Mother of God be the same as other women with respect to condition, while yet instantiating a clear difference as one who could stand out in "eminent and singular fashion?"[81]

We are again returned to Saidiya Hartman's *afterlives of slavery*, and what I would suggest as its corollary, the *afterbirth of surrogacy*—the legacy of refusal to see Black women as women, and even more so, the refusal to see Black women as mothers, and not as arbiters of threat and death.[82] What then must we imagine, theologically, for the Black mother's suffering to also not be offered as redemptive, to not be placed as a critical nexus of legibility in a political project of empathy or liberation, to not be an alternative modality of the surrogacy to which Delores Williams warns us is so deeply beholden to Black bodies with wombs, to not be reduced to the kenotic constraints of Paschal performativity? What might the church, the world, look like were we to hold space for the Black Madonna in all of her emanations? For the Black Madonna as *Mater dolorosa*, a mother who weeps and moans, who perhaps only wished *to mother*, not *to mother a "movement"*—without collapsing grief and trauma as primary register of legibility or mobilization? Are there different possibilities that can flow from the wounds of a pierced heart... or elsewhere, from bursting umbilical cords, leaking colostrum, from the site of the placenta? In other words, what is required, theologically, not just for Black mothers to be made well, but for us to see Black m(others)—those who gestate, nurture, and tend to Black life—as whole?

5
Women Are from Venus

Mistaken Identities

September 20, 1810
From the banks of the river Gamtoos, on the borders of Kaffraria, witnessed by those who were all greatly astonished. *The Morning Post* heralded her spectacular arrival—

THE HOTTENTOT VENUS—Just arrived (and may be seen between the hours of One and Five O'clock in the evening, at the No.225 Picadilly), from the Banks of the River Gamtoos, on the Borders of Kaffraria, in the interior of South Africa, a most correct and perfect Specimen of that race of people. From this extraordinary phenomena of nature, the Public will have an opportunity of judging how far she exceeds any description given by historians of that tribe of the human species. She is habited in the dress of her country, with all the rude ornaments usually worn by those people. She has been seen by the principal Literati in this Metropolis, who were all greatly astonished, as well as highly gratified with the sight of so wonderful a specimen of the human race. She has been brought to this country at a considerable expense, by Kendrick Cerar [sic], and their stay will be but short duration.—To commence on Monday next, the 24th inst.—Admittance, 2s each.

The Morning Post, September 20, 1810[1]

Just three years after the abolition of the British slave trade in 1807, Saartjie "Sara" Baartman, a young KhoiKhoi woman from the Camdeboo Region of South Africa, stepped onto British soil and into her new identity as "the Hottentot Venus." Far beyond what she could ever have known, her journey along the Atlantic would trace the line between "the sexual, the wondrous, and the ethnographic," a merger of parallel dimensions within a racialized colonial multiverse.[2] Literarti verified and Metropolis approved, all one needed to witness the Hottentot Venus take the stage were two shillings to rub together. Women, being of more delicate constitution, were only asked to give advance notice if they were planning to attend so that the show would be tailored appropriately.[3] Any ticket holder was invited to view the Hottentot, she who was the "truly transitional figure between man and ape,"[4] a naked savage and "*a most correct and perfect Specimen of that race of people.*" Her marketing as a lucrative scientific curiosity peaked the universality of her celebrity as she was strutted before audiences male and female, rich and poor, Catholic and Protestant, on a world tour that began in England, skirted Ireland, and captivated France.

Now you, too, could see the darkest heart of Africa right on Piccadilly square. Now you, too, could touch the past, could judge for oneself the nature of the (she-) beast. How close to man or ape would this woman, this monster, this *thing* actually be? The advertisement claimed the excess and difference of her body belonging to *that tribe*, a placeholder for an entire race whose skin marked the mysterious darkness emanating from the heart of Africa. The prophetic claims of the *Morning Post* instantiated the appetites of conspicuous consumption amongst a Public in which anyone could participate, offering their gaze and their analysis of whom—or more readily *what*—stood before them. She was strange and different, so much so that even the claim to her humanity was marred by its excess.

But the collision impact of these narratives was split with contraindications. The heralding of her exotic presence resonated at varying frequencies, as the idea of the Hottentot Venus danced frightfully across nineteenth-century British imaginations. Her appellation spoke of her irony. While sailors and travelers to the Cape arrived on the Southern tip of Africa ready to find out if the seafaring rumors—the wild tales of hyper erotic native, enslaved, and free Black women who could rub the salt from your wounds—were *actually* true, back in the London metropolis, the Hottentot stood as a spectacle of the primitive, an apparition of repulsion, a creature of such little cognition and such monstrous proportions who surely could *never* possess the sexual power of an *actual* Venus. Instead, "it was the figure of the *anti*-erotic that Baartman was reassuring to a European audience."[5] Cloaked in Black skin, even the nickname Venus was the kind that "licensed debauchery and made it sound agreeable."[6] Precisely as the performance of the Hottentot Venus was narrated through the lens of sexual desire and pleasure, Baartman was simultaneously desexed as an anomaly, a twisted engendering (if not *un*gendering) of her body as a commodity that itself marked the production of difference. Through her, one could enjoy a "vicarious pleasure," a perduring white gaze that sought fulfillment through the analysis of her body composition as grounding the "smug reassurance of [white] superiority."[7] Baartman was never meant to attain the normative virtues of anything good, anything beautiful, or anything true, other than grounding the fact of white supremacy. Never was she meant to be, "a beauty queen by English standards," instead only "a monstrosity, an aberration of nature, a grottesque [sic] freak."[8] Baartman's body anchored a certain sense of European identity and sexuality as the ideals of civilization were imagined through morality and decency. But yet, *and still*, people clamored for the opportunity to measure the curve of her breasts, to feel the tone of her behind, and to catch a secret glimpse of her "Hottentot apron," the mythically elongated labia she was presumed to possess.

Of course they did. The marketing subtleties of a *sexed* body, as opposed to a *sexy* body, drew the figure of the Black Venus into an aesthetic scale of approximation. With precise sophistication, her body measured "the differences between the social classes in 'this Metropolis' through the ambiguities attendant to the Hottentot Venus' humanity."[9] The pleasure and delight of such self-reassurance was meted out through the prospect of skin, a perfect alibi of sexual curiosity and fascination tucked beneath the guise of the biological and scientific.

In retrospect, the imagery of Sara Baartman looms most figuratively as the specter of both the terrors and traumas of the Black female body presumed available for consumption, a heuristic device cementing the visual politics that bind Black flesh to licentious sexuality. Baartman signifies the emergence and becoming of a pornotrope, the attenuated subjectivities between bodies and flesh, the deteriorating processes of objectification, of becoming a thing, where "the captured sexualities provide a physical and biological expression of 'otherness,' that place the Black female body as the preeminent site of racial and sexual difference."[10]

But such proceedings do not unfurl in vacuous, solitary accord. They are instead more clearly reflected in a complex theological tale of rescue, recovery, and abandonment, the varying attempts made by Baartman's contemporaries to rescue *her narrative*, redoubled by more contemporary criticism in Black studies and Black feminist scholarship to source the wounds generated by her disposability. In the preceding chapters I have suggested that the shifting coals between the imaginary of the Black Virgin and the Black Venus remain aglow with an imperial gaze fed a Christian theological imagination of the body and its consumption. "Women Are from Venus" now turns to *the* Black Venus, to the reassurances that the Black body provided against an emerging whiteness, to the anxieties and prescriptions that rest at the heart of a continued set of concerns and narratives around created order, and to the theological architecture of purity that synthesized her Black skin and female body as captive, even if not enslaved.

This chapter relinquishes the search for a historical Baartman to instead consider the making of an icon, the materialization of dark female flesh in the rise of the modern, and the fugitive assertions of Baartman that mark a praxis of freedom through struggle, to mark "the resistance of the object,"[11] while implicating Christian thought in the craft of the commodity. To do this requires we extrapolate the epistemologies built upon Baartman's buttocks, those that tether the relationship of theological thought to the exemplary global capitalist axiom: sex sells. Because before her untimely death in 1815, prior to the infamous dissection of her corpse, prior to the body cast that, affixed to a small platform, would make its way through exhibitions around the world; prior to the grotesque preservation and display of her brain and labia in the *Musee de l'Homme, a priori* to her immortal life as the (supposedly) definitive visual identification of a degenerate Black female sexual truth and trauma, Sara Baartman was the subject of a sex trafficking scandal.

142 IMMACULATE MISCONCEPTIONS

From the Bottom

> What makes the Hottentot so hot?
> Cowardly Lion
> *The Wizard of Oz*

If one has heard of the Hottentot Venus, it was likely with reference to her representation as an originary site of the sexual mythologies, tropes, and violence exercised over Black female flesh. Many are marginally familiar with her iconography—the early caricatures that exaggerated her features or depicted men fawning over her buttocks. She is the woman to which every reference to curvaceous celebrity, to which every critique of a culture of body modification and enhancement, all inevitably point. She is a reminder of every Black woman's silhouette, the rejoinder for augmented breasts, plumped lips, and injected behinds, the archival diagnostic of a Black woman's sexual disposability. And yet, is there more?

Baartman's life is readily redacted to her four-year stint as the Hottentot Venus, and is so frequently recounted from such a tight frame of analysis that it seems to make little difference that much of what is cited about her life is from an outdated set of source materials. Such narrative epistemologies constitute the economy of her icon, a legacy recounted and retold without recourse. This is what "we" thought we knew:

In 1810, a 22-year-old woman named Saartjie was smuggled into England. Baptized Sara Baartman while there, she was held against her will and exploited as the iconic visual of Black female sexuality marked by the size of her buttocks and her labia. She died tragically at the age of 25, where she was made fully available to the white Enlightenment thinker Georges Leopold Cuvier. Though she denied him the opportunity to examine her fully while she was alive, once she was dead he quickly organized a scientific escapade in the form of a proof texting dissection. Curvier oversaw the full casting of her body, and the preservation of her brain and genitals as living fossils of degeneracy. Her body and life were used to stabilize a legacy of endemic promiscuity that would "yield no truths," but would proliferate the idea of "legitimate quasi-theories of Black degeneration, degradation, and sexual deviance."[12]

The fabrication of Baartman as the Hottentot Venus was inured to such speculative clouds of disgust, amusement, and fascination that fogged the scientific imagination half-hearted and half-listening as they intuited and interpreted meaning even if contradicted by the human being fully within their view. But commodities are opportunities, not causes for care, and the construction of the fact of Baartman's body had her foundation staged in the racist science of the time. The Enlightenment return to the rational mind inspired dreams of the body and whiteness cemented in the concrete of colonialism, and Baartman stepped on stage in a world already swirling in the waters not just of Kantian philosophy, but of his racist anthropological assessments. It was Immanuel Kant's 1777 anthropological essays on race that offered the four classic phenotypical distinctions—white, Negro, Hun, and Hindustani. Herein Kant surmised a scale of existence, one even further reduced to solidify the nadir and apex of creation—"Negroes and whites are the base races," the "reason for assuming [this] is self-evident."[13] Kant too was taken with the female Hottentot, more particularly, her *pudenda*—the labia—in particular, though he reserved most of his writing attention for the Hottentots he classified as male.[14] Baartman's arrival came only three years after Kant's death, and already his significance and arrangement of the racial order pre-empted intrigue around the Hottentot body as site of hypothesis and probative discovery, impulses that undoubtedly fueled the incidents in the life of the Hottentot Venus.

The construction of truth is not limited to science, however, but to contemporary scholarship as well. For what has also failed to "yield truth" is the flattening of the Hottentot Event into a romantically tragic narrative, one that itself tropes a problematic narrative of oppression, subjection, and anti-Blackness. In the most prolific Baartman account to date, Clifton Crais and Pamela Scully note how the archive of Baartman's life was heavily determined by "the temptation of reading her history backward as a story of inevitable victimization."[15] This insistence has manifest in the numerous narrative details of Baartman's life that have been wrongly circulated since her reintroduction into the theoretical and popular canon.[16] The predominant narratives and citational practice of Baartman's representation are frequently rendered as explictly violent and wholly non-agential, emphasizing instead her naïveté, exacerbating the limits of her voice, ignoring the capacity for modalities of resistance or leverage, and priming the fragility and exoticism of her body as a corollary to her innocence all the more readily exploited, manipulated, and forced into slavery. Such tragic violence foregrounds the essentializing of Black women's experiences as literal flesh wound—originary, infected, perduring.

But genealogy excavates a more nuanced tale to be told. Arriving in London in her 30s, Baartman had already lived a rich and varied life. She knew the inner workings of rural life north of the Gamtoos River Valley, but had also navigated the urban trappings of Cape Town. She worked as a domestic servant. She was a lover. She was a mother who had given birth and experienced miscarriage. She spoke several languages. She was a musician, a skilled vocalist able to play several instruments. She had an incredible memory. She negotiated contracts and payments. When she arrived in London, she was the designer of the "native" conglomeration outfits that she wore. She loved carriage rides around the city on Sundays. She owned the rights to several of her pictures. She was baptized. She got married. She saw more of Europe than most Europeans ever did, much less to say the world. Baartman likely died closer to the age of 40, rather than the heavily cited 26 years of age.[17] Despite the obvious appeal of the image of the noble savage wronged by avaricious colonizing men, the trope of Sara Baartman as the eternally traumatized indigenous woman occludes a more complex rendering of her life.

In *The Black Body in Ecstasy*, Jennifer C. Nash examines a number of pioneering and formative texts that ground the "Black feminist theoretical archive," almost all of which cite the Hottentot Venus as "the paradigmatic case of racialized sexuality,"[18] the anchor to what Nash so helpfully describes as an "archive of pain."[19] From the moment of her performative inception, the Hottentot Venus bears the weight of the cyclical, repercussive violence exacted through the visual representation of Black women's bodies. The repeated citation of her trauma is so expected as to be cliché, but offers the definitive point of departure for feminist analysis and racial critique, a cautionary, centralized tale whose precedent is primary grounds for protest against the continued violent sexual depiction of Black women. Nash pushes us to more critically interrogate the archival claims to a shared and monolithic experience of trauma and injury as the precursor duly matched by the need to locate and employ a mode of recovery within the visual field. Such an antidotal task requires an investment in the very imaginary of representation and the power of the image, one that "enacts and enforces a view of visual culture that makes it impossible to theorize Black female pleasure from within the confines of the archive."[20] Nash is not working to negate the violence that Baartman experienced in life and death, rather, she argues we must not preclude acknowledging the ways pleasure and violence are often mutually constitutive. Even if rife with complexity, what is possible if one resists the assumption that the presence of agency somehow lessens the retributive claims that highlighting violence pursues?

The Black woman's body is not predestined for injury, yet the retellings of the Hottentot Venus eclipse all orbits but those that run tragic. Such a phenomena is a lesson learned in rote, a memory articulated through the histories of injustice and the powers of what bell hooks has more contemporarily termed "imperialist white-supremacist capitalist patriarchy."[21] In Baartman's case, it has proven productive and of great use-value to account primarily for the plural violence of her representation despite the instabilities and flux in her narrative. Perhaps this is because gray matters cannot gift us the justice we believe should be served, cannot extend us the legislations and legibility so often required in negotiations of jurisprudence and the nation state. Victims and perpetrators are scripted to battles fought in the arenas of the alleged, bound to the glaring light of narrative subjectivities. Shadows take first the form of doubt in the mire of interlocking oppressions, the power of their darkness enough to disrupt claims to legitimacy, retribution, or recovery. This of course depends on the color and content of the confessional subject, of the truth and virtue to which one is already imagined to naturally possess. It is as if oppression is governed by a one-drop rule, the hinted admixture of agency, the sheer potential for collusion enough to foreclose its properties. Polluted testimonies are of no use, and alibis must be either air-tight or exposed. Pleasure cannot preclude oppression. Miscegenation is the stuff of moral decay.

The citation of Baartman, or rather, the Venus, is critical because *she* is a Black Eve, the modern weathervane whose generative wounds are ever beholden to pain in the present, hermetically sealed from the possibilities of ambivalence beset by agency, much less, happiness. Though it bears strategic weight, the appeal of a romantic tragedy questions how we do or do not perceive oppression, and how the need to prove oneself as a victim determines the acceptable limits of one's agency. It also fails to challenge the moral implications of what womanist ethicist Katie Cannon describes as agency under constraint, who describes the ways classic ethical mores around the definitions and enactments of freedom, are most often inadequate to account for the material realities and negotiations of those facing a continuum of captivities.[22] Ironically, this logic hinges on the very rhetorical strategies employed by the white savior coalition who involved themselves in her legal case, those who tried to save her Black body from self-effacing demise, to serve and protect the decency and decorum of soon-to-be-Victorian England, to be the modern day abolitionists of their time, to send her back where she belonged—for her own sake, of course, to instantiate a sex slave refugee ban, to make London great again, a forgotten story which must be excavated. But what we must here note is the reality that the archives of pain, trauma, and representation are also so often responses to the denials of pain, the hollowing out of emotions and feelings and their effects, hauntings of the "afterlife of slavery,"[23] wherein we are all disciplined by fear and by trembling.

Which is dangerous when stories get true. For at some point between 1822 and 1850, the living museum of Sara Baartman's body was indeed mutilated postmortem and incarcerated in formaldehyde for the world to see. Under the racist scientific guise of discovery, the Hottentot Venus's skeleton, body cast, brain, and labia were placed on public display throughout Europe despite Baartman withholding consent to her body while she was alive. Her remains found a more permanent home in the *Musee de l'Homme*, rotating in and out of view alternately collecting dust until 1982, when the specimens were finally removed from public exhibition.[24] By then, Baartman had performed as the Hottentot Venus before millions. As Hortense Spillers described the ungendering of Black American women, we here in Europe can already bear witness to the displacement and distribution of the Black female body long before the American crucible "as a vestibular subject of culture, and as an instance of the 'flesh' as a primary or first-level 'body.'"[25] While there are many unknowns in Baartman's story, it is critical to shine light on the theological narrative that subtends her construction as the Hottentot Venus, to tell us more about what happened to her and why it happened as it did, and to point more broadly to the kinds of "radical imagining" we must necessarily attribute her life and story. Here first we must attend to the places where the pursuit of truth, goodness, mercy, and justice were imagined through her presence in London, and brought her case before the courts of whiteness.

Rapid Test

Presaging the mid-Atlantic slave trade, the conditions of European colonialism and the ramifications thereof rendered Black women's bodies objects of property, production, and reproduction through sexual violence and conquest. On multiple fronts, Christian theology was readily enacted through colonial expansion to buttress the architecture of racial distinction and cultural production. We know that Christian colonists aren't *exactly* known for minding the means to an end, particularly when eschatology and soteriology subtended the market calculations of slavery as an institution. Black *bodies* were justified as slave *bodies* through generous [white, Christian] assurances that their greatest good was being effected through slavery, the all too convenient theology, reinforced by baptismal formulation, that insisted the horrors of slavery, of Black people "now brought into some subjection," were but "a small matter in comparison of their souls, which would now possess true freedom for evermore."[26] How quickly one could truncate the "already-not-yet" to simply "*not yet*" when it came to the uses and denials of Black humanity.

By the time of Baartman's advent as the Venus, several Christians had grown a conscience about it, particularly the Clapham "Saints"—the cosmopolitan sect who briefly made their mission the Venus's rescue. The group was comprised of men (and one woman) of both money and influence in urban London who had a new theological agenda of liberation on their mind. These were the abolitionists, those who had a vocational calling that was dedicated certainly to the more humane treatment of all people, but whose commitments were also bolstered through their class, their vision of abolition a vehicle for a certain enactment of their English sense of moral superiority (particularly when compared to Americans). Under the leadership of William Wilberforce, the Saints successfully used their finances and clout to pressure British parliament to end the African slave trade in 1807. But laws don't always necessitate change; de facto often overrides de jure.

When the four abolitionists from the African Institute first came to see about Sara Baartman, they decidedly observed her unhappiness. They didn't have anything to say to her directly, but they collectively noted her solemn expression, her exasperated sighs as the minutiae evidencing her distress. They had been there before, but again they watched privately as her "Exhibitor" handled her as "any of the brute creation."[27] When one of the Saints finally asked Sara about the circumstances of her condition, she refused to answer. They heard in her silence not her resistance, but the resonance of their truth. The patricians left, certain they had just borne witness to slavery in supposed-to-be-free England.[28]

Sara Baartman, the first figure from Africa to "win public celebrity,"[29] was to be their viral video, the rescue mission that would catapult their profile in doing the abolitionist work of God. Convenient, as several of the *'saints'* had been cast as simply *'aint's'* in the months prior—this new case was perfect to quell the political controversies surrounding their personal activities, to help folks forget the questions raised about the private holdings (both land and people) that some of their most prominent members had between Jamaica and Sierra Leone, the suspicion that some of the abolitionists might actually be enslavers as well.

After the announcement of Baartman's arrival, the concern around her situation escalated swiftly and deliberately, as a strategic campaign promulgated by the Clapham Saints rallying against her public display was funneled through the news outlets of London. The back-and-forth conversation was calculated, incisive, and an incitement to court intervention (see Table 5.1). On October 11, three weeks to the day after the first *Morning Post* advertisement anticipated her full English debut, Zacharay McCauley, one of the Saints intent on seeing for himself, visited Cezar and Baartman. The following day, a letter of indictment and indignation serendipitously appeared in the *Morning Chronicle*. There, the writer claimed that Baartman—"wretched creature," "wretched object,"—was enslaved.[30] In the letter, the author lauds the wisdom of the newspaper editor before expertly feigning his own ignorance to the legal nuances of Britain's slave trade laws. The swift rhetorical plea allowed the writer to assert a juridical distinction between Baartman, whom he claimed to be a "poor slave," against "those beings who are sufficiently degraded to shew themselves for their own immediate profit, and where they act from their own free will."[31] "Those beings" was a clear reference to the carnival acts and their actors—dwarves, giants, exhibits of other 'exotic' races, and presumed prostitutes. Baartman would not garner sympathy if associated as being one of *them*, the "sufficiently degraded," as that would invalidate her as a worthy Christian cause. The appeal flattens Baartman's agency or complexity in service to her rescue, for one's choices, one's motives and ethics, *cannot* be ambiguous when a vision of liberation is bound to abject victimhood and the measure of one's deserving. It is a necessary gesture, a strategy still employed to evoke the kind of empathy and outrage necessary for legal recognition, particularly when her skin and body already testify against her. Baartman had to be better than the company she kept, had to be lexically shifted "from brutal savage to hapless simpleton," the preferred colonial subject.[32]

But while the argument ended there, it travelled by very specific route. The author doesn't claim the potential harm that *she* might be in, but rather narrates the harm that *she* is positioned to cause. The author writes of the danger *she* posed to society. The climax of the letter closes not on the problem of captivity, but the problem of her *indecency*, her "ribaldry" as that which is finally "contrary to every principle of morality and good order." What is most egregious in the Baartman exhibit is that she—her body, her display—offends the public. Only then does

148 IMMACULATE MISCONCEPTIONS

Table 5.1 Calendar of Events, Hottentot Venus, October 1810

\multicolumn{7}{c	}{October 1810}
Su	M	Tu	W	Th	F	Sa
30	1	2	3	4	5	6
7	8	9	10	11	12	13
				McCauley visits Baartman	*Morning Chronicle*: Letter to the Editor, signed "An Englishman"	*Morning Chronicle*: Response to "An Englishman," signed "Cezar" (likely Dunlop)
14	15	16	17	18	19	20
The Examiner: Letter from "A Constant Reader" with added editorial note	McCauley, Babington, and van Wageninge visit Baartman		*Morning Chronicle*: Letter to the Editor, signed "Humanitas" African Institute files affidavit	*Morning Post*: Letter to the Editor signed "A Man and a Christian"		*Morning Chronicle*: Response to Humanitas, signed "M. T."
21	22	23	24	25	26	27
The Examiner: Letter to the Editor, signed "Humanitas" (likely McCauley; and same from October 17)		*Morning Chronicle*: Second response from "Cezars" (Dunlop)	*Morning Chronicle*: Letter to the Editor, signed "Humanitas"			
28	29	30	31	1	2	3
The Examiner: Letter to the Editor, signed "Humanitas"	*Morning Post*: Letter to the Editor, signed "White Man"			Wm. Bullock files court affidavit		

the writer juxtapose the "offence to public decency" with "that most horrid of all situations, Slavery."[33] Signed only "An Englishman," the author effectively invokes an imagined community of common civility, couth, moral (and gendered) authority, and the political investment in respectability.

A response attributed to Hendrik Cezar was printed the very next day. In a show of editorial distance, the letter was introduced as being "from the person who exhibits this poor African female."[34] The notation was brief, but insisted that the exhibition was "for the joint benefit of both our families," and welcomed anyone with a need to speak to Baartman to confirm for themselves that this was truly the case.[35] Later encounters with Cezar would demonstrate the high unlikelihood that he had ever learned to read or write, much less that he had acquired fluency in the nuances of formal English conversation and the convention of editorial letter writing. It was far more likely that Dunlop wrote the fervent apology.

On Sunday, October 14, *The Examiner* printed a letter from "A Constant Reader," another Good Samaritan who expressed his desire "to state the case of a poor, unfortunate, friendless being . . . hoping by these means to attract the attention of some charitable person more powerful to assist her than I am."[36] The Constant Reader presents himself as a humble public servant, and paints a vivid narrative of his own naïveté and innocence that have compelled him to speak out. His description is of one transgressed, even assaulted by the seductive advertisements that enticed him beyond appeal—"the advertisements in the window caught my eye; and ignorant of what a sight I was to see,—a sight disgraceful both to decency and humanity,—I entered." There he witnesses shamble staging of an African setting from which Baartman climactically emerges when being called like a dog. As the reader-voyeur describes of his feeling:

> Never in my life did I feel my pity more strongly excited: with no other clothing than a tight dress, the colour of her skin, and a few rude ornaments, such as are worn by the nations of Southern Africa, the dreadful deformity of her person was fully displayed; and her face spite of the paint, with which, after the manner of her country, it was daubed, was strongly and deeply marked with misery.[37]

It is difficult to tell what arouses A Constant Reader most—his generous condolences, or the combination of tight dress, tawny skin, and tacky accessories that embellish "the dreadful deformity of her person." The relation of the reader's benevolence is fraught, a construction that relies on distance as the product of a wrenching narrative of betrayal into this torrid show, but requires the humanizing of the events to establish the foundation for his own salvific position. He *must* be offended by Baartman's body (and perhaps be willing to exacerbate the detail of events), and yet must disabuse and humanize the situation in order to make a universal appeal to rights and justice—"Will no one arise to protect her, because her colour and her form are different from our own?" The woman is in need of protection, but from what, and from whom is less clear. Is her protection for her own good, or for the society she contaminates? Even as an ambassador of good will, the need for intervention, and the power dynamics that perform intervention, are left uninterrogated. Never does he take ownership for the conditions of possibility, for those across the England countryside that would find such an attraction, so attractive. The letter itself ends with an appeal for intervention, particularly from the Missionary Society, who are likely also to be astonished by the tarnished civility produced by such poverty and abuse.

These rhetorics trade in the liberal politics of the newspaper and its readership; it's *constant* readers, as it were, so much so that the end of the letter is not the end of the article. The letter is accompanied by an editor's note that redresses Cezar's assertions in the *Morning Chronicle* edition featured the Friday before. There, restating Cezar's comments, the editors warn that he "must be listened to with caution, as we have been informed that on her first arrival in London, she was offered for sale by Capt. Cezar."[38]

Monday brought McCauley back around to see Sara Baartman, this time with his friends. Again, they learned so little as to be called nothing. Two days later, another letter appeared in the *Morning Chronicle* from a writer who signed himself "Humanitas," who questioned Cezar's false transparency around interviewing Baartman and called for a deeper investigation into the circumstances of her boarding ship and arriving in England.[39] That same day Zachary Macaulay, Thomas Babington, and Peter van Wagenige—members of the African Institution, "the object of which is the civilization of Africa"—officially filed their affidavit at Chancery Lane.[40] Culminating the one week anniversary from McCauley's first visit to Baartman, the *Morning Post* ran yet another letter from the editor on Thursday, October 18.[41] The weekend brought a response in the *Morning Chronicle* addressed to "Humanitas," questioning the authorship of the earlier responses from Cezar. The writer M.T. claimed to have met Cezar and indicated that Cezar actually knew very little English at all.[42] Importantly, the writer implied that perhaps Baartman was not the only person being manipulated in the situation.

The weekend brought another letter from "Humanitas," this time in the *Examiner*. In retrospect, it is very likely that McCauley himself was behind the benevolent pseudonym, and quite possibly the same "Humanitas" who wrote the letter to the *Morning Chronicle* just a few days earlier. The letter was eloquent and sophisticated, and rehearsed the numerous problems and discrepancies with the reportage on Baartman. The writer presses against the claims to Baartman's happiness and comfort as "the old rallying point" of justification, the interpretive gymnastics that argue that "the slaves are not so miserable as you think them to be, come and see them happy under our *kind and generous protection*."[43] He sees instead the scene of subjection, held pat beneath "the ascription of excess and enjoyment to the African effaces the violence perpetrated against the enslaved."[44] White dignity is now at stake, as the writer rallies those of the highest morale to the cause: "Let the honour of Englishmen rescue their character from the disgrace of keeping a foreigner, and a female too, in worse than Egyptian bondage."[45] He, too (or, if Macauley, *again*) calls for legal intervention (*habeas corpus*), calls for help by name (*that noble triumvirate Roscoe, Sharp and Clarkson*), and calls for institutional support (the Missionary Society) to intervene in a "disgusting, afflictive, and mortifying sight."[46]

On Tuesday, October 23, "Cezars" (Dunlop) responded yet again, but this time, with a different question of autonomy and self-determination: "Has she not as good a right to exhibit herself as an Irish Giant or a Dwarf?"[47] The question of work, of labor and profit, of the problematic assumption of "degradation" that the first Humanitas letter had condemned (of the exhibited, not of those who put their money where their awe and curiosity were) are brought to light. What was more displeasing—the danger of Baartman, or the reality of her profit? Cezar also announced the end of his public involvement in the exhibition. Given that his "mode of proceeding ... seems to have given offense to the Public, I have given the sole direction of it to an Englishman, who now attends."[48] Apparently having a white man in charge would clean up the show.

On Wednesday another Letter to the Editor from "Humanitas" ran in the *Morning Chronicle*, questioning the authorship of the letter signed Cezar and urging a response "for the sake of this country."[49] A final letter from yet another "Humanitas" appeared in the *Examiner* that Sunday, a response to Cezar's question. The writer argued that yes, the Hottentot Venus could perform as she liked, but it was naïveté, ignorance, or a suspicious combination of both if one thought she received any money from her exhibit. The impassioned writer described as such:

> after having run the gauntlet through the three capitals of England, Scotland, and Ireland, and traversed their provincial towns, dragged through them with greater barbarity than Achilles dragged the body of Hector at the foot of his chariot round Troy's walls, this miserable female will be taken back to the Cape; not enriched by European curiosity, but rendered poorer if possible than when she left her native soil.[50]

The *Morning Post* ran one more article from a "White Man" on Monday, October 29, culminating the print flurry over Baartman's circumstance, "a classic confrontation between heated humanitarianism and cold commerce, between the abolitionist conscience and the entrepreneurial ideal, between love and money."[51] At the end of the week, William Bullock, who Dunlop had offered a chance to buy giraffe skins along with offering the business of Baartman for sale, filed his affidavit on November 1. The case would be evaluated within a matter of weeks on November 26.

During preparations for the hearing, one of the court justices suggested that, on the grounds of indecency, criminal proceedings could be initiated against Cezar "for a breach of public decorum."[52] Full circle to the first moment of outcry, "public decency" was a legal category rooted in the outgrowth of the Protestant Reformation and the emergence of the Church of England as a convergence between the church and the state. The distinction between public and private marked the criminality of acts and behaviors that may not have usually fallen outside of the precedent for legal activity—which is to say, acts that "may or may not be illegal according to the prevailing legal provisions [may] become so when they are visible in the public domain instead of being confined to a private place, where that behavior could not directly harm the public."[53] When thrust beyond the confines of a private domestic space, the juridical distinctions around a plethora of actions were shifted into a new register of public (moral) safety, adjudicated through a lens of Christian decorum. From the fifth century, theologians like Augustine described the sacraments of the Christian church as outward and visible signs of an inward and invisible grace; but by the emerging Victorian period in England, the outward appearance of decency and conduct were signs not just of one's inner virtue and true Christian identity, but a critical aspect of a public, state-sanctioned agenda of civil performance: demeanor and conduct were appeals to pedigree, couth and decorum were markers of propriety, and all were linked to developing modalities of racial comparison, criminal surveillance and discipline.

Which is why, after the torrent of letters and public attention, the English courts first advised that there was a case for Sara Baartman, but only when brought before them as an incident of "public indecency," rather than that of illegal enslavement. When McCauley signed that first letter "An Englishman," he alluded to every one of the social mores of the time—mores coded through gender, citizenship, class, and the lens of *whiteness*. Invoking the authority of his social position, McCauley knew that the appeal of moral outrage around Sara Baartman was one that would be most effective when annotated. He problematized her presence as representing a crisis of character, refinement, and taste. She was a victim, but only in as much as she held the capacity to *victimize*, the capacity to "damage the welfare of the nation by vitiating its moral standards."[54] What found the most emphasis was that which found the most empathy—the pornotrope, the sexual innuendo, the erotics of her configuration—her need for more clothes, rather than questions of her labor and migration. The trail began and finally, the courts turned away from the media commentary to their supposed subject. Sara Baartman would have to speak to her situation—the Hottentot Venus was to have a hearing.

Trial and Error

Wounded by slavery.
A wretched object.
An unfortunate being.
Poor creature.
A helpless Black woman.

When the Clapham "Saints" offered their official depositions before the court, they got what they wanted. On November 28, 1810, Sara would finally speak. This was the moment to unveil the hidden truths of an exploited Hottentot, to confess to tales of trauma and pain, to plumb the depths of her bondage. The problem—one among many in the circumstance—was that that the words she spoke were not the ones such "Saints" had hoped to hear. Remaining just as elusive as her "apron," Sara failed them. Despite serious discrepancies in the dates, times, and languages of her supposed working contract, as well as the problem of whether or not she was ever actually paid for her labor (she wasn't); of whether or which languages she could speak or read, she—or at least, the *paraphrase* of what-she-supposedly-said in her three hour inquisition, her given Dutch testimony, taken in her second language because they couldn't find anyone who could accurately translate her first—*that* said that she said she had everything she needed. Her only complaint was that she often found it to be cold.[55] When Sara Baartman did not perform on the stand for these men, when she did not comply and rely upon their promises and goodwill within the first few weeks of coming upon foreign shores, when she did not attest to the narrative they had in mind, it was demonstrative. When she was not the kind of confessing subject the abolitionists wanted, *needed* her to be, they abandoned her completely. By not confirming in her confession, Sara Baartman was ultimately confirmed in her nature. The Hottentot Venus wasn't just a performance—it was her true, corrupt person.

One is pressed to ask why Baartman would cooperate otherwise—what is appealing about a call to confess to a room of wealthy, white men—the same kinds of men who gazed at her stocking covered body, even attempting prodding, groping her; Englishmen, speaking a language she didn't fully understand, who didn't understand the risks and realities of what her confession might mean, all of whom knew nothing about her? What the affidavits do not allow for are a reading of Baartman's archival refusal as practices of subversion, resistance, and fugitivity— "nimble and strategic practices that undermine the categories of the dominant."[56] Despite abolition being on trend for the Clapham Saints, this was not Baartman's first encounter with folks who saw her body before they saw her person. Did it matter that Hendrik Cezar—the Black South African man who exhibited her (and who may have at one time been her lover), the man who was the face of the operation, but not the white financier—was named as the defendant in the trial? Did it matter that the goal of her "self-appointed protectors"[57] was to repatriate her to the Cape, without a clear sense of why she left, nor the option of other circumstances (seeing as she would no longer have a job) for her to stay in Europe? Surely there was no lexical recognition, no T-Visa equivalents available to African women in 1810.[58] Baartman's resistance to the confines of juridical representation, the potential criminalization of the man who may have been her partner but who was nonetheless racialized and scapegoated in the scenario, point not to her ignorance but to her awareness that those rallying to her side could not inherently be trusted to support or sustain her, particularly given the complete eliding of any complexity to the conditions of her life in England. In the midst of the Saints' own controversies, and subsequently their own priorities and commitments, perhaps we can only take cues from the ways they interacted with—which is to say, the ways they *didn't* interact with Baartman. Perhaps she was keen to the fact that what they *really* wanted was to "rescue an African, not engage one."[59]

Laura Agustín coined the term "Rescue Industry" to describe the "modern-day" anti-trafficking machine, a movement of multiple actors—from lawyers and legislators to humanitarians and missionaries—who set out to *help*, to *save* the sexually vulnerable (usually women and children) who simultaneously find their own meaning in life in doing so. But for those who are "tired of living an anemic life,"[60] for those who want to be "the real heroes of the faith,"[61] the opportunity to "save" someone from "slavery" is a production funneled by, as Agustín describes, "non-self-critical helpers who assume they Know Better than the rest of us how we all ought to live."[62] This is nothing less than a charade of imperialism as benevolence and care, the promotion of freedom—the imaginary of freedom and abolition being, as Yvonne Zimmerman describes, rooted in Protestant morality—that turns rescue into an ideology, privileging the act over the accounts of people's actual lives, and failing to account for an intersectional analysis of a global sex trade that takes seriously concerns around race, class, gender, migration, social support, access, labor, and care in its considerations of sex.[63] Indeed the same racial logic that undergirded the civilizing mission of dark bodies in other worlds across the globe with the emergence of colonization and enslavement is that which continues on pervasively in the rescue industry today. Analyzing the legal facet of Sara Baartman's life in England—that which came before the scientific racism that dismantled and displayed her postmortem body—traces how the racially entrenched framework of rescue directly shaped the framework of intervention, the "acceptable" lens through which a "victim" will or won't be comprehended. For all intents and purposes, Baartman functions for us not as the site of Black representative trauma, nor a banner for sexual empowerment, but as the paradigm of the 'modern slave.'[64] *By definition*, Baartman fit the profile, the imagined demographic of the poor and helpless, the kinds of dingy, disadvantaged young girls constantly troped in the contemporary United States and elsewhere abroad continuing to replicate "white men saving brown women from brown men."[65] The false biographic details circulated as Baartman's story emphasize her youthfulness, her lack of exposure, her ignorance, and the savagery of her homeland—to this day, she remains captive to the narrations of anonymous white men's mouths rather than her own—"wretched object," "poor creature," "helpless." If only she had been the kind of rescued subject she was supposed to be.

Baartman instead continued to hide in plain sight, not even naked but clothed in a flesh toned body stocking, promulgating the illusions of capture while also tricking the system. Her continued refusals, met with her claims, point more deeply to an epistemology of strategic survival and self-preservation executed by repeated subversion of the mores of dominant culture. As womanist ethicist Katie Cannon describes, we must consider the "differences between ethics of life under oppression and [these] established moral approaches that take for granted freedom and a wide range of choices."[66] She continues, reminding that "the cherished ethical ideas predicated upon the existence of freedom and a wide range of choices proved null and void in situations of oppression."[67] However, Baartman's narrative reminds us that such performances are always negotiated with great risk. If, as Fred Moten describes, "Fugitivity . . . is a desire for and a spirit of escape and transgression of the proper and the proposed," we must not cede the strength required to sustain the consequences of transgression, even as they manifest a kind of freedom. By not playing the part of conveying her experience, her life through a lens of misery and pity, by not saying that she needed to be rescued, the tides of justification were turned completely against Baartman. The abject negligence of the Clapham Saints after her trial suggests they too concluded that Baartman was part and party to her own exploitation. In his assessment, Lindfors suggested that Baartman "may have been the victim of the cruelest kind of predatory ruthlessness, but her collusion in her own victimization is unmistakable."[68] Accusing her of falling prey to her own capitalist aspirations, he surmises her final defeat: "To put it plainly, she may have engaged in prostitution as well as exhibitionism. Her degradation may have been complete."[69]

The suggestion that Baartman worked as a prostitute is a conclusion that undermines the urgent concerns around the horizons of Baartman's labor, and reinforces the notion of a *proper* victim. A helpless Black woman indeed? Or otherwise? Perhaps really, just really, the rumors were true. Maybe she liked being touched, maybe she liked being seen. But let's think for a moment—so what if she did? Various critical archives have returned to Baartman as a generative sight of woundedness and trauma, conferring pain and perpetuating violent stereotypes particularly in reference to Black female sexuality as determined through the white gaze of Black women's bodies.[70] Understandably so, when coercion and consent are not always easily discerned, or when circumstances leave one "disempowered to consent."[71] But does this proceed as if pleasure and pain cannot ever coexist? As if empowerment and exploitation are only mutually exclusive categories? What if we consider Baartman a protagonist who exhibits a different account of moral agency even under the fathomless constraints of her condition? For as Katie Geneva Cannon wrote of the ethical realities of Black women's lives in the United States, "the real-lived texture of Black life requires moral agency that may run contrary to the ethical boundaries of mainline Protestantism. Black women may use action guides which have never been considered within the scope of traditional codes of faithful living."[72] The suggestion that Baartman—particularly as proxy for *any* Hottentot, any Black woman—was a prostitute was not exactly new, but there is no complexity to the social conditions either of prostitution or Black women's labor in the British context at the time. There is no discussion of prostitution as a form of labor, however protracted, much less a consideration of the economic conditions for Black women in foreign lands, where sex work might be a profitable option for someone who would need to work and make money. But as it is with the characterization of sex work writ large (under some umbrellas, Baartman's very display would have fallen into this category), the ascriptions of agency are used against the very subjects they help constitute. In Lindfors telling, we finally have the turn to the subject, all eyes are on Baartman. And yet, her agency is only granted in order to inversely magnify the inner depravity that condemns her to her own devices. Despite the impulse to resist delineating categories of pain and pleasure as exclusive, the suspicion and subsequent evaluation of pleasure is only intelligible through the lens of moral and character judgment. Pleasure remains possible only as perversion, an immoral and theologically conscribed concupiscence.

By the end of her trial, Baartman—Black, closer to nature, licentious, perceived as *willing to give herself away*—is not the Madonna but the whore, the Black Eve of debasement and disobedience, a specter of reprobation. As "Venus," she stood diametrically opposed to all things Virgin, holy, and pure. If she wasn't a victim, what else could she be? Baartman's Blackness foreclosed the ways in which one could perceive her oppression, the lack of her victimhood determined by her inability to meet the acceptable *limits* of one's agency. But the exploration of agency only undermines the significance of Baartman's pain if a limited moral framework through which we imagine injury and harm requires such diminishing, if she must be refused any interiority, if the only way to acknowledge harm and victimization is to eschew all complexity. But the reality is that Baartman's case far more accurately raises more questions about the tangled nuances inherent to the ideas of agency, liberation, captivity, voice, desire, resistance, commerce, and consumption that so often escape us in considering the subjectivity of (predominantly understood) anyone whose work might be considered sex work, and anyone who may—through violence or not—be involved in the global sex trade. It raises questions for us about the complexities of *sex* as well as *sex work*, at its most broadly defined, but also about the racialization of pleasure and sexual moralities that generate from a Christian theological landscape of sexual prudence and purity, where the echoing silences of complicity in market cycles fail to account for an imperial gaze materialized through race, gender, sex, and fetish commodity—what exactly made the market for Baartman's display in the first place? What Baartman's case questions for us are the enduring tropes of embodiment, the ways of seeing and encountering certain kinds of bodies, that often drive a liberatory praxis without disrupting the circulations of power that subtend subjection in the first place.

Behind the Curtain

> There is nothing more famous in natural history than the apron (*tablier*) of Hottentots, and, at the same time, no feature has been the object of so many arguments.
>
> George Cuvier

> Pay no attention to that man behind the curtain.
>
> *The Wizard of Oz*

In 1982, famed historian Stephen J. Gould found himself wandering the halls of the *Musee de l'Homme* in Paris. His good friend Carl Sagan had toured the collection and its findings years before, and the inspired Gould traced his colleague's journey through the "back wards" of natural history. He was on the lookout for the anatomical preservations of the famous scientist Paul Broca, the man who first figured out that brain functions were localized, and who was an assiduous collector of anatomical parts, most especially brains.[73] Broca thought that his collections and measurements of varied human anatomy would definitively answer the evolution of man, and finalize the hierarchy of being "from chimp to Caucasian."[74] His faith in the project was so great that he donated his own brain to his collection, the relics of quantitative pursuit, the predictable mode of scientific racism of the time. Gould was literally browsing through brains when he stumbled across an unexpected find. After rows and rows of jars containing the mushy organ tissue—all white, all male, still retaining boundedness to a clear biological inflection of race and science, "In three smaller jars," Gould writes, "I saw the dissected genitalia of three Third World women. I found no brains of women, and neither Broca's penis nor any male genitalia grace the collection."[75] The jars were labeled clearly: *une négresse, une péruvienne*, and *la Vénus Hottentotte*, that is, the Hottentot Venus.

What Gould had accidentally discovered was the time capsule of Georges Leopold Cuvier. On January 1, 1816, within mere hours of her death, Cuvier arranged for the dissection of Sara Baartman's body. Baartman had come to France in September 1814 to an audience primed and hungry for the most figurative caricature of the Hottentot Venus, every moment of her performance advertised to deliver savage delight. Expectations were high, as "both scientific and popular understanding placed her within an imaginary Khoekhoe culture that allowed for no learning, no movement, no history."[76] This was again the crafted projection of the atavistic and the primitive, the Black body as intermediary link in a chain of evolved hierarchy of being, a pristine and authentic primary text who could "reveal the supposed horrors of the primitive" or likewise recall "a primordial Eden of the noble savage."[77]

Cuvier, at the time a renowned professor, head of the *Muséum national d'histoire naturelle*, Napoleon protégé, and founder of the academic discipline of comparative anatomy, received one of the earliest invitations to come see the Hottentot Venus for himself.[78] He ignored the offer. In the meantime, Baartman continued the fantasy of the Hottentot Venus as her performance gained French renown, and where the expectations of her monstrosity, of her ugliness, and of her recorded "steatopygia" (the scientific explanation of her pathological "condition" of "enlarged" buttocks) were exacerbated to their fullest potential across the Francophone landscape. Here in Paris, the work her body did to anchor the superiority of white onlookers was exquisite: "It was as if the more modernity unhinged the accepted truths of religion, authority and historical change, the more people sought something absolutely certain and fixed."[79]

Things deteriorated quickly in January of 1815, when Henry Taylor, the man who travelled with Baartman to France and had worked as her exhibitor, exchanged hands with S. Reaux, the animal showman who would now take his place. Well-connected and an experienced entertainment businessman, under Reaux's auspices, the Hottentot Venus' audiences expanded in every direction. One can only gesture the multiple psychoanalytic renderings of his inventive modifications to her performances, including the collar he chose to parade her in through the homes of the Parisian elite. When Reaux inquired again as to if Cuvier would be interested in assessing the marvelous Hottentot Venus, this time, Cuvier wouldn't resist.

On the whole, the idea of the Hottentot was not simply a general reflection of sub-Saharan African people groups, but was singled out as a particular breed, a separate related race that was perhaps the "most ill-favored of all those that populate Africa."[80] More specifically, the differences between "Black Africans" and Hottentots were evidenced through the sex/gender distinction among females. Though travel literature and scientific assessment would both express various nuances of these differences, sometimes juxtaposing the presumptions of lewd sexuality and erotica of sub-Saharan African Black women with the supposed heavily oiled, smellier, uglier, animalistic Hottentots, the deepest fantasy around the Hottentot people were the curiosities of their sexual organs.[81] As Samuel Morton would write, the Hottentot was particular, if not exceptional, because the female Hottentot body was marked by "two very remarkable peculiarities or deformities: viz, humps behind their buttocks, like those on the backs of dromedaries, and a disgusting development of the *labia pudendi*."[82] Hottentot *females* were queer not only at the points of their imagined lack of delicateness (which is to say, a certain inversion of masculinities when compared to Hottentot *males*),[83] but at the site of their difference from others gendered as *women*. Hottentot "women," in the eyes of racial anthropology and ethnography, were (m)aligned by the connections their genitalia made to animality rather than a lens of their humanity. As Strother describes, "What first language, then supposed lack of religion, suggested could finally be *represented* for all to see in the genitals of the Hottentot woman."[84] In other words: "the female body held the secret."[85] So they thought. But this secret was enough to drive scientists mad, a mythology so committed to the "willful misunderstanding" of the Hottentot people in pernicious, pervasive, absurd and ludicrous ways that "one is tempted to qualify it as a collective hallucination."[86] Enlightenment thinkers from Kolb to Kant to Diderot, from Voltaire to Montesquieu and Rousseau had all taken great interest in the Hottentot's culture and history (or, to a degree, lack thereof), and Cuvier's fascination with classification would drive him to join the roster when he went to meet with Baartman that March.

After that meeting, under the supervision of Cuvier (who was at the time assisted by Henri de Blainville), Baartman agreed to be scientifically sketched for study. For three days she posed as her body was outlined from every angle and sightline, templates of her frame that would live on through space and time. However, despite Cuvier's pleas and insistent advances, Baartman refused to strip completely naked. She also defiantly refused to allow him to physically examine her body. As he would later mention in his dissection notes, "She keeps her apron [*tablier*] carefully concealed, either between her thighs or still more deeply, and it was only after her death we even knew she possessed it."[87] It is unclear how Cuvier reacted in person to Baartman's self-making, and her unwillingness to consent to his demands, but his satisfaction and avidness on the occasion of her death are cause for alarm, and his unrelenting sense of a right to Baartman's body. One can readily look to Cuvier's opening statement of his anatomical observations of Baartman's body, which betray his sexual imaginary around the Hottentot people as the heart of his entire exercise: "There is nothing more famous in natural history than the [*tablier*] apron of Hottentots."[88] Despite Baartman's clear refusals in life, she had no recourse to Cuvier's access to her body in death, nor could she speak to the way her body would come to be classified. But it is important to note that more than a perverse scientific fascination, Cuvier also brought a deeply religious worldview, a deeply Christian *theological* curiosity to the dissection table.

To understand this, we turn first to a question of translation foregrounding the "apron" obsession. Stephen Gould helpfully explains a critical mistake first made in a standard translation from the work of Carolus Linneaus (1707–78) whose racial classifications foregrounded the work of Cuvier in the years to come. Linnaeus' original work on the classification of human beings (*Homo sapiens*) included taxonomy of four distinct racial types, a paradigm that would inform opinions about racial hierarchy and supremacy that continue to endure even now, in an ever-racialized unfolding present. Of course, Linnaeus' classifications of Africans were, as expected, degrading and racist, but as Gould points out, included a reference to the *feminae sinus pudoris*. According to Gould, "this has usually been translated 'women are without shame—a slur quite consistent with the rest of his words.'"[89] However, the correct Latin for "without shame" is rendered *sine purdore*, not *sinus pudoris*. Gould notes the "ubiquity of the mistake" is likely due to poor or sloppy spelling in the medical Latin and suggests that Linnaeus' original observation was *not* a comment on Black women's sexuality, but that "Linnaeus was only saying that African women have a genital flap."[90] Cuvier renders Linaeus' *sinus pudoris* in French as *tablier*.

But the fascination with the *tablier* persisted anatomically as well, as the question of size and shape fell readily inside the ideas of anatomical measurement as indicative of the assumptions along a racial-aesthetic scale of comparison. Yes, the *tablier* was a site of assessment, a place of reference for assigning qualities of beauty, nature, humanity, and evolution by its proportions, a metaphor for the greater order of human being. Cuvier managed multiple intelligences as motivation for his investigation, his curiosity as Christian as it was "scientific." Cuvier's particular brand of Christianity is likely indeed why he is not as immediately resonant in or regularly cited in the historical archives. Though he falls among many contemporaries whose influence and infamy for racial pseudo-science inflect their dossiers, Cuvier's legacy remains more muted, "primarily because posterity has deemed incorrect the two cardinal conclusions that motivated his work in biology and geology—his belief in the fixity of species and his catastrophism."[91] Indeed, Cuvier was a Creationist, subscribing to a theology that insisted that the timeline of the earth could be interpreted through a "Mosaic chronology."[92] In a world where theology was regularly at odds with (though still arguably *informing*) scientific interrogation, Cuvier was a defender of the Church, affirming God's creation, the universality of the flood of Noah, and found in Scripture the Rosetta stone of scientific discovery. Indeed, in an apologetic reversal of sorts, Cuvier did not "invoke geology and non-Christian thought as window dressing for 'how do I know, the Bible tells me so.' Rather, he uses the Bible as a single source among many of equal merit as he searches for clues to unravel the earth's history."[93]

In the expansion of modernity, Christian theological justifications of Blackness were tied to the curse of Ham, and with women as the second "weaker" sex, the Black woman was readily an anomaly at the crossroads of two reckless paths. How would Cuvier imagine the woman of dark flesh through a biblical lens? Arguably through the *tablier*, as holy curtain to be torn in two, or perhaps, an altar meant for sacrifice. According to Gould, Cuvier was somewhat versed (if only anecdotally) with practices of female circumcision in Ethiopia. As "people of intermediate hue and geography," he assumed that the practice reflected the proportions of the labia as well, guessing Ethiopian women's genitals to measure somewhere "between curtains and full clearance."[94] Cuvier also conjectured that practices of circumcision were rooted in both the erotic and religious. He recounted stories of

Portuguese Jesuits converting the king of Abyssinia during the sixteenth century, who "felt that they were obliged to proscribe this practice [of female circumcision]" because they associated the practice as a remnant from Judaic traditions. But as the story goes, without circumcision, the young (Catholic) women could not find husbands, "because the men could not reconcile themselves to such a disgusting deformity."[95] Shortly thereafter, the Pope authorized the reestablishment of the custom.

Cuvier connected circumcision to sexuality, describing that, in the name of easier sexual access, "the negresses of Abyssinia are inconvenienced to the point of being obliged to destroy these parts by knife and cauterization (*par le fer et par le feu*)."[96] What Cuvier did not take into account was his own fetish for the ritual, his desire to cut and conquer, to have dominion over the woman of color's genitalia. Justified by both science and vocation, he too dreamed of circumcising (dare we say castrating?) the Hottentot. The fruit of her body was not a tree off limits in his scientific *jardin*, but readily available for his consumption. Her genitalia would be the sign and the mark of creaturely existence, but it would signify whether she was closer to the rest of the negro race, or to that of the orangutans. His tone after the autopsy seems satisfied, proud, with an air of superiority to lay claim to a kind of foundational theoretician vis-à-vis his findings of Baartman's body: "I have the honor to present to the Academy the genital organs of this woman prepared so as to leave no doubt about the nature of her *tablier*."[97] Of course what Cuvier 'found' wasn't an apron or a curtain, a remnant of some earlier Neanderthal function many had surmised. Instead, he solved the mystery quite plainly, concluding that the enlarged labia minora of the vagina left an exaggerated impression to the untrained eye. The rumors were a case of mistaken identity.

Cuvier's background provides a glimpse into the ways Christian ideas, as tied to Christian-colonial enterprise, were foundational to the shaping of the world in which Europe imagined itself. Though this world was made possible by scientific and philosophic interventions, though this world followed deeply in the path carved by the Enlightenment, there often remained a kind of theological superiority around the fixity to which ideas of the self were tied. The scientific language of developmental progress, of strivings for perfection, of ascendency and *racial* election, only mimic the theological cartography of salvation history, and reflect a social performance of Christianity that arose across the period of colonial expansion. Anne McClintock describes how the social hierarchies of imperial power created a relational dialectic between the colony and the metropole that effectively worked to engender colonial encounters. Taking a view toward the consumer racism that proliferated between Britain and the African continent in the nineteenth century, she describes how the metropole was a place of conspicuous consumption, a space where the imperial spectacle could be placed on display. Alternatively, the colony was a performative space of the opposite nature, an exhibition hall of the Victorian cult of domesticity. The two spaces worked together to strengthen their respective imaginaries by constituting the other—"as the domestic space became racialized, colonial space became domesticated."[98] McClintock takes Baartman as a critical example of the enacting of such Victorian subjectivity. The logics of pride, prudence, class, and civilized behaviors were ideas produced in and by the presence of the Black body in London. The Black female body, as a reproductive body, only escalated racial projections through what McClintock describes as *panoptical time*, the objective, knowing gaze cast over a fixed body and history from the point of invisibility, and *anachronistic space*, exemplified in the structure of the museum, where vision cast over the primitive and atavistic can be materialized, dismembered then re-membered in a particular way out of time, however disoriented or disorienting by the nostalgia of one's own attachments.[99]

The Baartman exhibitions were an amalgamation of scientific discovery, monstrous display, shock and awe, nostalgia and living museum, as the Hottentot Venus performed the atavistic within modernity. But what Cuvier's dissection unearthed was the desire for historical collapse, for a condensed, compacted meaning through which to experience both space and time. As the world was expanding, Cuvier and his colleagues wished for it to contract. Leaving no stone unturned, no skull unmeasured, no curtain un-lifted were all mechanisms of mastery and control in a world where dominance was most certainly in flux, and where *masters* were being undone. These are the terms in which we see Baartman's effect on the racial and gendered imaginations of Europe. Her presence as fetish object marks the intimacies between scientific racism and commodity racism, but her exploitation is elicited against the backdrop of Christianity and whiteness, for at the junction of panoptical time and anachronistic space lies salvation history, the Christian exceeding of the Jew, and the election of the (white) Christian. The exploration of the Black body was rife with modalities of creation and fall, of progression and possibility that situated her body within Christian thought, and returned to a theological ground zero—a Black woman who held the keys to the Kingdom.

Hindsight

> It is not wrong to go back for that
> which you have forgotten.
> *definition:* sankofa
> Asanta Adinkra symbol

Jars of genitals. We do not often think hard enough about the dynamics of incarceration, of the carceral properties of elements like formaldehyde, of what is left behind on shelves, of what curiosities are tucked away in dark cabinet corners, the backwards on back wards. If Baartman was put on celebrity display in life, she became even more iconic and ubiquitous in death, traveling the world in the form of a plaster body cast, or awaiting the random eyes who might look up and see her labia floating on a forgotten shelf in a museum.

Baartman's narrative is an unprecedented case of migration and movement particular to the realities of dark, eroticized female flesh, and how the mythologies of this flesh manifest in the market realities of labor. Her life speaks to the fabricated borders of countries and societies, demarcations between primitive and modern, colony and metropole, distinctions between Black and white, domestic and wild, dirty and clean. Hers is a story that muddles the lines of protection, precarity and pleasure, concerns flattened by the demand for confession, concerns undermined in the pursuit of science, where her resistance was part of a continued struggle for subjectivity in a world intent only on seeing the so-called 'Venus' in her.

I cited Baartman first as a paradigm of modern trafficking precisely because too many white Christian evangelically informed anti-trafficking organizations *fail to cite her*. This is likely because they do not know, which is an extension of the reality that one cannot know what one refuses to look for or to see. The case for modern slavery is distinct from the mid-Atlantic trade, but its hierarchy rests on a continued denial of the racial textures, the preceding tides of the trade that manifest in a global sex market, that spiral the production of certain kinds of bodies as commodity fetish, as being available for consumption. Expanding the narratives around what happened to Sara Baartman during those precious first weeks of the Venus' debut *makes visible* the *invisible*, the good intentions that pave roads in wrong directions, and the need to interrogate the theological frameworks of purity and decency that subtend moral convictions around what kinds of sex puts certain flesh on the market.

Citing Baartman as a paradigm of sex-trafficking discourse and as a sex-trafficked subject names the competing narratives, the multiple possibilities and the complexities of sexual desire, as well as the overlooked refusals, the explicit strategies of resistance despite the multiple ways race structured surveillance of Baartman's body. It also explicitly names race and the theological imagination as critical ideologies that subtend the conditions of the global sex trade. Naming these narratives do not preclude violence, the place of violence, the material realities of violence, the effects of violence, nor the importance of violence in the narrative of the global sex trade. But to name violence as singularly representative, or represented, in Baartman's story, or any story, is the precise moment in which a universal of sex and its moral attachments, as theological and ethical concepts, occludes the questions of power, justice, agency, and desire. Black life cannot be thought in the absence of desire, and silence does not foreclose the articulation of agency. And yet, where we have clear echoes of Baartman's own voice, too easily that voice is reduced to a semblance of the coerced. Such a project is encapsulated through the utter disregard for her body, disconnected from her dignity as a human, and split from consideration that she may be a person with a soul.[100] For the conditions of Baartman's life were related to her identity as a pure-but-*un*holy specimen, part of an authentic but unworthy people. Devastatingly the conditions of her death rendered her more captive than in life. What then must we make of what we have left, particularly the visual legacy of the Hottentot Venus?

In *Listening to Images*, Tina M. Campt reminds us of the complexities beholden to colonial ethnographic imagery. Highlighting the stunning and perplexing portraiture of Black South African women, Campt describes "the tense grammar of photographically stilled presentations of vulnerability twinned with proud defiance. . . . These images visualize a tense grammar of colonization and Black self-fashioning, as well as the tense relations of photographic subjects to the ethnographic gazes engendered by the history of colonial dispossession."[101] Though Campt considers the medium of the photograph, and the Christian missionary images produced much later in the century, the questions of performative "stillness," "muscular tension," and "stasis" she interrogates are witnessed in the lithographs of Baartman, more specifically, the two images that Baartman retained copyright over (see Fig. 5.1 and Fig. 5.2).[102] Can we listen to these images, as sites that narrate both the realities of confinement and captivity Baartman experienced through the mechanisms of her exhibition, while also pressing us into even the most fraught spaces of resistance, defiance, and refusal? Campt asks an even more nuanced question of her images, that must necessarily be asked of Baartman's: "What might be gained by uncoupling the notion of self-fashioning from the concept of agency?"[103] Which is to say, how might we read Baartman's subjectivity manifest through her self-fashioning "as complex articulations of self that resist easy categorization and refuse binary notions of agency versus subjection."[104] How might we proceed through archives that give no easy answers, that do not lend unilaterally toward abjection nor agency, but that offer repeated reminders of insistent refusal, intentional illusion, fugitive strategy as freedom, when liberation was a solipsis of white European colonial thinking, ever out of reach. Is it possible to render Baartman within a framework of womanist, fugitive possibility, as one whose life is also marked by "the Black woman's daring act of remaking her *lost innocence into invisible dignity*, her *never-practiced delicacy into quiet grace*, and her *forced responsibility into unshouted courage*?"[105] The only two images of Baartman I regularly reproduce are those that bear her name, her copyright, and perhaps in some way her approval. Though the archive cannot reveal if these were completely done without coercion, the marks of Baartman's resistance herein remain, and arguably wish to keep speaking.

Does Baartman lend us futurity? There are certainly moments where this is deeply intimated, but the severing of her corpse and her narrative speak to the unfairness to ask this of her legacy. The thought raises a different kind of theological question instead: What does it mean to consider the Christological implications of the dismembering of Baartman's body? Of the body held captive even in death? What does it mean that death as much as life function as a site, *for the Black body*, of identity production and difference? What is a theology of the posthumous—less

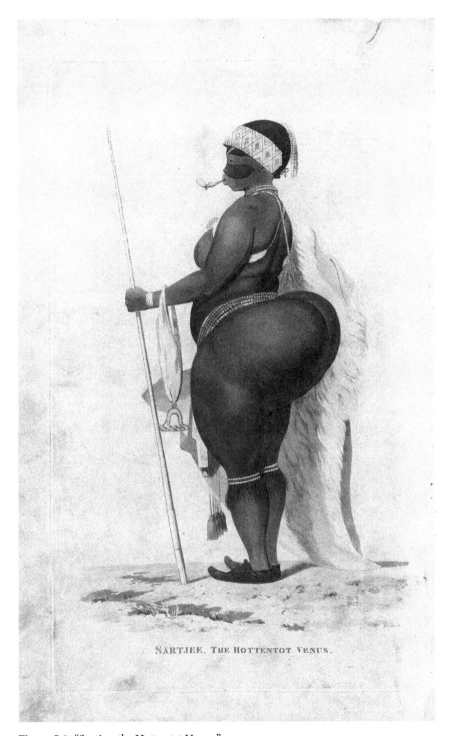

Figure 5.1 "Sartjee, the Hottentot Venus."
From Daniel Lysons, "Collectanea," © British Library Board, C.103.k.1, no. 103.

Figure 5.2 "Sartjee, the Hottentot Venus, Exhibiting at No. 225, Piccadilly." "Lewis Delin. Et. Sculpt. London, Published as the act directs March 14th, 1811, by S. Bartmaan, 225 Piccadilly."
From Daniel Lysons, "Collectanea," © British Library Board. C.103.k.1, no. 104.

of exhumation, but rather, the idea of the re-membering that constitutes the thought Resurrection? For if there is something to be said for pursuing victory over death, how might one recall social and material action that is an investment of Black life, an impulse to reorganize the attempts to swallow death's conditions. As did Baartman, we live in a world where some people are worth listening to, worth seeing, worth hearing—while others are duly ignored, or worse, violently silenced. Where Black bodies are still deemed monstrous, scary, are fetishized and feared. Where one can be an "abolitionist" without interrogating agency, choice, and consumption in one's own life, or the structural inequities that condition captivity around the world. Might there be a greater interrogation as to theological ideologies of salvation that expect that 'the poor' should be thankful, that 'the captive' should be grateful that there are those who would take time out of their day to wish to see them saved? Can we consider where the ethics and praxis of salvation—of soteriological, sexual imperialism—remain unnamed as forms of consumption themselves? What might Christian theology make of the claim that salvation has a price that has already been paid? In terms of her material conditions, then, from the beginning, Baartman didn't need to be *saved*, she needed to be *free*. Thus it must be *with* Baartman, not for Baartman, that a Christian theological discourse might begin to trace not only her own liturgies of hegemony, but also set forward to break the chains of her own captivity—by first recognizing those who have been made fugitive by her thought.

6
Following the Condition of the (M)other—or, At the Rim of the World

I think about us, women and girls, and I want to say something worth saying to a daughter, a friend, a mother, a sister—my self. And if I were to try, it might go like this:

Dear Us:

You were the rim of the world—its beginning. Primary. In the first shadow the new sun threw, you carried inside you all there was of startled and startling life. And you were there to do it when the things of the world needed words. Before you were named, you were already naming....

You did all right, girl.

"A Knowing So Deep"
Toni Morrison

Our visions begin with our desires.

Audre Lorde

Would you like to see in her how you are loved?

Julian of Norwich

To Be a Mother—*Fugitive*

mama.

Two syllables, bilabial nasal, lips pursed in smooth vibration pushing air through the nose. My infant child lingers with furrowed brow, puckered sound that requires the fullness of her face, every muscle guiding her mouth, a sputtering with force and dexterity as she attempts to tell me—in her own utterance—that she indeed knows who I am. A short string of enunciation lights her eyes in the sweetness of our own shared language.

Mama.

I wonder what Jesus called Mary, the woman who cradled her hands behind his neck as she fed him of her own body. Who rocked and swayed and hummed during interminable nights that slip out of the view of the infancy narratives. She who responded to his screams and his giggles, who tickled his belly and admired the tininess of his toes, who could discern the nuances of his needs from the chord progression of his cries. What lullabies did she sing? (For of course, we know that she sang.)

Jesus kicked her ribs and pressed his body against her organs as he stretched his limbs and expanded his lungs, rolling in the sacred baptismal of amniotic fluid. Her body drenched his need for "I thirst," allowed him to take and eat nourishment from the umbilical cord that supplied the cells forming and weaving together their holy tapestry from the creases and folds of her life.

Scripture records that Jesus referred to God with affection—*Abba*, Father. Scripture only records that Jesus referred to his mother as Woman. The absence of intimacy often feels conspicuous and peculiar, but perhaps should intimate that there are some Relations that simply can never be made legible in writing. How many miracles are overlooked because they were taken as mundane? Before the Christ we know cried Abba, he cooed *Immah*.

And when *his* life ended, as he breathed his last, he looked for *her*.

MAMA!

George Floyd annunciated his own murder before a crowd of witnesses who could not intervene without themselves being killed. Floyd's murderer's badge and gun flash toward the camera recording, his knee impinged on Floyd's neck, crushing soul and windpipe in suspended eternity.

8 minutes.
46 seconds.

How often it seems the author of time scribbles longform in the genre of horror. There are no containers large enough to collect the liters of Black blood crying out from the sidewalks and soil of this country, built with blood at the root, blood on the leaves. George Floyd pushes oxygen through tracheal obstruction to call out for his mother, to summon her, like a prophet desperate for ancestral strength, astral intervention, holy reckoning. In the weeks to come, the banner of his gruesome death will lead a cloud of witnesses closer to the world he deserved. A war of flesh and blood, of powers, of pandemics, of principalities.

How often the violence of this world demands us be subsumed by how people have died instead of how they have lived. So much in Christian thought centers on Crucifixion as the height of the theological narrative, a suffering often deemed necessary to salvation and thus a marker of redemption wholesale, as opposed to a pointing to the absurdities and harms that emerge when we assume thirsting for blood and power are equivocal to thirsting for righteousness. Perhaps the images of the suffering Christ proliferate because this is the violence we know, the violence we expect and have been formed to endure. For often we who have experienced pain and suffering, do in fact, at the least, simply, *wish to be seen*. Or remembered. Which must be considered cautiously, with the dangerous corollary, the desire *to be safe*.

Every day it seems we walk ever more closely to the precipice of the end. The collapsing of governments and capitals and currencies, the wars and rumors of wars, the genocides, the displacements, the diseases, the climate change—we are swallowed by catastrophe. Even to dare grasp the rosary, to feel the smooth cool of beads between palms gives way to the crushing weight of this world, the remaining shards splitting open slivers of wound upon wound, violence upon violence, memorial flowers kissed by fresh blood, the words of prayer unspeakable through the asphyxiation of human dignity.

Hail, Mary.
Pray for us sinners now, and at the hour of death.

In times like these, it seems the whole world sits in vigil with Mary at the Cross. But perhaps it is with her that we are asked to reimagine what might be yet possible in the liminal space of the *now but not yet*, to consider what it means *to still be* and *to birth*—even amid *stillbirth*—to think what sacred persists and remains, what is able to speak life amid a world committed to death. What is possible, particularly with regard to Black life, in the return to the birthing pool, the living waters of initiation, to proclamation, to annunciation, to joy. To plant seeds between the soils of systems and stratification, insisting still on new life and connection.

As the previous chapters have worked to retrace lost cartographies of possibility, we move to consider that any future we have left—especially for a theological imagination—requires seeing Black women as sacred figures, and accounting for how we have or have not been delimited by a theology of Mary that has not taken seriously her capacity for *Blackness(es)*—real and ontological and diasporic and shared—for as the Combahee River Collective has already insisted:

> If Black women were free, it would mean that everyone else would have to be free since our freedom would necessitate the destruction of all the systems of oppression.[1]

As such this chapter posits a Black Mariology, a pilgrimage with the Black Madonna, one that considers Marian thought beyond many of the normative claims to whiteness that masquerade themselves as finitely Christian, and instead expands the imaginary of Black *lifegiving* as Incarnational ethic. This chapter emphatically plays on the theological and legislative doctrine that emerged in the Virginia colonies of *partus sequitur ventrem*—the declarations that a Black child born into the world took on the status of their mother to determine if they were born enslaved or free, the blessing or curse of one's matrilineal begetting, a genealogy of the Black womb. This legality not only encouraged the sexual exploit of Black women, but attempted to curtail the imagination of Black futures, of Black life. The meditations in the chapter ask not only the question of what world it is that we are born into (never of our own choosing), but actively labors to pursue what dreams we can yet hear breathing at the rim of the world. Whether framed through negation, pathology, or crisis, *Black mothering* has functioned as a barometer for the ecology of Black life and death amidst anti-Blackness through the history of Christianity. Black Mariology then, considers a theology arising *from* the condition of the Black Mother, a theology *following* the condition of the Black Madonna, a theology *for* the consideration of all those who pursue justice and life at the spiritual intersections of the world, questioning the 'legislative doctrine' around our perceptions of Mary, as signposts to freedom. To consider that another theology is, perhaps, possible.

To Be a Mother—*Friend*

Heidegger begins his essay "Das Ding" (The Thing) with distance. Though he could not anticipate the exact contours of the digital information advances of the past decade alone, Heidegger aptly described how the proximity of nearness or farness dissipates, disintegrates into a lost notion as the "frantic abolition of all distances [that] brings no nearness."[2] The way that humans come to know the nature of nearness to something or someone is by attending to the things we perceive to be near to us. Ironically, such a form of measurement of proximity is always also a measure of distance away from the very thing itself. Such is the impulse of Heidegger's lecture:

> What is a thing? Man has so far given no more thought to the thing than he has to nearness. The jug is a thing. What is the jug? We say: a vessel, something of the kind that holds something else within it.[3]

How does one define the *thingliness* of the thing, when the concept of the thing is rather unknown? In the case of the jug, to perceive it as an object is in part to account for the materiality of its being, the seemingly constitutive fibers and particles that give shape to form. Earth and water adhere to become clay. A wet, unformed mass plops down, orbits the potter's wheel, melts into warm hands and folds back into itself again and again. There is careful arithmetic of the potter. Addition, then subtraction. Ply, carve, mold, seal and fire before the final vessel manifests in the fullness of its being. This is the thing, this is its thingness:

> The jug is a thing as a vessel—it can hold something. To be sure, this container has to be made. But it's being made by the potter in no way constitutes what is peculiar and proper to the jug insofar as it is qua jug. The jug is not a vessel because it was made; rather, the jug had to be made because it is this holding vessel.[4]

The earlier aspect ratio of nearness evolves from the intellectual presumption of the thing in its being known by its works, by the performativity of what it does as what is constitutive of its essence. The consciousness of the jug evolves in the execution of its purpose, of seeing it be the thing in the moment, a realized occupation of both space and time:

> We become aware of the vessel's holding nature when we fill the jug. The jug's bottom and sides obviously take on the task of holding. But not so fast! When we fill the jug with wine, do we pour the wine into the sides and bottom? At most, we pour the wine between the sides and over the bottom. Sides and bottom are, to be sure, what is impermeable in the vessel. But what is impermeable is not yet what does the holding. When we fill the jug, the pouring that fills it flows into the empty jug. The emptiness, the void, is what does the vessel's holding. The empty space, this nothing of the jug, is what the jug is as the holding vessel.[5]

The idea of the jug being empty is still constitutive that the jug is filled with, and thus contains, emptiness—as if emptiness were itself a thing. As Heidegger explains, the basics of science would indicate that there is not simply "empty" space, but a chamber of air that only comes to be displaced, one thing for another, upon the idea of filling the jug. What is the void, per se? Heidegger draws out our logics to their fault:

> We allowed ourselves to be misled by a semipoetic way of looking at things when we pointed to the void of the jug in order to define its acting as a container.... The vessel's thingness does not lie at all in the material of which it consists, but in the void that holds.[6]

The void is precisely what constitutes the jug unto itself, for even as the jug shapes the void, the void gives shape to the jug. The valuation of the jug is not effectively tied to the contents it holds, but to a capaciousness to be both empty and filled, to be in itself the very condition, the very thing that empties itself. As Fred Moten describes, "Perhaps the jug, as thing, is better understood as filled with an always already mixed capacity for content that is not made."[7] The void, the capacity for content, is that which gives the jug its thingness, but the quality of capaciousness itself cannot be thought a kind of purity of essence. Capacity exists only in its relationality, an already-not-yet anticipating the consummation of presence at an appointed time. The movement of pouring and filling, emptying—all signify the relations of the thing, the plexus impulse of matter, the infinite distance and nearness of electrons and protons, quarks and gluons, particles in exchange. This does not illumine the answer so much as it amplifies the weight with which Heidegger returns us to the question most crucial.

And yet, is the jug really empty?

While plausible, it is not likely the case that Heidegger had in mind any intentional reference to the historical metonymy of the jug and the womb. And yet, his analysis precisely describes the question of the theological conception of the womb and the thought of its purpose. The ancient world imagined the womb space as a vessel, an organic well that functioned as the holding cell of human life. Mary Foskett notes the predominant ancient Greek imagery of the uterus as "an inverted jug in need of unsealing (*kredemnon lysai*)."[8] She quotes Ann Ellis Hanson who, writing on the medical associations of the womb, describes that in ancient cultures:

> "Unsealing the wine jug" is expressed in the same terms as "violating the young girl" and "penetrating the city walls," for all three actions share a conspicuous visual similarity, whereby a rounded and sealed-off inner space is opened up and made available to the man who penetrates the protective barrier.[9]

Conquer and conquest of the weak feminine entity, of the fertile soil that is either reproductive body or reproductive land, is linked to penetration of the jug space, the breaking of a supposed seal of protection in order to fulfill a thirsting for that which might provide pleasure or profit therein. These ideas stand as both the precursor to and the process itself of consumption. Such corporeal, euphemistic projections of the womb in relationship to civility and society were not far from the thoughts of theologians, either. If in her decision to eat Eve was certified as the ultimate "unsealer," then Mary's womb alternatively would be carefully preserved, devoid of desire, airtight and indestructible. Her womb would be un-openable without being inoperable.[10]

Transposing Heidegger's jug with Mary's womb makes possible a reading of Mary's body, a body with a womb, beyond a sign in exchange—a no-thingness now filled—and a convenient instrumentality devoid of anything other than submission. Complicating the notion of barrenness, of no-thingness, might Mary instead be understood as a subject apart from the filling of her womb, as a very body marked by its capacity for content, and not the content itself?[11] The generative power and possibility of Mary's womb, theologically, are not solely predicated upon the moments of her being with child.[12] Her significance, then, is tied to something more than that which comes from her womb, and not the politics of what must be prevented from entering in.

The space of the womb, and of the womb imaginary, can be read in Scripture as marked by the certain element of friendship. Specifically, there are an ethics and politics of the womb articulated in and through women at the Annunciation. When the angel Gabriel—who is depicted frequently as a male, but as an angel, does not have a biologically sexed body—tells Mary that "The Holy Spirit will come upon you, and the power of the Most High will overshadow you," it is an undoubtedly intimate moment. Perhaps she noticed a change in her body, a somatic perception of molecular difference only she would be able to perceive. Perhaps she did not feel anything physical at all, her faith and trust enough of an incitement to ecstatic response. Mary is often theologically narrated in this moment here through the lens of her obedience, through the lens of what Jeanette Brooten described as the passivity understood to be the "natural" female role.[13] But it is also interesting to consider the narration of Mary through the lens of her will. She is a willing subject; she is a willful subject.[14] The contemporary perplexities of female agency are brought to mind in this moment: We live in a world where it remains difficult for some to believe that *no* means *no*. We do not live in a world where it is readily digestible when a woman's *yes* means *yes*.

As earlier chapters began to discuss, there seems to be a ubiquitous comfort in defense of the masculine, anthropomorphic language used to identify the Trinitarian God of the Christian faith—Father, Son, and Holy Spirit. The inclusion of feminine or gender-neutral language is readily resisted, particularly when it comes to the third person of the Trinity. As some have argued, this is perhaps rightly so, as the introduction of "she" or "her" into the language for God can have the effect of reinscribing the very gender binaries those who advocate for the language change wish to disrupt. But what keeps our theological anthropological imaginations from thinking that the Holy Spirit, in all of a bright cloud's ability to inhabit fluidity more than any of us, might offer for us a queer disruption of the normative roles of a cis*gendered male? Especially when, it would seem, the Trinitarian God is already disrupting normative frameworks of pregnancy and impregnation?

In the essay "Compulsory Heterosexuality and Lesbian Existence," the author, poet, and feminist critic Adrienne Rich condemned heterosexuality as a colonizing institution. Instead, she imagined a "lesbian continuum," a framework of "woman" identities that laid claim to a political subjectivity that could encompass but surpass the confines of sexuality as a series of intimate events alone. In her words, "As the term lesbian has been held to limiting, clinical associations in its patriarchal definition, female friendship and comradeship have been set apart from the erotic, thus limiting the erotic itself."[15] For Rich, lesbian existence was irreducible to bodies and pleasures, but inhabited an active politic of choice and resistance. Lesbian identity explored a refusal to accept or participate in dominant modes of patriarchal sexuality, instead holding the possibility of a new way of being together in the world.

Audre Lorde more deeply explored the notion and need for the erotic in her essay "The Uses of the Erotic as Power." Here she proclaimed:

> Our erotic knowledge empowers us, becomes a lens through which we scrutinize all aspects of our existence, forcing us to evaluate those aspects honestly in terms of their relative meaning within our lives. And this is a grave responsibility, projected from within each of us, not to settle for the convenient, the shoddy, the conventionally expected, nor the merely safe.[16]

For Lorde, the erotic is both an ontology and an epistemology, a way of being and a way of knowing embedded in knowledge of the self and a continuum of possibility not just of pleasure, but of compassion and community for Black women's lives. Lorde describes the ways the erotic functions—"providing the power which comes from sharing deeply any pursuit with another person," and grounding an "open and fearless underlining of my capacity for joy."[17] It requires one "feel deeply" every corner of their life with "deep participation."[18] One cannot engage the erotic from the sidelines. Perhaps this is why, "Translated in terms of African-American heritage from traditional African religions, one can say, '*The Spirit mounted Mary*'" (emphasis added).[19] The notions of the erotic are inherent to a consideration of Black women's capacity for love, pleasure, frolic, and delight—but also to power, and to the conscriptions around sexuality (for all) in the Black church experience, and sexuality (for all), period. Throughout this and her larger oeuvre, Lorde names the repeated ways that the interiority of Black life is externally refused, and yet is internally *suffused* through the practices of poetry, of resistance, of love, and of joy—on its own terms. There is a certain relational aspect of poetry, of survival, that even when it persists through isolation, it never operates alone.

Alongside Lorde's considerations, we can also take the work of Michel Foucault, who once described the searing beauty that resonates not within the boundaries of ecstasy tied to sex itself, but to the expanding universe of Rich's erotic—"friendship as a way of life."[20] Hesitant about the emerging sexual identity politics that yearn for a reduction of identities and identifications into their confessions, Foucault suggested that instead of asking about who a person was, or what their desires were, that it would be better to consider "What relations, through homosexuality, can be established, invented, multiplied and modulated?"[21] For Foucault the problem is not to "discover in oneself the truth of one's sex, but, rather, to use one's sexuality henceforth to arrive at a multiplicity of relationships. And, no doubt, that's the real reason homosexuality is not a form of desire, but something desirable.... The development toward which the problem of homosexuality tends is the one of friendship."[22]

What exactly is the nature of Mary's Relation to her own body, to her own pregnancy? What is her Relation to God, not as a form of desire, but as something itself desirable? The relation between God, and more specifically the person of the Holy Spirit who overshadows Mary, is one of deep and probing intimacy. It is a moment of union where the divine is wed to humanity, where new life is knitted together in her womb, where the Word is *from* flesh, *made* flesh. As the Introduction to this volume describes, theologically, Mary is not the singularity, but the multiplicity of existence as divinity proverbially wrecks itself upon the shores of the human. Her freeing consent, manifest in the squeezing together of bodies and the plunging into the unknown is the departure that Éduoard Glissant so vividly described as that when "one consents not to be a single being."[23] The consent is mutual, indeed, *for God so loved the world.*

In "The Body's Grace," Rowan Williams reflects that "The whole story of creation, incarnation and our incorporation into the fellowship of Christ's body tells us that God desires us, *as if we were God,* as if we were that unconditional response to God's giving that God's self makes in the life of the Trinity. We are created so that we may be caught up in this; so that we may grow into the wholehearted love of God by learning that God loves us as God loves God."[24] Being caught up in the love of God, or perhaps, to be overshadowed and covered by the love of God, represents the friendship and desire one understands to be the source of the Incarnation. And in the Annunciation of the body of her own Son, the grace of Mary's body becomes known to herself in a new way. This pronouncement of grace—*Ave Maria, Gracia Plena*—is the relation, the multiplicity of Mary's body not bound to the telos of giving birth, but inaugurated through the shadow-fire filling her body, the ecstasy of friendship as the way of New Life. What if the consideration for the Black mother, for all those bound up in Creation and the sacrality asserted by the Black Madonna, was not drowned in the apposite assignment of pain, but the free status of grace?

Mary's womb reconditions procreative sex—conception involving that which is *not-man* and a woman—to claim divine capacity as grounds for creation, birth, and possibility. There comes a different kind of consideration, around what wombs, organs, children, are truly for? Could it be that the vision of new life is one that veers away from human preservation, in order to rend itself toward an interdependent and ecologically grounded vision of *life* itself? For it is in the grounds of this *lesbian relation*, this sense of queer life and *kin*dom, the friendship between Mary and the Holy Spirit, the intimate coupling of a Trinitarian dialectic with the idea of Mary's own body's grace, that makes room for Christ's body and blood in the world. For indeed, not only is Mary considered the first disciple, she is also perhaps witness to the familial multiplicity, the *perichoresis,* of the Triune God, *Godself.* For it is not at Jesus's ritual baptism that we witness the descending presence of all persons of the Godhead, but in a quiet upper room, with the herald of the Lord with the voice of the first person, the overshadowing presence of the third, and the conception and presence of the Word Made Flesh. God in three persons, blessing Mary. Mary, witness to the Trinity, invited to dance.

Mary's womb then, is the consensual space of divine transgression, that which welcomes "She" who is wholly Other to her very self, modeling the very principle of ecclesial life. There was no Incarnational-immigration ban on Mary's womb. Rather, what takes place in Mary's body is not a single, individual action, but a communal enterprise, an embodiment of social conditions and relations that foreground the revolutionary as it manifests in and through her. Mary's body pronounces community in and of itself because it *is* Immanuel, God first with Mary, and God for and in the rest of the world. Mary, filled and empowered by the Holy Spirit, *is* now the condition of possibility that reimagines place, space, intimacy, and pleasure within her pregnancy. Her consent is her ascent to moral imaginary steeped in solidarity that weaves the fabric of the Church itself—life in the margins and love at the intersections.

To Be a Mother—*Flesh*

In the introduction to her work, *Image, Icon and Economy: The Byzantine Origins of the Contemporary Imaginary*, Marie-José Mondzain asks an intriguing question: "The visible world, the one given to us to see: is it liberty or enslavement?"[25] Mondzain's analysis of the place of the icon and iconography in the Christian tradition as a philosophy of the sacred image, sets to tease out the relation between the realms of visible and invisible meaning. For Mondzain, the image belongs to the category of that which is visible, while the icon points beyond the visible realm to that which is invisible, and that from which the visible derives meaning. Subsequently, the economy is the "*living* linkage" between the two. What is enlightening in this study is not just the historical narratives and controversies around the depictions of God, but how the idea of an image and its economy turns to a discussion of purity and, more specifically, virginity. Mondzain explains the capacity of Mary's body and fertility as such:

> ... in order for flesh to be capable of being fertilized by the Father's voice, it must already occupy a special place in the economic plan of the redemption. That body must already be in the image of what fertilizes it. It is also pure, virginal, and open to grace. ... What is at stake in the virginity of the Virgin is the purity of the image.[26]

It is an idea about primordial purity that Mondzain clings to, a cloying attraction to cleanliness that is representative of how the virginal body is interpreted, and both the lure and entrapment that come from the possibilities of virginal capacity. Speaking directly to the fifth-century loci of the Theotokos question, Mondzain claims that, "It is made clear [in Cyril's *Two Christological Dialogues*] that the christic economy cannot be separated from the virginal womb that bore it and to which it owes its visibility."[27] This is the positivist idea, that Mary, as *Theotokos*, is she who *bears* the economy. Mary is the embodied, living linkage between the seen and unseen. But there are risks requisite to this line of thinking, manifest by Mondzain as she makes a particularly *aesthetic* set of conclusions between the purity of virginity and the purity of Christ, he who is the ultimate image and icon:

> ... the immaculate womb of the invisible is opened to iconic life: panel, canvas, blank page, veil, vaults, unknown lands; in a word, endless space, no stain of inscription whatsoever, the body with no border of jurisdiction, the mirror empty of specularity.[28]

For Mondzain, this idea of an iconic life is a celebratory achievement, wherein woman becomes the "place of choice" for the harboring and regeneration of the entire economy. To this extent, she even reiterates the problem of theological descriptions that denaturalize the birth of Christ, as though he simply passed through Mary's body. She welcomes the way that Mary's womb renders her a blank space, a kind of *tabula rasa* that is perhaps *the* empty surface necessary for a new, better attempt at the perfection described in Genesis.

It is an interesting concept when placed against the insights of Gilles Deleuze, who reflects on the frustrations that artist Samuel Beckett felt between image and word:

> Beckett was less and less able to tolerate words. And he knew the reason for this growing intolerance from the beginning: the specific difficulty of "boring holes" in the surface of language so that, "what lurks behind it" might appear at last. You can do this on the surface of the painted canvas ... or on the surface of sound ... to allow the sudden appearance of the void or the visible per se, silence or the audible per se; but "Is there any reason why that terrible materiality of the word surface should not be capable of being dissolved ... ?[29]

Deleuze elaborates on the point:

> It is not only that words lie; they are so burdened with calculations and significations, with intentions and personal memories, with old habits that cement them, that their surface, barely broken, heals over again. It sticks together. It imprisons and suffocates us.... [Words] lack that "punctuation of dehiscence," that "disconnection" that comes from a groundswell peculiar to art.[30]

What "lurks behind" Mary's virginal body? This seems related to how we answer another question, which is, how is it that one describes the particularity of birth that is the dawning of the Incarnation? Mary's body takes on the task of punctiliar dehiscence, by giving birth, by that which breaks through the surface to "allow the sudden appearance of the void or the visible per se." Her womb witnesses the mature rupture, the splitting, that describes Christ's body as the site of God's inbreaking into the world, the flesh and blood of contact, of contamination, of transgression.

In Christian theological thought, the place of the image, of the icon, is critically present as a framework for anthropology, ontology, and relation. Humanity is created in the image of God (the *imago Dei*), all creation is fashioned in God's love and desire, and the lives we live, the stories we tell, the joys and pains we face, *together* have the capacity to draw us back in some way to the fundamental truth of human dignity. We are not only made in God's image, modeled in such a way to maintain the capacity for God's likeness through Jesus Christ. Christian thought understands that in the Incarnation, Jesus is the Word of God, the Word made flesh; in Christ, who is "the image of the invisible God,"[31] divinity is bound up with humanity in this God-Man. It is the Incarnation—God's very embodiment, presence, being with humanity—that grounds the justification for holy images.

Christ, as *the* Icon, ruptures, literally, the skin—*her* skin—of humanity; a unique punctuation of discourse, materiality, being, and time as the world has imagined it. In the Incarnation, Christ *disrupts* the *interruption* between things seen and unseen, transgressing the classifications that would necessarily sustain a rhetoric of purity. The breaking of bread at the Eucharistic feast resignifies Christ's breaking of the broken, the iconic rupturing of the rupture. In the ripping of flesh, in the shredding of skin, there is witness to the supplanting of the surface (or, to say, surface *reading*—and thus the problem of the gaze that settles upon, that renders). There are no blank spaces to be interpreted, no empty texts to be read.

Even Mondzain refers to the hybridized body of Mary as a "comical, organic monstrosity," but still comes to the conclusion that Mary's body functions derivatively: "A virginal, uterine space was thus defined by the economy."[32] Mondzain's concept of economy is a relation, and ultimately, a relation of purity. Her notion of economy does not encompass the presence nor the function of reproductive organs, nor the space of the womb, much less the processes of identification that cohere with human subjectivity. Which is to say, there is no account of the material, fleshly economy of Israel through which Mary's body is materialized.

This is precisely the problem Irigaray observed in the replacement of flesh and blood that "drills a hole through the female womb."[33] She, too, is describing the hollow surface—the configuration of the female womb is like a wall without studs. It can neither support nor feature hanging an image of any kind. What Mondzain misdiagnoses in her organization of Mary's virginity is the very presumption of the surface that Irigaray and Deleuze, vis-à-vis Beckett, find so tiring. A surface is not constituted by its contents, or the lack thereof; it is not ever blank, for the surface is a property already belonging to something. It is not the relation of purity, the idea of the sacredness of a place that situates or confers sacrality in relation. Rather, it is the sacredness of the thing that imbues its spatiality. The economy need not be sanctified to make space for the icon. The icon is that which sanctifies the economy. Mary's flesh and blood, not her virginity, are that which constitute the Icon.

Images of boring holes, of drilling wells, broaden the scope of our understanding of the importance of Mary's blood. For Irigaray, the holes that are poked through Mary's body move through her flesh because her flesh can neither contain nor support the substance of patriarchy. These holes pass through her, if you will, to deliver the Christ child without her body. For Deleuze, boring holes is an idea we can appropriate to interrogate the very concept of the womb as surface, for Mary comes to function as surface without substance. A white, pure canvas; a relation free of blood.

Throughout this text we have considered sensually the taste lingering on Eve's lips to whatever blood is left flowing in Mary's veins. When we considered the life force of food, and the implications of the act of eating, we discussed the terms under which an embodied act is constantly under the surveillance and discipline of certain normative conditions. In tracing the genealogy of blood and birth, a life force unto itself, it is arguably not just blood, but the act of *bleeding*, that comes to function theologically as a constitutive act of political subjectivity. We cannot begin to think about the meaning of the Incarnation, of the *Theotokos*, without taking seriously fertility and fecundity; the promises and sorrows of the body that undergoes *menstruation*—the menstruating body, the pregnant body, the bleeding body, the birthing body. Such abiding boundaries of the sacred are demarcated by the biological, which leaves us still with a perplexing question. If there is a certain sense that "bleeding out," however problematically so, signifies the (polluted or polluting) female body, why has the Christian relation to blood not been so readily witnessed in relation to bodies that bleed? For while Mary is fully human—again, it is *her* body that grants Jesus his human flesh and Palestinian Jewish identity—she also carries contact with the Divine, she carries within her the fullness of Divinity, the *imago Dei* itself. And yet, as described previously, she is not allowed to bear blood, hypothetical or literal. There is no space for Mary to be a *bleeding* body, despite the power of the blood that flows from her child.

Consideration of Mary's body and blood, and their theological significance, presses us toward a different, adapted set of relations that moves us from the functions of purity to the inhabitations of touch, to gesture, to sensing the energies and embodiments that flow in, between, and among living creatures. It is recognition, desire, acknowledgment. It is the offer of friendship, an invitation to faith. To this extent, this is perhaps a different lens through which the Christian tradition may yet effectively ask that the very notions of birth, life, and death be examined from the perspective of the Cross, from Christ the center. In moving toward this center, there must be a consideration that the *bleeding body* of Christ is a theological moment of aesthetic crossing, a moment that signals a "trans-gendered" act of embodiment that maintains the conditions of possibility for rupturing the theo-social vessels of bodily difference.

Christ, the *imago Dei*, is the image, the icon of One who is perpetually bleeding. This bleeding is not diseased, and not simply relegated to classifications of contaminant or detergent, but itself resists qualifications of the boundedness of life and death, of freedom and unfreedom, of body and flesh. Christ's bleeding body reanimates the theological thinking of intimacy, of intercourse, and is a discourse that pierces through the imaginaries of virginity as something that even exists. For it is the Incarnation itself that is the apex of reproduction anxiety and the inability to produce and control sexual knowledges. The coming of Christ disrupts every political notion of family, kinship, sovereignty, flesh, and blood, precisely because Jesus must *inhabit* a bleeding body in order to *become* a bleeding body. This inhabitation is a tabernacling, a taking up of space thought to be inhospitable and threatening if not policed. What Christian theology has not reckoned with is the full thought that it is Christ's blood, Mary's Palestinian, Jewish blood, this ritually unclean excrement, that is together shared in drink, and that the narrative of blood purity is displaced in the implications of institution, that "this is my blood, shed for you." In the words of the hymn,

> Down at the cross where my Saviour died,
> Down where for cleansing from sin I cried,
> There to my heart was the blood applied,
> Singing glory to His name!

To Be a Mother—*Fire*

Let us sing a song of Zion:

> Oh oh Mary
> Oh, Mary, don't you weep, don't you mourn
> Oh, Mary, don't you weep, don't you mourn
> Didn't Pharaoh's army get drowned?
> Oh, Mary, don't you weep
> Well, Satan got mad and he knows I'm glad
> Missed that soul that he thought he had
> Now, didn't Pharaoh's army get drowned?
> Oh, Mary, don't you weep
>
> God gave Moses the rainbow sign
> No more water, but fire next time
> Pharoah's army got drownded
> Oh Mary don't you weep

Mary wore three links of chain
Every link was freedoms name
Pharoah's army got drownded
Oh Mary don't you weep

The very moment I thought I was lost
The dungeon shook and the chains fell off
Pharoah's army got drownded
Oh Mary don't you weep

Oh, Mary, don't you weep

If we turn to the Marian story placed in the contemporary context, we might find a surprising image. Stripped of spiritual aura (and the confining identities that are often associated with the use of her body), Mary herself embodies "the least of these" in society through her own intersectional multiplicity of experiences. The material conditions of her everyday reality are not just the paragon of virtue, but are the paradigm of peril faced by so many, particularly those gendered and sexed as women, all over the world, particularly when one's identity is also Black, non-white, or white-but-adapted to racial logics through the economic and social intersections of global anti-Blackness. One does not need a search for some figment of a historical Mary, to see her allegorical imprint in the lives of so many who have been forgotten and forsaken all over the world, in a plethora of situations formed through capitalism, violence, and greed.

Think about it. Joseph was kind, but many men are not. Betrothed, had he found out about Mary's pregnancy without intervention, he could have had her arrested, or beaten, or sold. Found guilty in the desert then, she could have been subject to immeasurable ridicule, torture, and shame. Found guilty in the desert now, she might be burned or killed or disappeared by police—a massive irony given she would witness such terrors executed against her son. When Mary gave Christ the whole of his human flesh, perhaps she gave him the cell memory of her traumas, too?

If Mary were alive today, where would we find her? Under the rubble, among the targeted; unemployed or underpaid in a foreign land? An essential worker forced to show up through a pandemic? Giving birth in a slum, or on a street, or in a shelter, maybe even in a prison while still in shackles? Homeless, the extent of her poverty forcing her to give birth at whatever hospital-manger door will allow, while also calling social services to remove her child from her unfit arms? There is a story about unexpected provision in the accounts of the Nativity, but there is also a story about what is like to give birth under redoubled duress. Lacking resources, Mary wraps her son in pieces of scrap fabric, the leftovers, the trash of fast fashion we wouldn't bother to keep for our next homemade craft. For Mary, it is enough. For us, it should signal the anathema of greed.

If Mary were alive today, would she be a woman living under occupation, deprived of water, cut off from electricity, watching bombs fall or measuring breaks in encroaching gunfire as her baby kicks? If Mary were alive today, would her very existence make her a target for exploitation? Would the innocence of her youth protect her in a world where virginity is a privilege, not a right? Would she survive in a world, that does not see her body or life as graced, but as an imminent threat? Would her body be considered one of the *kinds* of bodies already deemed available for consumption?

And have we seen *her*? The Mary who is Palestinian, and Sudanese, and Congolese? The Black Madonna? The Trans-Madonna? Can Mary's capaciousness also retain the capacity for fine lines and wrinkles, for using a wheelchair, for being overweight or unattractive or depressed or a prostitute or imprisoned, marginalized from and by societal norms—and *still be sacred*? Have we seen *her*, the one who is *bearing* God right before our eyes? We celebrate the humble beginnings of our Lord by laying baby dolls in mangers, but have we stopped to think carefully enough about how *fully* Mary carried the Cross within her? While many Christians are able to imagine Christ's body as the one who is poor, incarcerated, hungry, or without a home (Matthew 25), Mary still too rarely, if at all, enters deeply into theological imagination as one inhabiting such spaces *without* also happening to *be* Divine. When we gloss Mary, we gloss what precarity looks like in the flesh.

There are other narratives, other witnesses, other angles and views to the life and witness of Mary, of the Black Madonna, of sacred flesh, that are necessary theological counterpoints for a Black Mariology that speaks beyond the confines of the Christian-colonial project. Like Christ, holy icons are haptic, breathing, active, the visual of faith and doctrine corresponding to the Word made flesh (thus why one *writes* rather than *paints* an icon). Icon theology teaches that there are no passive images; rather, we are constantly being acted upon, being drawn closer to God or pushed further away, making meaning. In encountering a holy icon, we are not meant to simply observe; we do not come to it, reach into it, bring ourselves to it. Rather, it is the icon, in its sacredness, that reaches out to us, changes us, brings us into an economy of Relation. We return to Mondzain's question: "The visible world, the one given to us to see: is it liberty or enslavement?"[34] Or, to be said another way, what are we being drawn toward in our considerations and consumption?

In his classic study *Iconology: Image, Text, Ideology*, W. J. T. Mitchell considers the "rhetoric of images" through two modes of inquiry, first to consider, "what to say about images," and second, "what images say."[35] He goes on to describe that "the critical study of the icon begins with the idea that human beings are created 'in the image and likeness' of their creator and culminates, rather less grandly, in the modern science of 'image making' in advertising and propaganda."[36] The continuum is one that makes meaning at every end. While icons reach out to us, drawing the worshipper closer to God, this economy, this field of relations, does not find a bounded or pure manifestation in relationship to the icon alone. Other images, immeasurably powerful, also reach out, also ask us to participate in their offering of the imaginary, in exerting an iconic force, an iconic function. Alas, in the wrong hands, without a sacred community, left to her own devices, even the icon, like anything, can become idol, in person or through a screen. What have we been taught, through image, through death? Are the things we see moving us toward liberty, or enslavement?

Icons meet us—or perhaps, we meet them—where we are. But in their very essence, they also lead us into a kind of *anamnesis*, a remembering of a future we have yet to behold, but are called to co-create. If Mary's womb is the space, where created and Uncreated embrace, collide in ineffable union, here also she is a model of the icon itself—"Every icon is rooted in the Incarnation, finding its fulfillment in the paschal light, and must henceforth be read from a resurrectional perspective."[37] Icons are meant to convey *Christian* vision—"of God, and one of a transfigured world"[38]—but one would be remiss to argue, that the energy and passion of the icon is *only* instructive for (or by) the confessional. What else might be rendered, in a world where the violence of crucifixion seems to predominate our imagination? Between liberty and enslavement, perhaps we recall the womanist theological commitment to survival in the here and now—if icons speak to our suffering, but also claim a sacred economy that brace us to resist and hope, perhaps the world needs the icon more than ever.

We consider again the Annunciation—a pronouncement of the gospel, of good news unexpected in a world there often seems to be none. Perhaps one of the most significant allusions of the Virgin Mary, often overlooked in the Latin and Protestant traditions, is her prefigurement in the burning bush and call to Moses at Mount Horeb. The inspiring account of Moses is found in the book of Exodus (3:1-6), where Moses is tending his flocks when there suddenly appears a miraculous sight. There is a bush there, completely enflamed, but it is not burning. It is filled with fire, but not consumed. As Moses comes closer to inspect the curious sight, God calls him by name, instructs him to keep his distance, and to take off his sandals—Moses is standing on holy ground. From the flames and leaves, the voice of God speaks to Moses—a moment of encounter, challenge, and transformation on sacred ground that challenges the presuppositions of what is or is not possible in Relation. Here God identifies God's self to Moses, and reveals God's holy name, I AM THAT I AM.

As early as the fourth century, Gregory of Nyssa captured the inferences of Mary in this moment of theophany and revelation in the life of Moses, where he described, "The light of divinity which through birth shone from her into human

FOLLOWING THE CONDITION OF THE (M)OTHER 185

Figure 6.1 *Virgin of the Burning Bush*, 19th c., Russian origin. Tempera and gold on wood, 36 x 31 cm. The Walters Art Museum, Baltimore.

life did not consume the burning bush, even as the flower of her virginity was not withered by giving birth."[39] However the iconic pattern and form of the *Theotokos of the Unburnt Bush* (*Neopalimaya Kupina*) did not grow in prevalence until the late sixteenth century, and most prominently in the Russian Orthodox tradition (see Fig. 6.1).[40] The icon is inspired by reading the narrative as prefiguring the body of Mary, she who is filled with the fire of the Holy Spirit, filled with Divinity and the promise of eternal life in her womb.

The icon itself is profoundly intricate, including multiple scenes and symbols throughout. The bush is represented by two rhombuses overlapping in the pattern of the star, a *slava* ("glory") that references the apocryphal idea of an eighth day of creation that inaugurates a new beginning of the world (often as signified in the Resurrection). The foregrounded layer is green, an allusion to the physical bush; the other star is an intense red, symbolic of the holy *unconsuming* fire. The green star (at times pigmented in shades of blue, a color reference to creation, or when decorated with stars, the Heavens), includes an array of angels, a reference to the reign of Mary as the Queen of Heaven, while the muddy red symbolizes earth. The interplay between the symbols of the physical elements (a material bush and divine fire), with the opposite color symbolisms (the green/blue Heavenly realm, the red representing created matter), further inflects the encounter between God and Creation, echoing again the mystery and revelation of the Incarnation. Here also we see divinity taken up in both the symbolism of *divine light* as well as *divine darkness*. The red points of the flame typically feature the symbols (the *tetramorph*) representing the four Evangelists who wrote the Gospels. The bush is flanked by eight rounded leaves or petals, where archangels stand in honor and reverence. The four corners of the icon are highlighted by prophetic scenes from the Hebrew Bible (Old Testament) that prefigure the Incarnation.[41] The example of the icon included here in Figure 6.1 (a later version, dating from the nineteenth century), depicts at the base what is referred to as the tree (or root, or rod, per theological tradition) of Jesse—King David's father and Mary's ancestor. The mandorla at the top displays Christ as the Ancient of Days, surrounded by the fiery seraphim.

At the center of the icon there is Mary, clothed in fiery raiment, with the blessed Christchild poised on her lap, a reminder of the Incarnation. Her position takes on the formula of the *Hodegetria* ("She who points the Way")—Jesus is held by his Mother in her left arm, and she gestures to her son with her right. Here we see a slight variation, where Mary also holds Jacob's ladder, an allusion to the connection between Heaven and Earth, the human and the Divine. Christ is not usually portrayed as an infant or with features signifying him as a child (similarly, Mary in Byzantine traditions is not generally portrayed as a young girl or with her head uncovered). He gestures in response to his Mother in sign—here, "He is shown blessing, a miniature child-adult, God-man from the beginning."[42]

The liturgical praxis of this image is certainly, upon first reading, clear veneration of the Theotokos and her ongoing significance to the Incarnation; Mary remains a critical link between the world that is and the world that is to come through her Son. Most exegete the unburnt bush itself in direct correlation to Mary's virginity, her innocence/sinlessness, and her purity, fire being a sign of her incorruptibility. If fire is a natural element that has the capacity to purify, or be the first cause toward a plan for regeneration and growth, the power of *divine* fire retains this capacity even more so. But in our contemporary moment, theological and otherwise, I would argue the significance of reading this as an icon *against* consumption—an icon that holds on to life, despite forces of fire that would seem by nature to only be able to destroy it (according to popular belief, the icon has the power to protect a home from fire). Mary's body and witness signal an intentional resistance to the temptation of globalization and the logics of consumption that mark certain kinds of bodies—which is to say, *certain people*—as disposable. While Mary's womb is filled with the fire of the Spirit, like the burning bush in Exodus, **she is filled but not consumed**. In a world where certain people too frequently are reduced to commodity, assumed expendable and exploitable, and thus made banal casualties of mass death or violence or greed, the icon of *Mary as the Unburnt Bush* resists, and reminds us it is divine calling to do the same. A profound sense of *Imitatio Mariae*, to name that the logics of consumption function as distortion, as antithetical witness to the image of God in the breadth of all human being. What in all creation—or perhaps, who in all creation—are we to consider, as less than holy ground? What injunctions of justice are there, to becoming pregnant with fire? To birth despite duress? In the words of Russian poet Max Voloshin:

> We perish but aren't dying
> Our souls are stripped and bare
> In flames but not consumed by fire
> That's the Unburnt Bush![43]

In his "Letter from a Region in My Mind," James Baldwin reflects on the ways Christianity—and in particular, white Christianity—has so readily lost the grounds for any claim to virtue or authority, her "domain of morals as chartless as the sea once was, and as treacherous as the sea still is."[44] It is a reminder that a return to icons, Scripture, documents, debates, doctrines, dogmas, councils, or the like *alone*—without a hermeneutic of community, accompanied by a hermeneutic of redress (as an ethical praxis of repentance)—are insufficient barometers of following Christ, if we take seriously how we are taught *to live*. The search for significance in a romanticized era or age, some sense of radical rediscovery or historical clarity as being *better than*, too often belies a certain sense of privilege and superiority, that one can simply make theology great again. Baldwin considers instead:

> It is not too much to say that whoever wishes to become a truly moral human being (and let us not ask whether or not this is possible; I think we must believe that it is possible) must first divorce himself from all the prohibitions, crimes, and hypocrisies of the Christian church. If the concept of God has any validity or any use, it can only be to make us larger, freer, and more loving. If God cannot do this, then it is time we got rid of Him.[45]

It was in response to a moment of despair that iconographer Mark Doox helped the world consider turning toward *Her* (see Fig. 6.2). What is at first most striking

188 IMMACULATE MISCONCEPTIONS

Figure 6.2 Mark Doox (b.1958), *Our Lady Mother of Ferguson and All Those Killed by Gun Violence*, 2015. Acrylic collage gold metal leaf on cradled wood board, 48 × 60 in. On long-term loan to the Cathedral of St. John the Divine, New York. Collection of Rev. Dr. Mark Bozzuti-Jones. The image appears courtesy of the artist.

are the notes of her beauty—the sonorous umber skin, wide spherical eyes, pronounced cheekbones, and broad nose round out the features far fuller than what the typical Byzantine style has made dogma. Her hands are lifted up in both veneration, revelation, and supplication before God. At first glance, one might mistake her for simply another version of an *Oranta* typology, or The Mother of God as

Sign. This Marian form is often referenced by the prophet Isaiah (whose words will be cited in the New Testament as confirmation of Christ's identity):

> [14] Therefore the Lord himself will give you a sign. Look, the young woman is with child and shall bear a son, and shall name him Immanuel. [15] He shall eat curds and honey by the time he knows how to refuse the evil and choose the good.

More broadly, *orante* depictions are numerous in Christian tradition, with forms dating back to the walls of the catacombs, depicting the soul in paradise. In the Marian formulation, she is imaged with the Christ on her lap, not depicted in the style referential of icons referencing the Gospels, but rather that of Christ-Emmanuel (Emmanuel meaning God-with-us), "the Logos who exists before time and history and is announced by the prophets."[46] This image of Christ usually appears with a broad forehead and the features of a more aged man. Particularly when placed above an altar, this image is also described as *platytera*, a reference to the expansion of Mary's womb, made 'more spacious than the heavens.'

But one quickly realizes we are not seated at the threshold of Heaven, but firmly planted here—in Ferguson, Missouri. Where the face and body of Christ would usually be, there is instead only a silhouetted son, full shadow, pure black, without feature. We do not see a child prefigured here as "an adult and kingly man," perhaps because this is a manifestation that is not promised to Black children in the United States. Similarly, we see no details of face or personhood at all—only the shadow outline of threat, a one-dimensional piece of paper fit for target practice. There are no gestures of blessing or consolation, no winged creatures assuring divinity. The gilded nimbus haloing his body—a signature of divinity—is breached by the crosshairs of a gun. The *orans* positions of both mother and child still reflect the outlines of a chalice, but this is no holy sign of sacrifice, no reference to sacrament (except perhaps, their sacramentality defiled). Instead, the Black Madonna and Child genuflect both the gesture and shout of protestors in the aftermath of the 2014 murder of Michael Brown: *Hands up, don't shoot!* This is *Our Lady Against All Gun Violence*.

The image grew to prominence as it was circulated on social media, and began to appear across the country at various protests to anti-Black violence and ongoing murders of Black people at the hands of the police. *Our Lady of Ferguson* became a compelling capture of a cultural zeitgeist that diagnosed the depths of racism's rootedness in American ideology, challenging a moral imaginary. If icons function as windows—divine instruments that are revealing, always doing the work of unveiling and drawing us closer to a certain truth—this icon certainly reminds the church of an oft unspoken lexicon of promulgation and collusion in the racist and colonial realities we still endure, and reminds us that to claim to follow Christ requires a different consideration of Blackness—*if one chooses to see*. This also requires the reciprocal impetus, that one endure the exfoliating work of also *being seen.* For what is perhaps less immediate in this icon's reception is the way the viewer, too, is part of the icon. The viewer serves as the source of the target. The viewer is the one who holds the gun in their hands. Not unlike viewing *The Rape of the Negress*, that to not experience the gravity of the scene, the choking "*sentiment du déshabillé*, is to say something about our participation and privilege in relationship to Black life. What do we choose to see, choose to do, in a world shaped by alternative facts, when we have distanced ourselves so vastly from one another, from community, and from truth? Who do we choose to be? To see this icon, is to be called out for the ways we, too, are bound up in the global complicities of vision and subjugation (or the conditions of possibility for such).

Baldwin's essay considers the despair, the retaliation, the failures of change without the threats of power and violence, and the legacies not only of sin but a theology of God's wrath and vengeance. At his close he reflects:

> When I was very young, and was dealing with my buddies in those wine- and urine-stained hallways, something in me wondered, *What will happen to all that beauty?* For black people, though I am aware that some of us, black and white, do not know it yet, are very beautiful. And when I sat at Elijah's table and watched the baby, the women, and the men, and we talked about God's—or Allah's—vengeance, I wondered, when that vengeance was achieved, *What will happen to all that beauty then?* I could also see that the intransigence and ignorance of the white world might make that vengeance inevitable—[47]

Our Lady of Ferguson is written in grief but drenched in light, with crosshairs unable to pin that which is at the center of the targeted Black life. Here still lies a sacred heart—encircled with a crown of thorns but alight with flame, emanating as both cross and organ are on fire. It is a cross, not a crucifix—a reminder of Resurrection. The suffering, the wounds, the trauma are all so very real—we do in fact bleed. And yet, the heart still beats. The heart still burns. The heart is still sacred. Blackness carries capacity for the divine, something a gun can deny, but not destroy. Blackness also carries capacity for the prophetic, a lesson for how to, in the words of the Isaiah passage, 'refuse the evil and choose the good.' As Baldwin writes:

> Everything now, we must assume, is in our hands; we have no right to assume otherwise. If we—and now I mean the relatively conscious whites and the relatively conscious blacks, who must, like lovers, insist on, or create, the consciousness of the others—do not falter in our duty now, we may be able, handful that we are, to end the racial nightmare, and achieve our country, and change the history of the world. If we do not now dare everything, the fulfillment of that prophecy, recreated from the Bible in song by a slave, is upon us: *God gave Noah the rainbow sign, No more water, the fire next time!*

There is something to be said of fire that is a sign of life, and the contradiction of fire as a force of death. A sacred heart, a burning bush, in fire but not on fire. Here we read, and are confronted with, two icons—one of an unburning fire, one of the will to a line of fire. And here we turn to the Black Madonna, a Sign of the times (*oranta*), one who asks us to gestate new worlds that expand our capacity and insist on possibility (*platytera*).

For though we may perish, we are not dying.

To Be a Mother—*Free*

It's the most wonderful time of the year. For even in the most Protestant of circles, out from the quiet shadows of humility, emerging from closets stuffed with seasonal tinsel and fake pine, she come into view. For Catholic traditions, despite her somewhat abiding presence, it is the Advent season where she actually claims the space of our twinkly attentions. Behold, like a star in the sky, a virginal figure appears. Draped in blue, perhaps only to distinguish from the blood-stained purples of Lent, her shape is swallowed both by the folds of fabric and the season. She admires her Son as She Who Is Ever-Virgin, an iconography that captures the most impossible of realities unseen, but also delimits that which might also be observed—Mary so rarely appears pregnant, there is no curvature in the lens of her hips, her stomach, or breasts, there is no nose spread wide or ankles swollen with fatigue. Her virginity hails postpartum and in perpetuity, but her body rarely bears the marks of stretched skin or perineal tears or rearranged organs, a chest engorged with milk or the loss of one's pelvic floor.

We have turned at several points throughout this text to the inimitable thought of Hortense Spillers and, even more specifically, her groundbreaking essay, *Mama's Baby, Papa's Maybe*. But to consider a Black Madonna, toward a Black Mariology, we must take seriously her analysis with the figure of Black Mary in mind, a braided reading in-line, after Hortense Spillers and alexis pauline gumbs:[48]

> Let's face it. She is **a marked woman**, and **everybody knows her name**. Mary and Madonna, Mother of Sorrows and Grace and Succor, Mother of Mercy, *Theotokos*, Mother of God, "My Homegirl," Queen of Heaven, Mediatrix, Blessed Virgin, Star of the Sea, Cause of Our Joy, Our Lady. Biblically she is often called simply Woman, which leads me wonder, if ever, her title was more simply, Mom. A **locus of confounded identities**, a **meeting ground of investments and privations** in the (inter)national treasury of theological wealth. My **church needs me** ... kind of ... "and if I were not here, I would have to be invented."

Mary was not, of course, historically, African-American. Nevertheless, the figure of Mary as she evolves and is imagined in this thing that for so long has just been called "the West" shares with the legacy of the enslavement for the Black woman in American the "**isolat[ion]**" of her "**overdetermined nominative properties**," the "**layers of attenuated meanings**," the "**crushing burden**" of birthing a child, who even if God, was first, his Mama's Baby. And at the time ... and beyond the crucifixes of Christendom, for some, still remains ... Papa's, maybe. But to say that Marian piety, by which is inferred Marian purity, lays critical gendered and sexual groundwork not only for that sense of "*perceived* **difference as a fundamental degradation or transcendence**," but most certainly of a politics that will clearly be invoked in melanin-rich encounter—"**We wonder the seeming docility of the subject.**"

This is not to speak of Mary in terms of literal acts of enslavement, though recent Black womanist scholarship has asked we consider the possibilities that Mary was indeed enslaved during her lifetime.[49] I am speaking to what Spillers infers as "**the symptoms of the sacred**," and the gestures of *capture* to Mary as the icon of the impossible, particularly in her pedagogical use as purveyor of colonial power, submission, and obedience, a certain kind of "**reproduction of mothering**" that subtends every aspect of *patriarchalized* **female gender** virtue, including the **vestibularity** of its exclusionary apparatus, *vis a vis* the incredibly queer invocation of being both *Virgin*—an imaginary—and *Mother*—an imaginary—and perhaps less frequently explored, and perhaps most intentionally diminished, to actually do so without the involvement of, (capital M) "Man,[50] a kind of "**displacement for other human and cultural features and relations, including the displacement of the genitalia**," any sense of desire, much less pleasure, that engenders future.

The theological turn here is to ask the question of this "**rule of gender and its application to African females in captivity**," and how such marginalizing justification are both a specter of the church, a deeply *un*holy Ghost, for which we much cosmologically account as a source of epistemic violence. If there are questions we must attend to, particularly when Mary is—or is not—Black, then they require a deep assessment of the normalizing hierarchies of gender and violence and capitalism and capture as a kind of divine right. I read moments of Mary's symbolic rendering along with Spillers here, and realize I have not come to the bulwark of specificity attendant to the American crucible. As described earlier, "Mary, sole progenitor of the *Word made Flesh*, somehow too stands only '*in the flesh,* **both mother and mother-dispossessed**.' Somehow, while she is espoused as the paragon of the traditional symbolic of female gender at its epitome and apex, she is actually **a different social subject.**"

I wonder. Can Black Mary, the Black Madonna, a different kind of Sapphire, retain a theological capacity that "**might rewrite after all a radically different text for empowerment.**"

I wonder, if we look more closely, if she already did.

The providence of origins is sheer with precarity. Birthed into worlds not of our own choosing, each cell and synapse immaculate, miraculous, begotten and made. Drenched with wonder the density of wisdom, we are ever perched on the brink of the ineffable, the possible. We mark birth and death with time, of course, but this is only the most meager of measures; each second, in actuality, a new start, a new end. These intermittent attentions we come to take for granted—the feigned fastidious, too readily muddled in the foregrounds of the mundane. So too, our origin stories. The stories that sear-stitch together our worlds and our wounds, our lives, our being. They do not begin with us, eukaryote, nor end when the drumbeat of aortas fade—no, we are ancestral in the truths that rip us apart at the seams, in the theological stops and starts of holiness and desire, the interrogations of life and possibility, the inbreaking of fabric and flesh with new freedoms. The annunciations of sorrows unending, survived by unspeakable joys.

And Mary said:

> My soul magnifies the Lord, and my spirit rejoices in God my Savior, for he has looked with favor on the lowly state of his servant. Surely from now on all generations will call me blessed, for the Mighty One has done great things for me, and holy is his name; indeed, his mercy is for those who fear him from generation to generation. He has shown strength with his arm; he has scattered the proud in the imagination of their hearts. He has brought down the powerful from their thrones and lifted up the lowly; he has filled the hungry with good things and sent the rich away empty. He has come to the aid of his child Israel, in remembrance of his mercy, according to the promise he made to our ancestors, to Abraham and to his descendants forever.

Though we have discussed the significance of the Magnificat and its lineage in the prophetic songs of women throughout Scripture earlier in this text, we return here now as 'we who believe in freedom.' For if there is a political theology of Mary, it begins here, with the call to revolution, with the clarity of resistance to structures of domination that would impede *life*.

We do not have many words of Mary, but what we do have, includes her song. Mary sings a song not just for herself, but as one who carries with and within her, the voices of her people. She will yet praise, she will yet rejoice, she will insist on new life. There is still, somewhere good news. In most scriptural translations, she is presented as the servant of the Lord, though Mitzi Smith's recent scholarship requires us seriously contend with the possibility that Mary was indeed enslaved, and following the condition of the mother, the source of Jesus's experiences (as for Smith, enslaved and manumitted) that will ground his life as "abolitionist Messiah."[51] It is an important consideration (one that would only emphasize the revolutionary perspective of her poetic frame) for a song too easily relegated to hymnody of praise and devotion. For Mary does not stop here. Instead, her exaltation is the gate through which she lays claim to a series of divine reversals, divine *refusals*, of the realities of injustice and oppression in the world—certainly as if ordained by God. The Magnificat becomes an invocation for any, as Pope John Paul II proclaimed in Zapopán, Mexico, "who do not passively accept the adverse circumstances of personal and social life and are not victims of alienation, as they say today, but who with her proclaim that God 'raises up the lowly' and, if necessary 'overthrows the powerful from their thrones.'"[52]

From Mary's great pleasure comes *the* promise, an enthrallment of *joy* that perhaps, in the words Black Christians in the United States context have exhorted for quite some time—*the world didn't give, and the world can't take away*. Here we also find that a commitment to liberation is critical element, if not essential component of what it means to ascent to God's plan. Here we have a Mary willing to stand in the tradition of those who proclaim and demand justice with freedom on their minds. It is not a paradox to rejoice and grieve, to inhabit the complexities of a world that will try to quiet both. We are returned to Audre Lorde's erotic imaginary, as it impresses upon us an ethical demand:

> In touch with the erotic, I become less willing to accept powerlessness, or those other supplied states of being which are not native to me, such as resignation, despair, self-effacement, depression, self-denial.[53]

Mary's Magnificat embodies the use of the erotic as power. We see this as Mary's song progresses into its fullest capacities and pronouncements. Mary's scriptural *yes*—her fiat, to 'Let it be unto me'—is cited along with God's (and Mary's taking up of God's) explicit *no*:

> Starting now God begins to register a resounding 'no' to any kind of sin that impedes or blocks the Kingdom of justice and freedom from arriving. God's 'no' resounds powerfully over the pride of the haughty, the ambition of the powerful, and the stuffed bellies of the rich.[54]

This is, for the global church, an indictment:

> If the church earnestly compares itself with the person and figure of Mary, such reflection will entail examining and discerning whether it has truly said 'yes' and whether it has had the courage to say 'no' at the right time.[55]

Mary's song—her *spiritual*—should subtend our solidarities. If we have considered the Black Madonna, with a womb that expands the capacity for being, impassioned with the fire and flame of this world without being consumed by it, then here we consider a Black Madonna who sings in the key of "doxological Blackness(es)," her song the break beat of protest.[56] Which requires us consider abolition as antiphon, as the grounds for Christ's origin stories, for freedom to be wrought even in the womb—for perhaps it was Mary who taught her son the songs of freedom.

We end—which is to say, we begin again—with Mary's freedom dreams. To contend that the womb is not a grave, to take the womb instead as Harriet Jacobs described, as "loophole of retreat," a respite from the configurations of what seemed impossible, in the creative kinship and commitments toward freedom, even when one must yet endure fugitive life.

We need a Mary who had as much capacity to laugh as she was made to weep. A Mary whose body was used to dance as much as it was made to mourn. A Mary of resistant joy as much as a Mary of sorrows. A Mary who sweats and tarries and groans, who bleeds and shrivels and aches, who delights and celebrates and luxuriates. Not because suffering is requisite to knowing joy, but because the human conditions of suffering are marked by the human capacity to resist it, or at least resist it as a totalizing eclipse of who we are. A Mary who leads with the reminders that advocacy, access, community, and support can find ways to remain verdant. That it is not our only job to attend to destruction, that our joy and grief can be met with rage. That even yet, we can follow the condition of the Mother—with tears and sweat and song and screams and hopelessness and dreams and exuberance—to the Way of Life.

And so too, to follow the condition of the Mother, in thinking about the dietary apparatuses of the world, about in(di)gestion, about how we monitor and determine morality by and think uncritically about what it means to consume, that being *consumer* has become *culture*. Mary requires us think about a world where it is possible to experience and be filled with, to take pleasure and ecstasy without destruction or annihilation, against catastrophic levels of consumption. To think a theological ethic of miraculous abundance and generosity and Relation in lieu of scarcities. Perhaps it is time to reclaim, to take, to eat of the same fruit as Eve in the Garden. Perhaps this is the fruit—desired, ingested, penetrating, dangerous, beautiful—recapitulated as the fruit of Mary's body. Not a blank slate inscribed upon, but one whose ink took part in writing the Word of God within her. One who speaks her own words, nurturing the spark of a revolution, a Magnificat that begins with joy and rejoicing and calling down the high places of the wicked.

What proceeds from Mary's womb is icon, is sacrament. Perhaps Jesus then only amplifies the words that Mary first instituted through her own show of sacrifice and love to nurture him at her bosom:

Take. Eat. This is my body.

For this—a commitment to sacrament over the sacrilege of squander—we must follow the condition of the Black Mother.

For to say that Mary is Black is to consider that God lives and moves and has being in Black bodies, in women's bodies, in Black women's bodies, in Black non-binary femme bodies, in cis-women's bodies, in trans-women's bodies, as of course, God invites divinity to transgress the perceived boundaries of flesh in the most beautiful and darkest and holiest of ways, and asks us to follow the way to also bearing God. *Blessed is the fruit of thy womb.*

To say that Mary is Black is to conjure the warmth of life interred with bone, like portents of the prophetic, the absorption of the ephemeral, the intensity of desire, the density of the universe. To quote Audre Lorde, "The white fathers told us, I think therefore I am; and the black goddess in each of us—the poet—whispers in our dreams, I feel therefore I can be free."[57]

To say that Mary is Black is to consider Black women as witnesses to the fullness of God, Black women as chosen by God, Black women as those who tarry and are present at every moment of Christ's ministry.

To say that Mary is Black is to consider she who survived a disparate maternal birth rate, brought life forth against circumstances and odds, lived and learned and loved as she who was persecuted but not abandoned, struck down but not destroyed, set aflame but not consumed.

To say that Mary is Black is to consider that, in as much as people could not recognize the Christ, they certainly could not recognize the precarity nor the joy of the body, of the life, of the womb God chose to anoint and grace.

For if Mary is Black, then Black female flesh is sacred and must be read against consumption and greed, against human indignity, against suffering and individualism, against scarcity. If Mary is Black, then 'deep calls to deep' the practice and proclamation of Black joy, the delight of divine darkness and Black life, the embrace of Black pleasure in "this here flesh" that must, Beloved, *be loved*.[58]

To say that Mary is Black is to say that Black wombs are holy hush harbors, that Black birth is liturgy, that Black *life* matters.

To say that Mary is Black is to affirm that Black love is infectious, that Black joy is contagious, that Black is beautiful, good, and true.

To say that Mary is Black is to say that God takes up residence and delights God's self among Black girls, among immigrants, among the trafficked, among the survivors, among those considered poor or despised, even among the dead and dying.

To say that Mary is Black is to say that the *very* birth of Black flesh is endemic to liberation, Black inhales and exhales holy arbiters of grace, incarnations of unfailing love.

To say that Mary is Black is to name the Divine creativity and connection of a woman of multiple religious belongings, a woman whose fugitive life was filled with border crossings and concealments, a woman who refused earthly affiliations, except to be always and ever be on the side of the oppressed.

To say that Mary is Black is to ponder the mystery, 'Woman as we are.'

To say that Mary is Black is to say that this is where you find God.

To say that Mary is Black is to say that anti-Blackness is anti-Christ.

To say that Mary is Black is to say that another world is possible.

To say that Mary is Black is to say that we can hear her breathing.

To say that Mary is Black is to lay claim to this future, here and now.

To say that Mary is Black is to pray, and then, to act.

To say that Mary is Black is to call upon freedom for us all.

Mary.
María.
Miriam.
Maryam.
Maryama.
Mario.

And in this world I must say,
That to say Mary is Black is to say that she is Indigenous.
That to say Mary is Black is to say that Mary is Palestinian. For in the words of June Jordan:

I was born a Black woman
and now
I am become a Palestinian.[59]

Mary is Black.

And we are reminded, that we *all* need images of Blackness that are sacred.
It turns out, we already have them.

If we are willing to see them as such.
Or as Mari Evans wrote in *I Am a Black Woman*:

> assailed
> impervious
> indestructible
> Look
> on me and be
> renewed.[60]

Taste, then.
And see.

Acknowledgments

I have had the great gift in life, and along the journey of this project, to have been so fiercely loved, supported, and championed by more people than I can possibly ever name, and in earnest, at times to always recall. My gratitude, however, is immense, as this book was birthed across multiple continents, loves, losses, transitions, illnesses, and joys—I am grateful for it, and simply to still be here. *Give thanks.*

For Granny, Mama Mabel, Grandma Nancy, Auntie Gloria, Grandma Nannie, and the lineages of mothers and aunties and fathers and ancestors who held me in their hearts and wombs long before I was here. Thank you for your gardens.

For my incredible parents, William and Anita Raye Adkins, thank you for raising me to live fearlessly and dream a world beyond what most eyes could see, even my own. Anything generous, loving, and kind in me, comes from you. I love you so much, Daddy! I love you so much, Moma! Alisa Beth, you are a far more talented, far more brilliant and far more lovely combination of the same set of genes. Thank you for the living reminder that my dreams pursue me. Bridgitte, thank you for swooping in with cape and enthusiasm on more than one occasion, and caring for me and my work through every storm, external or internal. Papa Turner, your sacrifices and love long before you knew my name, are the foundations of my possibility. For all of my family, extended and chosen, my love extends to every reach of our family tree, who share our roots in red clay against the backdrops of blue mountains. May we continue to bloom and thrive.

For incredible mentors and friends—at Duke, the first threads of this project emerged under the brilliance and guidance of thinkers who loved, challenged, and endlessly encouraged me. Forever Dr. Jennings, the echoes of your laughter (usually fueled by my behind-the-scenes and off-record playback) were the soundtrack of my studies. You never asked me to be anything other than myself, and gave me the space to figure out who that was. Thank you for always championing me, and humming along to every strung together sentence. To Robyn Wiegman, who truly taught me how to read theory, inhabit it, and think it, and who kept me from quitting; to Fred Moten, who pushed me to theorize theology; to J. Kameron Carter, who took the poetry of Black feminism seriously; to Mary Fulkerson, who first gave me space to say a word about Mary; to Gene Rogers, who remembered a shy girl from her undergraduate days, and told me then that it was always important to remain present in conversations I didn't understand—your hospitalities made room for me. To Brian Bantum and Gail Song Bantum, my "sixth men," who taught me that we are always worth each other's long hauls; you saw me first. To Leia Harper, Sarah Lance, and the friends and teachers at Sari Bari that changed my theology, all of it, and the ways I write and think in this world. To so many friends from that time, my gratitude to Denise Thorpe—I would not be so many things, including ordained, without you. SueJeanne Koh, with whom I have crossed more finish lines than I could imagine. To so many who cheered me on during such beloved Amsterdam years, most especially Michael Dunkley. To so many who have poured into me over the years, with love and hope, and who are still seeing about me—our ancestor Katie Geneva Cannon, ancestor Tammy Williams, Sharon Watson-Fluker, Evelyn Parker, Dianne Stewart, Kelly Brown Douglas, Matthew Wesley Williams—gratitude is inadequate to describe.

For incredible colleagues and friends, particularly those in the Theology department and African and African Diaspora Studies program at Boston College, who have supported my growth and read my drafts and taken my work and presence seriously. I do not have enough words to express the grace of my life, that has been manifest through the love and care and fierce intellect of M. Shawn Copeland (and by grand and holy capaciousness, Barbara Bzura). You helped keep me alive. I am honored to be able to learn (and laugh, loudly and unceasingly) with you. Andrew Prevot and Elizabeth Antus, your kindness and patience are the stuff of what is still good in this world, and I am thankful for your hospitality and friendship—you speak my sarcasm fluently, and made this space a home. I am particularly indebted to Jim Keenan, Kristin Heyer, and Mary Ann Hinsdale, for their mentorship, long walks, enthusiasm, wisdom, and trust. Nelly Wamaitha, you have made this journey one of grand laughter and decisive delight. The best is yet to come. Jonathan Howard and Alison Curseen, from Fred's classroom together to our first jobs as professors, I'm grateful for the way life brought us together time and time again. May we continue to share moments of serendipity along the way. To Martin Summers, my literal "day one," I truly admire you and grow always from your wisdom and counsel. To Régine Jean-Charles, a mentor and beloved sister and friend, who made me believe the fullness of an academic life was possible, while loving myself, fiercely. To Shawn McGuffey and Rhonda Frederick, gracious mentors who have kept me laughing and working (on books, and on my shoe game). To Richard Paul, for all of the ways you've kept my heart afloat and my receipts intact, you go above and beyond, I don't take it for granted. To Angela Ards, Latrica Best, Jovonna Jones, and Lorelle Semley, your presence and spirits have buoyed me here. To all of my students, graduate and undergraduate, who have made me better, and especially to those with greater brilliance coming after me—Kyle Johnson, Nathan Wood-House, Chanelle Robinson, Byron Wratee, Sarah Livick-Moses, and especially Maddie Jarret, who so graciously helped edit and support this manuscript in a multitude of ways—thank you for the reciprocity of being able to take part in your journey, and always entertaining my musings on the Black Madonna with excitement and rigor. Our futures are brighter because your work is on the way! I celebrate especially my dear undergraduate assistant, Sydney Fosnick-Davis, who labored lovingly with me on this project, and whose contributions have only made it (and me) that much better.

For the artists who have inspired me and so generously allowed me to be conversation with their brilliance—most especially, Lina Iris Viktor, Harmonia Rosales, and Mark Doox. I am indebted to the divine prescience and laughter of beloved nayyirah waheed. I extend my gratitude to Thomas Perridge, Nadine Kolz, Rachel Atkins, Vinothini Thiruvannamalai, and Timothy Beck, for the generosity of the early reviewers of this work, and to the entire team at Oxford University Press, for all of the ways they have guided this text to light.

For those who are my family, who happen to also be colleagues—Ashon Crawley, my beloved friend, thank you for living with me, friendship as a way of life. Some people ask to have their journals burned when they depart from this life; we will ask someone delete our endless hours of voice notes. Meredith Frances Coleman-Tobias (yes, always, the entire thing!), *Makidada*. Wherever you go, there I'll be. Know you keep fire kindled in my soul. Oluwatomisin Oredein, my Tomes, thank you for always seeing, and hearing, and reading, and listening, and revising, and dreaming with me, even when it is past both of our bedtimes. Kyrah Malika Daniels, my scholastic-sarcastic sacred initiatory beloved sister, know that I revel deeply in your wisdom and joy, showing up to places with unplanned matching outfits, and answering these calls from the deep together—*ayibobo!*

For the many friends and loved ones who have kept me between Boston and Newark, this book could not have happened without a village, especially Miyoshi Lee, Tracey Bey Johnson, Chrystal Williamson, Chanel Albert, Dorita Newsome-Dobbins, and Akosua Achampong.

And for my greatest loves.

To Sofia, Ezekiel, and Bella—you have made me who I am, as a mother and a person, and I am forever grateful for each of you. May you always know that Black is beautiful, and know it full well. To Judah Nwá, you are beyond precious, and as a pandemic baby, *built different*. Thank you for being so deeply everything I didn't know I needed—completely your own—and writing a new story inside of me. May every dream each of you dream become manifold reality. *So be it! See to it!*

To Timothy Levi—some things in life are simply *too good*, your love the epitome. Thank you for being peace, freedom, abundance, and mine. I love you, more.

And thank you, God—for this joy that I have, and for a life more beautiful than I could have ever imagined. May this book be an offering that brings us closer to a vision of love and justice befitting the sacred work in us all, across every manifestation. Amen.

Notes

Introduction

1. Translation from Wilda C. Gafney, *A Women's Lectionary for the Whole Church: Year W: A Multi Gospel Single-Year Lectionary* (New York: Church Publishing, Inc., 2021), 133.
2. Of the estimated ten to sixteen million stolen Africans who survived passage through the mid-Atlantic slave routes, it is estimated that anywhere from one-third to one-half of these survivors "landed in Brazil and between 60 and 70 percent ended up in Brazil or the sugar colonies of the Caribbean." Steven Mintz, "Historical Context: American Slavery in Comparative Perspective," https://www.gilderlehrman.org/history-resources/teacher-resources/historical-context-american-slavery-comparative-perspective. For comparison, "Only 6 percent arrived in what is now the United States," though "by 1860, approximately two-thirds of all enslaved men, women, and children in the Western Hemisphere lived in the American South."
3. Song of Songs 1:5.
4. Ivone Gebara and Maria Clara Bingemer, *Mary, Mother of God, Mother of the Poor* (Maryknoll, NY: Orbis Books, 1989), 157.
5. Audre Lorde, "Poetry Is Not a Luxury," in *Sister Outsider* (New York: Penguin Books, 2020), 24.
6. Ibid.
7. Édouard Glissant, *Poetics of Relation*, trans. Betsy Wing (Ann Arbor: University of Michigan Press, 1997), 5.
8. Ibid.
9. "It is the gift, the concept, the inhabitation of and living into *otherwise possibilities*. Otherwise, as word—otherwise possibilities, as phrase—announces the fact of infinite alternatives to what *is*. And what *is* is about being, about existence, about ontology." Ashon Crawley, *Blackpentecostal Breath: The Aesthetics of Possibility* (New York: Fordham University Press, 2016), 2.
10. Édouard Glissant, "Édouard Glissant in Conversation with Manthia Diawara," *Nka: Journal of Contemporary African Art* 28 (2011): 5.
11. Fred Moten, "Blackness and Nothingness (Mysticism in the Flesh)," *South Atlantic Quarterly* 112, no. 4 (2013): 745.
12. See Willie James Jennings, *The Christian Imagination: Theology and the Origins of Race* (New Haven: Yale University Press, 2010); Brian Bantum, *Redeeming Mulatto: A Theology of Race and Christian Hybridity* (Waco: Baylor University Press, 2010); J. Kameron Carter, *Race: A Theological Account* (Oxford: Oxford University Press, 2008).
13. Karl Barth, *Evangelical Theology: An Introduction* (Grand Rapids: Eerdmans, 1963), 49–50.
14. Michel Foucault, "Nietzsche, Genealogy, History," *Semiotext(E)* 3, no. 1 (1978): 1.
15. Ibid.
16. In *The Female Complaint*, Lauren Berlant describes female sexual identity as a genre in these terms, as well the implications of describing a kind of identity in these typological terms. Though she goes on to claim the problem of genre as a means to circumscribe identity, expectation, and performance of a part, I find that her imagery here is perhaps more pliable and more dynamic, particularly in describing theology as a way of reading or seeing, not of identifying a person. Lauren Gail Berlant, *The Female Complaint: The Unfinished Business of Sentimentality in American Culture* (Durham: Duke University Press, 2008), 4.
17. This concept is explored at length in Crawley, *Blackpentecostal Breath*.
18. Katie Cannon, "Wheels in the Middle of Wheels." *Journal of Feminist Studies in Religion* 8, no. 2 (1992): 129.
19. See M. Shawn Copeland, *Enfleshing Freedom: Body, Race, and Being* (Minneapolis: Fortress Press, 2010).
20. Fred Moten, "To Consent Not to Be a Single Being," *Harriet: A Poetry Blog* (2010).
21. Denise Ferreira da Silva, *Toward a Global Idea of Race* (Minneapolis: University of Minnesota Press, 2007).
22. Hortense J. Spillers, "Interstices," in *Black, White, and in Color: Essays on American Literature and Culture* (Chicago: University of Chicago Press, 2003), 195.

23. Ibid.
24. Ibid.
25. Fred Moten, *Stolen Life* (Durham: Duke University Press, 2018).
26. Gebara and Bingemer, *Mary, Mother of God, Mother of the Poor*, 88. Gebara and Bingemer have an extended discussion on the formulation and meaning of dogmatic tradition for the Roman Catholic Church, as well as their approach to revisiting the Marian Dogmas in a contemporary context in ch. IV "Marian Dogmas: Their Meaning Arising from the Poor and the 'Spirit' of Our Age" of their text.
27. Ibid., 93. Though they speak specifically to a Latin American context, this quote extends to thinking a Black Mariology.
28. James H. Cone, *A Black Theology of Liberation*. Fiftieth anniversary edition (Maryknoll, NY: Orbis Books, 2020), 8.
29. Ibid., 13.
30. Karen Baker-Fletcher, "More than Suffering: The Healing and Resurrecting Spirit of God," in *Womanist Theological Ethics: A Reader*, ed. Katie Geneva Cannon, Emilie M. Townes, and Angela D. Sims (Louisville, KY: Westminster John Knox Press, 2011), 158.
31. Delores Williams, *Sisters in the Wilderness*, 158.
32. Ibid.
33. Bingemer and Gebara speak of "God's 'endless' revelation of God in Mary" ... "the face of Mary of Nazareth has become manifold, like human yearnings, like the responses of love. Those responses are both so different and yet similar.... They spring from what is hoped, and from the unexpected, from encounter and from failure to connect, in grace and its absence ..." they continue, "This is why we can speak of different Marian traditions, of different ways of reading Mary's countenance, and they do not have to be mutually exclusive. Mary has moved beyond the situation of individuals who have only one history. She has many stories which merge into history, linking the lives of individuals and multitudes," Bingemer and Gebara, *Mary, Mother of God, Mother of the Poor*, 18.
34. Andrew Prevot, *Thinking Prayer: Theology and Spirituality amid the Crises of Modernity* (Notre Dame: University of Notre Dame Press, 2015), 304.
35. Ibid., 305.
36. Williams, *Sisters in the Wilderness*, 160.
37. Luce Irigaray, *Marine Lover of Friedrich Nietzsche* (New York: Columbia University Press, 1991), 185–86.
38. Cone, *Black Theology of Liberation*, 21.
39. Crawley, *Blackpentecostal Breath*, 2–10.

Chapter 1

1. Amanda Pipkin, *Rape in the Republic, 1609–1725: Formulating Dutch Identity* (Leiden: Brill, 2013), 93.
2. I use the term "Black woman" and "Black female flesh" in this chapter to mark the racial and gendered difference at work in the image, and the presumptions of the archive itself, acknowledging the limitations assumed in the language of "woman" and the ways that gendered and sexed difference is irreducible to the body, especially for someone of African descent within a frame of colonial violence.
3. Pipkin, *Rape in the Republic*, 94, n. 48.
4. Bob Haak, *The Golden Age: Dutch Painters of the Seventeenth Century*, trans. Elizabeth Willems-Treeman (New York: Stewart, Tabori & Chang, 1996), 326.
5. Ibid.
6. This painting was unidentified until 1940, when Jan Gerrit van Gelder noticed a distinctive, embellished "CB" in the lower right corner and realized it was the monograph of Delft painter Christiaen van Couwenbergh. Born in 1604, Couwenbergh (d. 1667) was a well-respected history painter, his contributions to the décor of the Oranjezaal in the Huis ten Bosch (the famous dome-ceiling room in the royal palace of the Netherlands) evidence of his elite status. Since Gelder's analysis, 88 works have been identified as belonging to Couwenbergh's oeuvre, including the 1632 oil painting known as *The Rape of a Negress*. J. G. van Gelder, "De Schilders Van De Oranjezaal," [Netherlands yearbook for history of art] *Nederlands kunsthistorisch jaarboek* 2 (1948–49) (118–64).
7. As per above, the closest approximations of both nakedness and/or rape in Couwenbergh's paintings are a painting of Potiphar's wife and Joseph, and a painting of Susanna. The Susanna scene centers her in the bath where, according to the apocryphal story from the book of Daniel in the Hebrew Bible, she is spied on by two voyeurs. The men at this point in the painting have no

physical contact with her, but the story indicates these two will later follow her and demand she have sex with them.
8. According to Haak, "Clues to patrons' wishes and demands are therefore scanty, a phenomenon in itself indicative of the religious, social, and political atmosphere in which the paintings originated. The Dutch Republic was newly Protestant and newly independent; the Calvinist Church eschewed adornment as a matter of principle and therefore did not patronize artists . . . the major customers were, rather, the citizens themselves and their civic organizations. Indeed, the greater number of paintings was created not on commission but for the free market." *The Golden Age*, 11.
9. Klaske Muizelaar and Derek L. Phillips, *Picturing Men and Women in the Dutch Golden Age: Paintings and People in Historical Perspective* (New Haven: Yale University Press, 2003), 4.
10. Note that, of the limited archive on the painting, no literature seems to mention the sitting chair and there is limited commentary on the presence of the pot. However, as Jan Steen's *Woman at Her Toilet* demonstrates, certain items deemed to be less respectable or lacking in good taste in paintings were frequently edited to be more acceptable. In *Woman at Her Toilet*, the original chamber pot was disguised as a more appropriate water pitcher, and a petticoat was included to drape over the bare thighs of the woman. The visibility of the chamber pot in *The Rape of the Negress* does seem to press an insistence of "real" humanity, including its aspects of stench and filth, into the frame of the interpretation. One cannot help but think of the Freudian relation between feces and gold, given this painting's center in the Golden Age.
11. Sandrine Le Bideau-Vincent, "Christian Van Couwenbergh," in *Peinture Flamande et Hollandaise ve–Xviiie Siècle* (Musee de la Ville de Strasbourg, 2009), 186.
12. As noted in an earlier footnote, in the one other painting that features a Black woman (*The Finding of Moses*), the Black woman is depicted with a head covering of similar style to the woman in *The Rape of the Negress*. Though the Black woman in the former scene is but one servant of Pharoah's daughter among two others (again, all three of whom are naked, the one who faces the painting audience covered from her lower waist to her thigh with a sheer fabric), the Black woman is the only one with a head covering. The archives rarely mention or interpret the bonnet on the woman's head in either of these images, or if there is a connection to the marking of someone who prostitutes—though the style is slightly different, the woman in Couwenbergh's *Brothel Scene* has a scarf over her hair, a notable exception for Couwenbergh's portraiture. As per *The Rape of the Negress*, I will also note here that there is little development on the significance or implications of the dressed man's costume as further detail that may elucidate Couwenbergh's choices here.
13. Hortense Spillers's analysis of patriarchalized gender is an extremely a helpful analytic for the ways the Black woman in this image is not granted the graces of being seen as a woman within patriarchal society, but as something outside of the category or demands of gendered performance or access. See Hortense Spillers, "Mama's Baby, Papa's Maybe: An American Grammar Book," *Diacritics* 17, no. 2 (1987): 65–81.
14. Diane Wolfthal, *Images of Rape: The "Heroic" Tradition and Its Alternatives* (Cambridge; New York: Cambridge University Press, 1999), 194–95.
15. Lotte C. van de Pol, "The Whore, the Bawd, and the Artist: The Reality and Imagery of Seventeenth-Century Dutch Prostitution," *Journal of Historians of Netherlandish Art* 2, no. 1/2 (2010). As Muizelaar and Phillips describe, "More than anything else, a woman's honor and respectability rested on her sexual behavior: virginity was expected of the unmarried, fidelity of the married. What was really at stake, however, was the honor of the men to whom women were related. A man's honor did not rest on his sexual conduct in the same way. In fact, he would often express his masculinity by trying to seduce the women of others. The head of the household was thus keenly aware of the need to exercise vigilance in regard to 'his' women. His own honor was defined by his success in doing so. Men considered women weak, pious, and sexually innocent, and thus requiring protection against the advances of other men. At the same time, they saw women as having an insatiable sexual appetite that derived from their physiology. . . . They were, after all, seen as daughters of Eve." Muizelaar and Phillips, *Picturing Men and Women*, 7.
16. Albert Blankert et al., exhibition catalogue *Hollands Classicisme in de zeventiende-eeuwse schilderkunst*, Rotterdam (Museum Boijmans Van Beuningen) and Frankfurt (Städelsche Kunstinstitut) 1999, 156, no. 24.
17. In his research, J. G. van Gelder realized that Couwenbergh painted the figure in his own likeness. This was not Couwenbergh's only attempt at interjection, his self-portraiture including himself at least once as Samson in a historical work with Delilah cutting his hair. Caravaggio and others did so similarly, as in *The Sick Bacchus*.
18. Wolfthal, *Images of Rape*, 191.

19. Charmaine Nelson, *Representing the Black Female Subject in Western Art* (New York: Routledge, 2010), 181.
20. Spillers, *Mama's Baby*, 67.
21. Nelson, *Representing the Black Female Subject in Western Art*, 180.
22. Edward Lucie-Smith, *Sexuality in Western Art* (New York: Thames and Hudson, 1991), 92.
23. Mariet Westermann, ed., *Making Home in the Dutch Republic* (Denver Art Museum and the Newark Museum, 2001), 18.
24. "As far as the producers were concerned, nearly all were men, usually from a relatively privileged segment of society. For most, the production of paintings was more a business than a channel of personal expression and creativity. Like other goods and services, paintings were produced "in the hope of arousing interest and finding a buyer" (Muizelaar and Phillips, *Picturing Men and Women*, 4).
25. After asking "Mais ce fait, quel est il?," Beyer cites a French *translation* of the two verses from the Song X portion of *Os Lusíadas* in original Portuguese. Victor Beyer, "Musee Des Beaux-Arts De Strasbourg. I. Un Tableau De Christiaen De Couwenbergh," *Revue du Louvre* XXII (1972). The English verses read: (45) "She had more stanzas sung in Siren-strain, lauding her Albuquerque's high renown, when she recalled the passionate deed, the stain on his white fame that o'er the world hath shone. The mighty Captain whom the Fates ordain to view his toils win Glory's lasting Crown, should ever 'prove him kind and loved compeer of his own men, not cruel judge severe.' (46) In days of hunger and of dire distress, sickness, bolts, arrows, thunder, lightning-glint, when the sore seasons and sad sites oppress his soldiers, rendering services sans stint; it seemeth salvage act of wild excess, of heart inhuman, bosom insolent, to make last penalty of Laws atone for sins our frailty and our love condone. (47) Abominable incest shall not be his sin, nor ruffian rape of virgin pure, not e'en dishonour of adultery, but lapse with wanton slave-girl, vile, obscure: If urged by jealous sting, or modesty, or used to cruelty and harshness dour, Man from his men mad anger curbeth not, his Fame's white shield shall bear Black ugly blot." Luís de Camões, *Os Lusiadas (The Lusiads)*, trans. Richard Francis Burton and Isabel Burton, 6 vols. (London: B. Quaritch, 1880), 378–79. Note that the English translation here reflects the gradual diminishing of the act against the enslaved Black woman here as a "lapse."
26. W. Maier-Preusker, "Christiaen Van Couwenbergh (1604–1667). Oeuvre und Wandlungen eines Holländischen Caravaggisten," *Wallraf-Richartz Jahrbuch* 52 (1991): 196. ("Hier rüstet sich ein zum Bade bereiter Mann, eine Negerin 'weißzuwaschen', wird aber von einem zweiten Mann ob dieses vergeblichen Unterfangens lachend verspottet.")
27. See discussion specifically in Wolfthal, *Images of Rape*. Also see chapter on religious and mythological figures in Muizelaar and Phillips, *Picturing Men and Women*.
28. Writing on the eroticized depictions of the post-rape suicide of Lucretia, Carol M. Schuler suggests, "As an eroticized version of an historical theme, the suicide of Lucretia joins numerous classical and biblical subjects similarly transformed by sixteenth-century artists. Indeed, one consistent feature of sixteenth-century Northern erotic art is the placement of the sexualized female in the context of a legendary schema. In such scenes a distortion of the spirit, if not the actual facts, of the story provides an opportunity for the representation of nude, or semi-nude, Judiths, Susannas, Eves, and others." Carol M. Schuler, "Virtuous Model / Voluptuous Martyr: The Suicide of Lucretia in Northern Renaissance Art and Its Relationship to Late Medieval Devotional Imagery," in *Saints, Sinners, and Sisters: Gender and Northern Art in Medieval and Early Modern Europe*, ed. Jane L. Carroll and Alison G. Stewart (Aldershot: Ashgate, 2003), 11.
29. In the 1999 exhibition catalogue, Albert Blankert too insists this must be an episode from a story but concedes that "This painting has baffled experts right from the start. Yet another effort was made to interpret it for the present exhibition catalogue but unfortunately with no result." Blankert et al., *Hollands Classicisme*, 156–59, no. 24.
30. For more on the gendered legalities of property in the Netherlands and the contemporary understanding of rape, see van der Heijden (2000), 623–44.
31. Pipkin, *Rape in the Republic*, 3.
32. Régine Jean-Charles, "They Never Call It Rape: Critical Reception and Representation of Sexual Violence in Marie Vieux-Chauvet's *Amour, Colère et Folie*," *Journal of Haitian Studies* 12, no. 2 (2006): 4.
33. Blankert et al., *Hollands Classicisme*, 159.
34. Wolfthal, *Images of Rape*, 191.
35. Haak, *The Golden Age*, 326.
36. "These are the poles of iconoclasm in 1566: on the one hand, disorderly destruction, plundering and theft, with motives that were violent or mercenary; on the other hand, controlled and

sometimes systematic iconoclasm, often for sound theological reasons, with little if any theft and some saving on the grounds of the artistic merit of particular works of art." David Freedberg, "Art and Iconoclasm, 1525–1580: The Case of the Northern Netherlands," in *Kunst Voor De Beeldenstorm*, ed. J. P. Filedt Kok, W. Halsema-Kubes, and W. Th. Kloek (Rijksmuseum, Amsterdam: Staatsuitgeveri: 's-gravenhage, 1986), 75. For more on the Dutch iconoclasm, see Angela Vanhaelen, *The Wake of Iconoclasm: Painting the Church in the Dutch Republic* (University Park: Pennsylvania State University Press, 2012). For more on the intensification of Catholic faith in the Protestant republic, see Charles H. Parker, *Faith on the Margins: Catholics and Catholicism in the Dutch Golden Age* (Cambridge, MA: Harvard University Press, 2008).

37. See appendix B in Charles Warren Currier, *Carmel in America a Centennial History of the Discalced Carmelites in the United States* (Baltimore: John Murphy, 1890), 370–76.
38. Theirs was not the only Marian statue to be hidden. At the same time, a statue of Our Sweet Lady (or, Our Lady of Den Bosch) was also hidden and smuggled to Brussels for safekeeping. She was returned in 1853 and now rests in St. John's cathedral in Den Bosch.
39. Pavel Florensky, *Iconostasis* (Crestwood, NY: St. Vladimir's Seminary Press, 1996), 69.
40. Ibid., 134.
41. Ibid., 91.
42. Monique Scheer, "From Majesty to Mystery: Change in the Meanings of Black Madonnas from the Sixteenth to Nineteenth Centuries," *American Historical Review* 107, no. 5 (2002): 1413.
43. Ibid., 1419.
44. For the history of this term and its erasure, please see Moya Bailey and Trudy, "On Misogynoir: Citation, Erasure, and Plagiarism," *Feminist Media Studies* 18, no. 4 (2018): 762–68.
45. Nelson, *Representing the Black Female Subject in Western Art*, 179.
46. "Without doubt, the doctrine of election and reprobation must stand or fall together." George Whitefield, "Letter to Wesley, from Bethesda in Georgia" (December 24, 1740).
47. Ibid.
48. Willie Jennings, *The Christian Imagination: Theology and the Origins of Race* (New Haven: Yale University Press, 2011), 34.
49. Wolfthal, *Images of Rape*, 197.
50. Viktor Shklovsky, *Theory of Prose*, trans. Benjamin Sher (Elmwood Park, IL: Dalkey Archive Press, 1990), 10.
51. Elaborating on Shklovsky's observations, Rey Chow suggests that, "While 'art as a device' defamiliarizes an object in such a way as to make us notice its perceptible quality (such as the stoniness of a stone), 'laying bare' suggests, rather, a return to an original condition lying behind a set of numbing habits to automatized conventions—an original condition, that is, of *unadorned nakedness*." Rey Chow, *Entanglements: Or Transmedial Thinking about Capture* (Durham: Duke University Press, 2012), 26.
52. Shklovsky, *Theory of Prose*, 10.
53. Saidiya Hartman, "Venus in Two Acts," *Small Axe* 12, no. 2 (2008): 2.
54. Ashon Crawley, "Harriet Jacobs Gets a Hearing," *Current Musicology* 93 (2012): 34.
55. Ibid., 33.
56. Hilda Graef, *Mary: A History of Doctrine and Devotion* (Notre Dame, IN: Ave Maria Press, 2009), 39.

Chapter 2

1. Most biblical scholars follow the documentary hypothesis in understanding that the creation accounts in the book of Genesis are edited and redacted from two different sources. Genesis 1:1–2.3 is attributed to the school of priests identified as source "P," while Genesis 2:4–3:24 is attributed to the Yahwist (denoted by the use of the divine name YHWH/Yahweh), source "J."
2. Gen 1:26–28 (New Revised Standard Version).
3. Gen 2:22–25 (emphasis added).
4. The Yahwist (or Jahwist) source is considered to have been composed around 950 BCE, during the rule of David and Solomon.
5. For the purposes of clarification, I use the names Adam and Eve to distinguish the narrative characters throughout, though Eve here is not yet named.
6. Though for our purposes "grammatical gender is not sexual identification," I will note here that, given the insistence on sexuality for the other actors in this unfolding drama, the attention to the serpent's grammatical *maleness* is a conspicuously understated a point. Phyllis Trible, *God and*

the *Rhetoric of Sexuality* (Philadelphia: Fortress Press, 1978), 80. One can also refer to the complicated gendering and racialization of the serpent in Stokes's "Someone's in the Garden with Eve."
7. In her brilliant article "Blaming Eve Alone," Julie Faith Parker offers an incredible genealogy of the absence of the prepositional phrase עמה ("with her"), especially from English translations of Genesis 3:6b (ויאכל עמה גם־לאישה ותתן) "and she gave also to her husband *with her* and he ate." Her research emphasizes the circulation of multiple discourses placing blame and responsibility of banishment from the Garden of Eve upon Eve alone (and thus, "woman"). With a thoroughly detailed analysis of multiple translations as well as translation committee discussion, she concludes: "The myth of 'the fall' has become so firmly embedded in our collective conscience with only the woman as the culpable character that translators may convey the story accordingly, without realizing that they are contradicting the Hebrew text. Yet, while discerning translators' motivations for specific decisions can be speculative, assessing the effect of these translations is not." Julie Faith Parker, "Blaming Eve Alone: Translation, Omission, and Implications of עמה in Genesis 3:6b," *Journal of Biblical Literature* 132, no. 4 (2013): 729–47.
8. Early examples of feminist exegesis name Adam as a victim to his own ineptitude, a demonstrative point in arguing male identity as that which is less qualified for leadership positions within a social hierarchy. Though this made a tactical point critical to the time, my argument here is to destabilize rather than denigrate the idea of the male in the text.
9. Gayle Rubin, "The Traffic in Women: Notes on the 'Political Economy' of Sex," in *Deviations: A Gayle Rubin Reader* (Durham: Duke University Press, 2012), 34.
10. In City of God (*De Civitate Dei*), Augustine asks "And what is the origin of our evil will but pride?" (14:13). For Augustine, though Eve was fully deceived by the devil-cum-serpent, Adam deliberately followed Eve, with intents both valiant and selfish, into prideful disobedience (14:14). See Augustine, *City of God* (Harmondsworth: Penguin Books, 1972). As John Cavadini describes, for Augustine, "the defining moment is when Adam fully and deliberately decides—despite not being deceived—to disfigure by sin the spousal fellowship he and Eve had already been given by God." John C. Cavadini, "Spousal Vision: A Study of Text and History in the Theology of Saint Augustine," *Augustinian Studies* 43, no. 1/2 (2012): 135.
11. Citing several key interlocutors, Monique Wittig describes: "A materialist feminist approach shows that what we take for the cause or origin of oppression is in fact only the *mark* imposed by the oppressor; the "myth of woman," plus its material effects and manifestations in the appropriated consciousness and bodies of women. Thus, this mark does not preexist oppression . . . sex is taken as an 'immediate given,' a 'sensible given,' 'physical features,' belonging to a natural order. But what we believe to be a physical and direct perception is only a sophisticated and mythic construction, an '*imaginary formation*.' . . ." Monique Wittig, "One Is Not Born a Woman," *Feminist Issues* 1, no. 1 (1981): 48.
12. Jennings, *The Christian Imagination: Theology and the Origins of Race*. Throughout our discussion I will refer to Jennings's notion of *displacement* as critical to our understanding the multifaceted optics of race and sex as they emerge in the new world.
13. The task of reading the Genesis texts with a hermeneutic of suspicion, particularly with regard to Eve, is made possible by a number of now classic feminist and womanist Biblical interventions. A much-abbreviated list includes: Phyllis Trible, "Eve and Adam: Genesis 2–3 Reread," *Andover Newton Quarterly* 13 (1973); *God and the Rhetoric of Sexuality*; Carol L. Meyers, *Discovering Eve: Ancient Israelite Women in Context* (New York: Oxford University Press, 1988); Elaine H. Pagels, *Adam, Eve, and the Serpent* (New York: Random House, 1988); Athalya Brenner, ed., *A Feminist Companion to Genesis* (Sheffield: Sheffield Academic Press, 1993); Karen Baker-Fletcher, *Sisters of Dust, Sisters of Spirit: Womanist Wordings on God and Creation* (Minneapolis: Fortress Press, 1998); Kristen E. Kvam, Linda S. Schearing, and Valarie H. Ziegler, *Eve and Adam: Jewish, Christian, and Muslim Readings on Genesis and Gender* (Bloomington: Indiana University Press, 1999); Joseph Abraham, *Eve, Accused or Acquitted?: An Analysis of Feminist Readings of the Creation Narrative Texts in Genesis 1–3* (Cumbria: Paternoster Press, 2002); Anne Lapidus Lerner, *Eternally Eve: Images of Eve in the Hebrew Bible, Midrash, and Modern Jewish Poetry* (Waltham, MA: Brandeis University Press, 2007); Gay L. Byron and Vanessa Lovelace, eds., *Womanist Interpretations of the Bible: Expanding the Discourse* (Atlanta, GA: SBL Press, 2016).
14. Few would likely be comfortable with considering practices of bestiality in the garden, but later moments in Genesis have inferred that human beings may have had intimate and even sexual contact beyond themselves, perhaps with celestial beings. The Genesis 6:4 reference to the Nephilim as "sons of God" is ambiguous and disputed, but it claims that these beings reproduced with the "daughters of men." At minimum, there is an indication here of broader ethos around sex and relationship than contemporary forms of heteronormative monogamy.

15. For a helpful engagement with how Christian thought shifted the ideas around sex and sexual morality, see Kyle Harper, *From Shame to Sin: The Christian Transformation of Sexual Morality in Late Antiquity* (Cambridge, MA: Harvard University Press, 2013).
16. "The question before us, then, is not about the motion of bodies, without which there could not be sexual intercourse; but about the shameful motion of the organs of generation, which certainly could be absent, and yet the fructifying connection be still not wanting, if the organs of generation were not obedient to lust, but simply to the will, like the other members of the body. Is it not even now the case, in 'the body of this death,' that a command is given to the foot, the arm, the finger, the lip, or the tongue, and they are instantly set in motion at this intimation of our will? And (to take a still more wonderful case) even the liquid contained in the urinary vessels obeys the command to flow from us at our pleasure, and when we are not pressed with its overflow; while the vessels, also, which contain the liquid, discharge without difficulty, if they are in a healthy state, the office assigned them by our will of propelling, pressing out, and ejecting their contents. With how much greater ease and quietness, then, if the generative organs of our body were compliant, would natural motion ensue, and human conception be effected; except in the instance of those persons who violate natural order, and by a righteous retribution are punished with the intractability of these members and organs! This punishment is felt by the chaste and pure, who, without doubt, would rather beget children by mere natural desire than by voluptuous pruriency; while unchaste persons, who are impelled by this diseased passion, and bestow their love upon harlots as well as wives, are excited by a still heavier mental remorse in consequence of this carnal chastisement." Augustine, "On Marriage and Concupiscence," in Vol. 5: *St. Augustine: Anti-Pelagian Writings*, ed. Philip Schaff. A Select Library of the Nicene and Post-Nicene Fathers of the Christian Church: 1st Series (Grand Rapids, MI: Eerdmans, 1978), II.53 (XXXI).
17. Trible, "Eve and Adam: Genesis 2-3 Reread," 74-81. Emphasizing the literal Hebrew word play between Adam, the earth creature, literally *ha-'adam*, and created from the earth, *ha-'adama*. In this creation account we are faced with what many early interpreters understood as *'adam* the androgyne, not the man Adam. There is a long tradition of accounting for androgyny, and taking as fact its presence, in both Jewish midrash and early Christian interpretations.
18. Jay F. Rosenberg, *Thinking Clearly about Death* (Englewood Cliffs, NJ: Prentice-Hall, 1983), 21-22.
19. Georges Bataille, *Death and Sensuality: A Study of Eroticism and the Taboo*, trans. Mary Dalwood (New York: Walker, 1962), 14.
20. For this reason, as the writer interjects, a man leaves his mother and father. Adam has no mother and father that we know of, but the charge to journey and relocate, the leaving and cleaving, the revolutions of separation and joining and return wrapped in the command suggest too that one changes in relation to oneself as well as to an other, to one's gathered community.
21. Bataille, *Death and Sensuality*, 18.
22. Ken Stone, "The Garden of Eden and the Heterosexual Contract," in *Bodily Citations: Religion and Judith Butler*, ed. Ellen T. Armour and Susan M. St. Ville (New York: Columbia University Press, 2006), 65.
23. Judith Butler, *Gender Trouble: Feminism and the Subversion of Identity* (New York: Routledge, 1999), 7. Though beyond the scope of space here, it would be interesting to further analyze Butler's contentions and their scriptural applications in conversation with Simone de Beauvoir and Luce Irigaray.
24. Ibid., 33.
25. Rubin, "The Traffic in Women," 180.
26. For more information and an even wider compilation of primary source materials, see James Kugel's highly integral discussion of "Blame It on the Woman" in Kugel, *Traditions of the Bible: A Guide to the Bible as It Was at the Start of the Common Era*, 100-102.
27. Flavius Josephus, *Jewish Antiquities*, Vol. 1: *Books 1-3*, trans. H. St J. Thackeray. Loeb Classical Library 242 (Cambridge, MA: Harvard University Press, 1930), 23.
28. Ibid.
29. Though anomalous in his own right, Ben Sira (or Sirach, as he is known in Greek) hinted as early as 200 BCE at this line of thinking (Sir 15:14, also 25:24). There are numerous other examples of similar themes that arise. The texts of the Sibylline Oracles and Pseudo-Philo's *Biblical Antiquities*, texts contemporary to the aftermath of the Temple destruction, make their own citations of blame and responsibility: "But the woman first became a betrayer to him [Adam]. She gave, and persuaded him to sin in his ignorance" (Sibylline Oracles 1:42-43); "But the man transgressed my ways and was persuaded by his wife, and she was deceived by the serpent. And then death was ordained for the generations of men." (Pseudo-Philo, *Biblical Antiquities* 13:10). Another text,

likely written in the same period, 2 Enoch: "In such a form he [the devil] entered paradise and corrupted Eve. But he did not contact Adam" (2 Enoch (J) 31:6). And yet it is the pseudepigraphic writing by the Latin title *The Life of Adam and Eve* (known in Greek as *The Apocalypse of Moses*) that most thoroughly express contempt with Eve: "Oh evil woman! Why have you wrought destruction among us?" (*Apocalypse of Moses*, 21:6); "And Adam said to Eve, "What have you done? You have brought upon us a great wound, transgression and sin in all our generations" (*Life of Adam and Eve*, 44:2). For more on the importance of these unique texts, see Gary A. Anderson, Michael E. Stone, and Johannes Tromp, eds., *Literature on Adam and Eve: Collected Essays*. Studia in Veteris Testamenti Pseudepigrapha (Leiden and Boston: Brill, 2000). These tests demonstrate the rendering of Eve circulating at the time of Christianity's advent.

30. Philo, *On the Creation. Allegorical Interpretation of Genesis 2 and 3.*, trans. G. H. Whitaker and F. H. Colson. Loeb Classical Library 226 (Cambridge, MA: Harvard University Press, 1929), 119 (§51). Interestingly, on the note of pleasure and desire, Philo and Josephus were some of the earliest scholars to describe the sins of Sodom and Gomorrah as related to homosexuality. Prior to their assertions, commentaries frequently assumed the sins were illicit sexual acts between men and women.
31. Ibid., 122 (§52).
32. For a helpful discussion of Eve's absorption after Eden, particularly in relation to the birth of Seth, see the Conclusion in Lerner, *Eternally Eve*.
33. Given the strength of Paul's own Hebrew lineage, this is not unusual as Sarah and Abraham are frequently referenced as the faithful, model progenitors of Israel in lieu of raising Adam and Eve to spiritual prominence as the first created.
34. Gary A. Anderson, *The Genesis of Perfection: Adam and Eve in Jewish and Christian Imagination* (Louisville: Westminster John Knox Press, 2001), 84.
35. See Tina Beattie, *Eve's Pilgrimage: A Woman's Quest for the City of God* (London and New York: Burns & Oates, 2002).
36. Before his more austere season of life, Augustine lived for around 15 years with his unnamed concubine before leaving her and their son behind. The once expert practitioner of the Manichean "rhythm method" of contraception (which he later condemned) was later betrothed to a 12-year-old girl while in his 40s. As Margaret Miles aptly describes, "Human beings seem perennially to exhibit more hostility toward practices they themselves engaged in than those known only by hearsay." Margaret R. Miles, *Rereading Historical Theology: Before, during, and after Augustine* (Eugene: Cascade Books, 2008), 146.
37. In the opening footnote on Augustine's prominence, Bonaiuti described "the success of the Augustinian doctrine" as "amazing." Ernesto Bonaiuti, "The Genesis of St. Augustine's Idea of Original Sin," *Harvard Theological Review* 10, no. 2 (1917).
38. Ibid., 163.
39. Jesse Couenhoven, "St. Augustine's Doctrine of Original Sin," *Augustinian Studies* 36, no. 2 (2005): 367.
40. Augustine, *City of God* 13.14.
41. In "On the Good of Marriage" (*De Bono Coniugali*) Augustine suggests "For necessary sexual intercourse for begetting is free from blame, and itself is alone worthy of marriage. But that which goes beyond this necessity, no longer follows reason, but lust." (11) He describes that one does not "exact" but rather "yield(s)" sexual pleasure for the sake of the other within the union. However, a few thoughts later he becomes more explicit, stating that "For, whereas that natural use, when it pass beyond the compact of marriage, that is, beyond the necessity of begetting, is pardonable in the case of a wife, damnable in the case of a harlot; that which is against nature is execrable when done in the case of an harlot, but more execrable in the case of a wife.... But, when the man shall wish to use the member of the wife not allowed for this purpose, the wife is more shameful, if she suffer it to take place in her own case, than if in the case of another woman" (12). The phrase "contrary to nature" figures heavily here and in "On Marriage and Concupiscence" (*De Nuptiis et Concupiscentia*). "On the Good of Marriage," in Vol. 3: *On the Holy Trinity; Doctrinal Treatises; Moral Treatises*, ed. Philip Schaff. A Select Library of the Nicene and Post-Nicene Fathers of the Christian Church: 1st Series (Grand Rapids, MI: Eerdmans, 1978), 11–12. For more on this see also nn. 17, 42.
42. Augstine, *The Confessions* 2.4, 9.
43. Annamarie Jagose, *Orgasmology* (Durham: Duke University Press, 2013).
44. Amey Victoria Adkins-Jones, "Stretched Beneath a Pear Tree: Womanist Considerations of Augustine's *Confessions*." Unpublished manuscript: Duke University, last modified June 28, 2023.
45. Beattie, *Eve's Pilgrimage*, 25.

46. Kyla Wazana Tompkins, *Racial Indigestion: Eating Bodies in the 19th Century* (New York: New York University Press, 2012), 5. Tompkins will further explore the notions of the edible black subject, as well as how bodies inscribed by race are often bodies inscribed by food.
47. Ibid., 1.
48. See examples like Gen 30:27, Lev 19:26, Num 23:23.
49. Yvonne Chireau, *Black Magic: Religion and the African American Conjuring Tradition* (Berkeley: University of California Press, 2006), 3.
50. Ibid., 2
51. Suzanne Preston Blier, "Truth and Seeing: Magic, Custom and Fetish in Art History," in *Africa and the Disciplines: Contributions of Research in Africa to the Social Sciences and Humanities*, ed. Robert Bates, V. Y. Mudimbe, and Jean O'Barr (Chicago: University of Chicago Press, 1993). Qtd in ibid., 2.
52. Chireau notes elsewhere the gendered difference between the perceptions of conjurers (the "cunning man" versus the "witch").
53. Ibid., 3.
54. Kameelah L. Martin, *Conjuring Moments in African American Literature: Women, Spirit Work, and Other Such Hoodoo* (New York: Palgrave Macmillan, 2013), 2.
55. Mason Stokes, *The Color of Sex: Whiteness, Heterosexuality, and the Fictions of White Supremacy* (Durham: Duke University Press, 2001), 83.
56. Ibid., 87.
57. Ibid., 83.
58. Ibid., 87.
59. Ibid.
60. Charles Carroll, *The Tempter of Eve; or, the Criminality of Man's Social, Political, and Religious Equality with the Negro, and the Amalgamation to Which These Crimes Inevitably Lead. Discussed in the Light of the Scriptures, the Sciences, Profane History, Tradition, and the Testimony of the Monuments* (St Louis: The Adamic Publishing Co., 1902), 402.
61. See Carroll, *The Tempter of Eve*, 402–6; See Stokes, *The Color of Sex*, 97.
62. Stokes, *The Color of Sex*, 98.
63. Ibid., 98. Here it is important to note Stokes's footnote here, reminding us that "the tempter's lack of femininity cannot be fully separated from her lack of humanity" (n. 20).
64. Ibid., 99–100.
65. Ibid., 100.
66. See Hortense Spillers, "*Mama's Baby, Papa's Maybe?*" and additional discussions throughout the text.
67. Stokes, *The Color of Sex*, 102. Stokes's discussion here in relationship to Ida B. Wells and the antilynching campaign is an incisive analysis of Carroll's work and context.
68. Hartman, *Lose Your Mother*, 17.
69. Ibid., 5.
70. Dionne Brand, *A Map to the Door of No Return: Notes to Belonging* (Toronto: Vintage Canada, 2002), 6.
71. Ibid., 8.
72. Patricia Hill Collins, *Black Feminist Thought*, 129.
73. Martin, *Conjuring Moments*, 84.
74. Eugene F. Rogers, *After the Spirit: A Constructive Pneumatology from Resources outside the Modern West* (Grand Rapids, MI: Eerdmans, 2005), 113.
75. "But when the fullness of time had come, God sent his Son, born of a woman, born under the law. . . ." Galatians 4:4.
76. Raymond E. Brown, Paul J. Achtemeier, and United States Lutheran-Roman Catholic Dialogue (Group), *Mary in the New Testament: A Collaborative Assessment by Protestant and Roman Catholic Scholars* (Philadelphia: Fortress Press, 1978), 23.
77. Ignatius, "Epistle to the Traillians," in *The Apostolic Fathers, Justin Martyr, and Irenaeus*, ed. Alexander Roberts et al. The Ante-Nicene Fathers: Translations of the Writings of the Fathers Down to A.D. 325 (Grand Rapids: Eerdmans, 1978), X.
78. "Epistle to the Ephesians," ibid., XIX.
79. Ibid., XVII.
80. Irenaeus, "Against Heresies," ibid., III.22.4.
81. Ibid.
82. Clare Hemmings, *Why Stories Matter: The Political Grammar of Feminist Theory* (Durham: Duke University Press, 2011), 170.

83. Note here that, even once key Reformers like Luther, Calvin, and Bucer move away from the emphasis on virginity and asceticism in lieu of arguing women's honor and virtue as established through motherhood and domestic responsibility, virginity will still be disciplined by the institution of marriage. The idea of obedience that subtends the early church turn to virginities also subtends the turn to what may be considered a kind of Protestant maternal sexuality.
84. Tertullian, "On the Apparel of Women," in Vol. 4: *Tertullian, Part Fourth; Minucius Felix; Commodian; Origen, Part First and Second*, ed. Alexander Roberts et al. The Ante-Nicene Fathers: Translations of the Writings of the Fathers Down to A.D. 325 (Grand Rapids: Eerdmans, 1978), I.1.
85. "On the Flesh of Christ," in Vol. 3: *Latin Christianity: It's Founder, Tertullian*, ed. Alexander Roberts et al. The Ante-Nicene Fathers: Translations of the Writings of the Fathers Down to A.D. 325 (Grand Rapids: Eerdmans, 1978), XVII. To note, Tertullian implies that it is not just sexual acts but sexual desires/thoughts that are sinful. There is no space to think of self-pleasure or even an erotic imaginary apart from the destruction of *mankind*.
86. Irenaeus, "Against Heresies," III.22.4, emphasis added.
87. Jerome, "To Eustochium," in Vol. 6: *Jerome: The Principal Works of St. Jerome*, ed. Philip Schaff and Henry Wace. A Select Library of Nicene and Post-Nicene Fathers of the Christian Church: 2nd Series (Grand Rapids, MI: Eerdmans, 1978), XXII.21.
88. Some speculate that this theory, drawn from Freudian psychoanalysis, has roots in Judeo-Christian theology itself, the image of the Madonna being Mary herself. However, it may be considered that the early doctors of the Christian church only instantiated theologically what was culturally latent at the time, and which has persisted.
89. Sigmund Freud, "On the Universal Tendency to Debasement in the Sphere of Love," in *The Freud Reader*, ed. Peter Gay (New York: W. W. Norton & Company, 1989), 397.
90. It is important to note here that this trope will be skewed along lines of racial and class encounter in modernity, a topic for further analysis within the Christian imagination. See Hortense J. Spillers, "Mama's Baby, Papa's Maybe: An American Grammar Book," *Diacritics* 17, no. 2 (1987): 65–81; "All the Things You Could Be by Now if Sigmund Freud's Wife Was Your Mother: Psychoanalysis and Race," *Critical Inquiry* 22, no. 4 (1996).
91. Sigmund Freud, *Three Essays on the Theory of Sexuality* (New York: Basic Books, 2000), 89.
92. Miles chronicles the interesting disappearance of Marian images depicting the nursing of Jesus from holy iconographies. While she narrates the secularization of the breast in relationship to the rise of the medical and pornographic industries, the ecclesial shift toward "modesty" in this regard is ripe for Freudian analysis. See Margaret R. Miles, *A Complex Delight: The Secularization of the Breast, 1350–1750* (Berkeley: University of California Press, 2008).
93. Irenaeus, *Proof of the Apostolic Preaching*, trans. Joseph P. Smith. Ancient Christian Writers (Westminster, MD: Newman Press, 1952), 33.
94. The Catholic doctrine of the Immaculate Conception, a long-standing tradition affirmed by Pope Pius IX in *Ineffabilis Deus* (1854) asserts that Mary did not participate in original sin. Instead, she received sanctifying grace from the moment of her inception that lasted throughout her life.
95. Vladimir Tumanov, "Mary versus Eve: Paternal Uncertainty and the Christian View of Women," *Neophilologus* 95, no. 4 (2011): 511.
96. Tina Beattie, *God's Mother, Eve's Advocate: A Marian Narrative of Women's Salvation* (London and New York: Continuum, 2002), 183.
97. Mary F. Foskett, *A Virgin Conceived: Mary and Classical Representations of Virginity* (Bloomington: Indiana University Press, 2002), 28.
98. Lisa Isherwood, *Introducing Feminist Theology* (Sheffield: Sheffield Academic Press, 1993), 63.
99. "The female gender was identified as the embodiment of carnality, sex, and evil by the early church fathers, while virginity was upheld as a virtue for young girls and women. Women were told to follow the example of the Virgin Mary, so that they could overcome the penalties of sexuality and marriage associate with the sin of Eve to become worthy brides of Christ." Pui-lan Kwok, *Postcolonial Imagination and Feminist Theology* (Louisville, KY: Westminster John Knox Press, 2005), 11.
100. Amy-Jill Levine, "Introduction," in *A Feminist Companion to Mariology*, ed. Amy-Jill Levine and Maria Mayo Robbins (London and New York: T & T Clark International, 2005), 5.
101. Maria Mar Perez-Gil, "Mary and the Carnal Maternal Genealogy: Towards a Mariology of the Body," *Literature and Theology* 25, no. 3 (2011): 301.
102. Mari Kim, *Eros in Eden: A Praxis of Beauty in Genesis 3*. PhD diss. Emory University, 2010.
103. Ibid., 191.

104. Ibid., 196.
105. Jane Schuyler considers Michelangelo's proximity to the Medici in Florence, where he would have been readily exposed to the translations and conversations of the mystical Jewish traditions of the cabala, including the narratives of Lilith. In her analysis of Michelangelo's depiction, she notes of the serpent that "Her female sex and twinship with blond Adam suggests that she is, instead, yet another in the cabalistic cast of characters in Michelangelo's scenes—the awesome Lilith." Jane Schuyler, "Michelangelo's Serpent with Two Tails," *Source: Notes in the History of Art* 9, no. 2 (1990), 23.
106. The earliest references to this story are located in the Alphabet Ben-Sirach, composed between 700 and 1000 BCE.
107. Caption, https://www.harmoniarosales.art/catalogue/eve-and-lilith.
108. Harmonia Rosales, "Eve and Lilith . . . we are one and the same." Photo of Eve and Lilith progress. *Instagram*. December 15, 2020. https://www.instagram.com/honeiee/p/CI1p775BaSL/?img_index=1.
109. Kim, *Eros in Eden*, 90.
110. Wives will remain subject to their husbands, slaves will remain subject to their masters. The scriptural premise that there is no longer Jew or Greek, slave or free, male and female (Gal. 3:28) will be applied to the eschaton instead of the everyday. As Luther comes to describe Eve as having been "very free" (a bad thing!), we will see analogues to La Jau's baptism, requiring slaves to make oaths of a theoretical teleology of freedom, one only earned in the life to come through obedience and submission during the tenure on Earth. The call to submission as a mechanism of God's order all traces back to a Garden from which we are all barred entry.

Chapter 3

1. Byron's study describes the modulating ideas of the Egyptian, Ethiopian, and Black/Blackness as markers of ethnic difference and identification of the ethnic other in early Christian theological development. See Gay L. Byron, *Symbolic Blackness and Ethnic Difference in Early Christian Literature* (New York: Routledge, 2002).
2. See Exodus 23:26; Deuteronomy 7:14.
3. For a brilliant analysis of the nuances of Christian writers' varying ideas of how God's volition, sexual intercourse, and giving birth as having various capacities to open or close the womb and constitute or maintain virginal integrity, see Julia Lillis, *Virgin Territory, Virgin Territory: Configuring Female Virginity in Early Christianity*. University of California Press, 2023.
4. Luke 1:20.
5. Fred Moten, *In the Break* (Minneapolis: University of Minnesota Press, 2003), 85.
6. Luke 1:25.
7. Luke 1:28.
8. Luke 1:34.
9. The lack of clarity around Mary's virginity includes the absence of its mention in Mark or John, and Matthew's questionable lexical translation from the book of Isaiah (see discussions in previous chapters). However, scholarly consensus generally confirms that the author of Luke understood Mary to have been a virgin at the time of the Annunciation, despite varying accounts about her relationship status with Joseph. As will be seen in a few paragraphs with quotations from Matthew, several theories about the relationship of Mary to Joseph emerged to further explain Gabriel's message to Mary and harmonize the gospel accounts. Some interpreters understood Mary to be ritually married to Joseph, but not yet living with him, while others understood Joseph and Mary to be in a "spiritual marriage," based on Joseph's protestation to the arrangement given his age in the *Protoevangelium of James*. Some have argued that Mary had already consecrated herself to virginity, and interpret her response as bearing the adamant tone of a determined postulant. For further references, explanations and citations, see discussion in Brown, Achtemeier, and United States Lutheran-Roman Catholic Dialogue (Group), *Mary in the New Testament*, 114–16.
10. Ibid., 122.
11. Ibid., 125.
12. Jerome, *To Eustochium*, 38.
13. Clarissa W. Atkinson, *The Oldest Vocation: Christian Motherhood in the Middle Ages* (Ithaca: Cornell University Press, 1991), 111.
14. The song outlined in Luke 1:46–55 is known as the Song of Mary, the Canticle of Mary, the Ode to the Theotokos (in Eastern traditions) or simply the Magnificat (Latin for "my soul magnifies," the first words of the verse).

15. Matthew 1:19.
16. Matt. 1:25.
17. Luke 1:60.
18. Luke 1:63.
19. John Anthony McGuckin, *St. Cyril of Alexandria: The Christological Controversy: Its History, Theology, and Texts*, trans. John Anthony McGuckin. Supplements to Vigiliae Christianae (Leiden and New York: Brill, 1994), 21.
20. Socrates, *The Ecclesiastical History of Socrates, Surnamed Scholasticus, or the Advocate: Comprising a History of the Church, in Seven Books, from the Accession of Constantine, A.D. 305, to the 38th Year of Theodosius Ii., Including a Period of 140 Years*. Bohn's Ecclesiastical Library (London: H. Bohn, 1853), VII.29.
21. Ibid.
22. Ibid. Immediately thereafter, Socrates describes Nestorius' statements as revealing his foolish, hot-tempered, and pompous character.
23. Edward Rochie Hardy, "Introduction to the First Letter of Nestorius to Celestine," in *Christology of the Later Fathers*, ed. Edward Rochie Hardy and Cyril Charles Richardson (Philadelphia: Westminster Press, 1954), 346. Arianism, deemed by then a heresy, was a line of thinking associated with and promulgated earlier in the third century by Arius, a priest from Alexandria. Like the fortunes of many heresiarchs, it would only take the quarreling over one of his central teachings to earn him the title of heretic: "there was a time when the Son was not." It was a question of who exactly Jesus was, and what kind of a Savior could save. According to Arius, scripture described Jesus as a man who suffered and experienced the realities of humanity—hunger, thirst, learning, and change—while also modeling a way of life reliant upon the Holy Spirit for guidance and strength. Jesus was indisputably human, and necessarily so, as he served as a paragon how to faithfully follow God amid the human condition. For Arius and many others, logic did not naturally follow that a being could be completely human and completely divine at the same time, nor did it need to; the Son was still God, inimitable and unique, resurrected in power and glory. Rather, for Arius, Scripture pointed to an understanding of Christ as a created being, brought into creation by the will of the Father and subsequently, subordinate to the Father within a divine hierarchical scheme: "He [the Son] is the Only-begotten God." The matter was settled on paper when emperor Constantine convened the first ecumenical meeting of the church at the Council of Nicea (325), which formulated the result of their findings—and several direct condemnations of Arius' teachings about the nature of Christ—as part of the first version of the Nicene Creed: Light of Light, very God of very God, begotten, not made, being of one substance with the Father (*homoousion toi Patri*) ... came down and was incarnate and was made man. But while this perhaps made headway in terms of understanding the Christian doctrine of the Trinity, the finer details about the nature of Christ were not so readily accounted for. How exactly did divinity and humanity converge? The percolating minds of the fifth century were wrapped around this very question, for many upon which Mary, the point of partial origin, was an unstable tipping point. And with Nestorius dutifully dedicating himself to cleaning house, folks who were less than thrilled with his manner of politics took advantage of the fact.
24. McGuckin, *St. Cyril of Alexandria*, 24. See also Socrates, *The Ecclesiastical History of Socrates, Surnamed Scholasticus, or the Advocate: Comprising a History of the Church, in Seven Books, from the Accession of Constantine, A.D. 305, to the 38th Year of Theodosius Ii., Including a Period of 140 Years*, VII.29.
25. *Purkaia* is a word associated with lighting a funeral pyre. See *The Ecclesiastical History of Socrates, Surnamed Scholasticus, or the Advocate: Comprising a History of the Church, in Seven Books, from the Accession of Constantine, A.D. 305, to the 38th Year of Theodosius Ii., Including a Period of 140 Years*, VII.29; McGuckin, *St. Cyril of Alexandria*, 87; Susan Wessel, *Cyril of Alexandria and the Nestorian Controversy: The Making of a Saint and of a Heretic* (Oxford and New York: Oxford University Press, 2004).
26. The *gynaikeia*, or "women's section," was a gallery area specifically designed to keep women out of the main sanctuary area of the church. For Holum, the gendered architecture of the Church can readily be traced to a clear logic where "dogma had a convenient explanation: woman was the daughter of Eve, and through Eve sin had entered the world." Kenneth G. Holum, *Theodosian Empresses: Women and Imperial Dominion in Late Antiquity* (Berkeley: University of California Press, 1982), 140.
27. Ibid., 145.
28. "La reine Pulchérie fut irritée contre lui et lui dit: 'Laisse-moi entrer selon ma coutume.' Mais il lui dit: 'Ce lieu ne doit être foulé que par les prêtres.' Elle lui dit: 'Est'ce parce que je n'ai pas enfanté

Dieu?' Il lui dit: 'Toi tu as enfanté Satan' et il la chassa de la porte du Saint des saints. Elle partit irritée, alla trouver l'empereur et lui raconta la chose. L'empereur lui dit: 'Par ta vie, ma soeur, et par la couronne qui est sur ta tête, je ne cesserai pas avant d'avoir tiré vengeance de lui.' Depuis ce jour il n'eut plus aucun crédit près de l'empereur." Nestorius, *Le Livre D'héraclide De Damas*, trans. Paul Bedjan (Paris: O. Harrassowitz, 1910), appendix I, 364. Cf. "Elle lui dit, 'Pourquoi n'ai-je pas enfanté Dieu!'" in "Lettre À Cosme," in *Patrologia Orientalis* (Paris: Firmin-Didot, 1916), 279. See discussion also in Wessel, *Cyril of Alexandria and the Nestorian Controversy*, 101–2; *Leo the Great and the Spiritual Rebuilding of a Universal Rome* (Leiden and Boston: Brill, 2008), 265. Though a precise date is not given, if the event occurred during the first Easter celebration under Nestorius' bishopric, the date would have been April 15, 428—a mere five days after his ordination. See Holum, *Theodosian Empresses: Women and Imperial Dominion in Late Antiquity*, 153.
29. Nestorius, *Le Livre D'héraclide De Damas*, Appendix I, 363; "Barhadbeshabba," in *Patrologia Orientalis* (Paris: Firmin-Didot, 1913), 565–66.
30. "Barhadbeshabba," 528.
31. McGuckin, *St. Cyril of Alexandria*, 26.
32. "Une femme belliquese," is footnoted by Nau with the more literal and more aggressive "une fille des combats." Nestorius, *Le Livre D'héraclide de Damas*, 89.
33. Ibid. See also notes in *The Bazaar of Heracleides*, trans. G. R. Driver and Leonard Hodgson (Oxford: Clarendon Press, 1925).
34. *Acta Conciliorum Oecumenicorum*, ed. Eduard Schwartz et al., 4 vols. (Berolini: de Gruyter, 1914–40), I, 4, 5; "Ad Johannen Antiochenum," in *Nestoriana: Die Fragmente Des Nestorius*, ed. Friedrich Loofs (Halle a. S.: Niemeyer, 1905), 185; "Doctrina Pietatis (Erster Sermon gegen das Theotokos)," in *Nestoriana: Die Fragmente des Nestorius* (Halle a. S.: Niemeyer, 1905), 251–52; *Le Livre D'héraclide de Damas*, 91–92; Friedrich Loofs, *Nestorius and His Place in the History of Christian Doctrine* (Cambridge: Cambridge University Press, 1914), 28–32.
35. Socrates, *The Ecclesiastical History of Socrates, Surnamed Scholasticus, or the Advocate: Comprising a History of the Church, in Seven Books, from the Accession of Constantine, A.D. 305, to the 38th Year of Theodosius Ii., Including a Period of 140 Years*, 7.32.
36. Proclus, "Homily I: De Laudibus S. Mariae," in *Acta Conciliorum Oecumenicorum*, ed. Eduard Schwartz et al. (Berolini: de Gruyter, 1914), I.1.1, 103–7. Translation found in Luigi Gambero, *Mary and the Fathers of the Church: The Blessed Virgin Mary in Patristic Thought* (San Francisco: Ignatius Press, 1999), 235. See also Proclus, "Homily I," in *Proclus of Constantinople and the Cult of the Virgin in Late Antiquity Homilies 1–5, Texts and Translations*, ed. Nicholas Constas, Supplements to Vigiliae Christianae (Leiden and Boston: Brill, 2003), 137–47; *Patrologiæ Cursus Completus, Series Græca*, ed. J. P. Migne (Paris: 1857–66), 65.680C-92B.
37. Fragments present in Nestorius, *Nestoriana: Die Fragmente des Nestorius*, trans. Friedrich Loofs (Halle a. S.: Niemeyer, 1905), microform, 337–38. See McGuckin, *St. Cyril of Alexandria*, 31. On the theory of Nestorius being interrupted, see Franz Xaver Bauer, "Proklos von Konstantinople: Ein Bietrag zur Kirchen und Dogmengeschichte des 5 Jahrhunderts" (microform, Universität München 1919).
38. *Patrologiæ Cursus Completus, Series Græca*, Paschal Homily 17, 77.76–78.
39. Cyril, "Letter to the Monks of Egypt," in *St. Cyril of Alexandria: The Christological Controversy: Its History, Theology, and Texts*, ed. John Anthony McGuckin. Supplements to Vigiliae Christianae (Leiden and New York: Brill, 1994), 245; *Patrologiæ Cursus Completus, Series Græca*, 77.9–40; *Acta Conciliorum Oecumenicorum*, I.1.1, 10–23. Cf. "Cyril to Monks in Egypt," in *St. Cyril of Alexandria Letters 1–50*. Fathers of the Church (Washington, DC: Catholic University of America Press, 1987).
40. "Letter to the Monks of Egypt," 252.
41. This incident is reported in the gathered compendium from Cyril to Celestine. See "Letter to Pope Celestine," 277; *Patrologiæ Cursus Completus, Series Græca*, 77.80–85; *Acta Conciliorum Oecumenicorum*, I.1.5, 10–12. Cf. "To Celestine."
42. Nestorius, "First Letter of Nestorius to Celestine," in *Christology of the Later Fathers*, ed. Edward Rochie Hardy and Cyril Charles Richardson (Philadelphia: Westminster Press, 1954), 348; *Nestoriana: Die Fragmente des Nestorius*, 165–68; *Acta Conciliorum Oecumenicorum*, I, 2; 12–14.
43. "First Letter of Nestorius to Celestine."
44. Anne Anlin Cheng, *Second Skin: Josephine Baker & the Modern Surface* (Oxford and New York: Oxford University Press, 2010), 118.
45. Cf. "Third Letter of Cyril to Nestorius" in McGuckin, *St. Cyril of Alexandria*, 266–75.
46. Cyril, "Third Letter of Cyril to Nestorius," 350.

47. For more on Cyril's lens of redemption in relationship to the Adam-Christ typology, see Robert L. Wilken, "Exegesis and the History of Theology: Reflections on the Adam-Christ Typology in Cyril of Alexandria," *Church History* 35, no. 2 (1966).
48. Cyril, "Third Letter of Cyril to Nestorius," 350.
49. Ibid., 352–53.
50. Wessel, *Cyril of Alexandria and the Nestorian Controversy*, 39.
51. See discussion (including texts and translations of several letters) in ibid., 39–45.
52. Socrates, *The Ecclesiastical History of Socrates, Surnamed Scholasticus, or the Advocate: Comprising a History of the Church, in Seven Books, from the Accession of Constantine, A.D. 305, to the 38th Year of Theodosius Ii., Including a Period of 140 Years*, 7.13.
53. Edward Gibbon, The History of the Decline and Fall of the Roman Empire (Project Gutenberg, 1845). Ebook. IV.47.ii.
54. Maria Dzielska, *Hypatia of Alexandria*, trans. F. Lyra (Cambridge, MA: Harvard University Press, 1995), 53. Elsewhere Jennifer Knust helpfully discusses the history of *sophrosyne* as a uniquely feminine virtue, primarily relating to chastity and purity. See Jennifer Wright Knust, *Abandoned to Lust: Sexual Slander and Ancient Christianity* (New York: Columbia University Press, 2006), 37–40.
55. Gibbon, *The History of the Decline and Fall of the Roman Empire*, vol. 4, ch. XLVII.
56. As the story goes, a group of Christian monks from out of town were particularly zealous for their cause, and with a penchant to "fight on Cyril's behalf," apprehended Orestes in the streets. Things quickly devolved, Orestes was hit in the head by a rock thrown from a monk (Ammonius), so Orestes arrested and tortured him. Ammonius did not survive. Socrates, *The Ecclesiastical History of Socrates, Surnamed Scholasticus, or the Advocate: Comprising a History of the Church, in Seven Books, from the Accession of Constantine, A.D. 305, to the 38th Year of Theodosius Ii., Including a Period of 140 Years*, 7.14.
57. Gibbon, *The History of the Decline*, vol. 4, ch. XLVII. Several ancient sources witnessed and recorded the events, including Socrates, John of Nikiu, and Damascius.
58. In a tract from John Toland's literary history of the events, he titled his account "Hypatia: Or, the history of a most beautiful, most virtuous, most learned, and every way accomplished lady; who was torn to pieces by the clergy of Alexandria, to gratify the pride, emulation, and cruelty of their Archbishop, commonly but undeservedly styled St. Cyril." John Toland, *Tetradymus* (London: J. Brotherton and W. Meadows, 1720), 101–36. For more on the complexities of the Hypatia story, see the excellent account in Dzielska, *Hypatia of Alexandria*.
59. Wessel, *Cyril of Alexandria and the Nestorian Controversy*, 216.
60. G. Christopher Stead, "Rhetorical Method in Athanasius," *Vigiliae Christianae* 30, no. 2 (1976): 132. The application of the term to Nestorius' rhetorical method is cited in Wessel, *Cyril of Alexandria and the Nestorian Controversy*.
61. Cyril, "Homily V," in *Cyril of Alexandria and the Nestorian Controversy: The Making of a Saint and of a Heretic* (Oxford and New York: Oxford University Press, 2004), 304; *Acta Conciliorum Oecumenicorum*, I.I.2, 93.
62. The witness is given in the *Coptic Acts of Ephesus. Koptische Akten Zum Ephesinischen Konzil Vom Jahre 431*, trans. Wilhelm Kraatz (Leipzig: J. C. Hinrichs, 1904), 47, 49–50. Cited in Wessel, *Cyril of Alexandria and the Nestorian Controversy*, 217.
63. *Cyril of Alexandria and the Nestorian Controversy*, 217.
64. Drake paraphrases the thought of Chrysostom in *Adversus Iudaeos* (*Against the Jews*), a series of sermons given in Antioch, 386 CE. Susanna Drake, *Slandering the Jew: Sexuality and Difference in Early Christian Texts* (Philadelphia: University of Pennsylvania Press, 2013), 1, 97–98.
65. In her argument, Drake offers a genealogy of the emergence of the Jewish subject as sexually deviant. This theme, which she traces through the reading practices of Scripture and the exegetical claims of early doctors of the church, emerged most clearly by the third and fourth centuries, heightened in the post-Constantinian era. By then, growing emphasis on the spiritual interpretation of the Bible for Christians over the literal interpretation that was associated with the Jews (as witnessed in theologians like Origen) mapped onto ideas about celibacy and temperance as spiritual qualities of Christians, over and against the carnality, fornication, and even how the notions of marriage and reproduction were seen as qualities of Jews. The slander and invective toward the Jews that Drake carefully cites is necessarily thought through for our discussion of the fifth century. Ibid.
66. Ibid., 3.
67. Ibid., 99.
68. Glissant, "Édouard Glissant in Conversation with Manthia Diawara," 5.

NOTES 217

69. Raniero Cantalamessa, *Mary: Mirror of the Church* (Collegeville, MN: Liturgical Press, 1992), 57. Cantalamessa is drawing a distinction between the use of *Dei Genetrix* and *Theotokos*, for their unique values of attributing Mary as the Mother of God.
70. Proclus, "Homily I."
71. Margaret R. Miles, *The Word Made Flesh: A History of Christian Thought* (Malden, MA: Blackwell, 2005), 109.
72. Of the twelve anathemas given, only the first mention anything about Theotokos. See "The Third Letter of Cyril to Nestorius" and "Explanation of the Twelve Chapters" in McGuckin, *St. Cyril of Alexandria:*, 273–4; 82–93.
73. Jaroslav Pelikan, *Mary through the Centuries: Her Place in the History of Culture* (New Haven: Yale University Press, 1996), 1.
74. Miles, *The Word Made Flesh*. See also comments in *Carnal Knowing: Female Nakedness and Religious Meaning in the Christian West* (Boston: Beacon Press, 1989), 210, n. 7.
75. Leo I, "Letter Xxviii. To Flavian, Commonly Called 'the Tome,'" in Vol. 12: *Leo the Great, Gregory the Great*, ed. Philip Schaff. A Select Library of the Nicene and Post-Nicene Fathers of the Christian Church: 2nd Series (Grand Rapids, MI: Eerdmans, 1978).
76. Reproduced in Eamon R. Carroll, "Mary in the Documents of the Magisterium," in *Mariology*, ed. Juniper B. Carol (Milwaukee: Bruce Publishing, 1955), 13.
77. IX Pius, "Ineffabilis Deus" (1854). Excerpts reprinted in Sarah Jane Boss, ed., *Mary: The Complete Resource* (London and New York: Continuum, 2007), 279–80.
78. Luce Irigaray, *This Sex Which Is Not One* (Ithaca: Cornell University Press, 1985), 180.
79. Chris Weedon, "Subjects," in *A Concise Companion to Feminist Theory*, ed. Mary Eagleton (Oxford: Blackwell, 2003), 123.
80. Jane Schaberg, *The Illegitimacy of Jesus: A Feminist Theological Interpretation of the Infancy Narratives* (Sheffield: Sheffield Phoenix Press, 2006), 71.
81. Tumanov, "Mary versus Eve," 514.

Chapter 4

1. "We celebrate our history, but our future is in jeopardy as a genocidal plot is carried through abortion," said Life Always board member Stephen Borden. "We have seen the heartbreaking effects of opportunists who happen to be black abortionists perpetuating this atrocity. It's not just babies who are in danger; it's also their mothers and our society at large." https://www.theroot.com/views/re-ppnyc-statement-abortion-billboard-targeting-african-americans-nyc (accessed April 23, 2015).
2. Annie Waldman, "How Hospitals Are Failing Black Mothers," *ProRepublica* December 21, 2017, https://www.propublica.org/article/how-hospitals-are-failing-black-mothers (accessed February 28, 2021).
3. Jennifer C. Nash, *Birthing Black Mothers* (Durham: Duke University Press, 2021), 20.
4. Ibid., 4.
5. Dorothy Roberts, *Killing the Black Body: Race, Reproduction, and the Meaning of Liberty* (New York: Pantheon Books, 1997), 82.
6. Christina Sharpe, *In the Wake: On Blackness and Being* (Durham: Duke University Press, 2016), 26.
7. Ibid., 28.
8. Ibid., 28.
9. "How does one mourn the interminable event?" Ibid., 19.
10. Patrice D. Douglass, "Black Feminist Theory for the Dead and Dying," *Theory & Event* 21, no. 1, (2018): 106.
11. See Leo Bersani, *Is the Rectum a Grave? and Other Essays* (Chicago: University of Chicago Press, 2009), 29–30.
12. As Barbara Newman points out, Hildegard was writing before the official establishment of the doctrine of the Immaculate Conception. She stood in a theological tradition that understood the partial sanctification of Mary in her own mother's womb to have been completed or fulfilled during the Annunciation. Barbara Newman, *Sister of Wisdom: St. Hildegard's Theology of the Feminine* (Berkeley: University California Press, 1987).
13. Hildegard of Bingen, *Scivias* quoted in ibid., 175–76.
14. See M. Cobb, "An Amazing 10 Years: The Discovery of Egg and Sperm in the 17th Century," *Reproduction in Domestic Animals* 47 (2012).
15. Newman has suggested that, "When Hildegard wrote about the daughters of Eve—living women in their concrete psychosexual being—the prophet turned physician; and the reader may be

startled to find pages of frank, original discussion of female physiology and passion, with scarcely a nod toward theological interpretation." Newman, *Sister of Wisdom*, 121. However, scholars like Bruce Holsinger suggest an influential intertwining of Hildegard's musical compositions and theological resonances with her natural writings. See ch. 3 in Bruce Holsinger, *Music Body and Desire in Medieval Culture: Hildegard of Bingen to Chaucer* (Stanford: Stanford University Press, 2022).
16. Bruce Holsinger, *Music Body and Desire in Medieval Culture: Hildegard of Bingen to Chaucer* (Stanford: Stanford University Press, 2001), 117.
17. Isaiah 1:18.
18. See full text of Hildegard, *Cum processit factura* reproduced in Newman, *Sister of Wisdom*, 275.
19. Hildegard's vision in *Scivias* of the Apocalypse features the figure of the church exposed "from the waist to the place that denotes the female," with "various scaly blemishes;" from this image of the vagina emerges "a black and monstrous head ... it has fiery eyes, and ears like an ass, and nostrils and mouth like a lion." The vision extends to include that "a great mass of excrement adheres to the head, which raises itself upon a mountain and tries to ascend the height of Heaven," a reign of stench and terror (Book 3, Vision 11). Hildegard's vision is of a monster born from within the Church, but her later reflections on the demonic figure as one who practices Jewish ritual leaves open this interpretation. See Richard K. Emmerson, "The Representation of Antichrist in Hildegard of Bingen's *Scivias*: Image, Word, Commentary, and Visionary Experience," *Gesta* 41, no. 2 (2002): 95–110. For the reception history of the book of Revelation, see Judith L. Kovacs, Christopher Rowland, and Rebekah Callow, *Revelation: The Apocalypse of Jesus Christ* (Malden, MA: Blackwell, 2004).
20. In her contemporary biography of Hildegard, Fiona Maddocks notes that "It is perhaps no coincidence that several centuries later the revival of interest in Hildegard at the time of the 750th anniversary of her death in 1929 was linked to a stirring of interest not only in the Catholic Church but also in German national identity at the end of the Weimar Republic." Fiona Maddocks, *Hildegard of Bingen: The Woman of Her Age* (New York: Doubleday, 2001), 85.
21. Hildegard, *Causae et curae*; translated and discussed in Holsinger, *Music Body and Desire in Medieval Culture*, 101.
22. Ibid.
23. Hildegard, *O quam preciosa*, translated in Holsinger, *Music Body and Desire in Medieval Culture*, 103–4.
24. Hildegard of Bingen, *Scivias*, quoted in Newman, *Sister of Wisdom*, 176.
25. Ibid.
26. See n. 19 above on the Apocalyptic vision.
27. Tertullian, "On the Flesh of Christ."
28. Michael L. Power and Jay Schulkin, *The Evolution of the Human Placenta* (Baltimore: Johns Hopkins University Press, 2012), 31.
29. *Revelations* 7.21 in Marguerite Tjader Harris, ed., *Birgitta of Sweden: Life and Selected Revelations*, The Classics of Western Spirituality (New York: Paulist Press, 1990), 203–4.
30. See John 20:7.
31. Ibid.
32. Maria Mar Perez-Gil, "Mary and the Carnal Maternal Genealogy: Towards a Mariology of the Body," *Literature and Theology* 25, no. 3 (2011): 299. Along similar lines, Margaret Miles elsewhere chronicles the disappearance of the breast from holy iconography, particular evidenced through the missing images of Jesus nursing as a baby. She helpfully narrates the secularization of the breast in relationship to the rise of medical and pornography industries, but traces this from an ecclesial shift toward "modesty." See Miles, *A Complex Delight*.
33. Margaret Whitford, *Luce Irigaray: Philosophy in the Feminine* (London and New York: Routledge, 1991), 118.
34. Luce Irigaray, *Sexes and Genealogies* (New York: Columbia University Press, 1993), 16.
35. As described, many Christians popularly confuse the Immaculate Conception as referring to Christ's conception in the womb of Mary, rather than Mary's conception in the womb of her mother Anne.
36. Pius, "Ineffabilis Deus."
37. Mary Douglas, *Purity and Danger: An Analysis of the Concepts of Pollution and Taboo* (London: Ark, 1984), 2.
38. Ibid., 5.
39. Ibid., 2–4.

40. Michel Foucault, *Discipline and Punish: The Birth of the Prison* (New York: Vintage Books, 1995), 135–69.
41. Multiple discourses of pathology and criminality would come to be formed around those seen as savages, barbarians and whores. Ibid., 136.
42. Gloria Anzaldúa, *Borderlands: The New Mestiza = La Frontera* (San Francisco: Aunt Lute Books, 1991), 3.
43. Brian Bantum, *Redeeming Mulatto: A Theology of Race and Christian Hybridity* (Waco: Baylor University Press, 2016), 100.
44. Reproduced in Carroll, "Mary in the Documents of the Magisterium."
45. Sarah Jane Boss, *Mary*, New Century Theology (London and New York: Continuum, 2004), 102.
46. Ibid.
47. Robyn Wiegman and Elizabeth A. Wilson, "Introduction: Antinormativity's Queer Conventions," *differences* 26, no. 1 (2015): 16.
48. John 1:1–18.
49. John 20:24–29.
50. Sarah Jane Boss, *Empress and Handmaid: On Nature and Gender in the Cult of the Virgin Mary* (London: Cassell, 2000), 197.
51. For a more thorough account of the notion of Mary's dimension, particularly as it resonated in and after the fifth century, see Stephen J. Shoemaker, *Ancient Traditions of the Virgin Mary's Dormition and Assumption*, Oxford Early Christian Studies (Oxford: Oxford University Press, 2002).
52. I intentionally recall imagery of female circumcision as its function, particularly as ritual, continues to be a critical topic for feminist discourses, particularly at the intersections of gender, race, class, religion, and globalization. If one is willing to narrate the violence that Mary's virginity, held before woman as ideal, perpetrates, then the connection specifically to two common forms of female circumcision—that of removing or splicing the clitoris, and that of suturing the vaginal opening that must be reopened for childbirth—becomes explicitly applicable. I do not mean to lessen the intensity of lived women's experiences of circumcision, but I do find it an important analytic given the link between divinely ordained modesty and purity for women that is expressed and policed by men directly, or women who are in exchange among men for the pleasures and desires of men. In these cases, circumcision remains in quotation marks to denote the distinction between theorizing the subject and the questions of contemporary lived religious and cultural practices. See Wynter, "'Genital Mutilation' or 'Symbolic Birth?': Female Circumcision, Lost Origins, and the Aculturalism of Feminist/Western Thought"; Rogaia Mustafa Abusharaf, *Female Circumcision: Multicultural Perspectives* (Philadelphia: University of Pennsylvania Press, 2006). See also brief discussion in Saba Mahmood, *Politics of Piety: The Islamic Revival and the Feminist Subject* (Princeton: Princeton University Press, 2005), 85–86.
53. "The symbol of *Mater Admirabilis* ... offer[s] a construction of womanhood which extols the virginal mother, removed from her sexuality, and following a life of self-sacrifice under the control of the male hierarchy of the church. As Mary was removed from sexuality with conception taking place only by the intervention of God rather than via her partner, so too were wives within the Catholic Church encouraged to consider intercourse as being for procreation rather than sexual pleasure. This life of self-sacrifice required ... sublimation of any feeling of resistance." Christine Trimingham Jack, "Sacred Symbols, School Ideology and the Construction of Subjectivity," *Paedagogica Historica* 34, no. 3 (1998): 788.
54. The demand for male circumcision was religiously instituted as a sacrificial marker of identity in Genesis 17. Removal of the foreskin was a physical sign of God's covenant with the chosen people of Israel. It was a permanent sign of covenant sealed in human flesh and blood, a commitment and kinship belonging that was not inherently a biological trait. When Paul wrote in his epistles about bodies, sex, and flesh—the words that would be interpreted as references to Jewish sexuality—references to "Israel according to the flesh" were far more specific in context. Much more literally, *kata sarka* directly recalled the practices of circumcision and sacrifice associated with Jewish identity. Unlike the instructions of the Torah, the New Covenant demanded a circumcision of the heart—a kinship beyond the lineages of birth that did not require a physical sign. As Paul wrote in the book of Romans, a "real circumcision is a matter of the heart—it is spiritual and not literal" (Rom 2:29). The Christian emphasis on the spiritual, interior interpretation and existence distanced what was perceived to be a Judaic barbarism that relied on blood and painful sacrifice to consummate relationship with God.
55. Rogers, *After the Spirit: A Constructive Pneumatology from Resources Outside the Modern West*, 106–7.

56. See Spillers, "Mama's Baby," 65. Where Spillers is speaking about the material violence and slave relations of a physical, historically grounded experience of captivity, her analysis of the delimitation of being at the hands of another give shape to the way naming and marking are claims to secure identity, particularly of the reproductive body.
57. Ibid. Interestingly enough, Spillers's broader analysis begins with the Moynihan report, which centered an idea of forced matriarchy as the root cause of black-identified social pathology. The identification of a child through the lineage of the mother is noted because it is "it is so far out of line with the rest of American society," that it "seriously retards the progress of the group as a whole." This American, Anglicized vision identifies the Black female-mother as a usurper of power and authority of the Black father, an atavistic practice that explains the supposed criminality and perversity of a racialized existence.
58. Willie James Jennings, *The Christian Imagination: Theology and the Origins of Race* (New Haven: Yale University Press, 2010).
59. See Delores S. Williams. *Sisters in the Wilderness: The Challenge of Womanist God-Talk* (Maryknoll, NY: Orbis Books, 1993).
60. Spillers, *Mama's Baby*, 67.
61. It is important to note that Williams's analysis in *Sisters in the Wilderness* anticipates contemporary ethical concerns around surrogacy, and most particularly the contemporary question of "womb tourism" and the rise of the surrogacy industry, through her commentary on the imaginary of Black women as "strong breeders" in the 1980s.
62. Williams, *Sisters in the Wilderness*, 161.
63. Ibid., 162.
64. Stephen J. Shoemaker, *The Life of the Virgin: Maximus the Confessor* (New Haven: Yale University Press, 2012), 52.
65. Ibid., 65–66.
66. Ibid.
67. Ibid.
68. Ibid., 101.
69. Ibid., 106.
70. Emmett Till's gruesome kidnapping and murder at just 14 years old in Money, Mississippi. Severely beaten, eye gouged out, shot in the head, and dumped in the Tallahatchie River, his murder in 1955 galvanized a generation of the civil right movement, in part due to his mother, Mamie Till-Mobley's insistence, that people bear witness to what the two white men who murdered her son had done.
71. Fred Moten, "Black Mo'nin'," in *Loss: The Politics of Mourning*, ed. David L. Eng and David Kazanjian (Berkeley: University of California Press, 2003), 59. As he will also describe, "Black mo'nin' is the phonographic content of this photograph," 65.
72. Courtney R. Baker, *Humane Insight: Looking at Images of African American Suffering and Death* (Chicago: University of Illinois Press, 2015), 72.
73. Ibid., 5.
74. Ibid., 75.
75. Ibid.
76. Stephanie Buckhanon Crowder, *When Momma Speaks: The Bible and Motherhood from a Womanist Perspective* (Louisville, KY: Westminster John Knox Press, 2016), 53.
77. Ibid.
78. Spillers, *Mama's Baby*, 80.
79. Alexis Pauline Gumbs, *Spill: Scenes of Black Feminist Fugitivity* (Durham: Duke University Press, 2016), 7.
80. Imani Perry, "Stop Hustling Black Death: Samaria Rice Is the Mother of Tamir, Not a 'Mother of the Movement.'" *The Cut*. May 24, 2021. Retrieved October 10, 2021, from https://www.thecut.com/article/samaria-rice-profile.html.
81. Pope Paul VI, *Lumen Gentium* (*Dogmatic Constitution on the Church*) (1965).
82. In *Lose Your Mother*, Saidiya Hartman writes "If slavery persists as an issue in the political life of black America, it is not because of an antiquarian obsession with bygone days or the burden of a too-long memory, but because black lives are still imperiled and devalued by a racial calculus and a political arithmetic that were entrenched centuries ago. This is the afterlife of slavery—skewed life chances, limited access to health and education, premature death, incarceration, and impoverishment. I, too, am the afterlife of slavery," 6.

Chapter 5

1. "The Hottentot Venus," *Morning Post*, November 27, 1810, 2. Note also that the Hottentot *female* was distinguished as far more barbaric and apelike than the Hottentot male, reinforcing a broader prevailing narrative of the female gender, across races, as being closer to nature.
2. Clifton C. Crais and Pamela Scully, *Sara Baartman and the Hottentot Venus: A Ghost Story and a Biography* (Princeton: Princeton University Press, 2009), 72.
3. Ibid., 78.
4. Zoe S. Strother, "Display of the Body Hottentot," in *Africans on Stage: Studies in Ethnological Show Business*, ed. Bernth Lindfors (Bloomington: Indiana University Press 1999), 10.
5. Ibid., 2.
6. Hartman, *Lose Your Mother*, 143. Hartman speaks of a young girl called Venus who died on board the *Recovery*, a slave ship, at the hands of Captain John Kimber in 1972. Because there was little witness to her story, and as she did not fit the narrative of chastity William Wilberforce ascribed to the other enslaved Black girl—"a virgin persecuted by a monster"—she was rarely spoken of, another murder unproven and acquitted on the waters of the Atlantic. Hartman expounds upon this story in "Venus in Two Acts."
7. Stephen Jay Gould, "The Hottentot Venus," *Natural History*, October 1982. Gould mentions that women likely were sufficiently quelled by the latter in absence of the former, though I would argue that the idea of an absent vicarious pleasure is founded upon the presumptions of heterosexual desire and not necessarily upon the reality of the experience.
8. Bernth Lindfors, "Courting the Hottentot Venus," *Africa: Revista Trimestrale di Studi e Documentazione dell Istituto Italo-Africano* 40, no. 1 (1985): 132.
9. Carlos A. Miranda and Suzette A. Spencer, "Omnipresent Negation: Hottentot Venus and Africa Rising," *Callaloo* 32, no. 3 (2009): 912.
10. As described elsewhere, captivity functions as a logic of both desire and identity for Spillers: "The captive body is reduced to a thing, to *being* for the captor; in this distance *from* a subject position the captured sexualities provide and physical and biological expression of 'otherness'; as a category of 'otherness' the captive body translates into a potential for pornotroping and embodies sheer physical powerlessness that slides into a more general 'powerlessness' resonating through various centers of human and social meaning." Spillers, "Mama's Baby, Papa's Maybe," 67.
11. Fred Moten, *In the Break: The Aesthetics of the Black Radical Tradition* (Minneapolis: University of Minnesota Press, 2003), 14.
12. M. Shawn Copeland, *Enfleshing Freedom: Body, Race, and Being* (Minneapolis: Fortress Press, 2010), 12.
13. Immanuel Kant, "Of the Different Human Races," in *The Idea of Race*, ed. Robert Bernasconi and Tommy Lee Lott (Indianapolis: Hackett Publishing Co., 2000), 12. In his work on Kant, J. Kameron Carter argues the stake of this racial spectrum. Carter notes the way Kant eventually narrates the lineal root genus of the human species. According to Carter, "In contrast to his lengthy accounts of the origins of 'Negros, Huns and Hindustani,' in which he is clear they are races [*rassen*]," when it comes to his narrations of white bodies, Kant inflects a series of other terms, from "*Gestalt* (form) to *Abartung* (deviation) to *Schlag* (kind)." But not race. "As he sees it, whites are a group apart. They are a 'race' that is not quite a race, a race that transcends race precisely because of its 'development progress' (*fortgang*) toward perfection." Carter, *Race*, 84 (Kant quoted), 88.
14. "Kant believed that it was the armchair scientist alone who could be relied upon to offer an adequate account of the Hottentots, not the travellers who saw them with their own eyes, let alone the Hottentots themselves." Robert Bernasconi, "Silencing the Hottentots: Kolb's Pre-Racial Encounter with the Hottentots and Its Impact on Buffon, Kant, and Rousseau," *Graduate Faculty Philosophy Journal* 35, no. 1/2 (2014): 105.
15. Crais and Scully, *Sara Baartman and the Hottentot Venus*, 4.
16. Crais and Scully point out that scholars relied heavily on the work of Percival Kirby, a Scottish musicologist whose work on South African instruments and composition is well renown. His research in the 1940s and 1950s eventually included several articles on Sara Baartman, which became the horizon of truth around Baartman's life: "Scholars used Kirby's work as gospel, assuming that nothing could be found out about Sara Baartman's life in South Africa: her colonial history either remained of no interest or was presumed inaccessible." Ibid. See also Clifton Crais and Pamela Scully, "Race and Erasure: Sara Baartman and Hendrik Cesars in Cape Town and London," *Journal of British Studies* 47, no. 2 (2008); Percival R. Kirby, "The Hottentot Venus," *Africana Notes and News* 6, no. 3 (1949). As I later discuss, I have similar concerns around the introduction of Sara

Baartman into the more contemporary American theoretical canon, particularly through the citation of Sander Gilman.
17. The label in the Museum of Man in Paris actually stated that Baartman died at the age of 38.
18. Ibid., 30.
19. Jennifer C. Nash, *The Black Body in Ecstasy: Reading Race, Reading Pornography* (Durham: Duke University Press, 2014).
20. Ibid., 31.
21. bell hooks, *The Will to Change: Men, Masculinity, and Love* (New York: Atria Books, 2004), 17.
22. Katie G. Cannon, *Black Womanist Ethics* (Eugene: Wipf and Stock, 2006), 2.
23. Hartman, *Lose Your Mother*, 6.
24. See Gould, "The Hottentot Venus."
25. Spillers, "Notes on Brooks and the Feminine," 149.
26. Gomes Eanes de Zurara, *The Chronicle of the Discovery and Conquest of Guinea* (Project Gutenberg, 1896), Ebook. See discussion in Copeland, *Enfleshing Freedom*, 27. On the convincing nature of such logic, as evidenced by renowned poet Phyllis Wheatley, a young Black American woman most definitely a slave, was also marketed as an "exotic curiosity" for her intelligence, referred to Africa as the "land of errors," and expressed gratitude for slavery expediting her Christian conversion. See Anne Applegate, "Phillis Wheatley: Her Critics and Her Contribution," *Negro American Literature Forum* 9 (1975): 123.
27. Crais and Scully, *Sara Baartman and the Hottentot Venus*, 90. Rebutting a number of incorrect quotes and highly cited data on Baartman's life—in particular that she left South Africa as a young girl, and thus died in her early twenties—Crais and Scully have published a groundbreaking biography that challenges much of the historical reference to Baartman, providing the most comprehensive evaluation of her life to date.
28. The Act for the Abolition of the Slave Trade was passed in British parliament on March 25, 1807. While the act deemed it illegal to participate in the slave trade between British colonies, the slave trade continued throughout the Caribbean until 1811. Slavery itself was not abolished in England until the Slavery Abolition Act of 1833.
29. Crais and Scully, *Sara Baartman and the Hottentot Venus*, 80.
30. An Englishman, "Letter to the Editor," *Morning Chronicle*, October 12, 1810.
31. Ibid.
32. Strother, "Display of the Body Hottentot," 12.
33. Englishman, "Letter to the Editor."
34. "Response to an Englishman (Attr. To Hendrik Cezar)," ibid., October 13, 1810.
35. Ibid.
36. A Constant Reader, "The Female Hottentot," *The Examiner*, 14 October 1810.
37. Ibid.
38. Ibid.
39. Humanitas, "Female Hottentot," *Morning Chronicle*, October 17, 1810, 3.
40. Affidavit, Public Record Office No. KB1/36, pt. 2 reprinted in Strother, "Display of the Body Hottentot," 43–45.
41. "A Man and A Christian", "Hottentot Venus," *Morning Post*, October 18, 1810, 3.
42. M.T., "To Humanitas," *Morning Chronicle*, October 20, 1810.
43. Humanitas, "The Female Hottentot," *The Examiner*, October 21, 1810.
44. Saidiya V. Hartman, *Scenes of Subjection: Terror, Slavery, and Self-Making in Nineteenth-Century America* (New York: Oxford University Press, 1997), 26.
45. Humanitas, "The Female Hottentot."
46. Ibid.
47. "To the Editor of the Morning Chronicle (Attr. To Hendrik Cezar)," *Morning Chronicle*, October 23, 1810, 4.
48. Ibid.
49. "To the Editor of the Morning Chronicle," ibid., October 24, 1810.
50. "Letter to the Editor," *The Examiner*, October 28, 1810.
51. Lindfors, "Courting the Hottentot Venus," 138.
52. See discussion in ibid., 141. Accounts from the court proceedings can be found in "The Hottentot Venus," *Bell's Weekly Messenger*, November 25, 1810; "The Hottentot Venus," *Observer*, November 25, 1810; "The Hottentot Venus," *Morning Chronicle*, November 26, 1810; "The Hottentot Venus," *Times*, November 26, 1810; "The Hottentot Venus."
53. David J. Cox et al., *Public Indecency in England 1857–1960: "A Serious and Growing Evil"*.

54. Ibid. An example of this is prostitution, which was not itself illegal, and as such its legal pursuit and claims were framed through the lens of behavior rather than morality. On the "managing [of] prostitution through imaginative use of the law in England and Wales," see Ruth Mazo Karras, *Common Women: Prostitution and Sexuality in Medieval England* (New York: Oxford University Press, 1996); Felix Driver, "Moral Geographies: Social Science and the Urban Environment in Mid-Nineteenth Century England," *Transactions of the Institute of British Geographers* 13, no. 3 (1988). Driver helps to elucidate that this very model was inherent to the organization and visionary schema for the modern city. For more on the cultural nuances of this, see G. J. Barker-Benfield, *The Culture of Sensibility: Sex and Society in Eighteenth-Century Britain* (Chicago: University of Chicago Press, 1992); Steven Marcus, *The Other Victorians: A Study of Sexuality and Pornograhy in Mid-Nineteenth-Century England* (New York: Basic Books, 1966).
55. Crais and Scully, *Sara Baartman and the Hottentot Venus*, 100.
56. Tina M. Campt, *Listening to Images* (Durham: Duke University Press, 2017), 32.
57. Sadiah Qureshi, *Peoples on Parade: Exhibitions, Empire, and Anthropology in Nineteenth Century Britain* (Chicago: University of Chicago Press, 2011).
58. Commonly referred to as simply the "T-Visa," the T Nonimmigrant Status is a protective designation for those who are or who have been identified as victims of human trafficking. It allows survivors and their immediate family to legally remain and work in the United States if they assist in the investigation or prosecution of a trafficker. It was created in October 2000 with the passing of the Victims of Trafficking and Violence Protection Act (VTVPA).
59. Worth noting is the focus on Sara, despite the very obvious two young Black boys who also shared her residence, and to whom Sara also referred in her eventual testimony. Apparently their stories were not quite as compelling as Sara's, though Crais and Scully also suggest that the Saint Macaulay was wary to open an investigation because of a similar controversy involving several boys he brought to England from Sierra Leone. See discussion in Crais and Scully, *Sara Baartman and the Hottentot Venus*, 89.
60. Haugen and Hunter, *Terrify No More*, cover quote.
61. Ibid.
62. Laura Agustín, https://www.lauraagustin.com/becoming-aware-of-awareness-raising-as-anti-trafficking-tactic. See also *Sex at the Margins: Migration, Labour Markets and the Rescue Industry*. (New York: Zed Books), 2007.
63. For a timely and incisive analysis of the connections between American government interests in anti-trafficking with respect to Christian morality, see Yvonne C. Zimmerman, *Other Dreams of Freedom: Religion, Sex, and Human Trafficking* (Oxford: Oxford University Press, 2013).
64. Samantha Pinto helpfully contextualizes the legal contracts surrounding Baartman in the "Venus at Work" chapter of *Infamous Bodies: Early Black Women's Celebrity and the Afterlives of Rights* (Durham: Duke University Press, 2020).
65. Spivak, *Can the Subaltern Speak?*, 93.
66. Cannon, *Black Womanist Ethics*, 2.
67. Ibid.
68. Lindfors, "Courting the Hottentot Venus," 148.
69. Ibid.
70. For a more developed critique of the place of the Hottentot Venus in the Black feminist theoretical archive, particularly the reliance of narratives on traumatic assessments of the visual, see "Archives of Pain" in Nash, *The Black Body in Ecstasy*.
71. Yvette Abrahams, "Disempowered to Consent: Sara Bartman and Khoisan Slavery in the Nineteenth-Century Cape Colony and Britain," *South African Historical Journal* 35 (1996). Elsewhere, Crais and Scully also resist the insistence on Baartman as an object only, noting that such a narration quickly slips into a project that "renders her as a kind of classic noble savage victimized by Europe and unable to negotiate the challenges of modernity." Crais and Scully, "Race and Erasure," 303.
72. Cannon, *Black Womanist Ethics*, 2.
73. It is worthy to note that Broca was a great inspiration to Sagan, perhaps the world's greatest astrophysicist, such that he wrote an entire book on the subject, Carl Sagan, *Broca's Brain: Reflections on the Romance of Science* (New York: Random House, 1979).
74. Gould, "The Hottentot Venus."
75. Ibid.
76. Crais and Scully, *Sara Baartman and the Hottentot Venus*, 116. See also discussion in Crais and Scully, "Race and Erasure."

77. Crais and Scully, *Sara Baartman and the Hottentot Venus*, 117. For more on this narrative see discussion in Strother, "Display of the Body Hottentot"; François-Xavier Fauvelle-Aymar, *L'invention Du Hottentot: Histoire Du Regard Occidental Sur Les Khoisan, Xve-Xixe Siècle*, Histoire Moderne (Paris: Publications de la Sorbonne, 2002).
78. Henry Taylor, the man travelling with Baartman in Paris and promoting and managing her appearances, notified the museum of her presence and invited Cuvier personally to attend her afternoon showing on 13 September at the Neuves-des-Petits-Champs. Gérard Badou, *L'énigme De La Vénus Hottentote* (Paris: JC Lattès, 2000), 101–2; Crais and Scully, *Sara Baartman and the Hottentot Venus*, 123.
79. *Sara Baartman and the Hottentot Venus*, 125.
80. "... cette race paraît être la plu disgraciée de toutes celles qui peuplent l'Afrique. Les Hottentots manquent d'intelligence et d'activité." "Hottentots," in *Larousse Great Universal Dictionary of the Nineteenth Century* (Paris: Larousse, 1886–90), 19.1.
81. In particular, Duchet emphasized Hottentots and other Black Africans as two separate races, the former being a more primitive animal than the latter. He also differentiated the races via the notion of female embodiment. See discussion in Michèle Duchet, "Racisme Et Sexualité Au Xviiie Siècle," in *Ni Juif Ni Grec: Entretiens Sur Le Racisme*, ed. Léon Poliakov (Paris: Mouton, 1978), 132–34; Strother, "Display of the Body Hottentot," 3, 11, 16–18.
82. Samuel George Morton, *Crania Americana: Or, a Comparative View of the Skulls of Various Aboriginal Nations of North and South America* (Philadelphia: Dobson, Simpkin, Marshall, 1839), 90.
83. Hottentot men were often imagined to be beautiful creatures but flawed with regard to the excision of one testicle. Strother describes the early travelogue emphasis on the *dissymmetry* of the male and female Hottentot, as in but one example, where the calm, shapely, and thoughtful man is juxtaposed with the woman, "knock-kneed, with simian proportions, and pendulous breasts ... unfocused eyes and silly grin," indicative of a lack of mental faculty. Strother, "Display of the Body Hottentot," 11.
84. Ibid., 21.
85. Crais and Scully, *Sara Baartman and the Hottentot Venus*, 133.
86. Strother, "Display of the Body Hottentot," 1.
87. "Elle tient son tablier soigneusement cache, soit entre ses cuisses, soit plus profondément, et ce n'est qu'apres sa mort qu'on a su qu'elle le possédoit." Georges Cuvier, "Extrait D'observations Faites sur le Cadaver d'une Femme Connue à Paris et à Londres Sous le Nom de Vénus Hottentote," *Mémoires du Muséum d'histoire naturelle* 3 (1817): 265.
88. "Il n'est rien de plus celebre en histoire naturelle que le tablier des Hottentottes." Ibid., 259.
89. Gould, "The Hottentot Venus."
90. Ibid.
91. "The Stinkstones of Oeningen," *Natural History*, June 1982.
92. Ibid.
93. Ibid.
94. "The Hottentot Venus," *Natural History*, October 1982.
95. Ibid.
96. Ibid.
97. "J'ai l'honneur de présenter à l'Académie les organes génitaux de cette femme préparés, de manière à ne laisser aucun doute sur la nature de son tablier." Cuvier, "Extrait D'observations Faites sur le Cadaver d'une Femme Connue à Paris et à Londres Sous le Nom de Vénus Hottentote," 266.
98. Anne McClintock, *Imperial Leather: Race, Gender, and Sexuality in the Colonial Conquest* (New York: Routledge, 1995), 36.
99. Ibid.
100. Indeed, Cuvier would later reenact the Las Casas and the Valladolid debate around whether or not American Indians, as they were identified, had souls, and whether or not conversion was justification for violence in fighting acts considered against nature.
101. Campt, *Listening to Images*, 50.
102. "We think that Baartman sought to render her depictions with verisimilitude, even if the overall design of the poster was out of her control. And she went one step further. Both aquatints record S. Baartman as the publisher, not Alexander Dunlop or Hendrik Cesars. In a move most unusual for the time, the subject of a print managed to hold the copyright. Sara was the official publisher of the famous depictions. Sara had the rights to her own representation. In a context far from her choosing, she helped to fashion an icon for public consumption. It is highly unlikely that Sara Baartman saw any of the royalties from the sale of her image. And the meaning of her being

listed as publisher is hard to determine. The first poster, made early in her stay in England, might well have more genuinely represented her participation in the wider marketing of the production. By March 1811, however, she was contractually under Dunlop's authority, which makes one suspicious of her being named as publisher. Dunlop had reasons, in the wake of the court case about Baartman's liberty, to list her as publisher of the second print too. This might allay fears among members of the public that she was indeed particularly exploited. As in so many aspects of this history, we cannot easily resolve such questions." Crais and Scully, *Sara Baartman and the Hottentot Venus*, 75–78.
103. Campt, *Listening to Images*, 59.
104. Ibid., 74.
105. Cannon, *Black Womanist Ethics*, 17. Cannon quotes and will continue to expand upon the descriptions of Black women writers configured by Mary Burgher (author italics are in the original), which she applies to her analysis of Zora Neale Hurston.

Chapter 6

1. The Combahee River Collective Statement, reprinted in *Home Girls: A Black Feminist Anthology*, ed. Barbara K. Smith (New Brunswick: Rutgers University Press, 2000), 270.
2. Martin Heidegger, "The Thing," in *Poetry, Language, Thought* (New York: Perennial Library, 1975), 163.
3. Ibid., 164.
4. Ibid., 166.
5. Ibid.
6. Ibid., 167.
7. Fred Moten, "The Case of Blackness," *Criticism* 50, no. 2 (2008): 184.
8. For more on the womb as a jug, see Foskett's analysis in Foskett, *A Virgin Conceived: Mary and Classical Representations of Virginity*, 34. Hanne Blank also helpfully notes the reference to the "upside-down jug." Noting the virginal logics that subtend the medical theorization of the hymen, she reflects that the womb was described as having "a functional resemblance to a *krater*, the cup or jar in which wine was mixed with water before being drunk. A jug without a stopper easily spills. A lid with a hole in its middle is hardly a lid at all." Blank, *Virgin*, 47. See also Kathleen Coyne Kelly, *Performing Virginity and Testing Chastity in the Middle Ages*. Routledge Research in Medieval Studies (London and New York: Routledge, 2000).
9. Ann Ellis Hanson, "The Medical Writer's Woman," in *Before Sexuality: The Construction of Erotic Experience in the Ancient Greek World*, ed. David M. Halperin, John J. Winkler, and Froma I. Zeitlin (Princeton: Princeton University Press, 1990), 327.
10. "You are the devil's gateway: you are the unsealer of that (forbidden) tree." Tertullian, "On the Apparel of Women." For more on this see the discussion of Tertullian in "In Search of Our Mother's Garden."
11. This line of thinking I hope to develop elsewhere regarding a constructive theology for those experience infertility.
12. I am drawing from Kristeva's notions of Lacan and the mirror stage, though this line of thought is open to further development utilizing both of these theorists.
13. Bernadette J. Brooten, *Love between Women: Early Christian Responses to Female Homoeroticism* (Chicago: University of Chicago Press, 1996).
14. Sara Ahmed, *Willful Subjects* (Durham: Duke University Press, 2014).
15. Adrienne Rich, *Compulsory Heterosexuality and Lesbian Existence* (Chicago: University of Chicago Press, 1980).
16. Audre Lorde, "Uses of the Erotic: The Erotic as Power," in *Sister Outsider* (New York: Penguin Books, 2020), 45.
17. Ibid., 44.
18. Ibid., 45.
19. Williams, *Sisters in the Wilderness*, 168.
20. Michel Foucault, "Friendship as a Way of Life," in *Ethics: Subjectivity and Truth. The Essential Works of Michel Foucault, 1954–1984*, ed. Paul Rabinow (New York: New Press, 1997). The April 1981 interview appeared first in the French magazine *Gai Pied*.
21. Ibid., 137.
22. Ibid., 138.
23. Glissant, "Édouard Glissant in Conversation with Manthia Diawara," 5.

24. Rowan Williams, "The Body's Grace," in *Sexuality and the Christian Body: Their Way into the Triune God*, ed. Eugene F. Rogers (Oxford and Malden, MA: Blackwell, 1999).
25. Marie-José Mondzain, *Image, Icon, Economy: The Byzantine Origins of the Contemporary Imaginary* (Stanford: Stanford University Press, 2005), 3.
26. Ibid., 100.
27. Ibid., 31.
28. Ibid., 100.
29. Gilles Deleuze and Anthony Uhlmann, "The Exhausted," *SubStance* 24, no. 3 (1995): 21–22.
30. Ibid.
31. Col 1:15.
32. Mondzain, *Image, Icon, Economy*, 101.
33. Irigaray, *Sexes and Genealogies*.
34. Marie-José Mondzain, *Image, Icon, Economy: The Byzantine Origins of the Contemporary Imaginary* (Stanford: Stanford University Press, 2005), 3.
35. W. J. T. Mitchell, *Iconology: Image, Text, Ideology* (Chicago: University of Chicago Press, 1986), 1–2.
36. Ibid., 2.
37. Michel Quenot, *The Resurrection and the Icon* (Crestwood, NY: St. Vladimir's Seminary Press, 1997). 43.
38. Ibid., 45.
39. Gregory of Nyssa, *The Life of Moses*, trans. Everett Ferguson and Abraham J. Malherbe (New York: Paulist Press, 1978), 59. Other early writers like John Chrysostom and Theodoret of Cyrus will draw similar conclusions.
40. For an extensive discussion of the symbols of this type of icon, as well as her Greek counterpart, see David Coomler, "Spirits of Fire and Ice: The Unburnt Thornbush Icon," *Icons and Their Interpretation*, August 6, 2015. Accessed August 28, 2019. https://russianicons.wordpress.com/2015/08/06/spirits-of-fire-and-ice-the-unburnt-thornbush-icon-2/.
41. "Virgin of the Burning Bush: The Walters Art Museum," *The Walters Art Museum*. Accessed February 20, 2023. https://art.thewalters.org/detail/6972/virgin-of-the-burning-bush/.
42. Katherine Sanders, "Symbols in Icons: The Theotokos." Accessed October 12, 2023. https://katherinesandersicons.com/blog/symbols-in-icons-of-mary-the-theotokos-panagia.
43. "[Мы погибаем, не умирая, / Дух обнажаем до дна. / Дивное диво—горит, не сгорая, / Неопалимая Купина!]." From Maximilian Voloshin's 1919 poem "Neopalimaya Kupina," the title poem of his censored and in-flux collection of poems about the Russian revolutionary period. This translation is taken from an epigraph found "The Symbolism and Meaning of the Unburnt Bush Icon of the Mother of God," *St. Elisabeth Convent Blog*, October 10, 2018. Accessed December 20, 2023. https://catalogueofstelisabethconvent.blogspot.com/2018/10/the-symbolism-and-meaning-of-unburnt.html.
44. James Baldwin, "Letter from a Region in My Mind." *The New Yorker*, November 9, 1962. Accessed January 11, 2022. https://www.newyorker.com/magazine/1962/11/17/letter-from-a-region-in-my-mind.
45. Ibid.
46. Giovanna Parravicini, ed., *Mary, Mother of God: Her Life in Icons and Scripture*, trans. Peter Heinegg (Liguori, MI: Liguori/Triumph, 2004), 19.
47. Baldwin, *Letter from a Region*.
48. Direct citations from Spillers's *Mama's Baby* are in bold, though the intermittent phrases contain several riffs on the structure and content of the original essay, which could be read in tandem. This reading is directly inspired by the work and structural approach of Alexis Pauline Gumbs's *Spill*.
49. Mitzi J. Smith, "Abolitionist Messiah: A Man Named Jesus Born of a *Doulē*," in *Bitter the Chastening Rod: Africana Biblical Interpretation after Stony the Road We Trod in the Age of BLM, SayHerName, and MeToo* (Lanham: Lexington Books/Fortress Academic, 2022), 53–70.
50. See Sylvia Wynter, "Unsettling the Coloniality of Being/Power/Truth/Freedom: Towards the Human, after Man, Its Overrepresentation—An Argument," *CR: The New Centennial Review* 3, no. 3 (2003): 257–337.
51. Mitzi Smith contends that the Gospel of Luke "Presents Jesus as the child of an enslaved mother . . . God chose a Galilean *doulē* (enslaved female) named Mary to conceive a male child called Jesus whom the Spirit anointed in her womb to be an abolitionist, as announced in his inaugural sermon: "The Spirit of Yahweh is upon me because he has anointed me to bring good news to the poor . . . sent me to proclaim release to the captives and recovering of sight to the blind [conscientization is the precursor to activism] and to let the oppressed go free (4:18 NRSV)" (55).

Following the condition of the mother, Smith is clear that "Any child born of an enslaved woman, is a slave, living but always dying in stigmatized Black(ened) flesh," and resists the ways *doulē* or *doulos* have lost their meanings, given the euphemistic and "strategically translated as 'servant' in Luke" (56). This extends to Mary's self-identification as *doulē* while speaking with Gabriel at the time of the Annunciation, as well as in her proclamation of the Magnificat. See Mitzi J. Smith, "Abolitionist Messiah: A Man Named Jesus Born of a *Doulē*," 55–6.
52. John Paul II, Homily at Zapopán, January 30, 1979, https://www.vatican.va/content/john-paul-ii/en/homilies/1979/documents/hf_jp-ii_hom_19790130_messico-zapopan.html.
53. Lorde, *Uses of Erotic*, 46.
54. Gebara and Bingemer, *Mary, Mother of God, Mother of the Poor*, 169.
55. Ibid., 170.
56. Andrew Prevot, *Thinking Prayer: Theology and Spirituality amid the Crises of Modernity* (Notre Dame: University of Notre Dame Press, 2015), 304–5.
57. Lorde, *Poetry Is Not a Luxury*, 26.
58. Toni Morrison, *Beloved: A Novel* (New York: Vintage International, 2004), 100.
59. June Jordan, "Moving toward Home (1982)," reprinted in Valerie Kinloch, *June Jordan: Her Life and Letters* (Westport, CT: Praeger Publishers, 2006), 119.
60. Mari Evans, "I Am a Black Woman," in *I Am a Black Woman: Poems by Mari Evans* (New York: William Morrow and Co., 1970), 12.

Bibliography

"A Man and A Christian." "Hottentot Venus." *Morning Post*, October 18, 1810.
Abraham, Joseph. *Eve, Accused or Acquitted?: An Analysis of Feminist Readings of the Creation Narrative Texts in Genesis 1–3*. Cumbria: Paternoster Press, 2002.
Abrahams, Yvette. "Disempowered to Consent: Sara Bartman and Khoisan Slavery in the Nineteenth-Century Cape Colony and Britain." *South African Historical Journal* 35 (1996): 89–114.
Abusharaf, Rogaia Mustafa. *Female Circumcision: Multicultural Perspectives*. Philadelphia: University of Pennsylvania Press, 2006.
Acta Conciliorum Oecumenicorum, edited by Eduard Schwartz, Johannes Straub, Rudolf Schieffer, and Catholic Church. 4 vols. Berlin: de Gruyter, 1914–40. [In Greek and Latin.]
Adkins, Amey Victoria. "Black/Feminist Futures: Reading Beauvoir In black Skin, White Masks." *South Atlantic Quarterly* 112, no. 4 (2013): 697–723.
Adkins, Amey Victoria. "Stretched beneath a Pear Tree: Womanist Considerations of Augustine's *Confessions*." Unpublished manuscript: Duke University, last modified June 28, 2023.
Agustín, Laura María. *Sex at the Margins: Migration, Labour Markets and the Rescue Industry*. New York: Zed Books, 2007.
Ahmed, Sara. *Willful Subjects*. Durham: Duke University Press, 2014.
Alhambra Decree (the Edict of Expulsion). March 31, 1492.
Althaus-Reid, Marcella. *Indecent Theology: Theological Perversions in Sex, Gender and Politics*. New York: Routledge, 2000.
Anderson, Gary A. *The Genesis of Perfection: Adam and Eve in Jewish and Christian Imagination*. Louisville, KY: Westminster John Knox Press, 2001.
Anderson, Gary A., Michael E. Stone, and Johannes Tromp, eds. *Literature on Adam and Eve: Collected Essays*. Studia in Veteris Testamenti Pseudepigrapha, vol. 15. Leiden and Boston: Brill, 2000.
Anzaldúa, Gloria. *Borderlands: The New Mestiza = La Frontera*. San Francisco: Aunt Lute Books, 1991.
Applegate, Anne. "Phillis Wheatley: Her Critics and Her Contribution." *Negro American Literature Forum* 9 (1975): 123–26.
Atkinson, Clarissa W. *The Oldest Vocation: Christian Motherhood in the Middle Ages*. Ithaca: Cornell University Press, 1991.
Augustine. *City of God*. Harmondsworth: Penguin Books, 1972.
Augustine. *The Confessions*. Translated by Maria Boulding. New York: Vintage Books, 1998.
Augustine. "On Marriage and Concupiscence." In Vol. 5: *St. Augustine: Anti-Pelagian Writings*, edited by Philip Schaff, 258–309. A Select Library of the Nicene and Post-Nicene Fathers of the Christian Church: 1st Series. Grand Rapids, MI: Eerdmans, 1978.
Augustine. "On the Good of Marriage." In Vol. 3: *On the Holy Trinity; Doctrinal Treatises; Moral Treatises*, edited by Philip Schaff, 397–413. A Select Library of the Nicene and Post-Nicene Fathers of the Christian Church: 1st Series. Grand Rapids, MI: Eerdmans, 1978.
Badou, Gérard. *L'énigme De La Vénus Hottentote*. Paris: JC Lattès, 2000.
Bailey, Moya, and Trudy. 2018. "On Misogynoir: Citation, Erasure, and Plagiarism." *Feminist Media Studies* 18, no. 4: 762–68.
Baker, Courtney R. *Humane Insight: Looking at Images of African American Suffering and Death*. Urbana: University of Illinois Press, 2015.
Baker-Fletcher, Karen. "More than Suffering: The Healing and Resurrecting Spirit of God," in *Womanist Theological Ethics: A Reader*, ed. Katie Geneva Cannon, Emilie M. Townes, and Angela D. Sims, 155–79. Louisville, KY: Westminster John Knox Press, 2011.

Baldwin, James. "Letter from a Region in My Mind." *The New Yorker.* November 9, 1962. Accessed January 11, 2022. https://www.newyorker.com/magazine/1962/11/17/letter-from-a-region-in-my-mind.
Bantum, Brian. *Redeeming Mulatto: A Theology of Race and Christian Hybridity.* Waco: Baylor University Press, 2010.
Barker-Benfield, G. J. *The Culture of Sensibility: Sex and Society in Eighteenth-Century Britain.* Chicago: University of Chicago Press, 1992.
Barry, Kathleen. *Female Sexual Slavery.* Englewood Cliffs, NJ: Prentice-Hall, 1979.
Barry, Kathleen. *The Prostitution of Sexuality.* New York: New York University Press, 1995.
Barth, Karl. *Evangelical Theology: An Introduction.* Grand Rapids, MI: Eerdmans, 1963.
Bataille, Georges. *Death and Sensuality: A Study of Eroticism and the Taboo.* Translated by Mary Dalwood. New York: Walker, 1962.
Bauer, Franz Xaver. "Proklos von Konstantinople: Ein Bietrag zur Kirchen und Dogmengeschichte des 5 Jahrhunderts." Microform. Universität München, 1919.
Beattie, Tina. *Eve's Pilgrimage: A Woman's Quest for the City of God.* London and New York: Burns & Oates, 2002.
Beattie, Tina. *God's Mother, Eve's Advocate: A Marian Narrative of Women's Salvation.* London and New York: Continuum, 2002.
Beauvoir, Simone de. *The Second Sex.* Translated by Constance Borde and Sheila Malovany-Chevallier. New York: Alfred A. Knopf, 2010.
Berlant, Lauren Gail. *The Female Complaint: The Unfinished Business of Sentimentality in American Culture.* Durham: Duke University Press, 2008.
Bernasconi, Robert. "Silencing the Hottentots: Kolb's Pre-Racial Encounter with the Hottentots and Its Impact on Buffon, Kant, and Rousseau." *Graduate Faculty Philosophy Journal* 35, no. 1/2 (2014): 101–24.
Bernstein, Elizabeth. "The Sexual Politics of the 'New Abolitionism.'" *differences* 18, no. 3 (2007): 128–51.
Bersani, Leo. *Is the Rectum a Grave? and Other Essays.* Chicago: University of Chicago Press, 2009.
Beyer, Victor. "Musee Des Beaux-Arts De Strasbourg. I. Un Tableau De Christiaen De Couwenbergh." *Revue du Louvre* XXII (1972): 297–300. [In French.]
Bideau-Vincent, Sandrine Le. "Christian Van Couwenbergh." In *Peinture Flamande Et Hollandaise Xve-Xviiie Siècle,* 186–87: Musee de la Ville de Strasbourg, 2009. [In French.]
Blank, Hanne. *Virgin: The Untouched History.* New York: Bloomsbury, 2007.
Blier, Suzanne Preston. "Truth and Seeing: Magic, Custom and Fetish in Art History," in *Africa and the Disciplines: Contributions of Research in Africa to the Social Sciences and Humanities,* ed. Robert Bates, V. Y. Mudimbe, and Jean O'Barr, 139–66. Chicago: University of Chicago Press, 1993.
Bonaiuti, Ernesto. "The Genesis of St. Augustine's Idea of Original Sin." *Harvard Theological Review* 10, no. 2 (1917): 159–75.
Boss, Sarah Jane. *Empress and Handmaid: On Nature and Gender in the Cult of the Virgin Mary.* London: Cassell, 2000.
Boss, Sarah Jane. *Mary.* New Century Theology. London and New York: Continuum, 2004.
Boss, Sarah Jane, ed. *Mary: The Complete Resource.* London and New York: Continuum, 2007.
Brand, Dionne. *A Map to the Door of No Return: Notes to Belonging.* Toronto: Vintage Canada, 2002.
Brenner, Athalya, ed. *A Feminist Companion to Genesis,* vol. 2. Sheffield: Sheffield Academic Press, 1993.
Brooten, Bernadette J. *Love between Women: Early Christian Responses to Female Homoeroticism.* Chicago: University of Chicago Press, 1996.
Brown, Raymond E., Paul J. Achtemeier, and United States Lutheran-Roman Catholic Dialogue (Group). *Mary in the New Testament: A Collaborative Assessment by Protestant and Roman Catholic Scholars.* Philadelphia: Fortress Press, 1978.
Butler, Judith. *Gender Trouble: Feminism and the Subversion of Identity.* New York: Routledge, 1999.

Byron, Gay L. *Symbolic Blackness and Ethnic Difference in Early Christian Literature*. New York: Routledge, 2002.
Camões, Luís de. *Os Lusiadas (the Lusiads)*. Translated by Richard Francis Burton and Isabel Burton, 6 vols. London: B. Quaritch, 1880.
Campt, Tina. *Listening to Images*. Durham: Duke University Press, 2017.
Cannon, Katie G. *Black Womanist Ethics*. Eugene: Wipf and Stock, 2006.
Cannon, Katie G. "Wheels in the Middle of Wheels." *Journal of Feminist Studies in Religion* 8, no. 2 (1992): 125-32.
Cantalamessa, Raniero. *Mary: Mirror of the Church*. Collegeville, MN: Liturgical Press, 1992.
Carroll, Charles. *The Tempter of Eve; or, the Criminality of Man's Social, Political, and Religious Equality with the Negro, and the Amalgamation to Which These Crimes Inevitably Lead. Discussed in the Light of the Scriptures, the Sciences, Profane History, Tradition, and the Testimony of the Monuments* (St Louis: The Adamic Publishing Co., 1902), 402. Accessed February 12, 2022. https://archive.org/details/tempterofeve01carr/mode/2up.
Carroll, Eamon R. "Mary in the Documents of the Magisterium." In *Mariology*, edited by Juniper B. Carol, 1-50. Milwaukee, WI: Bruce Publishing, 1955.
Carter, J. Kameron. *Race: A Theological Account*. Oxford: Oxford University Press, 2008.
Cavadini, John C. "Spousal Vision: A Study of Text and History in the Theology of Saint Augustine." *Augustinian Studies* 43, no. 1/2 (2012): 127-48.
Cheng, Anne Anlin. *Second Skin: Josephine Baker & the Modern Surface*. New York: Oxford University Press, 2010.
Chireau, Yvonne. *Black Magic: Religion and the African American Conjuring Tradition*. Berkeley: University of California Press, 2006.
Chow, Rey. *Entanglements: Or Transmedial Thinking about Capture*. Durham: Duke University Press, 2012.
Cobb, M. "An Amazing 10 Years: The Discovery of Egg and Sperm in the 17th Century." *Reproduction in Domestic Animals* 47 (2012): 2-6.
Cohen, Shaye J. D. *The Beginnings of Jewishness: Boundaries, Varieties, Uncertainties*. Hellenistic Culture and Society. Berkeley: University of California Press, 1999.
Collins, Patricia Hill. *Black Feminist Thought: Knowledge, Consciousness, and the Politics of Empowerment*. New York: Routledge, 1991.
Cone, James H. *A Black Theology of Liberation*. 50th anniversary ed. Maryknoll, NY: Orbis Books, 2020.
Copeland, M. Shawn. *Enfleshing Freedom: Body, Race, and Being*. Minneapolis: Fortress Press, 2010.
Couenhoven, Jesse. "St. Augustine's Doctrine of Original Sin." *Augustinian Studies* 36, no. 2 (2005): 359-96.
Cox, David J., Kim Stevenson, Candida Harris, and Judith Rowbotham. *Public Indecency in England 1857-1960: "A Serious and Growing Evil"*. New York: Routledge, 2015.
Crais, Clifton C., and Pamela Scully. *Sara Baartman and the Hottentot Venus: A Ghost Story and a Biography*. Princeton: Princeton University Press, 2009.
Crais, Clifton C., and Pamela Scully. "Race and Erasure: Sara Baartman and Hendrik Cesars in Cape Town and London." *Journal of British Studies* 47, no. 2 (2008): 301-23.
Crawley, Ashon. *Blackpentecostal Breath: The Aesthetics of Possibility*. New York: Fordham University Press, 2016.
Crawley, Ashon. "Harriet Jacobs Gets a Hearing." *Current Musicology* 93 (2012): 33-55.
Crowder, Stephanie Buckhanon. *When Momma Speaks: The Bible and Motherhood from a Womanist Perspective*. Louisville, KY: Westminster John Knox Press, 2016.
Currier, Charles Warren. *Carmel in America a Centennial History of the Discalced Carmelites in the United States*. Baltimore: John Murphy, 1890.
Cuvier, Georges. "Extrait D'observations Faites sur le Cadaver d'une Femme Connue à Paris et à Londres Sous le Nom de Vénus Hottentote." *Mémoires du Muséum d'histoire naturelle* 3 (1817): 259-74. [In French.]
Cyril. "Cyril to Monks in Egypt." Translated by John I. McEnerney. In *St. Cyril of Alexandria Letters 1-50*, 13-33. Fathers of the Church. Washington, DC: Catholic University of America Press, 1987.

Cyril. "Homily V." Translated by Susan Wessel. In *Cyril of Alexandria and the Nestorian Controversy: The Making of a Saint and of a Heretic*, 303–6. Oxford and New York: Oxford University Press, 2004.

Cyril. "Letter to Pope Celestine." Translated by John Anthony McGuckin. In *St. Cyril of Alexandria: The Christological Controversy: Its History, Theology, and Texts*, edited by John Anthony McGuckin, 276–79. Supplements to Vigiliae Christianae. Leiden and New York: Brill, 1994.

Cyril. "Letter to the Monks of Egypt." Translated by John Anthony McGuckin. In *St. Cyril of Alexandria: The Christological Controversy: Its History, Theology, and Texts*, edited by John Anthony McGuckin, 245–61. Supplements to Vigiliae Christianae. Leiden and New York: Brill, 1994.

Cyril. "Third Letter of Cyril to Nestorius." In *Christology of the Later Fathers*, edited by Edward Rochie Hardy and Cyril Charles Richardson, 266–75. Philadelphia: Westminster Press, 1954.

Cyril. "To Celestine." Translated by John I. McEnerney. In *St. Cyril of Alexandria Letters 1–50*, 60–64. Fathers of the Church. Washington, DC: Catholic University of America Press, 1987.

Daly, Mary. *The Church and the Second Sex*. Boston: Beacon Press, 1985.

Deleuze, Gilles, and Anthony Uhlmann. "The Exhausted." *SubStance* 24, no. 3 (1995): 3–28.

Douglas, Mary. *Purity and Danger: An Analysis of the Concepts of Pollution and Taboo*. London: Ark, 1984.

Douglass, Patrice D. "Black Feminist Theory for the Dead and Dying." *Theory & Event* 21, no. 1 (2018): 106–23.

Drake, Susanna. *Slandering the Jew: Sexuality and Difference in Early Christian Texts*. Philadelphia: University of Pennsylvania Press, 2013.

Driver, Felix. "Moral Geographies: Social Science and the Urban Environment in Mid-Nineteenth Century England." *Transactions of the Institute of British Geographers* 13, no. 3 (1988): 275–87.

Duchet, Michèle. "Racisme Et Sexualité Au Xviiie Siècle." In *Ni Juif Ni Grec: Entretiens sur le Racisme*, edited by Léon Poliakov, 127–38. Paris: Mouton, 1978. [In French.]

Dzielska, Maria. *Hypatia of Alexandria*. Translated by F. Lyra. Cambridge, MA: Harvard University Press, 1995.

Eilberg-Schwartz, Howard. *God's Phallus and Other Problems for Men and Monotheism*. Boston: Beacon Press, 1994.

Evans, Mari. *I Am a Black Woman: Poems by Mari Evans*. New York: William Morrow and Co., 1970.

Fanon, Frantz. *Black Skin, White Masks*. Translated by Richard Philcox. New York: Grove Press, 2008.

Fauvelle-Aymar, François-Xavier. *L'invention Du Hottentot: Histoire du Regard Occidental sur les Khoisan, Xve–Xixe Siècle*. Histoire Moderne. Paris: Publications de la Sorbonne, 2002. [In French.]

Florensky, Pavel. *Iconostasis*. Crestwood, NY: St. Vladimir's Seminary Press, 1996.

Foskett, Mary F. *A Virgin Conceived: Mary and Classical Representations of Virginity*. Bloomington: Indiana University Press, 2002.

Foucault, Michel. *Discipline and Punish: The Birth of the Prison*. New York: Vintage Books, 1995.

Foucault, Michel. "Friendship as a Way of Life." Translated by Robert Hurley. In *Ethics: Subjectivity and Truth. The Essential Works of Michel Foucault, 1954–1984*, edited by Paul Rabinow, 135–40. New York: New Press, 1997.

Foucault, Michel. "Nietzsche, Genealogy, History." *Semiotext(E)* 3, no. 1 (1978): 78.

Freedberg, David. "Art and Iconoclasm, 1525–1580: The Case of the Northern Netherlands." In *Kunst Voor De Beeldenstorm*, edited by J. P. Filedt Kok, W. Halsema-Kubes, and W. Th. Kloek, 69–84. Rijksmuseum, Amsterdam: Staatsuitgeverij: 's-gravenhage, 1986.

Freud, Sigmund. "On the Universal Tendency to Debasement in the Sphere of Love." In *The Freud Reader*, edited by Peter Gay, 394–99. New York: W. W. Norton & Company, 1989.

Freud, Sigmund. *Three Essays on the Theory of Sexuality*. New York: Basic Books, 2000.

Fulkerson, Mary McClintock. "Sexism as Original Sin: Developing a Theacentric Discourse." *Journal of the American Academy of Religion* 59, no. 4 (1991): 673.

Gafney, Wilda C. *A Women's Lectionary for the Whole Church: Year W: A Multi Gospel Single-Year Lectionary.* New York: Church Publishing, Inc., 2021.

Gambero, Luigi. *Mary and the Fathers of the Church: The Blessed Virgin Mary in Patristic Thought.* San Francisco: Ignatius Press, 1999.

Gebara, Ivone, and Maria Clara Lucchetti Bingemer. *Mary, Mother of God, Mother of the Poor.* Maryknoll, NY: Orbis Books, 1989.

Gelder, J.G. van. "De Schilders Van De Oranjezaal." *Nederlands kunsthistorisch jaarboek* 2: (1948–49) (1949): 118–64. [In Dutch.]

Gibbon, Edward. *The History of the Decline and Fall of the Roman Empire*, vol. 4. Project Gutenberg, 1845. Ebook. https://www.gutenberg.org/cache/epub/25717/pg25717-images.html.

Gilman, Sander L. "The Jewish Nose: Are Jews White? Or, the History of the Nose Job," in *The Other in Jewish Thought and History: Constructions of Jewish Culture and Identity*, eds. Laurence J. Silberstein and Robert L. Cohn, 364–401. New York: New York University Press, 1994.

Gilman, Sander L. *Jewish Self-Hatred: Anti-Semitism and the Hidden Language of the Jews.* Baltimore: Johns Hopkins University Press, 1986.

Glissant, Édouard. "Édouard Glissant in Conversation with Manthia Diawara." *Nka: Journal of Contemporary African Art* 28 (2011): 4–19.

Glissant, Édouard. *Poetics of Relation.* Translated by Betsy Wing. Ann Arbor: University of Michigan Press, 1997.

Gould, Stephen Jay. "The Hottentot Venus." *Natural History,* October 1982, 20–28.

Gould, Stephen Jay. "The Stinkstones of Oeningen." *Natural History,* June 1982, 6–13.

Graef, Hilda. *Mary: A History of Doctrine and Devotion.* Notre Dame, IN: Ave Maria Press, 2009.

Gregory of Nyssa. *The Life of Moses.* Translated by Everett Ferguson and Abraham J Malherbe. New York: Paulist Press, 1978.

Gumbs, Alexis Pauline. *Spill: Scenes of Black Feminist Fugitivity.* Durham: Duke University Press, 2016.

Haak, Bob. *The Golden Age: Dutch Painters of the Seventeenth Century.* Translated by Elizabeth Willems-Treeman. New York: Stewart, Tabori & Chang, 1996.

Hanson, Ann Ellis. "The Medical Writer's Woman." In *Before Sexuality: The Construction of Erotic Experience in the Ancient Greek World*, edited by David M. Halperin, John J. Winkler, and Froma I. Zeitlin, 309–38. Princeton: Princeton University Press, 1990.

Hardy, Edward Rochie. "Introduction to the First Letter of Nestorius to Celestine." In *Christology of the Later Fathers*, edited by Edward Rochie Hardy and Cyril Charles Richardson, 346–48. Philadelphia: Westminster Press, 1954.

Harper, Kyle. *From Shame to Sin: The Christian Transformation of Sexual Morality in Late Antiquity.* Cambridge, MA: Harvard University Press, 2013.

Harris, Marguerite Tjader, ed. *Birgitta of Sweden: Life and Selected Revelations.* The Classics of Western Spirituality. New York: Paulist Press, 1990.

Hartman, Saidiya V. *Lose Your Mother: A Journey along the Atlantic Slave Route.* New York: Farrar, Straus and Giroux, 2007.

Hartman, Saidiya V. *Scenes of Subjection: Terror, Slavery, and Self-Making in Nineteenth-Century America.* New York: Oxford University Press, 1997.

Hartman, Saidiya V. "Venus in Two Acts." *Small Axe* 12, no. 2 (2008): 1–14.

Haugen, Gary A., and Gregg Hunter. *Terrify No More.* Nashville: W. Publishing Group, 2005.

Hayes, Diana L. *And Still We Rise.* Mahwah, NJ: Paulist Press, 1996.

Heidegger, Martin. "The Thing." Translated by Albert Hofstadter. In *Poetry, Language, Thought*, 163–86. New York: Perennial Library, 1975.

van der Heijden, Manon. "Women as Victims of Sexual and Domestic Violence in Seventeenth-Century Holland: Criminal Cases of Rape, Incest, and Maltreatment in Rotterdam and Delft." *Journal of Social History* 33 no. 3 (2000): 623–44.

Hemmings, Clare. *Why Stories Matter: The Political Grammar of Feminist Theory*. Durham: Duke University Press, 2011.
Holsinger, Bruce. *Music Body and Desire in Medieval Culture: Hildegard of Bingen to Chaucer*. Standford: Stanford University Press, 2001.
Holum, Kenneth G. *Theodosian Empresses: Women and Imperial Dominion in Late Antiquity*. Berkeley: University of California Press, 1982.
hooks, bell. *The Will to Change: Men, Masculinity, and Love*. New York: Atria Books, 2004.
Ignatius. "Epistle to the Ephesians." In *The Apostolic Fathers, Justin Martyr, and Irenaeus*, edited by Alexander Roberts, James Donaldson, A. Cleveland Coxe, Allan Menzies, Ernest Cushing Richardson, and Bernhard Pick, 45–58. The Ante-Nicene Fathers: Translations of the Writings of the Fathers Down to A.D. 325. Grand Rapids, MI: Eerdmans, 1978.
Ignatius. "Epistle to the Trallians." In *The Apostolic Fathers, Justin Martyr, and Irenaeus*, edited by Alexander Roberts, James Donaldson, A. Cleveland Coxe, Allan Menzies, Ernest Cushing Richardson, and Bernhard Pick, 66–72. The Ante-Nicene Fathers: Translations of the Writings of the Fathers Down to A.D. 325. Grand Rapids, MI: Eerdmans, 1978.
Irenaeus. "Against Heresies." In *The Apostolic Fathers, Justin Martyr, and Irenaeus*, edited by Alexander Roberts, James Donaldson, A. Cleveland Coxe, Allan Menzies, Ernest Cushing Richardson and Bernhard Pick, 309–567. The Ante-Nicene Fathers: Translations of the Writings of the Fathers Down to A.D. 325. Grand Rapids, MI: Eerdmans, 1978.
Irenaeus. *Proof of the Apostolic Preaching*. Translated by Joseph P. Smith. Ancient Christian Writers. Westminster, MD: Newman Press, 1952.
Irigaray, Luce. *Marine Lover of Friedrich Nietzsche*. New York: Columbia University Press, 1991.
Irigaray, Luce. *Sexes and Genealogies*. New York: Columbia University Press, 1993.
Irigaray, Luce. *This Sex Which Is Not One*. Ithaca: Cornell University Press, 1985.
Isherwood, Lisa. *Introducing Feminist Theology*. Sheffield: Sheffield Academic Press, 1993.
Jack, Christine Trimingham. "Sacred Symbols, School Ideology and the Construction of Subjectivity." *Paedagogica Historica* 34, no. 3 (1998): 771–94.
Jagose, Annamarie. *Orgasmology*. Durham: Duke University Press, 2013.
Jennings, Willie James. *The Christian Imagination: Theology and the Origins of Race*. New Haven: Yale University Press, 2010.
Jerome. "The Perpetual Virginity of Blessed Mary (against Helvidius)." In Vol. 6: *Jerome: The Principal Works of St. Jerome*, edited by Philip Schaff and Henry Wace, 756–76. A Select Library of Nicene and Post-Nicene Fathers of the Christian Church: 2nd Series. Grand Rapids, MI: Eerdmans, 1978.
Jerome. "To Eustochium." In Vol. 6: *Jerome: The Principal Works of St. Jerome*, edited by Philip Schaff and Henry Wace, 101–38. A Select Library of Nicene and Post-Nicene Fathers of the Christian Church: 2nd Series. Grand Rapids, MI: Eerdmans, 1978.
Johnson, Willis. "The Myth of Jewish Male Menses." *Journal of Medieval History* 24, no. 3 (1998): 273–95.
Josephus, Flavius. *Jewish Antiquities*, Vol. 1: *Books 1–3*. Translated by H. St J. Thackeray. Loeb Classical Library 242. Cambridge, MA: Harvard University Press, 1930.
Kant, Immanuel. "Of the Different Human Races." In *The Idea of Race*, edited by Robert Bernasconi and Tommy Lee Lott, 8–22. Indianapolis: Hackett Publishing Co., 2000.
Karras, Ruth Mazo. *Common Women: Prostitution and Sexuality in Medieval England*. New York: Oxford University Press, 1996.
Kelly, Kathleen Coyne. *Performing Virginity and Testing Chastity in the Middle Ages*. Routledge Research in Medieval Studies. London and New York: Routledge, 2000.
Kempadoo, Kamala, and Jo Doezema. *Global Sex Workers: Rights, Resistance, and Redefinition*. New York: Routledge, 1998.
Kempadoo, Kamala, Jyoti Sanghera, and Bandana Pattanaik. *Trafficking and Prostitution Reconsidered: New Perspectives on Migration, Sex Work, and Human Rights*. Boulder, CO: Paradigm Publishers, 2005.
Kinloch, Valerie. *June Jordan: Her Life and Letters*. Westport, CT: Praeger Publishers, 2006.

Kim, Mari. *Eros in Eden: A Praxis of Beauty in Genesis 3*. Emory University, PhD dissertation, 2010.
Kirby, Percival R. "The Hottentot Venus." *Africana Notes and News* 6, no. 3 (1949): 55–61.
Knust, Jennifer Wright. *Abandoned to Lust: Sexual Slander and Ancient Christianity*. New York: Columbia University Press, 2006.
Koptische Akten zum Ephesinischen Konzil vom Jahre 431. Translated by Wilhelm Kraatz. Leipzig: J. C. Hinrichs, 1904.
Kovacs, Judith L., Christopher Rowland, and Rebekah Callow. *Revelation: The Apocalypse of Jesus Christ*. Malden, MA: Blackwell, 2004.
Kugel, James L. *Traditions of the Bible: A Guide to the Bible as It Was at the Start of the Common Era*. Cambridge, MA: Harvard University Press, 1998.
Kvam, Kristen E., Linda S. Schearing, and Valarie H. Ziegler. *Eve and Adam: Jewish, Christian, and Muslim Readings on Genesis and Gender*. Bloomington: Indiana University Press, 1999.
Kwok, Pui-lan. *Postcolonial Imagination and Feminist Theology*. Louisville, KY: Westminster John Knox Press, 2005.
Leo I. "Letter Xxviii. To Flavian, Commonly Called 'the Tome.'" In Vol. 12: *Leo the Great, Gregory the Great*, edited by Philip Schaff, 100–10. A Select Library of the Nicene and Post-Nicene Fathers of the Christian Church: 2nd Series. Grand Rapids, MI: Eerdmans, 1978.
Lerner, Anne Lapidus. *Eternally Eve: Images of Eve in the Hebrew Bible, Midrash, and Modern Jewish Poetry*. Waltham, MA: Brandeis University Press, 2007.
Levine, Amy-Jill. "Introduction." In *A Feminist Companion to Mariology*, edited by Amy-Jill Levine and Maria Mayo Robbins, 1–14. London and New York: T & T Clark International, 2005.
Lillis, Julia. *Virgin Territory, Virgin Territory: Configuring Female Virginity in Early Christianity*. Berkley: University of California Press, 2023.
Lindfors, Bernth. "Courting the Hottentot Venus." *Africa: Revista Trimestrale di Studi e Documentazione dell Istituto Italo-Africano* 40, no. 1 (1985).
Loofs, Friedrich. *Nestorius and His Place in the History of Christian Doctrine*. Cambridge: Cambridge University Press, 1914.
Lorde, Audre. "Poetry Is Not a Luxury," in *Sister Outsider*, 24–27. New York: Penguin Books, 2020.
Lorde, Audre. "Uses of the Erotic: The Erotic as Power," in *Sister Outsider*, 41–48. New York: Penguin Books, 2020.
Lucie-Smith, Edward. *Sexuality in Western Art*. New York: Thames and Hudson, 1991.
Maddocks, Fiona. *Hildegard of Bingen: The Woman of Her Age*. New York: Doubleday, 2001.
Mahmood, Saba. *Politics of Piety: The Islamic Revival and the Feminist Subject*. Princeton: Princeton University Press, 2005.
Maier-Preusker, W. "Christiaen Van Couwenbergh (1604–1667). Oeuvre und Wandlungen Eines Holländischen Caravaggisten." *Wallraf-Richartz Jahrbuch* 52 (1991): 163–236. [In German.]
Marcus, Steven. *The Other Victorians: A Study of Sexuality and Pornograhy in Mid-Nineteenth-Century England*. New York: Basic Books, 1966.
Martin, Kameelah L. *Conjuring Moments in African American Literature: Women, Spirit Work, and Other Such Hoodoo*. New York: Palgrave Macmillan, 2013.
McClintock, Anne. *Imperial Leather: Race, Gender, and Sexuality in the Colonial Conquest*. New York: Routledge, 1995.
McGuckin, John Anthony. *St. Cyril of Alexandria: The Christological Controversy: Its History, Theology, and Texts*. Translated by John Anthony McGuckin. Supplements to Vigiliae Christianae. Leiden and New York: Brill, 1994.
Meyers, Carol L. *Discovering Eve: Ancient Israelite Women in Context*. New York: Oxford University Press, 1988.
Miles, Margaret R. *Carnal Knowing: Female Nakedness and Religious Meaning in the Christian West*. Boston: Beacon Press, 1989.
Miles, Margaret R. *A Complex Delight: The Secularization of the Breast, 1350–1750*. Berkeley: University of California Press, 2008.

Miles, Margaret R. *Rereading Historical Theology: Before, during, and after Augustine.* Eugene, OR: Cascade Books, 2008.
Miles, Margaret R. *The Word Made Flesh: A History of Christian Thought.* Malden, MA: Blackwell, 2005.
Miranda, Carlos A., and Suzette A. Spencer. "Omnipresent Negation: Hottentot Venus and Africa Rising." *Callaloo* 32, no. 3 (2009): 910–33.
Mondzain, Marie-José. *Image, Icon, Economy: The Byzantine Origins of the Contemporary Imaginary.* Stanford: Stanford University Press, 2005.
Morrison, Toni. *Beloved: A Novel.* New York: Vintage International, 2004.
Morton, Samuel George. *Crania Americana: Or, a Comparative View of the Skulls of Various Aboriginal Nations of North and South America.* Philadelphia: Dobson, Simpkin, Marshall, 1839.
Moten, Fred. "Black Mo'nin'." In *Loss: The Politics of Mourning,* edited by David L. Eng and David Kazanjian, 59–76. Berkeley: University of California Press, 2003.
Moten, Fred. "Blackness and Nothingness (Mysticism in the Flesh)." *South Atlantic Quarterly* 112, no. 4 (2013): 737–80.
Moten, Fred. "The Case of Blackness." *Criticism* 50, no. 2 (2008): 177–218.
Moten, Fred. *In the Break: The Aesthetics of the Black Radical Tradition.* Minneapolis: University of Minnesota Press, 2003.
Moten, Fred. "To Consent Not to Be a Single Being." *Harriet: A Poetry Blog,* February 15, 2010.
Muizelaar, Klaske, and Derek L. Phillips. *Picturing Men and Women in the Dutch Golden Age: Paintings and People in Historical Perspective.* New Haven: Yale University Press, 2003.
Nash, Jennifer C. *Birthing Black Mothers.* Durham: Duke University Press, 2021.
Nash, Jennifer C. *The Black Body in Ecstasy: Reading Race, Reading Pornography.* Durham: Duke University Press, 2014.
Nestorius. "Ad Johannen Antiochenum." Translated by Friedrich Loofs. In *Nestoriana: Die Fragmente des Nestorius,* edited by Friedrich Loofs. Halle a. S.: Niemeyer, 1905. https://www.poetryfoundation.org/blog/uncategorized/53342/to-consent-not-to-be-a-single-being.
Nestorius. "Barhadbeshabba." Translated by François Nau. In *Patrologia Orientalis,* 565–66. Paris: Firmin-Didot, 1913.
Nestorius. *The Bazaar of Heracleides.* Translated by G. R. Driver and Leonard Hodgson. Oxford: Clarendon Press, 1925.
Nestorius. "Doctrina Pietatis (Erster Sermon gegen das Theotokos)." Translated by Friedrich Loofs. In *Nestoriana: Die Fragmente Des Nestorius,* 249–63. Halle a. S.: Niemeyer, 1905.
Nestorius. "First Letter of Nestorius to Celestine." In *Christology of the Later Fathers,* edited by Edward Rochie Hardy and Cyril Charles Richardson, 346–48. Philadelphia: Westminster Press, 1954.
Nestorius. *Le Livre D'héraclide De Damas.* Translated by Paul Bedjan. Paris: O. Harrassowitz, 1910.
Nestorius. "Lettre À Cosme." Translated by François Nau. In *Patrologia Orientalis.* Paris: Firmin-Didot, 1916.
Nestorius. *Nestoriana: Die Fragmente des Nestorius.* Translated by Friedrich Loofs. Halle a. S.: Niemeyer, 1905.
Nelson, Charmaine. *Representing the Black Female Subject in Western Art.* New York: Routledge, 2010.
Newman, Barbara. *Sister of Wisdom: St. Hildegard's Theology of the Feminine.* Berkeley: University California Press, 1987.
Pagels, Elaine H. *Adam, Eve, and the Serpent.* New York: Random House, 1988.
Parravicini, Giovanna ed. *Mary, Mother of God: Her Life in Icons and Scripture.* Translated by Peter Heinegg. Liguori, MI: Liguori/Triumph, 2004.
Parker, Charles H. *Faith on the Margins: Catholics and Catholicism in the Dutch Golden Age.* Cambridge, MA: Harvard University Press, 2008.
Parker, Julie Faith. "Blaming Eve Alone: Translation, Omission, and Implications of עמה in Genesis 3:6b." *Journal of Biblical Literature* 132, no. 4 (2013): 729–47.

Patrologiæ Cursus Completus, Series Græca. Edited by J. P. Migne. Paris: 1857–66.

Pelikan, Jaroslav. *Mary through the Centuries: Her Place in the History of Culture.* New Haven: Yale University Press, 1996.

Perez-Gil, Maria Mar. "Mary and the Carnal Maternal Genealogy: Towards a Mariology of the Body." *Literature and Theology* 25, no. 3 (2011): 297–311.

Philo. *On the Creation. Allegorical Interpretation of Genesis 2 and 3.* Translated by G. H. Whitaker and F. H. Colson. Loeb Classical Library 226. Cambridge, MA: Harvard University Press, 1929.

Pinto, Samantha. *Infamous Bodies: Early Black Women's Celebrity and the Afterlives of Rights.* Durham: Duke University Press, 2020.

Pipkin, Amanda. *Rape in the Republic, 1609–1725: Formulating Dutch Identity.* Leiden: Brill, 2013.

Pius, IX. "Ineffabilis Deus." 1854.

Pol, Lotte C. van de. "The Whore, the Bawd, and the Artist: The Reality and Imagery of Seventeenth-Century Dutch Prostitution." *Journal of Historians of Netherlandish Art* 2, no. 1/2 (2010).

Power, Michael L., and Jay Schulkin. *The Evolution of the Human Placenta.* Baltimore: Johns Hopkins University Press, 2012.

Prevot, Andrew L. *Thinking Prayer: Theology and Spirituality amid the Crises of Modernity.* Notre Dame: University of Notre Dame Press, 2015.

Proclus. "Homily I." In *Proclus of Constantinople and the Cult of the Virgin in Late Antiquity Homilies 1–5, Texts and Translations,* edited by Nicholas Constas, 125–272. Supplements to Vigiliae Christianae. Leiden and Boston: Brill, 2003.

Proclus. "Homily I: De Laudibus S. Mariae." In *Acta Conciliorum Oecumenicorum,* edited by Eduard Schwartz, et al., 103–7. Berlin: de Gruyter, 1914.

Quenot, Michel. *The Resurrection and the Icon.* Crestwood, NY: St. Vladimir's Seminary Press, 1997.

Qureshi, Sadiah. *Peoples on Parade: Exhibitions, Empire, and Anthropology in Nineteenth Century Britain.* Chicago: University of Chicago Press, 2011.

Resnick, Irven M. "Medieval Roots of the Myth of Jewish Male Menses(*)." *Harvard Theological Review* 93 (2000): 241.

Rich, Adrienne. *Compulsory Heterosexuality and Lesbian Existence.* Chicago: University of Chicago Press, 1980.

Roberts, Dorothy E. *Killing the Black Body: Race, Reproduction, and the Meaning of Liberty.* New York: Pantheon Books, 1997.

Rogers, Eugene F. *After the Spirit: A Constructive Pneumatology from Resources outside the Modern West.* Grand Rapids, MI: Eerdmans, 2005.

Rose, E. M. *The Murder of William of Norwich: The Origins of the Blood Libel in Medieval Europe.* Oxford: Oxford University Press, 2015.

Rosenberg, Jay F. *Thinking Clearly about Death.* Englewood Cliffs, NJ: Prentice-Hall, 1983.

Rubin, Gayle. "The Traffic in Women: Notes on the 'Political Economy' of Sex." In *Deviations: A Gayle Rubin Reader,* 33–65. Durham: Duke University Press, 2012.

Rubin, Gayle. "The Trouble with Trafficking: Afterthoughts on 'the Traffic in Women.'" In *Deviations: A Gayle Rubin Reader,* 66–86. Durham: Duke University Press, 2012.

Sagan, Carl. *Broca's Brain: Reflections on the Romance of Science.* New York: Random House, 1979.

Schaberg, Jane. *The Illegitimacy of Jesus: A Feminist Theological Interpretation of the Infancy Narratives.* Sheffield: Sheffield Phoenix Press, 2006.

Scheer, Monique. "From Majesty to Mystery: Change in the Meanings of Black Madonnas from the Sixteenth to Nineteenth Centuries." *American Historical Review* 107, no. 5 (2002): 1412–40.

Sharpe, Christina Elizabeth. *In the Wake: On Blackness and Being.* Durham: Duke University Press, 2016.

238 BIBLIOGRAPHY

Shklovsky, Viktor. *Theory of Prose*. Translated by Benjamin Sher. Elmwood Park, IL: Dalkey Archive Press, 1990.

Shoemaker, Stephen J. *Ancient Traditions of the Virgin Mary's Dormition and Assumption*. Oxford Early Christian Studies. Oxford: Oxford University Press, 2002.

Silva, Denise Ferreira da. *Toward a Global Idea of Race*. Minneapolis: University of Minnesota Press, 2007.

Smith, Mitzi J. "Abolitionist Messiah: A Man Named Jesus Born of a *Doulē*," in *Bitter the Chastening Rod: Africana Biblical Interpretation after Stony the Road We Trod in the Age of BLM, SayHerName, and MeToo* (Lanham, MD: Lexington Books/Fortress Academic, 2022), 53–70.

Socrates. *The Ecclesiastical History of Socrates, Surnamed Scholasticus, or the Advocate: Comprising a History of the Church, in Seven Books, from the Accession of Constantine, A.D. 305, to the 38th Year of Theodosius Ii., Including a Period of 140 Years*. Bohn's Ecclesiastical Library. London: H. Bohn, 1853.

Spillers, Hortense J. "All the Things You Could Be by Now if Sigmund Freud's Wife Was Your Mother: Psychoanalysis and Race." *Critical Inquiry* 22, no. 4 (1996): 710–34.

Spillers, Hortense J. "Interstices." In *Black, White, and in Color: Essays on American Literature and Culture*, 152–75. Chicago: University of Chicago Press, 2003.

Spillers, Hortense J. "Mama's Baby, Papa's Maybe: An American Grammar Book." *Diacritics* 17, no. 2 (1987): 65–81.

Spivak, Gayatri Chakravorty. "Can the Subaltern Speak?" In *Marxism and the Interpretation of Culture*, edited by Cary Nelson and Lawrence Grossberg, 271–313. Urbana: University of Illinois Press, 1988.

Stead, G. Christopher. "Rhetorical Method in Athanasius." *Vigiliae Christianae* 30, no. 2 (1976): 121–37.

Stokes, Mason. *The Color of Sex: Whiteness, Heterosexuality, and the Fictions of White Supremacy*. Durham: Duke University Press, 2001.

Stone, Ken. "The Garden of Eden and the Heterosexual Contract." In *Bodily Citations: Religion and Judith Butler*, edited by Ellen T. Armour and Susan M. St. Ville, 48–70. New York: Columbia University Press, 2006.

Strother, Zoe S. "Display of the Body Hottentot." In *Africans on Stage: Studies in Ethnological Show Business*, edited by Bernth Lindfors, 1–61. Bloomington: Indiana University Press 1999.

Teman, Elly. *Birthing a Mother: The Surrogate Body and the Pregnant Self*. Berkeley: University of California Press, 2010.

Tertullian. "On the Apparel of Women." In Vol. 4: *Tertullian, Part Fourth; Minucius Felix; Commodian; Origen, Part First and Second*, edited by Alexander Roberts, James Donaldson, A. Cleveland Coxe, Allan Menzies, Ernest Cushing Richardson, and Bernhard Pick, 24–53. The Ante-Nicene Fathers: Translations of the Writings of the Fathers Down to A.D. 325. Grand Rapids, MI: Eerdmans, 1978.

Tertullian. "On the Flesh of Christ." In Vol. 3: *Latin Christianity: It's Founder, Tertullian*, edited by Alexander Roberts, James Donaldson, A. Cleveland Coxe, Allan Menzies, Ernest Cushing Richardson, and Bernhard Pick, 521–54. The Ante-Nicene Fathers: Translations of the Writings of the Fathers Down to A.D. 325. Grand Rapids, MI: Eerdmans, 1978.

Toland, John. *Tetradymus*. London: J. Brotherton and W. Meadows, 1720.

Tompkins, Kyla Wazana. *Racial Indigestion: Eating Bodies in the 19th Century*. New York: New York University Press, 2012.

Trible, Phyllis. "Eve and Adam: Genesis 2-3 Reread." *Andover Newton Quarterly* 13 (1973): 74–81.

Trible, Phyllis. *God and the Rhetoric of Sexuality*. Philadelphia: Fortress Press, 1978.

Tumanov, Vladimir. "Mary versus Eve: Paternal Uncertainty and the Christian View of Women." *Neophilologus* 95, no. 4 (2011): 507.

United Nations General Assembly. "Protocol to Prevent, Suppress and Punish Trafficking in Persons, Especially Women and Children, Supplementing the United Nations Convention against Transnational Organized Crime." November 15, 2000.

United States Department of State. *Trafficking in Persons Report*. Annual.

Vanhaelen, Angela. *The Wake of Iconoclasm: Painting the Church in the Dutch Republic*. University Park: Pennsylvania State University Press, 2012.

VI, Pope Paul. *Lumen Gentium (Dogmatic Constitution on the Church)*. 1965.

Weedon, Chris. "Subjects." In *A Concise Companion to Feminist Theory*, edited by Mary Eagleton, 111–31. Oxford: Blackwell, 2003.

Wessel, Susan. *Cyril of Alexandria and the Nestorian Controversy: The Making of a Saint and of a Heretic*. Oxford and New York: Oxford University Press, 2004.

Wessel, Susan. *Leo the Great and the Spiritual Rebuilding of a Universal Rome*. Leiden and Boston: Brill, 2008.

Westermann, Mariet, ed. *Making Home in the Dutch Republic*. Art & Home: Dutch Interiors in the Age of Rembrandt. Denver Art Museum and The Newark Museum, 2001.

Whitefield, George. "Letter to Wesley, from Bethesda in Georgia." December 24, 1740.

Whitford, Margaret. *Luce Irigaray: Philosophy in the Feminine*. London and New York: Routledge, 1991.

Wiegman, Robyn, and Elizabeth A. Wilson. "Introduction: Antinormativity's Queer Conventions." *differences* 26, no. 1 (2015): 1–25.

Wilken, Robert L. "Exegesis and the History of Theology: Reflections on the Adam-Christ Typology in Cyril of Alexandria." *Church History* 35, no. 2 (1966): 139–56.

Williams, Delores S. *Sisters in the Wilderness: The Challenge of Womanist God-Talk*. Maryknoll, NY: Orbis Books, 1993.

Williams, Rowan. "The Body's Grace." In *Sexuality and the Christian Body: Their Way into the Triune God*, edited by Eugene F. Rogers, 17–36. Oxford and Malden, MA: Blackwell, 1999.

Wittig, Monique. "One Is Not Born a Woman." *Feminist Issues* 1, no. 1 (1981): 47–54.

Wolfthal, Diane. *Images of Rape: The "Heroic" Tradition and Its Alternatives*. Cambridge and New York: Cambridge University Press, 1999.

Wynter, Sylvia. "'Genital Mutilation' or 'Symbolic Birth?': Female Circumcision, Lost Origins, and the Aculturalism of Feminist/Western Thought." *Case Western Reserve Law Review* 47, no. 2 (1997): 501–52.

Wynter, Sylvia. "Unsettling the Coloniality of Being/Power/Truth/Freedom: Towards the Human, after Man, Its Overrepresentation—An Argument." *CR: The New Centennial Review* 3, no. 3 (2003): 257–337.

Zimmerman, Yvonne C. *Other Dreams of Freedom: Religion, Sex, and Human Trafficking*. Oxford: Oxford University Press, 2013.

Zuckoff, Aviva Cantor. "The Lilith Question." *Lilith* 1, no. 1 (1976): 5–10.

Zurara, Gomes Eanes de. *The Chronicle of the Discovery and Conquest of Guinea*. Project Gutenberg, 1896. Ebook.

Index

For the benefit of digital users, indexed terms that span two pages (e.g., 52–53) may, on occasion, appear on only one of those pages.

abolition, abolitionist 139–40, 145, 146–47, 151–52, 153–55, 164–67
abortion 109–12
abyss 5–6, 7, 10–11, 19, 37, 109
Adam and Eve 39, 42, 46–47, 48–49, 52, 53–55, 63
   typology of 74–75, 119
   see also Eve
afterlife of slavery, afterlives of slavery 137–38, 145
Annunciation 19, 20–22, 67, 82–83, 87, 90, 103–4, 118, 122, 170, 174, 176, 184, 193
anthropology, theological 4, 7, 14–15, 29–30, 65, 66, 78, 108, 132, 174
Aparecida, Our Lady 1–3, 10
Assumption 13–14, 128
atonement 52, 132, 135–37 *see also* cross; crucifixion
Augustine 46–47, 54–57, 60–62, 152

Baartman, Saartjie (Sara) 18–19, 139–67
   background 139–43, 145–46
   Cuvier, Georges 157–62
   dissection and display 157–58, 159, 160–63
   London exhibition 139–40, 143–44
   iconography 62–63, 144–45, 163, 164–67
   newspaper and media concerns in London 146–52
   trafficking 153–57, 163–64
   see also Hottentot Venus
Baldwin, James 187, 190
baptism, baptismal, baptize 1, 3, 28, 34, 71–72, 92, 116, 142, 143–44, 146, 169, 176
beauty 8, 75–76, 80, 100, 127, 140, 160, 187–89, 190
birth
   Adam and Eve 47
   birth control 55
   Blackness and birth 16, 18, 113, 131–32, 135–37, 143–44, 196, 197
   Bridget's vision 120–22
   childbirth and pain 51, 128, 129, 132–35
   divine birth 67–68, 70, 71, 89, 94, 95, 96, 97, 98–99, 103, 108, 117, 127, 178

gender 80, 103–4
Hildegard's vision 118, 119–20
Mary and birth 19, 178–79, 180, 182–83, 184–85, 186–87
theological significance of birth 19, 48, 68, 81, 82, 86, 88, 90, 117, 124–25, 170, 176, 180, 193
virgin birth 81, 106–7, 116–17, 124, 126
see also pain; surrogacy; *Theotokos*
Black feminism, Black feminist 4, 7, 12, 17, 19, 34–35, 141, 144
Black Madonna 4, 7–8, 10–11
   Black women's lived experiences 132, 135–38
   loss of relationship to Black people 17, 33–34, 37
   Our Lady Aparecida 2, 3
   Our Lady Kupfergasse 31–33
   Our Lady of Ferguson 189–90
   significance for theology and Black Mariology 13–14, 15, 16, 19, 79
   see also other named Madonna figures
Black Mariology 4, 7–8, 13–16, 19, 170–71, 183, 191
bleeding body 126, 180–81
blood
   Blackness 6, 116, 169–70
   of Christ 103, 176, 178–79, 181, 191
   Mary 10–11, 66, 103, 118, 120, 121, 122–23, 128–29, 134–35, 179–81
   purity 17, 73, 118–19, 120, 121–22, 125, 126
   see also bleeding; menstruation
borders 124–25
Bridget of Sweden 117, 120–21, 123

Cannon, Katie 10, 145, 155–57
captive, captivity 23–24, 34, 35, 37, 59, 68, 130–33, 141, 147–49, 154–55, 156–57, 163–67, 192
Carmelites 30, 31, 37
Carroll, Charles 17, 60–63
Chalcedon, Council of 106–7, 126
circumcision 128–29, 161
Clapham Saints 146, 147, 153–55

242 INDEX

Combahee River Collective 170
conjure, conjurer 17, 26–27, 59, 65–66, 196
consent 21, 65, 103–4, 111, 145–46, 155–56, 159, 177
   not to be a single being 6, 7, 10–11, 19, 74, 103, 176
Couwenbergh, Christiaen van 22–25, 26–27, 28, 29–30, 34, 36, 57–58
Crawley, Ashon 6, 19, 37
cross 8, 92, 101, 130, 132, 134–35, 137, 170, 180, 181, 183, 190 *see also* crucifixion
crucifixion 71, 128, 133–34, 170, 184 *see also* cross
Cuvier, Georges 142, 157–62
Cyril of Alexandria 92, 96, 97–105, 106, 177–78

Deleuze, Gilles 178, 180
diaspora 5, 6–7, 45, 108, 137
disobedience 17, 52, 54–55, 60–62, 65–66, 69–70, 73, 74, 156–57
Divine Motherhood 13–14, 82
door of no return 5, 7, 19, 64
Douglas, Mary 123, 124–25
doxological Blackness 16, 194–95

enslave, enslaved, enslavement, enslaver
   Aesop's fable of Ethiopian 28
   Black women 12, 27, 65, 130–32, 140, 141, 147, 150–51, 152, 154–55, 170–71, 192
   Brazil and *Our Lady of Aparecida* 2–3
   colonialism and slavery 29–30, 64
   Josephus 50–51
   liberty 177, 183–84
   magic and power 43
   Mary 192, 193–94
   racial justification for 59–60
   sin 52
   virginity 103–4
Ephesus, Council of 17–18, 82, 104–5, 106–7
erotic, eroticized 9, 11–12, 21–22, 23–24, 25, 28, 36–37, 51, 55, 56–58, 75–76, 140, 152, 158–59, 160–61, 163, 174–75, 194 *see also* Lorde, Audre
Eve 17, 36, 39, 41–42, 43, 45, 46–47, 48–50, 51–55, 56–57, 58, 63, 66, 78–79, 85, 103–4
   Black/Blackness 18–19, 76, 79, 122, 130–31, 145, 156–57
   conjure 58–63
   Eve in relationship to Mary 64, 66, 68–75, 79, 81–83, 105–6, 107–8, 119, 122–23, 124–25, 128–29, 135, 173, 195
   Eve's virginity 65, 94
   Lilith 75–78
   Mother of All Living 45, 66, 75–76, 78–79
   race 59, 60–62, 63, 65–66
Eve and Lilith 17, 75–79

Ferguson, Our Lady of 189–90
fire
   Alexandrian church 100
   Arian chapel 93
   the fire next time 190–91
   Unburnt bush 184–87
   theological significance 19, 96, 172, 176, 181–91
   see also *Ferguson, Our Lady of*; *Unburnt Bush, Theotokos of*
Floyd, George 169
Foucault 39
   docile bodies 124
   friendship as a way of life 175
   genealogy 9
freedom 4, 9–10, 13, 14–16, 18–19, 31, 52–53, 66, 73–74, 103–4, 107–8, 128, 132, 135, 141, 145, 146, 154–55, 164, 170–71, 181, 182, 193, 194–95, 197
Freud 72–73
friendship 10–11, 43, 88–89, 174–75, 176, 180
fugitive, fugitivity 12–13, 19, 33–34, 37, 141, 164–67, 168–71, 195, 197

gender 9, 11–12, 17, 18–19, 34–35, 39–40, 43–44, 45, 46–47, 49–50, 54–55, 56–57, 59–63, 65–66, 69, 76, 79, 80–82, 108, 128, 137, 147–49, 152, 154–55, 156–57, 158–59, 174, 180, 182, 192
   genitalia 40, 46–47, 60, 62–63, 80, 84, 119, 157, 158–59, 161, 192
   race and gender 18–19, 21–22, 65, 130–32, 158–59, 162, 192
   sex and gender 45, 46–47, 49–50, 59–60, 80–81
   ungendering 63, 131–33, 140, 145–46
Glissant, Édouard 5–7, 74, 176
Gould, Stephen 157–58, 159–61

Hagar 14–15, 131–32
Hartman, Saidiya 64, 109, 137–38
Heidegger, Martin 171–74
Hildegard of Bingen 117, 118–20, 121
Hottentot Venus 18–19, 62–63, 139–67 *see also* Baartman, Saartjie
hybridity 126, 130
Hypatia 100–1, 103–5

icon, iconography 4, 7–8, 10, 13–14, 16, 18–19, 31–34, 37–38, 39–40, 63, 76, 78, 107–8, 130, 141, 142, 162–63, 168–69, 177–78, 179, 181, 187–90, 191, 192, 195
   iconic 37, 133–34, 183–84
   iconoclasm 17, 30–31, 34, 35–36
   see also Black Madonna, specific named icons
Ignatius of Antioch 68

Immaculate Conception 1–2, 3, 11, 13–14, 15–16, 67–68, 82–83, 122–23
Incarnation 3, 7, 13, 16, 52, 68, 86–87, 96, 105–7, 125, 126, 127–28, 137, 170–71, 176, 177, 178–79, 180, 181, 184, 185–87, 197
injustice *see* justice
inviolable, inviolability 33–34, 39, 108, 127
Irenaeus of Lyon 69–71, 74–75, 99
Irigaray, Luce 107–8, 121–22, 179–80

Jerome 72, 87
joy 9–10, 13, 19, 56–57, 88–89, 113, 135, 170, 175, 179, 191, 193, 194, 195, 196
justice 3, 7, 8, 9–10, 14–15, 113, 115, 131–32, 135–37, 144–46, 149–50, 163–64, 170–71, 186–87, 193–94

Kim, Mari 75–76, 78–79
Kupfergasse, Our Lady of, 31–34

Lateran Council 73, 106–7, 126
lesbian 174–75, 176
liberation 3, 7, 13, 14–15, 19, 137–38, 146, 147, 156–57, 164, 194, 197
Lilith 46, 60, 79
Lorde, Audre 4, 80, 168, 175, 194, 196

magic 53–63, 66, 75–76
Magnificat 13–14, 67, 88, 193–95
Mammy 131–32
Mariology 13–14 *see also* Black Mariology
Mater Dolorosa 18, 117, 133–38
maternal mortality 112, 116–17
menstruation 118, 180 *see also* bleeding; blood
Michelangelo 56–57, 60, 76
misogynoir 4, 17–18, 34–35, 113
Moten, Fred 7, 10–11, 12–13, 155, 172–73
mothering 46–47, 76, 103–4, 125
    Black mothering 18, 111, 113, 116–17, 131–32, 135–37, 170–71, 192

Nash, Jennifer 112–13, 115, 116–17, 137, 144
Nestorian controversy 17–18, 82, 91–92, 104–5
Nestorius 92, 93–97, 98–99, 101–2, 103–5, 106

pain 66, 108
    Black women and pain 26–27, 37–38, 113, 114–15, 117, 132–33, 135–37, 144, 145, 153, 155–57, 176
    mothering and grief 18, 134–37
    in relationship to childbirth 18, 44, 51, 81, 82–83, 85, 117–23, 124, 127, 128, 129, 132–35
partus sequitur ventrem 109, 115, 170–71
penis 46–47, 56, 62–63, 65, 157
    see also genitalia; vagina
pieta 37–38

polygenesis 17, 59–60
Proclus 96–97, 104, 108
Pulcheria 93–95, 96, 97, 101, 102, 103–5, 106
purity 4, 11–12, 58–59, 80–81, 101, 102, 123, 127–28, 186–87
    blood 17, 73, 108, 116, 118, 125, 180–81
    cleanliness 15–16, 119, 121, 123, 124–25, 130
    idea/ideal 7–8, 108, 117, 124, 127, 179
    moral 24, 35–36, 100
    race 18, 33–34, 35, 37, 60, 63, 65, 91–92, 128–29, 130–31, 141, 156–57, 163, 172–73, 192
    scale 72, 81–82
    virginity 17–19, 33–34, 54–55, 69–70, 74, 82, 122, 126, 130–31, 177–78

queer 6–7, 10–11, 17, 19, 47, 56–58, 59, 62, 65, 73–74, 75–76, 103–4, 158–59, 174, 176, 192
queer alimentarity 56–58
see also lesbian

race
    class 35–36
    classifications 65, 142–43, 157, 161
    colonialism 5, 6–7, 29–30, 79, 91–92, 139–40, 147, 158–59
    gender 9, 11–12, 17, 21–22, 34–35, 39–40, 65–66, 81–82
    reproduction 15, 46–47, 103, 112, 113
    separation of 60–62
    sex/desire 11–12, 18–19, 29–30, 60, 63, 82, 154–55, 156–57
    theology 7, 15, 91–92, 163–64
    see also racial, racialized
racial, racialized 4, 8, 11–12, 15–16, 25–26, 34–35, 57–58, 154–55, 163, 182, 190
    anxiety 52–53, 59, 60–62, 75–76
    formation 64, 116, 130–31, 146
    hierarchy 21, 33, 79, 143, 152, 158–62
    identity 57–58, 59–60
    imaginary 116, 117
    optic 21, 111–12
    purity 35, 60, 65, 73, 116, 129
    sex 65, 80–81, 141, 144, 156–57
rape 12, 20, 27–29, 132
    Rape of the Negress 17, 22–24, 26, 28–30, 34–35, 36, 37–38, 189–90
recapitulation 69, 70, 74–75, 76–78, 99
Relation
    Mary 176
    method 9–10, 11, 16, 19
    Poetics of Relation 5–6
    purity 123–24, 179–80
    Theology-in-relation 5–14, 39–40, 183, 184, 195
    see also Glissant

reproduction 17–18, 39, 46–48, 103, 118–19, 121–22, 146, 181
  Blackness 37, 109–11, 115, 116–17, 122, 131–32, 192
rescue industry 154–55
Rosales, Harmonia 17, 75–79

serpent
  dialogue in Genesis 41–42, 43–44, 45, 48–49
  Eve's deception 51, 52, 56, 71
  gender 56–58, 76
  Lilith and Eve 76–78
  race and gender 60–63
  serpent as good creation 75
  see also Lilith; polygenesis
Sharpe, Christina 113–15
silence, silenced
  in the Garden of Eden 47–48
  in relationship to sound 57–58, 163–64, 178
  theological significance 84–85, 90, 134–35
  women learning in or being silenced 52, 73–74, 146, 164–67
sin 3, 17, 194
  Adam and Eve 51, 53–55, 60
  Mary and Eve 71–72, 73, 78, 79, 122–23
  original sin 54–55, 60, 86–87, 107–8, 120, 122, 124–25, 128
  sin and salvation 52, 106, 134–35, 181, 190
Sistine chapel 56 *see also* Michaelangelo
slavery 12, 60, 130, 137–38, 143, 145, 146, 147–49, 153, 154–55, 163
  see also afterlives of slavery; enslavement
Spillers, Hortense 12, 63, 65, 130–32, 145–46, 191–92
suffering 17, 18, 20, 45, 108, 132–35, 170, 184, 187, 195, 196
  in relationship to Black mothering 112–13, 115, 117, 127, 128, 129, 137–38
  see also *Mater dolorosa*
surrogacy 18, 117, 131–32, 137–38 *see also* Williams, Delores

Tertullian 20, 70–72, 120
Theotokos 15–16, 17–18, 66, 78–79, 92, 95–97, 98–99, 101, 103, 105–6, 108, 121, 126, 127, 131, 132–33, 177–78, 180, 184–85, 186–87, 191 see also *Unburnt Bush, Theotokos of the*
Till, Emmet 135–37
Till-Mobley, Mamie 135–37
trafficking 18–19, 43, 65, 141, 154–55, 163–64
Trinity 19, 21, 68, 174, 176

Unburnt Bush, Theotokos of the 19, 184–87

vagina
  gender and genitalia 45–53, 65, 66, 74, 119
  Hottentot Venus 161
  vaginal birth 66, 119–20, 121, 125
  see also genitalia; penis
Virgin, virginity 3, 11, 14–15, 66, 72–74, 79, 82, 84, 91–92, 96, 103–4, 107–8, 117, 118, 131, 137, 191
  aieparthenos 73
  Biblical texts 67–68
  Black Virgin 3, 31–34, 37, 121, 131, 141, 191, 192
  early Church discussions 68–72, 96, 97, 98–99, 102–3, 104, 105, 106–8
  Eve and virginity 65, 66, 70–72, 73–75, 79
  Hypatia 100, 103–4
  Mary 81, 82, 86–87, 89, 119, 120, 121, 124–25, 126, 127–29, 133–34, 137, 184–85, 187
  parthenos 86–87
  perpetual 13–14, 17–18, 73–74, 106–7, 119, 126, 127, 130, 137, 191
  practices of devotion 2–3, 96
  privilege 183
  Pulcheria 94–95, 103–4
  purity 17–18, 20, 27–28, 81, 82, 130–31, 177–79, 181
  see also birth; Black Madonna; purity

Williams, Delores 14–15, 131–32, 137–38
womanist theology 4, 7, 14–15, 18–19, 117, 164, 184, 192
womb
  Black Madonna 13–14, 132–33, 196
  gender 82
  grave 18, 109–17, 135, 195
  imaginary 18, 74, 115, 116–17, 132–33, 137–38, 174, 177, 184–85, 194–95, 196
  jug 173–74
  Mary 11, 68, 70, 71, 86, 88, 90, 91, 98–99, 119, 120–21, 124–25, 176–77, 184–85, 186–87
  open and shut (closed) (barrenness) 82–83, 84, 89
  purity 54–55, 73, 74, 119, 120, 121–23, 128–29, 130, 134–35
  race 18, 82, 109, 111–12, 115, 116–17, 125, 131–32, 170–71
  slave ship 11
  space 11, 69, 82, 108, 109, 177–78, 179–80, 184, 189
  theological significance 10–11, 13, 16, 54–55, 105–7, 189